Michèle Barrett teaches sociology at the City University, London, England, and is a member of the *Feminist Review* collective. She is author of *Women's Oppression Today* (1980) and, with Mary McIntosh, of *The Anti-social Family* (1982).

Roberta Hamilton is at Queen's University, Kingston, Ontario, where she teaches sociology and history and is co-ordinator of women's studies. She is author of *The Liberation of Women* (1978).

The Politics of Diversity:

Feminism, Marxism and Nationalism

Edited by

Roberta Hamilton and Michèle Barrett

Verso is the imprint of **New Left Books**

Canadian
Cataloguing in Publication Data

Main entry under title:
The Politics of diversity: feminism, marxism
and nationalism
    Bibliography: p.
    ISBN 0-920094-28-7
    1. Feminism—Canada.   2. Women and socialism—
Canada.   I. Hamilton, Roberta   II. Barrett,
Michèle
HQ1233.P64   1987   305.4′0971   C86-090314-1

Published in Canada by Book Center Inc.

British Library
Cataloguing in Publication Data

The politics of diversity.—(Questions for feminism)
    1. Women—Canada—Social conditions
    2. Women in politics—Canada
    I. Barrett, Michèle   II. Hamilton, Roberta
    III. Series
    305.4′2′0971   HQ1453

First published 1986
©Verso 1986

Verso 6 Meard Street London W1

Filmset in 10/11pt Times by
Papyrus Printers and Stationers Limited, Thetford, Norfolk

Printed in Great Britain by
Thetford Press Limited, Thetford, Norfolk

ISBN 0-86091-164-0
ISBN 0-86091-876-9 Pbk

Contents

Racism, Ethnicity, Nationalism

Acknowledgements

Permission to reprint articles from the following publications is gratefully acknowledged,

Meg Luxton, 'Two Hands for the Clock: Changing Patterns in the Gendered Division of Labour in the Home', no. 12 (Fall 1983); Patricia Connelly and Martha MacDonald, 'Women's Work: Domestic and Wage Labour in a Nova Scotia Community', no. 10 (Winter 1983); Angela Miles, 'Economism and Feminism: Hidden in the Household; A Comment on the Domestic Labour Debate', no. 11 (Summer 1983); Pat Armstrong and Hugh Armstrong, 'Beyond Sexless Class and Classless Sex: Towards Feminist Marxism', no. 10 (Winter 1983) and 'More on Marxism and Feminism: A Response to Patricia Connelly', no. 15 (Fall 1984); Patricia Connelly, 'On Marxism and Feminism', no. 12 (Fall 1983); all in *Studies in Political Economy* (Ottawa).

Roberta Hamilton, 'Working at Home', vol. 7, no. 1 (Fall 1981); Bruce Curtis, 'Rejecting Working at Home', vol. 8, no. 1 (Fall 1982); Roberta Hamilton, 'Reply to Curtis', vol. 8, no. 1 (Fall 1982); Jane Gaskell, 'Conceptions of Skill and the Work of Women: Some Historical and Political Issues', vol. 8 no. 2; Michèle Jean and Marie Lavigne, 'Le Phénomène des Yvettes: analyse externe', vol. 6, no. 2 (Spring 1981); Jacqueline Lamothe and Jennifer Stoddart, 'Les Yvettes ou: comment un parti politique traditionnel se sert encore une fois de femmes', vol 6, no. 2 (Spring 1981); all in *Atlantis* (Halifax).

Ruth Roach Pierson, 'Women's Emancipation and the Recruitment of Women into the War Effort', in Susan Mann Trofimenkoff and Alison Prentice, eds. *The Neglected Majority*, Volume 1, Toronto 1977.

Mary O'Brien, 'Hegemony and Superstructure: A Feminist Critique of Neo-Marxism', in Jill McCalla Vickers, ed., *Taking Sex Into Account: The Policy Consequences of Sexist Research*, Ottawa 1984.

Mary O'Brien, 'Feminism and Revolution', in Angela Miles and Geraldine Finn, eds., *Feminism in Canada: From Pressure to Politics*, Montreal 1982.

Nadia Fahmy-Eid and Nicole Laurin-Frenette, 'Théories de la famille et rapports famille/pouvoirs dans le secteur educatif au Québec et en France, 1850–1960'; Marie Lavigne, 'Réflexions feministes autour de la fertilité des Québecoises'; in Nadia Fahmy-Eid and Micheline Dumont, eds., *Maîtressses de maison, maîtresses d'ecole*, Montreal 1983.

Susan Russell, 'The Hidden Curriculum of School: Reproducing Gender and Class Hierarchies, in Meg Luxton and Heather Jon Maroney, eds., *Women's Jobs, Women's Struggles: Feminism and Political Economy*, Toronto 1986.

Roberta Hamilton, 'The Collusion with Patriarchy: A Psychoanalytic Account', *Alternate Routes*, no. 6 (1983), (Ottawa).

Heather Jon Maroney, 'Embracing Motherhood: New Feminist Theory', *Canadian Journal of Political and Social Theory*, vol. 9, nos. 1–2 (1985), (Montreal). Reprinted in Marilouise and Arthur Kroker, eds., *Feminism Now: Theory and Practice*, Montreal 1985.

The editors extend particular thanks to Bonnie Fox and Wally Seccombe for their contributions, written for this volume at short notice; also to Nicole Laurin-Frenette, Marie Lavigne and Jennifer Stoddart for their attention to the translations. We are also grateful to many of the contributors for revisions of their work, and to all of them for permission to reprint. We would also like to thank Geoffrey Smith in Kingston, Mary McIntosh in London, and Anne Phillips of the Verso 'Questions for Feminism' series, for their advice and comments.

Translations

Joy Holland: Nadia Fahmy-Eid and Nicole Laurin-Frenette, 'Théories de la famille et rapports famille pouvoirs dans le secteur educatif au Québec et en France, 1850–1960'; Michèle Jean and Marie Lavigne, 'Le phénomène des Yvettes: analyse externes'; Jacqueline Lamothe and Jennifer Stoddart 'Les Yvettes ou: comment un parti politique traditionnel se sert encore une fois des femmes'.

David Macey: Marie Lavigne 'Réflexions féministes autour de la fertilité de Québecoises'.

Introduction

The work published in this book has been written in Canada, where an extremely active and lively feminist movement has confronted both the realities of women's oppression and the adequacy or otherwise of existing socialist analyses of that society. These articles represent a flourishing Canadian socialist-feminist literature, which has a great deal to offer people elsewhere who want to confront the patriarchal dimensions of capitalist society and move forward with the project of a feminist transformation of socialist analysis and strategy.

Surprisingly little of this work is known in Britain or the United States. Ignorance about, and apathy and prejudice towards, intellectual debates going on within Canada is fairly common. Certainly the Paris – New York – London communication system of modern thought does not often take time to stop in Toronto or Montreal for longer than it takes to unload its latest ideas. Much of the time the assumption that Canada is a pale imitation of the United States, or a neatly untangled cross between the USA and Britain, passes itself off as an understanding of the country.

The relative isolation of Canadian work is, however, a clue to why these particular debates around feminism and socialism are of such interest to others. For Canadians talk to each other – indeed shout at each other – across barriers of theory, analysis and politics that in Britain, for example, would long since have created an angry truce of silent pluralism. Thus some of the exchanges in this book, notably the detailed criticisms of Marxist concepts from what in Britain at least would be identified as a 'radical feminist' position, reopen questions that have elsewhere been abandoned unresolved. Another feature of this willingness to engage, even where considerable disagreement is evident, is the participation of men in some of these arguments. There is an open-mindedness in the conduct of these debates that reflects the scale and diversity of Canada as a country and the need for solidarity among its progressive movements.

The contributors to this book write from within a political culture built on the recognition rather than the denial of division and differences between people. The articles focus not only on the social relations, structures and ideologies that create and consolidate the disadvantage and oppression of women. These authors also seek to analyse, and contest, the connections between gender and other social hierarchies and divisions. Questions of class and nationality figure most centrally, but the interrelations of ethnicity, generation and religion are also addressed. The essays seek not only to explain, and to change, the processes that divide the sexes: they illuminate too the various ways in which women are divided from each other.

Apprehending that diversity, without becoming totally distracted by it, has become the greatest challenge of feminist work today. In Canada this task has been undertaken with greater solidarity and less suspicion between activists and intellectuals, academics and reformers than has been the case in Britain or the United States.

Feminism in Britain has for some time been divided on the question of nationalism and imperialism, with many socialist – feminists in disagreement as to the nature of the political relationship between, for example, feminism and the republican struggle in Northern Ireland. More recently, and derived initially from the extensive debates on this topic in the USA, but now expressing the concerns of an autonomous black feminist movement in Britain, it is the issue of racism that has come to dominate British feminist politics. The explosive, and divisive, character of these political engagements can hardly be denied. Yet the question of the basis upon which we can move forward, of what hope for solidarity there might be and on what issues alliances can be formed with integrity – all these remain open questions. The contribution of a set of debates from a feminist movement that has engaged with political and cultural difference from its inception can only be positive in this context. And lessons might be learned in Canada, too, from the traditional centrality of the Anglo-French conflict in what was essentially a white feminist movement in Canada for many years. Now the issue of racism, as opposed to nationality, is more apparent in the struggles of Amerindian women and others who are victims of racism on the basis of their colour or ethnicity.

In this introduction we try to situate this body of work for a wider readership, and we begin with a section describing and analysing the development of feminism in Canada as a political movement. This we believe useful in understanding the political context of the debates that follow. Then we discuss each of the book's sections in turn. The first two sections focus on the 'feminism and Marxism' debate and on the intersection of gender and class relations in capitalist societies such as contemporary Canada. The next two sections deal on a broader canvas with the social diversity of Canada and the political implications of this for feminism. Finally we raise some questions about sexuality, motherhood and the political project of feminism that dovetail clearly with their sister debates in Britain and the United States.

The section 'Home and Workplace' brings together articles that address this connection in specific historical and detailed empirical research. As such it complements the growing body of work in feminist history on this important topic.[1] The second section, entitled 'Towards Feminist Marxism?', deals with the extremely animated recent Canadian debate about domestic labour; we include brief retrospective pieces on this from two of the most important protagonists, Bonnie Fox and Wally Seccombe. Also in this section is a more general debate about feminism and Marxism, sparked off by an article in which Pat Armstrong and Hugh Armstrong call for a rethinking of Marxism that would enable us to deal with questions of biology and human reproduction.[2]

In the section 'Racism, Ethnicity, Nationalism' we address particularly the question of nation, and the effects of Québec nationalism on the emergent feminist movement in Canada. Differences of ethnicity and the question of racism are dealt with more briefly. The general processes through which women's oppression and disadvantages are recreated, by the educational system and the definitions at play in the division of labour, are explored in two articles on the theme of 'The Social Reproduction of Gender'. The concluding sections deal with two areas of lively contemporary debate within feminism internationally – the possibility of developing a critical feminist perspective within psychoanalytic theory, and the new emphasis on revalorizing motherhood. The book concludes with a brief polemic from

Mary O'Brien on feminism's engagement with revolutionary political praxis.

The Development of the Women's Movement in Canada

Perhaps no population of feminists has been more continually aware of the many deep social divisions between women than the one to which the authors of this collection belong. They are Canadian – but we should say immediately, to illustrate our point, that they are Canadian and Québecoise feminists. For they are citizens of a single state whose very creation in 1867 confirmed the subordination of the French to the English and their confinement, as a people, to the geographical area of Québec. Like the military defeat over a century earlier, this political conquest provided fertile ground for the continuing development of nationalism. This culminated in the 1970s in a social and electoral challenge to the very legitimacy of the Canadian state, a challenge which we can be sure, if history is any guide, is only in temporary retreat.[3]

But nationalism did not have the whole field of politics to itself in Québec in the 1970s. That exciting decade also witnessed the incredible developments of the women's liberation movement, and the growing realization that between feminists and nationalists – many of whom were both – there could be both exhilarating alliances as well as potentially devastating contradictions. French and English feminists in Québec recognized their different interests almost before they acknowledged the extent and depth of their joint struggle.[4] Canada's two nations have gone on to produce two women's liberation movements, two feminist literatures and two markedly different political agendas. Very little of what is written in one language is translated into the other and indeed the articles originally written in French in this anthology had to be translated for this volume. The cost of translation, which, ironically, has skyrocketed as a result of the federal state's policy in favour of bilingualism, has made communication between French and English feminists even more difficult.

A belief in undivided sisterhood was never very marketable in Canada; consequently its passing produced little disillusionment. Indeed, feminists in Canada have been particularly willing to tolerate diversity, understand split loyalties, negotiate compromises as well as engage in common struggles. French and

English feminists have worked together to found journals, women's centres, political alliances, research institutions and academic associations. But it hasn't been easy. Yet to write of the 'unequal union' between French and English,[5] and its consequences for feminists is to pass over a greater inequality, a far deeper repudiation of a people and its way of life. For while the French and English claim to have discovered North America; they in fact conquered it.[6] And part of the process, through which the indigenous people were systematically dispossessed of their land, involved the passing of the Indian Act in 1876 by the Canadian state, through which some were declared 'Indian' and others – with mixed French-Indian parentage (the Métis) – were not. That meant their exclusion from even the slim and tenuous treaty rights negotiated by 'pure' Indians. It was, therefore, an overtly racist Act. But it was also sexist. For Indian women who married white men automatically became enfranchised (Indian people did not get the vote in Canada until 1960) and therefore had their name struck from the band list. As Non-Status Indians they lost all benefit of treaty, their right to live or hold property on reservations. White women married to Indian men took their place.

The organized feminist movement has backed the long – and recently successful – struggle for reinstatement of Indian women who lost their status through marriage,[7] yet the scarce resources of the bands, including land, have not been expanded to accommodate those who may now move back. The Canadian state has responded to a feminist demand, but in a way that forces the poor and wronged to pay the cost of righting the racist and sexist laws and policies instituted over a century ago. And the category Métis – with all the rights and privileges pertaining thereto – remains untouched.[8]

Feminists in Canada have had more than the experience of national hierarchies and racist practices to sharpen their appreciation of diversity. Some of the contributors to this volume live over four thousand miles from each other. Getting together for conferences (leaving aside a revolution) is a formidable task that is enormously expensive in both time and money. But the problems are more than mere distance. As Patricia Connelly and Martha MacDonald explain in their article, the various regions of the country are linked by complex relations of dependence and exploitation that are mediated and organized politically through the provincial governments within Canada. These economic and political relations – and inequalities – have been mirrored in the women's liberation movement and have sharpened the effects of geographical distance.

Much feminist political work has been provincially based, and its fortunes have risen and fallen with different governments in the provinces. The New Democratic Party (NDP) has committed far more state resources to feminist-sponsored work during its one term of office in British Columbia, its longer term in Saskatchewan and its present mandate in Manitoba, than have the Conservatives or the Liberals in their much lengthier administrations. Needless to say little has come from the Social Credit, Canada's closest equivalent to the Thatcher and Reagan regimes, now wreaking havoc in British Columbia.[9] Many feminists are members of the NDP and have an integral – though continually contested – role within it.[10] Its demise in British Columbia in 1975 had a devastating effect on feminist services: shelters for battered women, rape crisis centres, abortion services and myriad women's centres all suffered. The early days of the Parti Québecois government in Québec in 1976 also produced some heady times for feminists. Some feminists' demands were taken on board by the government, although the end result in many cases was the recuperation by the state of these feminist services.[11]

Across these regional differences feminists in Canada have also collectively confronted the federal state: the long struggle over the law on abortion, pressuring for resources for feminist projects, the mobilization around the constitution and the inclusion of a sex equality clause, for example.[12] In doing this they have had a rather remarkable document on which to draw. For in 1967 the Liberal federal government of Lester Pearson, bowing to pressure from middle-class women's groups, had set up a Royal Commission on the Status of Women.[13] Although this was motivated by a desire to shelve the issue, the upshot was rather different. The Commission hearings, held throughout the country, helped mobilize women's groups and individual feminists to meet, present evidence and press their claims on a wider audience.[14] The Commission, which began as a laughing stock of the press, eventually contributed to a remarkable shift in public attitudes towards feminist issues and its final report proved radical and critical enough to be of longer-term use to feminists.

Of course the Commission report has been criticized by both socialist and radical feminists for its essentially liberal feminist agenda.[15] Yet taken together, had they been implemented, the proposals would have revealed a glimpse of what Zillah Eisenstein has called the 'radical future' of liberal feminism.[16] That most of the report's major recommendations were shelved or instituted in only piecemeal fashion was not surprising. But in the aftermath of the Royal Commission feminists formed their only national organization, the National Action Committee on the Status of Women,[17] which brings together a highly diverse range of women's groups, primarily to lobby the government.

The Commission certainly raised expectations about the potentially emancipatory role of the state. Yet its failure did not produce a commensurate realization of the limitations of state intervention. Feminists in Canada, though in many cases doubtful, have not given up on the role the state might play in producing sex equality. The largest mobilization in Canada in recent years concerned a successful struggle to include a sex discrimination clause in the Human Rights section of the recently patriated Canadian Constitution. Although the campaign was remarkably well organized, feminists were not agreed about its relevance: Québec feminists and socialist feminists, for different if overlapping reasons, looked at the federal state in far more oppositional terms.[18]

Their appreciation of the role of the state in capitalist societies has led socialist feminists to react in anguish to the current most popular feminist struggle in Canada – as elsewhere – against pornography. No issue divides the feminist movement in Canada as publicly as the analysis and policy proposals surrounding pornographic material. Pressure for censorship by many feminists has been countered by others who cannot be persuaded that increased state control is any solution. But the issue is also informed by feminists coming down with different emphasis on the 'pleasure or danger' potential of female sexuality.[19]

The most remarkable and long-term contribution of Canadian feminists to the popular dissemination of information and attitudes about sexuality has come from the Montreal Health Press. With roots at McGill University in the late 1960s, this feminist collective developed a mass market for its publications on birth control, sexual assault, venereal disease, and soon – reflecting the present age of the late 1960s feminist cohort – the menopause. Informed by sexual and class politics, as well as by feminist theoretical work, their publications have sold millions of copies, reaching more young women in Canada than all other feminist work put together.[20]

Debates between socialist, radical and liberal feminists go back to the late 1960s in Canada. The movement's first anthology, *Women Unite!*, encompassed writings from the broad range of perspectives. The editorial collective, in its introduction to the book, pointed out a major – and abidingly significant – difference between the women's liberation movement as it was developing in Canada and in the United States. That difference was and is socialism.[21] Many Canadian feminists had experienced an earlier political education in the left wing of the NDP and in the Student Union for Peace Action, a hybrid of the Campaign for Nuclear Disarmament and the New Left. These women were socialists, fast becoming feminists: they were becoming socialist-feminists.

Socialist-feminists insist that class divisions in Canadian society are as salient as those of sex, and their attention has turned to the interaction of gender and class inequalities. Both in their academic and political work they have focused on working-class women, who are now (at least partly through the organizing efforts of socialist-feminists) at the centre of much feminist activity. Trade-union organization, union policies and union negotiating demands have all been dramatically, if unevenly, affected by these struggles.[22]

Like the sex divide, these class issues permeate the other divisions that Canadian feminists have encountered. The nationalist movement in Québec has been the location for fragile alliances and some bitter splits between socialists, social democrats, the middle class and the petite bourgeoisie, many of the latter being conservative or even right-wing nationalists.[23]

Feminists have fought a brilliant, if ultimately a losing, battle for a place on the ground floor of this aggregate *indépendantiste* movement. Of course, too, class divisions permeate all the regional disparities: it is perhaps easier to be a liberal feminist in metropolitan Toronto than in poorer areas such as the Maritime Provinces of the Atlantic coast.

Like all aspects of Canadian life the women's liberation movement has been structured not only by these internal divisions but by the country's economic, political and cultural dependence on the United States. Many early 'Canadian' feminists moved north with their husbands and lovers who were draft-resisters against the war in Vietnam. Like most Americans, they wanted to see

Canada as an extension, albeit a temporarily safer one, of their own country. In addition, many of them brought a feminism drawn from early radical feminism in the United States, leaving little space for analysis and reflection about American imperialism in Canada. Feminist literature was coming in from the United States and from England as quickly as it was written, and the women's movement threatened to become a rather colonized affair.

In fact, for several good reasons that has not happened. First, however much Canada may appear to outsiders to be similar to the United States, it is in fact different in all the ways we have suggested and more. When Canadian and Québecoise feminists came to organize they encountered those differences – as had many socialists, nationalists and intellectuals before them. The struggle against the law restricting abortion provides a vivid illustration. In 1970 the 'Abortion Caravan' focused on the role of the federal state in controlling female sexuality. Women trekked across the country to Ottawa and chained themselves to seats in the gallery of the House of Commons. But the law gave so much power to doctors and hospital boards that the fight had to be made in both local and provincial venues. Here, of course, there were significant class and regional discrepancies. Women in large urban centres had better access to abortion facilities than their rural sisters. Women from the Maritime Provinces often had to travel, if they could raise the money, far inland to Montreal.

Abortion politics took a particularly interesting and courageous turn in that city, where traditionally the English hospitals had been prepared to approve and perform abortions while the French hospitals would not. But from 1967 Dr Henry Morgentaler, working closely with a women's centre, operated a private abortion clinic in Montreal. Clandestine yet well-known, his work finally led to his arrest in 1970. Three juries found him innocent; the state appealed and obtained convictions. The Liberal government of Robert Bourassa was about to press charges a fourth time when in November 1976 it lost power to the Parti Québecois. That party, which had been effectively infiltrated by feminists, announced that it would not proceed with another trial. Women across the country had mobilized to raise funds for Dr Morgentaler's enormously high legal expenses. In the past few years he opened clinics in Ontario and Manitoba, has been arrested again, and is currently facing trial, with medical colleagues, in both places. In the course of his dramatic odyssey (Morgentaler's campaign has included the screening on Canadian television – provocatively on Mother's Day – of an abortion operation), feminists have had to come to terms with an important turn of events. For Québec – once used as an excuse by federal governments reluctant to change laws on divorce, birth control and other so-called moral issues that invariably pertain to the behaviour and freedom of women – is now the province with the easiest access to abortion. Dr Morgentaler, whose clinics face angry 'Right to Life' mobs in the rest of the country, now operates his clinic quietly in Montreal. The paradox of this situation, when the religious (Catholic) heritage of Québec would lead one to expect relatively greater opposition to abortion than in English Canada, is explicable in terms of the alliance between nationalism and feminism at a particular period.

Even on an issue such as abortion – which may once have seemed like a straightforward 'feminist' question – feminists in Canada have had to take account of national, regional and class differences as well as federal and provincial jurisdictions. (Their experience has been mirrored by the developing recognition in both the United States and Britain that abortion forms only one aspect of a more general struggle for reproductive freedom for women, and one that varies significantly for black women, white women and women of colour.) Many of the differences that are so important in Canada derive from the country's colonial past, and from its subsequent 'silent surrender' to the domination of the United States. This history of colonization, and the extreme character of economic and political dependence within North America as a whole, have encouraged the development of a strong tradition of work in Canada on 'political economy'.[24]

The study of political economy in Canada has traditionally been much broader than what is usually understood by this term elsewhere. It is not necessarily Marxist in orientation. As the editors of *The New Practical Guide to Canadian Political Economy* note: 'As practised in Canada, political economy is not simply a discipline, nor is it merely a preserve for a single political or ideological tradition.'[25] For several decades liberal social scientists have taken a stronger interest in the economy and in relations of material determination in Canada than they do in Britain or the United States. In recent years this tradition of political economy has been encountered and refashioned by Marxists as part of the regeneration of socialism in Canada since the

1960s. When feminists in Canada came to develop their analysis of that society, they found that they had a far richer and more sophisticated set of materialist debates from which to begin.

Some of the pioneering work on how feminists should begin to theorize women's work on capitalism, and how to understand the ways in which women's work in the home related to the organization of capitalism more generally, was originally developed in Canada. Peggy Morton, Margaret Benston and Wally Seccombe are authors who played a crucial part in sparking the so-called 'domestic labour debate' in the late 1960s and early 1970s.[26] Many feminists have argued since that the orientation of this work was too much towards Marxism rather than feminism, and that this perspective failed to generate an understanding of women's oppression *as women*, and by men. These debates have taken place in Canada too, and some of them are reflected in this volume. Yet it must be said that the strong historical, empirical and materialist character of the political economy tradition in Canada helps to shape a version of the debate evoking wider interest than these abstract and sometimes rather technical debates. Of particular interest has been the substantial body of work undertaken on the relationship between home and workplace in Canadian society, and it is to this that we turn next.

Home and Workplace

The articles in this part of the book have a specific contribution to make to international knowledge about the realities of women's 'double day' as paid workers and as houseworkers in modern capitalist societies. They also engage directly with a debate, about the theoretical and political relationship between feminism and Marxism, that has been running for some years in Britain and the United States. This work has a sharp relevance to debates outside Canada on these subjects, and it is noticeable that the distinctive strengths of the 'political economy' tradition in Canadian socialist thought gives these essays a specifically materialist inflection.

Canadian feminists have explored the relationship of home and workplace, and of the home *as* workplace, in historical and contemporary detail. Perhaps the finest example of a full-length analysis of housework in relation to wage work is the study by Meg Luxton, whose theoretical framework is matched by an unusually vivid participant ethnography. Luxton studied a city in northern Manitoba, reconstructing the evolution of domestic life through the three generations of settlers, and documenting the current household division of labour. The town of Flin Flon was an exemplary casebook of the 'family wage' system in operation: it was geographically isolated, completely dominated by one employer (the Hudson Bay Mining and Smelting Company, invariably referred to as 'the Company'), and this employer refused to employ wives. So Luxton found there the perfect type of a domestic situation where the male wage supported the whole household. In Luxton's book the fascinating material used to recreate the fabric and texture of everyday existence in such households is integrated with a theoretical analysis of domestic labour similar to that elaborated by Wally Seccombe in 1974.[27]

Perhaps the most interesting aspect of Luxton's study, from a contemporary British point of view, is the discussion of the political dynamic inherent in the women's position as dependants. In the 1934 strike at the mine the women formed a support committee, worked collectively with each other, ran and supported picket lines, renegotiated relationships with husbands – and subsequently found that the men's union tried to ease them back into their previous roles when the strike was over. The parallels with the massive mobilization of women in support of the 1984 – 5 strike in Britain of the National Union of Mineworkers are interesting.[28] For in both cases, one local the other a major national strike, the women were organizing independently, *as women*, in order to defend a family and community organization in which they were ultimately completely dependent upon men. This dilemma is often regarded as a crucial contradiction for socialist-feminism, forming a gulf between working-class women who see their interests as integrally bound up with the family and the fortunes of a male breadwinner, and the supposedly 'middle-class' demands of the feminist movement for much greater independence from men and the family. Luxton's book ends on a relatively optimistic note, citing an instance where a successful strike was backed by a women's group that took on board a relationship with women's liberation politics.

In 1981 Meg Luxton went back to Flin Flon to see whether the domestic division of labour between men and women had changed. She found that to some extent working-class women were contesting men's traditional power in the household and that some men were taking more responsibility in the home. But, as she argues, these developments are only part of a situation where other couples adopted quite different strategies, some of them reinforcing the ideological pressure on women to assume complete domestic responsibility.

In contrast to the 'male breadwinner' model of household, Patricia Connelly and Martha MacDonald selected for detailed study an economic situation where working-class households had never managed on one male wage. Their research on a fishing community in Nova Scotia covers the period (roughly 1950 – 70) when the basis of fishing as commodity production gave way to the increasingly wage-earning market economy, reflecting the uneven development of the rural sector in Canada. Connelly and MacDonald show that the extent to which women engage in wage labour at the fish plant, and the categories of women who do so, relate directly to the fortunes of the male-controlled fishing operation and to a variety of local economic factors. Patricia Connelly had previously set out in *Last Hired, First Fired* a straightforward application of the Marxist concept of an industrial reserve army to the wage labour of women.[29] In the present study this question is approached in a more empirical fashion, and from the point of view of the women workers' own motivations and interests rather than those of the employers. It is concluded that women's domestic labour remains, as does independent commodity production, in a restricted form in the wage economy but one that serves in important ways to underwrite the costs of reproduction of labour.

These two examples of detailed research projects illustrate some points of general relevance. British readers of Luxton's book and of the Connelly and MacDonald article printed here, will notice a congruence between their theoretical positions and those associated with attempts by socialist-feminists in Britain in the 1970s to re-work the Marxist concept of social reproduction.[30] This concept, as developed in British work at least, derived principally from the work of Louis Althusser and is one whose fortunes have declined with the eclipse of 'Althusserianism' in general. Yet it must be said that few analyses of the Althusserian 'moment' have deployed the concept in the context of such meticulous and open-minded research as is the case here.

Secondly, both articles printed in this collection illustrate the continuing importance, and empirical character, of the 'domestic labour debate' in modern Canadian socialist-feminist work. This sociologically and historically informed treatment of the question of domestic labour contrasts sharply with the abstract and theoretical way in which the subject was developed – and abandoned – in Britain in the 1970s, and we say more about this below.

Thirdly, the examples throw an interesting light on the debate about the 'family wage'. Jane Humphries has argued that it was in the interests of the working-class family in the nineteenth century to fight for a 'family wage' earned by a male breadwinner, and thus create the opportunities for the creation of use value in the home from domestic labour and the raising of the family's standard of living.[31] The debate on this subject has been heated and has centred on the question of whether working-class *women's* interests were served by such an arrangement.[32] A secondary theme of the debate, however, has been the question of whether such a 'family wage system' has ever really existed on any substantial scale. In Britain it might be argued that only among the 'labour aristocracy' – the exclusive, male, skilled craft unions – has the male wage ever been enough to support a dependent family at home. For the majority of working-class households, the employment of the wife and older children has been a necessity. Luxton's original study was of the pure 'family wage' instance, though the follow- up shows a distinct weakening of this model. Connelly and MacDonald's research reminds us that the notion of an omnipotent 'male breadwinner' was and is in many cases more a myth than a description of reality.

These issues are historically interesting but are also relevant for understanding the present changes in relations between home and workplace. This is underlined by Susanne Mackenzie's article, which gives a fascinating account of how the economic restructuring of recent years has redrawn the definitions of both home and workplace. Writing as an urban geographer, she discusses the ways in which women are, as a result of the present recession and growth of the informal economy, adopting various strategies to maintain their household resources. In doing so they are significantly shifting relations between home and community and in many cases collectivizing work previously done in isolation in the home. Frequently, too, they are redefining their homes as a workplace for more than purely domestic labour, hence altering the relations between home work and wage earning.

These changes form an integral part of the decline of formal employment outside the home and the large-scale expansion of the informal home-based economy. In Britain the left and feminists have had to come to terms with this in a particularly dramatic form through the effects of government policies explicitly geared to fostering casual labour. Feminists studying work have increasingly, in recent years, turned towards these ambiguous 'twilight' areas and the informal economy to understand the situation. Angela Coyle's work on the effects of privatization policies on women workers is one example; others are the major study of women's part-time work by Veronica Beechey and Tessa Perkins and the research by Sheila Allen and Carol Wolkowitz on women home-workers.[33]

Canadian research on women in the labour market and in the home has for a decade been informed by the work of Pat Armstrong and Hugh Armstrong. The Armstrongs have documented and analysed the movement of women in and out of paid employment, emphasizing the fact that women work because they need the money. This research contradicts the conventional wisdom – still powerful even today in government circles – that women can dispense with their earnings.

This conventional wisdom is one of the threads of Ruth Pierson's article on women's recruitment to the war effort in 1939 – 45. Faced with labour shortages, the Canadian government undertook a systematic campaign to convince first single women, then married women without children, and finally women with children to register for employment: the appeal was, naturally, to patriotism. But again Pierson shows that many women took the jobs because they desperately needed the money, and so they had to be forced out of them in 1945. A memo from the Minister in Québec shows the official line as a stark one by any standards: 'Now that the war is over,' he wrote, 'I would be inclined to close these Day Nurseries immediately, but I feel that a month's notice to parents would only be fair.' The Armstrongs have shown that even without day care centres, women with children have persisted – at great personal cost and with astonishing resilience – in maintaining their position in the labour force.[34]

Towards Feminist Marxism?

In this second section we move on to the more general and theoretical treatment of issues concerning home and workplace and how these should be formulated in an analysis of capitalism. As is probably well known, Canadians led the field in the so-called 'domestic labour debate' of the early 1970s. It must be said, however, that the context and meaning of this debate varies significantly between Britain and Canada.[35] In Britain the debate became almost exclusively concerned with technical disputes within a set of Marxist categories, for example, about whether domestic labour could be said to be value producing or not. As we shall see, some of the Canadian literature on this topic also takes the form of this kind of doctrinal controversy, and perhaps too it can be said that some of it takes Marxism rather than feminism as its point of reference. The difference, however, is that the debates as they developed in Canada formed part of a much broader project to understand the oppression of women in modern capitalist society in greater empirical and historical detail. So we do not have an abstract and technical debate that exists in isolation; we have a much richer and broader research-based tradition of enquiry into political economy into which the more theoretical debate is inserted. To give readers outside Canada a flavour of this, it seemed logical to precede the more general discussion of domestic labour with some examples of the specific work done in the research tradition.

We start the section on these questions with the specific question of domestic labour, and move towards more wide-ranging issues on the relationship of Marxism and feminism. In 1980 the Women's Press in Toronto published a collection entitled *Hidden in the Household*, edited by Bonnie Fox. It contains a variety of essays through which a debate was conducted on how to move forward on the analysis of domestic labour in capitalism. One noted contributor was Wally Seccombe, who had in 1974 published a path-breaking article in *New Left Review* theorizing domestic labour in terms of the daily and generational reproduction of the labour force, that is the commodity of labour power. Seccombe's article generated considerable debate,[36] though various feminists argued that it centred on the relationship between domestic labour and capitalism at the expense of an emphasis on women or gender relations. *Hidden in the Household* contained two major essays by Seccombe, in which he elaborated with much greater precision and sophistication his argument that capitalist reproduction requires the private sphere of the domestic household for its maintenance and as a condition of its existence. *Hidden in the Household* is a starting point for much of the recent discussion about how to theorize the domestic economy in Canada, and many of the pieces reprinted here refer back and summarize the arguments presented by the contributors to that book. For this reason, and since *Hidden in the Household* has been available since 1980, we decided to solicit brief comments from its editor Bonnie Fox and from Wally Seccombe.

Roberta Hamilton published in 1981 a review article on the general theme of domestic labour in which she sought – some thought invidiously – to distinguish sharply between the approach taken in *Hidden in the Household* and the methodology and theory of Meg Luxton's historical study, *More than a Labour of Love*. Although she suggested Luxton was somewhat neglectful of feminist arguments about the benefits of the domestic division of labour to men, Hamilton argued that Luxton's respect for the experiential reality of women's lives precluded any interpretation that was pre-given by the use of particular conceptual categories. This latter was the charge she made against the application of Marxist concepts to domestic labour by the authors of *Hidden in the Household*. Bruce Curtis rose to defend the collection, arguing that Hamilton's critique rested on a dogmatic rejection of theory and a romantic appropriation of the voice of personal experience as the clue to understanding the nature of women's oppression. Whether or not this error was made can be left to the reader to decide; more salient is the substantive critique that Hamilton made of the 'domestic labour' school of thought.

Hamilton argued, in parallel with Eva Kaluzynska's criticism of the domestic labour debate in Britain,[37] that the central focus of this area of work had shifted significantly in political terms. Thus what had begun as an effort to understand the oppression of women, which required a new understanding of how and why work in the home was so important and intractable to change, became less and less about women and more and more about what was required by capitalism as a system of production. It increasingly became a debate purely within Marxist conceptual categories, rather than a debate about whether those concepts could be used to illuminate the oppression of women. Roberta Hamilton saw this as tending to mystify the underlying issue: 'the debate has provided some Marxists with a neat and tidy way to suppose that they are dealing with "the woman question" even as they studiously avoid such an encounter.' So the central point at issue in this debate about domestic labour – as indeed in the more general debate about feminism and Marxism – is whether Marxist categories do, or could, adequately encompass the specific character of women's oppression and the relations between women and men.

The feminist critique of the explanatory claims of Marxist concepts in relation to gender, and in particular the tendency to think that an analysis of domestic labour is an explanation of women's oppression, is put yet more strongly in the piece by Angela Miles reprinted here. *Hidden in the Household* again forms the focal point of the argument. In the course of her fundamental critique of the approach of this book Angela Miles, a radical feminist, raises a series of cogent objections to the habitual styles of Marxist and Marxist-feminist theorizing, giving her article a much broader relevance. Socialist and Marxist-feminists have often argued that their particular strength is in analysing the form taken by women's oppression under different modes of production, in varying periods of history and cultures. It is often acknowledged that this provides some corrective to the tendency within radical feminism for the development of universalistic and ahistorical, even biologistic, arguments. Miles draws attention in a salutary way to the dangers of the classic socialist-feminist position, which is that the general causes of oppression are ignored or skirted around in the attempt to theorize and understand the historical variations found. The crucial question for socialist-feminism then becomes: to what extent are men, or capitalism, responsible for women's oppression? Miles does not believe that the contributors to the domestic labour debate, at least, have shown that it is capitalism rather than men that 'cause' the oppression of women: 'To illustrate that women's oppression takes specific forms under capitalism is *not* to prove that it is derivative.'

On this salient point we move towards more general questions about the devolpment of Marxist-feminism and the difficult project of transforming Marxist theory in the light of feminist insights. Pat and Hugh Armstrong, whose studies on women's employment we have already mentioned, have reopened this general question with a sustained argument that Marxism requires rethinking in the light of consideration of biological reproduction. Reviewing the Marxist tradition as well as the history of the domestic labour debate, they propose, in the later sections of their article, a new orientation towards the capitalism/

gender relationship – one which locates procreation at the heart of a Marxist understanding of capitalism as a mode of production. The Armstrongs stress the social character of childbirth and procreation, but insist that at the highest level of generality we can speak of a sexual division of labour that is integral to the reproduction of capitalism. This argument is premised on the analysis of capitalism as resting on free wage labour, which in turn – a point emphasized in Seccombe's analysis – rests on a private sphere and the separation of the workplace from the arena of reproduction of labour power. Hence, Pat and Hugh Armstrong argue, the sexual division of labour (at the basic level of women, not men, having babies) is 'central to capitalism' and not an historical or contingent matter. Clearly, they agree, the form taken by that division of labour, or particular kinds of family, are examples of what must be investigated historically as wide variation will occur. But at the most general level they propose that biological reproduction forms part of the definitional requirements of capitalism.

Patricia Connelly takes issue with this argument and suggests, in line with Michèle Barrett's book,[38] that the sexual division of labour is best analysed as part of an historically constituted social formation rather than as a theoretical prerequisite of capitalism. Connelly's contribution, and the reply from Pat and Hugh Armstrong, moves the debate on to three related questions. The first is whether such matters should, methodologically, be constituted as theoretical or as historical problems; the second is on the competing analytic claims of traditional Marxist and feminist theories (Connelly defends against Angela Miles the analytic primacy of the concept of mode of production); the third is the question of how to theorize gender ideology in a non-reductionist way.

These three issues also form the nexus of debate in the recent *New Left Review* exchanges about 'sex and class' that followed the review article, by Johanna Brenner and Maria Ramas, of *Women's Oppression Today*.[39] Brenner and Ramas are principally concerned with what they see as the undue weight attached by Barrett to ideology, but their second theme is that of biological reproduction as a determinant of the disadvantaged position of working-class women in the nineteenth century. Recasting the debate over the 'family wage' and in whose interests women were excluded from equal participation in productive labour, Brenner and Ramas argue that the exigencies of childbirth and lactation require greater attention than previously given. Michèle Barrett's reply on this point could find some point of entry to the questions raised in the Armstrong/Connelly exchange: how can we theorize as class specific a phenomenon such as the procreative division of labour which is consistent in all social classes? And if it cannot be theorized in terms specific to the working class, in what sense is it an essential precondition of the reproduction of that class rather than any other? The question of biology is one to which socialist-feminists must pay much greater attention, but clearly the issues remain at present unresolved.

A quite distinctive contribution to this last project has been made by the Canadian feminist Mary O'Brien, with whose essay we conclude this section of the anthology. O'Brien's work draws both on the Marxist tradition and on an analysis of the enormously unequal roles played by women and men in biological reproduction. In her book *The Politics of Reproduction*, she analyses 'the lengths to which men have gone to ameliorate the uncertainty of paternity, both conceptually and institutionally'.[40] O'Brien is unusual – perhaps more so in Britain than in Canada – in combining a rigorous and critical interrogation of Marxist theory and politics with an interest in male control over female reproductive labour that is more often associated with a radical feminist position. O'Brien's critical engagement with the hegemony theory of Antonio Gramsci provides an illustration of her imaginative eclecticism. Insightful to some, idiosyncratic to others, it reveals the distance travelled by Canadian feminists in their dialogue with Marxism.

Racism, Ethnicity, Nationalism

Clearly socialist politics and a strong political economy tradition have influenced the work of Canadian feminists. They have taken account in their work of relations of domination between Canada and the United States, of exploitative relations between classes and of disparities between different regions of the country. All these, they argue, have shaped the relations between women, men and children within the household; this includes people's choice of survival strategies, the relation between wage work and domestic work, and the connection between 'public' and 'private' worlds. In doing this feminists have questioned, altered and expanded the terms in which the country's social relations and development had formerly been understood.

This is illustrated by the attention that feminist historians have paid to the significance of ethnic and racial inequality in Canada. How white women, themselves dependent on their adventuring husbands, contributed to the development of structured racist inequalities between whites and Amerindians has been explored in Sylvia Van Kirk's thoughtful book, *Many Tender Ties: Women in Fur Trade Society*.[41] Today Indian women organize against the new forms of gender inequality that have been induced by the laws of the Canadian state which determines who does and does not have Indian 'status'.

The theme of racism is also taken up by Carol Lee Bacchi in her book *Liberation Deferred: The Ideas of the English Canadian Suffragists*.[42] Bacchi argues that many feminists wanted the vote to protect 'Canada' against the immigrant and French hordes threatening to overrun the country. Racism – despite the pious beliefs of many Canadians – has a long history in Canada. Women, from their contradictory location as dependants of men and members of privileged ethnic groups, and also and explicitly as feminists, have been involved in the building of racist inequalities and ideologies.

Oppressive conditions do not necessarily breed progressive politics, even among those who do, in some ways, break with their times. Yet once again arguments are being made and popularized, this time by feminists, about female essentialism and the special virtues of women. Feminists' involvement with social purity movements, as Bacchi and others have argued, clearly has created problems for women on the 'wrong' side of the class and race divides. Many 'first-wave' feminists in Canada simply assumed their superiority to the next generation of immigrant women taking their places in the country. John Porter has since conclusively shown that the formation of Canadian society through successive periods of immigration created a 'vertical mosaic' of discrete groups retaining their identity and history – and not the 'melting pot' culture of the USA.[43] Many of the early feminists, it seems, were determined to keep things that way.

Roxana Ng emphasizes the contemporary significance of this category of 'immigrant women' in Canadian society. Just as first-wave feminists were anxious to establish and perpetuate such a category to fill their needs for domestic servants, so the immigrant counselling service of today helps to produce appropriately labelled kinds of labour for the job market from its clients. In so doing the agency consolidates the work already begun by the racist and class-prejudiced immigration laws of Canada. The political ambiguity of the situation lies in the fact that the agency does also prepare its clients to support themselves and their dependants in an arena that offers few satisfactory options.

In writing the history of women in Canada, feminists have added new chapters to the ongoing work of understanding relations between Amerindians and whites, between successive groups of immigrants and the indigenous population. In addition, and with a much higher political profile in the last few decades, their work has transformed understanding of French-English relations and explored some complex connections between feminism and nationalism.

If there is one thing everyone – at least everyone who wrote about it – has believed about French women in Québec, it was that they produced many children. This belief contributed to English Canadian fears of 'race suicide'. Indeed, through the high francophone birth rate they feared the conquest itself might be subverted. While the English had won the military encounter on the Plains of Abraham in 1759, they were in danger of losing the war being conducted not on battle fields but in the bedrooms of French Canada. Why the French women had so many children seemed quite clear to the English: they were single-minded dupes of the Catholic church – poor, uneducated victims of their reactionary, priest-ridden society.

French intellectuals, both clerical and lay, turned this francophobic argument on its head. French women did indeed have many babies, but this represented the apogee of female virtue, combining as it did the interests of family, church and national survival. The continued French presence on this hostile English continent was attributed to the love, sacrifice and reproductive powers of the women. This was the 'revenge of the cradle'.

This clerico-national response was first developed in the years following the First World War, when it became apparent that the urban birth rate was falling. Québec's nationalists, as Susan Trofimenkoff has shown,[44] blamed a variety of foreign imports for this problem: capitalism, urbanization, protestantism – and feminism. What would happen to the nation if women began to foresake their most important tasks of child bearing and child rearing? French feminists in Québec responded by articulating a strongly Christian position: women only wanted what was necessary to perform their Christian duties properly and with dignity.[45]

There were, however, other reasons for the circumspect way in which French feminists behaved and expressed their criticisms of their situation. While some middle-class English women were expanding their horizons through education, professional and volunteer work, French lay women continued to face serious competition from the religious orders. Nuns – the heroines of New France, and many of them were quite extraordinary – had traditionally dominated these fields and retained their control as the work expanded.[46] Clearly the first wave of feminism in Québec was severely restricted by the repressive package of clerico-nationalist ideology on motherhood, family and pro-natalism.

Nadia Fahmy-Eid and Nicole Laurin-Frenette provide an analysis of the historical role of the church in Québec where 'a traditional alliance between family and church [contributed] to the containment of state power'. Like many Québec intellectuals Fahmy-Eid and Laurin-Frenette are informed by French Structuralism and, in particular, the Althusserian analysis of the role of the state in capitalist society. But they are critical of both its content and method, partly because of the need for an historical analysis. Furthermore, they argue, the pivotal role of the church in some modern capitalist societies is simply ignored. Certainly they make clear that it is impossible to understand Québec society, the role of women, family ideology or the early history of feminism without grasping the extent of power wielded by the Catholic Church.

The modern wave of feminism found dramatically more congenial ground in Québec. In the 1960s a 'quiet revolution' had deposed the church from its key guardianship of culture, language, religion and nation. A thoroughly secular provincial government had expanded state control into education, social services and health care. Women moved into the labour force, albeit into the same kinds of jobs – and occupational ghettos – as women elsewhere in the country. The contradiction between an apparent educational equality for women and men, and the continued reproduction of an extremely unequal division of labour, was becoming more clearly obvious. The birth rate had dropped dramatically too. By 1961 it was lower in Québec than in any other province in the country and, far from being the catalyst of the drop, as earlier nationalists had feared, feminism seems ironically to have been its beneficiary. It was only later, from the late 1960s, that growing numbers of women in Québec became feminist activists. This time it was not the clerics but the demographers who blew the whistle: the nation was courting disaster if women did not take to child bearing on a grander scale again.

It is at this point that a feminist historian, Marie Lavigne, took on the whole question of women and the birth rate in Québec. In the article reprinted here she looks closely at Québec's demographic history and concludes that within every generation since the turn of the century more women chose to have fewer children. She shows that the decline in the birth rate paralleled that of non-francophone women in the rest of the country. Furthermore, when the number of women who chose not to have children by taking up the religious life is recalled, the automatic conflation of French women with motherhood and numerous children must be challenged.

This challenge is not just to 'history' as already written. Contemporary political culture and policies still rest on the assumption that families have been large and that the nation is in danger if women flag in their reproductive efforts. For example, in 1981 the Parti Québecois promised increased support for the nuclear family in its election campaign: that meant financial rewards for having children, not more childcare places. (By and large offering more monetary incentives for having children is a policy that has not worked very well – if every women has her price it must be higher than the pro-natalists imagine.[47]) This illustrated the return of some traditional assumptions about women and the family to the nationalist movement in Québec. This followed a period in the mid-1970s when a progressive alliance developed between feminists and nationlists within the Parti Québecois. Of course, many nationalists were male and middle-class, but for a few years their political rhetoric was more general and generous. The nationalist appeal had to be broad and social democrats, socialists, trade unionists and feminists worked together towards the election in 1976 of the Parti Québecois.

From 1976 to 1981 the Cabinet of the Parti Québecois government included Lise Payette, latterly as a full Minister of State (for 'la condition féminine'). No feminist had achieved such high position in any federal or provincial government in Canada.

After her appointment to this portfolio she declared: 'I entered politics to work for the cause of women. It is revolutionary, the women's dossier. If there is a revolution in progress it is that one. The phenonmenon is not Québecois, it is world-wide.'[48] The extent of Payette's disillusionment can be seen in her auto-biography, significantly called *Le Pouvoir? Connais Pas!* (col-loquially, 'Power? Don't Ask Me!'), where she observed that 'It has not been possible to be in power among men. I have some-times had the illusion of having a bit of the action. I know now, however, that governments cannot, as long as they are com-posed in the majority by men, be feminist.'[49] Feminist disen-chantment with the Parti Québecois was symbolized by her announcement in 1981 that she would not run in the next elec-tion.

The sequence of events that led to Payette's resignation as Minister are often described as 'the Yvette phenomenon'. This fascinating political episode requires a little background expli-cation. First, the referendum on the independence of Québec. Central to the Parti Québecois' package of election priorities in 1976 was the promise to hold a referendum on Québec's future status. The question finally formulated asked for a mandate to negotiate 'sovereignty association' – a term used to convey poli-tical independence with economic association – with the rest of Canada. The pre-referendum opinion polls showed that the government's biggest obstacles to a 'yes' vote were the English and women.[50] The women were Payette's challenge. How could she avert the danger that it would be women, encouraged through the years to maintain their traditional role, who would respond to tradition and support the status quo with a vote for no change?

Lise Payette addressed the women of Québec in a speech on 9 March, arguing that women, including herself, had been brought up to be 'Yvettes' and that it was time to change. Yvette was the little girl in the primary school readers who helped her mother in the kitchen while her brother, Guy, did exciting things outside. Feminists, including Payette, had failed to get these sexist readers out of the schools and they were still the standard fare. Payette added another line to her speech; she said that Claude Ryan, the leader of the Provincial Liberal Party, was the kind of man who wanted women to remain 'Yvettes'. 'He is, moreover,' she continued fatefully, 'married to an Yvette.'

Payette's famous *faux pas* affected the outcome of the referendum, led to her own resignation and contributed to the breakdown of the fragile feminist-nationalist alliance. Four feminist historians of the Québec Collectif Clio (Michèle Jean, Jacqueline Lamothe, Marie Lavigne and Jennifer Stoddart) have analysed the political significance of the Yvette phenomenon. For it was Payette's alleged attack on Québec mothers that gave the 'no' lobby their most powerful card and, at the same time, disorganized and silenced their opponents. The image of the mother, as defender of the nation, with all its ideological force, was quickly captured for an anti-feminist position and – given the identification of feminism and nationalism in this conjuncture of events – that meant for an anti-nationalist vote.[51]

The reliance on maternalism in all the interpretations of national survival in Québec was a crucial factor in the 'Yvette' situation, but the difficulty that progressives have in articulating alternative visions of personal life is a broader problem. The New Right in the United States is distinctively different from similar ('pro-family') movements in Canada or Britain – mainly because of the powerful role of religious fundamentalism in the USA. But progressives in all these countries share the difficulty of finding anything to replace the emotional force of the old loyalties and moralities.

The referendum decision not to give the government a mandate to negotiate exerted a heavy strain on the feminist-nationalist alliance. Payette's success in cabinet had been based on her colleagues' belief that she had her finger on the pulse of Québec's women. After the Yvette débâcle they saw no electoral advantage in listening to her advice. Although she drafted a feminist programme on women and the family for the 1981 election, the Premier (Levesque) chose to stake out a different position for the Parti Québecois. He had listened to public discourse over the Yvette affair and opted for a strong defence of the traditional nuclear family.[52]

Women, including some feminists, continued to work in and with the Parti Québecois until its defeat in 1985. But this last term of office was not a spectacular dénouement for the alliance that had created such hope less than a decade earlier. It was not just the feminists who were disillusioned. The nationalist cause was also abandoned as the Parti Québecois tried unsuccessfully to persuade voters that they could do 'business as usual' just as well as the Liberals.

Yet the issue of babies and national survival remains. When feminist and nationalist forces rebuild in Québec, as they inevitably will, they will have the history of a progressive alliance and the mystery of its fragility and collapse to contemplate. The apparent contradiction between feminist emphasis on women's autonomy and independence, and the anxiety about national 'survival', will also have to be confronted.

The Social Reproduction of Gender

Lise Payette's struggles over the Yvettes at least had one positive consequence. The Minister of Education, horrified by what had been unleashed, ordered that all the 'Yvette' books be taken out of schools. Yet as we know, schools have many, and more subtle, ways of providing a gendered educational experience. In an article based on her research in a predominantly middle-class, urban, high school, Susan Russell demonstrates the school's collaboration in actively reproducing gender inequality through the behaviour, expectations and attitudes of teachers and guidance counsellors. Male students who do well are 'bright', females who excel 'work too hard'. But there is more to the problem: topics that interest girls because they touch their lives directly are often not regarded as 'knowledge', as legitimate subjects for study and discussion. The growth of women's studies in Canadian universities has not been matched in primary and secondary schools and current debates about the curriculum bypass this issue.

Just as the interests of women students are often dismissed in school, so also is the work they are likely to find when they enter the labour market. Jane Gaskell's article counters the argument that women are badly paid because they are unskilled. Developing some themes familiar in Britain from the work of Anne Phillips and Barbara Taylor on this topic,[53] Gaskell argues that the designation of work as 'skilled' or 'unskilled' results from struggles at work in which men have had greater bargaining power than women. Challenging the simplified view that women should improve their skills and enter 'masculine' jobs, Gaskell argues that women must continue to press for proper recognition of the work they do.

Subjectivity, Sexuality, Motherhood

Canadian feminists have taken up many of the current issues that are being debated in feminism elsewhere, and in particular there has been a resurgence of interest in the politics of sexuality and motherhood. In Britain, and to a large extent elsewhere too, feminists working with psychoanalytic theory have tended to be particularly interested in Freud, initially from the reassessment provided in Juliet Mitchell's rightly influential *Psychoanalysis and Feminism*.[54] Subsequent re-workings of Freud based more closely than Mitchell on the work of Jacques Lacan have proved perhaps even more attractive to many feminists on both sides of the Atlantic, particularly those interested in questions of culture and representation.[55] In Britain the Freud/Lacan dominance in the work of those feminists who pursued a psychoanalytic approach has recently been complemented by a new appropriation of the work of Melanie Klein and others more in the 'humanist' rather than structuralist stream within psychoanalysis. It seems likely that debates about the political implications for feminism of psychoanalytic theory will continue, since the Kleinian inspired approach has been criticized for locking women into traditional sexual and maternal identities at least as rigidly as the Freudian model was accused of doing.[56]

In this context it might be argued that the psychoanalytic tendency discussed in Roberta Hamilton's article is more critical, in social and political terms. Hamilton goes back, through the work of the Canadian theorist Gad Horowitz, to Marcuse's distinction between 'basic' and 'surplus' repression, examining the implications of this for normative heterosexuality and the denigration of femininity in modern capitalist society. Horowitz argues that surplus repression – that is, repression beyond what is strictly necessary to subjugate the psyche to the social – includes the prohibition of non-reproductive sexuality, and in particular homosexuality, in order to redirect libidinal energy towards labour. The need for intensive labour in capitalist society both underlines the salience of this point and indicates the potential for change in a future epoch with lesser need for toil. Hamilton argues that the form taken by this surplus repression can provide a clue to the understanding of misogyny and the denigration of femininity by both women and men, and this is examined through a re-presentation of the classic psychosexual stages of Oedipal socialization for both boys and girls.

The following quotation from Horowitz epitomizes the critical character of the position speculatively sketched out by Hamilton: 'revolutionary movements which do not revolutionize the psychosexual structure formed by surplus repression must fail, for this psychosexual structure is both product and source of domination.' Perhaps this partakes of the revolutionary romanticism with which Marcuse and the 'sexual liberation' of the 1960s are now so closely identified. But it is salutary to see that genuinely progressive appropriations of psychoanalysis continue, confronted as we are with a Paris fashion for 'taking back femininity' and, in London, newly respectable forms of heterosexism.[57]

Some comparable issues are raised in Heather Jon Maroney's closely argued review of the recent debate about motherhood in feminist writings. Maroney provides critical discussion of such writers as Nancy Chodorow and Dorothy Dinnerstein and explores the Canadian feminist Mary O'Brien's theories of the politics of reproduction. Maroney concludes by posing the central political question for feminism of the new tendency to embrace motherhood: does it mean a return to the 'separate spheres' of earlier feminisms and does it rest on essentialist ideas about women's natural qualities?

Heather Jon Maroney offers an interesting escape route for feminists who reject the conservatism of the 'new feminist essentialism'[58] but who are none the less convinced by many of the arguments coming from the feminist 'motherhood problematic' that has developed alongside more positive personal attitudes towards the bearing and rearing of children. Maroney draws attention to the difference between the old and limited 'separate spheres' idea and the revolutionary ambitions of a 'second wave' feminism whose 'radical transformative project is to create a feminized world'. She regards the new theories of motherhood as a means to reject altogether the metaphor of 'separate spheres', since they propose such a fundamental extension of the feminine sphere 'until it becomes coterminous with the human totality'. This is no feminist separatism, but an argument based on a fuller understanding of what Maroney (using Mary O'Brien's work) calls the alienated 'male reproductive condition'.

Maroney's article is one of very few that confronts the conflict – theoretical and strategic – between traditional Marxist assumptions, modern feminist theory and the recent ecological and peace movements. She brings out the relevance of the new motherhood theory for issues of planetary survival and what she calls 'biospheric renewal', emphasizing the need for a profound re-thinking of the Marxist political tradition in the light of these issues. Given the facile assumptions often made about the women/peace connection, and the equally dogmatic rejections of this made from an unbendingly anti-essentialist position, Maroney's rigorous and rational discussion stands out like a landmark in the political debate.

Feminism and Revolution

By way of a conclusion we reprint a brief essay by Mary O'Brien. Her work is well known in Canada, but less so in Britian and the United States. As Maroney points out, O'Brien's achievement has been a brilliant transposition of the Marxist notion of alienation from the production process to the sphere of biological reproduction. Her theorization of male and female reproductive conditions, and of 'generically' divided reproductive conciousness, suggests the need for a dialectic knowledge of reproduction analogous to a Marxist knowledge of production. No doubt some will regard the general emphasis on biological reproduction, not to mention the specific arguments raised, as more characteristic of radical than of socialist feminism. Certainly Mary O'Brien's work might easily fall into the category of 'dualist' analysis that has been developed to try to theorize the place of women's oppression in capitalism.[59]

One danger of the 'dualistic' mode is that it can obscure the gender/class relation by setting up two distinct systems: one related to women and family and the other to class and production. Dorothy Smith has argued against the 'sectioning off' of social relations that include women, because this ignores the 'gender-saturated' quality of *all* social relations. She emphasizes that gender relations are an integral part of the constitution of classes.[60] But if Mary O'Brien's analysis is dualistic, it none the less recognizes the historical interrelation of production and reproduction. Also it is an argued theoretical position, one that insists that the twofold subject being analysed requires what Joan Kelly called a 'doubled vision'.[61]

The theme of biological reproduction – its political significance and the dificulties of its theorization – calls up the sex and class debate in the second section, and some of the issues about gender and nationality in the third. Mary O'Brien's essay encapsulates the originality, and the diversity, of Canadian feminist work.

Home and Workplace

Two Hands for the Clock: Changing Patterns in the Gendered Division of Labour in the Home

Meg Luxton

> When I first got a job, I just never had any time, what with looking after the children and the housework. But now my husband has started to help me. He cooks and picks up the kids and is even starting to do other stuff! What a difference! Before, I used to feel like the second hand on the clock–you know, always racing around. Now, with his help, it feels like there are two hands for the clock – his and mine - so I get to stop occasionally.

More and more married women with young dependent children are employed outside the home. Studies conducted in the early and mid-1970s suggested that when married women took on paid employment, their husbands did not respond by increasing the amount of time they spent on domestic labour. These studies reached the general conclusion that married women were bearing the burden of the double day of labour almost entirely by themselves.[1]

Underlying women's double day of labour is the larger question of the gendered division of labour itself. The gendered division of labour, and particularly women's responsibility for domestic labour, have been identified as central to women's oppression in the capitalist societies as a whole, and specifically to women's subordination to men within families.[2] Women's changing work patterns have posed sharply questions about domestic labour. What is actually being done in the home? Is it sufficient? Who is actually doing it? Who should be doing it? This in turn has raised further questions about the existing unequal power relations between women and men.

In the paid labour force, some women's groups, particularly within the union movement, have organized campaigns centred on such specific issues as equal pay and equal access to jobs.

Their efforts are a challenge to the existing divisions of work between women and men.[3] Such changes in the definition and distribution of women's work raise the question of whether or not attitudes toward the gendered division of labour in the family household are also being challenged. Has there been any comparable redefinition of men's work roles? And further, has there been any redistribution of work inside the family household? As women learn to drive electrohauls, shovel muck, and handle the heat of coke ovens, are men learning to change diapers, comfort an injured child, or plan a week's food within the limits imposed by a tight budget?

A recent Gallup poll on the sharing of general housework is suggestive. The poll, conducted across Canada in August 1981, reports that, during the years 1976 to 1981, Canadians changed their opinions substantially about whether husbands should share in general housework. When asked the question, 'In your opinion, should husbands be expected to share in the general housework or not?' 72 per cent responded 'yes' in 1981 as compared with 57 per cent in 1976. Only 9 per cent (11 per cent of all men and 7 per cent of all women) replied that men should not share the work.

However, changes in attitudes do not necessarily indicate changes in behaviour. The Gallup poll goes on to suggest that there has apparently been little change in what husbands do. It also implies that women and men disagree on the extent to which men are helping regularly. In 1976, 44 per cent of men polled said they helped regularly with housework, while, in 1981, 47 per cent said they did. By contrast, in 1976, 33 per cent of women polled said men regularly helped while, in 1981, 37 per cent of women polled said men regularly helped.[4]

Flin Flon Revisited

In 1976–7 I investigated women's work in the home through a case study of one hundred working-class households in Flin Flon, a mining town in Northern Manitoba.[5] Five years later, in 1981, I carried out a follow-up study to discover whether or not changes had occurred over the preceding five years. As Flin Flon is a small, fairly remote, single-industry town, it is not a Canadian pace-setter. Changes occurring in Flin Flon probably indicate more widespread developments. While this case study does not dispute the finding of earlier studies (that when married women get paying jobs they continue to do most of the domestic labour), it does suggest that the situation is considerably more complex than had previously been perceived. It illustrates some of the factors underlying the emergence of the different patterns of attitudes and behaviours reflected in the Gallup poll. It also shows that in some working-class households, important changes in the division of labour are beginning to occur, as women exert pressure on their husbands to take on more domestic labour.

In the first study, I interviewed women of three generations. The first generation set up households in the 1920s and 1930s, the second in the 1940s and 1950s, and the third in the 1960s and 1970s. With just a few exceptions, women of the third generation were the ones with young children under the age of twelve. Just over half the women interviewed had held paid work outside the home for some period after their marriage. None of them, however, had worked outside the home while their children were young. Most had worked for pay before their children were born, but then had not worked for pay again until the children were of school age. Regardless of whether or not they held paid jobs outside the home, these women identified themselves primarily as housewives and considered domestic labour their responsibility. They generally maintained that they did not expect their husbands to help with domestic labour. Those few men who did some work were praised as wonderful exceptions.

In the follow-up study I sought out only women of the third generation and was able to locate forty-nine of the original fifty-two. In striking contrast to the previous study, I found that these women, all of whom had children twelve years of age or less, were for the most part working outside the home for pay. Over half of these women had pre-school children, and nineteen had had another baby between 1976 and 1981. Despite their continued childcare responsibilities, forty-four women had full-time employment. Of these, fourteen said they would prefer to be in the home full-time; nine said they would prefer part-time paid work; and almost half (21) said they were satisfied with the situation they were in. Four women had part-time paid work. Of these, two were satisfied while one wanted, but had not yet been able to find, a full-time paid job. One wanted to return to full-time domestic labour, but could not afford to quit her job. Only one woman was still working full-time in the home and she said she was there by choice.

What emerged from the interviews was that regardless of whether or not they wanted to be employed, these women were changing their identification of themselves as being primarily housewives. As one of the women who was working for pay full-time, but who wished she could stay at home, put it:

> I am a housewife. That's what I always wanted to be. But I have also been a clerk for years so I guess I'm one of those working mothers – a housewife, a mother and a sales clerk.

Given the demands of their paid work, these women were forced to reorganize their domestic labour in some way. Both interviews and time budgets showed that the attitudes women have towards their work responsibilities (both paid and domestic) affect the way they reorganize domestic labour. A key factor was the extent to which they were willing to envisage a change in the gendered division of labour inside the family household.

Labour-force participation did not necessarily reflect their approval of 'working mothers'. In 1981, all of the women were asked what they thought about married women who had dependent children and who worked outside the home. Seven flatly opposed it under any circumstances, although all of them were in that situation. Nine did not think it was right for them personally, although they felt such a decision should be made on an individual basis. Eight women said it was fine if the woman needed the money, although they opposed mothers working outside the home for any other reasons.[6]

In contrast over half of the the women interviewed (twenty-five) maintained that mothers with dependent children had every right to work outside the home if they wanted to. Many of them (fourteen) went further and argued that it was better for mothers to be working outside the home. For these women, ecomonic need was only one of several valid reasons that women would take paid employment.

There was a direct correspondence between the attitudes these women expressed toward paid employment for mothers and their views on the gendered division of labour in the home. All of the women were asked who they thought should be responsible for domestic labour. Their responses show three distinct strategies in balancing the demands of domestic labour, paid employment and family. I have identified these distinct positions, based on their conceptualization of appropriate gender relations, as follows: separate spheres and hierarchical relations; separate spheres and co-operative relations; shared spheres and changed relations.[7]

Separate Spheres and Hierarchical Relations

Seven respondents (14 per cent) advocated a strict gender-based division of labour. They flatly opposed women working outside the home because doing so would both violate women's proper role and detract from their ability to do domestic labour. These women argued that men, as males, were breadwinners and were 'naturally' also household or family heads. Women were to be subordinate to their husbands – this was described by several women as 'taking second place to my husband'. They argued that women's wifely duties included acquiescence in relation to their husband's demands and putting their families' needs before their own. These women maintained that they themselves held paid jobs outside the home only because their earnings were crucial. They intended to stop work as soon as the 'emergency' was over.

They insisted that their paid work must never interfere with their ability to care for their husbands and children or to run their households. Because they assumed that domestic labour was entirely women's responsibility, they did not expect their husbands to help. They maintained that boy children should not be expected to do anything at all around the house and argued that they were teaching their girl children domestic labour skills, not because the mothers needed help, but as training for the girl's future roles as wives and mothers. Accordingly, these women sustained the full double day of labour entirely by themselves.

To deal with the contradiction between their beliefs and their actions, these women worked even harder at their domestic labour. In what appears to be a rigorous overcompensation, they actually raised their standards for domestic labour. They were determined to behave as though paid work made no difference to their domestic performance. Many of them insisted, for example, that every evening meal include several courses made from scratch as well as home-made desserts.

As a result, these women set themselves up in a never-ending vicious circle and ran themselves ragged. Their fatigue and resulting irritability and occasional illness only served to convince them that their original prognosis was correct: paid employment is bad for women and harmful to their families.

Separate Spheres and Co-operative Relations

Seventeen women (35 per cent) said that women and men are different. Each gender moves in a separate sphere and marriage, in uniting a woman and man, requires co-operation between the two spheres, with each person pulling his or her own weight. These women considered it acceptable for women to 'help out' by earning money when necessary but, they argued, women's real work was in the home.

There were two identifiable currents within this general position. Nine women advocated full-time domestic labour for themselves though they agreed that might not be the best option for all women. These women maintained that they should not be working outside the home because they thought it interfered with their family responsibilities. While they were more flexible in their attitudes than those in the first group of women, they argued generally for the maintenance of the gendered division of labour. Particularly in their childrearing attitudes and behaviour, they adhered to a strict notion that boys should not be expected to engage in domestic labour while girls should be encouraged to do so.

Like the first group of women, these women also did most of the domestic labour on their own. Their way of trying to cope with the enormous strain this created, however, was to ease up their standards for domestic labour. They were much more willing to purchase 'convenience foods' or to eat in restaurants. They talked about doing less around the house and about feeling vaguely disappointed that they could not keep their place nicer. They were, however, prepared to accept that they could not work outside the home and continue to do full-time domestic labour as well.

Taking a slightly different approach, eight women stated that paid work was acceptable for women with children, if the women's income was necessary for her household economy. While these women also indicated that they were in favour of maintaining a traditional gendered division of labour, they often engaged in contradictory practices. They would argue that domestic labour was women's work, but in day-to-day activities they frequently asked their husbands to lend a hand, and they all expected their boy children as well as the girls to learn and take on certain domestic tasks.

To a large extent, it appears that the discrepancy between their beliefs and their behaviour lies in an experienced necessity. Unlike those who argued for hierarchial relations, these women were unwilling to become 'superwomen'. They acknowledged the pressures on them and were willing to ask for help. The extent to which they asked for, and received, assistance varied from household to household. In most cases, children had been assigned chores such as washing the dishes or setting the dinner table which they were expected to do on a regular basis. Husbands were not assigned regular jobs but were usually expected to 'lend a hand' when they were specifically asked.

Towards Shared Spheres and Changing Relations

Twenty-five women – just over half the sample (51 per cent) – stated that regardless of necessity, women with young children had the right to paid employment if they wanted it. For them, wives and husbands were partners who should share the responsibilities for financial support and domestic labour. They supported the idea of changing the division of labour and in practice they were instituting such changes by exerting increasing pressure on their husbands and children to redistribute both the responsibility for, and the carrying out of, domestic labour. As it is these women who are challenging the existing ideology and practice of the gendered division of labour, and especially the place of women and men in the family home, I want to look more closely at the changes they have enacted in the last five years.

A Redistribution of Labour Time

While the women who argued for separate spheres were defending a gendered division of labour within the household, statements made by the third group reflected the trends indicated in the Gallup poll. When these twenty-five women were asked in the 1976 study if they thought husbands should help with domestic labour, most agreed that they did not expect their husbands to do anything, although six said their husbands actually did help. By 1981, however, they unanimously insisted that husbands should help out and all said their husbands did some domestic labour on a regular basis.

An examination of time budgets for these households shows that men have in fact increased the amount of time they spend on domestic labour. By themselves, the figures seem to be quite impressive; men increased their domestic labour time from an average of 10.8 hours per week in 1976 to 19.1 hours in 1981 – an increase of 8.3 hours.

By contrast, in 1976 full-time housewives spent an average of 63 hours per week on domestic labour while women working a double day spent an average of 87.2 hours per week working, of which 35.7 hours were spent on domestic labour. In 1981, women doing both jobs averaged 73.9 hours per week, of which 31.4 hours were spent on domestic labour. This is a decrease of only 4.3 hours per week. While one would not expect a direct hour for hour substitution for one person's labour for another, there is a discrepancy between the increase in men's work and the relatively insignificant reduction in women's work. Women on an average were spending 12.3 hours a week more than men on domestic labour. Furthermore, there is a discrepancy between the women's insistence that domestic labour should be shared equally and the actual behaviour of household members. These discrepancies generate considerable tension between wives and husbands – tension which reflects the power struggle inherent in the redistribution of domestic labour.

Women's and Men's Domestic Labour

The women who wanted their husbands to be more involved have developed a variety of strategies and tactics with which to get the men to take on more work. These range from gentle appeals to fairness or requests for assistance to militant demands for greater (or equal) participation. In a few cases, women discussed the situation with their husbands and they mutually agreed on a sharing of tasks that both partners considered fair and reasonable. In the majority of cases, however, negotiations appeared to be out of the question. Instead the couples seemed locked into tension-generating, manipulative power struggles.

For the women, the impetus to change comes first from the pressures of their two jobs. It is fuelled further when they compare their experiences with those of their husbands. Some contrasted their own working time at home with their husband's leisure time.

> I come home from work dead tired and I still have to cook and be with the kids and clean up. And he just lies around, drinking beer, watching TV and I get so mad, I could kill him.

Others compared the standards their husbands expected from their wives with those the men held for themselves. They noted that when living alone, some men kept their households immaculately clean; others lived in a total mess. Whatever their standards for themselves, when the women were around, men changed their behaviour, altered their expectations and pressured the women to meet male standards.

> When my husband is on his own, he's quite happy to live in a pig sty. Mess doesn't bother him. But the minute I get back he insists that he can't live in the house unless it's spotless.
>
> Before we were married he lived on his own and his place was so clean and tidy. But as soon as we got married, he somehow never felt he could clean up. It was all up to me.

Despite the obvious interest these women have in redistributing domestic labour, and despite their motivating anger, there are numerous forces operating which make it difficult for women to insist that their spouses actually share the work.

Because inequalities in the division of labour are based on male power, when women demand equalization of the work, they are challenging that power. Some women were afraid that if they pushed for more male participation, they would provoke their husbands' anger and rage. At least one woman said her husband had beaten her for suggesting he help with domestic labour.

While there is evidence to suggest that when women have paid employment they increase their own power in marriage, all of these women earned considerably less than their husbands. As a result, the men retained economic power (breadwinner power). Men can also use their greater earnings as a justification for not doing domestic labour. They often argued that with their earnings they discharged the responsibility to the household. Under present circumstances it is up to the individual women to initiate changes in the patterns of domestic labour. For many, economic dependency makes it difficult to challenge their husbands.

Furthermore, the actual task of getting men to do domestic labour is often difficult. If women want their husbands to begin doing domestic labour, they must be prepared to take responsibility not only for overcoming male resistance but also for helping the men overcome both the accumulated years of inexperience and the weight of traditional assumptions about masculinity. Generally, the women assumed that their husbands were unfamiliar with domestic labour and therefore neither knew what needed doing nor had the necessary skills to carry out the work. Taking on this training of resisting and unskilled workers is often in itself an additional job.

When men do start doing domestic labour, women begin to lose control. Domestic labour has traditionally been the one sphere of female control and power. For most women, the kitchen is the closest they ever come to having a 'room of one's own'. It is difficult for many women to relinquish this, particularly if they are not compensated for that loss by gains made elsewhere – for example in their paid work. While the women were uniformly pleased that their husbands had increased their contribution, they were troubled by the way domestic labour was being redistributed.

Men and Domestic Labour

That men increase the amount of time they spend on domestic labour does not in itself convey much about changing work patterns. Most significantly, it was still assumed that women were primarily responsible for domestic labour and that men were 'helping out'. When women do domestic labour they often juggle several tasks at once. One of the ways that men have increased the amount of time they spend on domestic labour is by taking over some of that simultaneous work. Many women reported that their husbands were willing to watch the children while the women prepared dinner or did other household chores. While such actions obviously relieved some of the pressures and tensions on women, they did not reduce the amount of time required of women for domestic labour.

Often when men (and children) took on certain tasks, they ended up generating even more domestic work. A number of women indicated that their husbands cooked, but when they did so they seriously disrupted the orderliness of the kitchen, emptying cupboards to find something and not putting things back, of using an excessive number of dishes in the preparation. Another commonly cited example was that when men agreed to look after the children, they actually paid more attention to their visiting friends or the TV. Unattended, the children ran 'wild' through the house so that when the woman returned she had to spend a great deal of time tidying the house and calming the children. Further, many women pointed out that getting their husbands to do domestic labour required a considerable amount of their time and energy. Sometimes, women argued, it took more work to get the man to do the work than it did to do the work themselves.

Furthermore, men tended to take over certain specific tasks which had clearly defined boundaries. They did not take on the more nebulous, ongoing management tasks and they rarely took responsibility for pre-task planning. For example, a number of men did the grocery shopping on a regular basis but they insisted that the women draw up the basic list of things needed. Some men would do the laundry, if all the dirty clothes were previously collected and sorted and if the necessary soap and bleach were already at hand.

A recurring theme throughout the interviews was that men preferred jobs that involved working with machinery. A number of men were willing to do the vacuuming because they enjoyed playing with the vacuum cleaner. One women described how her husband had refused to cook until they purchased a food processor. After that he was forever reading the recipe book and planning new techniques for meal preparation. Several women noted that their husbands had increased their participation in meal preparation after they bought microwave ovens.

The redistribution that is occurring is selective. The husbands tend to take the path of least resistance. The trend has been for men to take on those tasks that are the most clearly defined, or sociable and pleasant ones, while leaving the more ill-defined or unpleasant ones to the women. Repeatedly women noted that their husbands had taken on reading the children a bedtime story and staying with them until they fell asleep, thus 'freeing' the women to wash the dishes and tidy the kitchen. Men were often willing to feed their infant children or take older ones to the park, but on the whole they would not change soiled nappies or wash their children's hair. They would wash the dishes but not the kitchen floor or the toilet. One man would vacuum the living-room rug but refused to do the stairs because they were too awkward.

A number of women expressed concern about this pattern. They noted that when men took on the more pleasant aspects of domestic labour, they were left with the most onerous and boring tasks. They were particularly concerned when the man took on more of the playtime with children. As one woman expressed it:

> I'm really glad he's spending more time with the children. They really enjoy it. But it's beginning to make me look like the meany. Daddy plays with them and tells them stories and other nice things while I do the disciplining, make them wash up, tidy their toys and never have time to play because I'm cooking supper.

One of the most significant transformations of men's involvement in domestic labour has been in the area of childcare. While most fathers have always spent some time with their children, particularly with older children, increasingly they are doing more of the day-to-day care-giving, especially with younger children. Perhaps the most significant change of all has been with the birth process itself.[8] In 1976 only 4 out of 25 men had been present at the birth of at least one of their children. However, of the babies born between 1976 and 1981, 10 of the 19 new fathers had been present at the birth (and only 2 of these were of the original 4). The wives indicated that they felt very strongly that having their husbands involved in the birth also drew the men into the whole process of pregnancy, childbirth and infant care. Men who were willing to attend the birth were subsequently more inclined to get up at night with the baby, to take over certain feedings and to be generally more involved with their small babies.

Despite this very promising shift, women were still responsible for overall childcare. All twenty-five women said it was up to them to arrange day-care for their children when they worked outside the home. If the childcare arrangements fell through on any particular day, it was the woman who had to get time off work to stay home, although this can in part be explained by her lower pay and in part by his unavailability when underground.

Furthermore, men 'babysat' their own children – something that women never did. The implication of this typical reference was that the children were the responsibility of the mother, and the father 'helped out'. This attitudinal difference was often carried out in behaviour as well. Women repeatedly described situations where men would agree to watch the children, but would then get involved in some other activity and would ignore the children. As children grew up, they learned from experience that their mothers were more likely to be helpful, and so they would turn to the woman rather than the man for assistance, thus actively perpetuating the traditional division of labour.

The ambivalent and often reluctant way in which these men have moved into domestic labour reflects a combination of valid reasons and invalid excuses. In 'The Politics of Housework', Pat Mainardi describes with biting sarcasm the various forms of male resistance developed in response to a wife's attempt to share housework:

> Husband: 'I don't mind sharing the work, but you'll have to show me how to do it.'
> Meaning: I'll ask a lot of questions and you'll have to show me everything every time I do it because I don't remember so good. And don't try to sit down and read while I'm doing my jobs because I'm going to annoy the hell out of you until it's easier to do them yourself.[9]

Flin Flon women described various forms of male behaviour that were obviously intended to resist attempts to draw them into domestic labour. The majority of resisters took a subtle approach (passive resistance) similar to the ones satirized by Mainardi. One woman described how their kitchen sink was directly in the centre of the kitchen counter. Normally the draining board sat on the left-hand side and the dirty dishes were stacked on the right. Her husband maintained he was unable to do the dishes as he was left-handed and the sink was designed for right-handed people. Some women talked suspiciously of the way household machinery 'broke down' when their husbands tried to use it. Several women told of incidents where their husbands agreed to do the work but then repeatedly 'forgot' to do it, complained when the women 'nagged' them about it, and finally told the women to do it themselves if they did not like the way the men did it. One man explained his position quite clearly:

> Look, I'm not interested in doing stuff around the house. I think that's her job, but since she's working she's been on my back to get me to help out so I say, 'sure I'll do it'. It shuts her up for a while and sometimes I do a few things just to keep her quiet. But really, I don't intend to do it, but it prevents a row if I don't say that.

For men to take on domestic labour meant that they had to give up some of the time they had previously spent on their own enjoyments. Within certain limits this may not be much of a sacrifice, but at some point a man's increasing involvment in domestic labour starts eroding his ability to engage in other activities he values highly. There is a substantial difference between washing dishes and watching TV, and in having to come home early from drinking with one's mates at the pub because one has to cook dinner.

Because the majority of men have, until recently, not been expected to do domestic labour, they have not been taught either implicitly, the way girls learn via their dolls and play kitchens, or explicitly, through 'helping' mother or in home economics classes. As a result, they often lack knowledge and are unskilled and awkward. Working at a job for which one is ill-prepared often generates feelings of anxiety, inadequacy and incompetence which are easily translated into a generalized reluctance to continue the job.

Some men expressed a willingness to do domestic labour but they were afraid that if it were publicly known that they did 'women's work', they would be subjected to teasing and ridicule. One man, for example, quite enjoyed doing the vacuuming. However, there were no curtains on the windows, so the interior of the house was visible from the street. As a result, he did the vacuuming on his knees so that no one would see him! Other men were willing to do tasks inside the house but steadfastly refused to do those tasks that were 'women's work' outside in public (hanging washing on the line, for example).

This fear of public ridicule was illustrated by two neighbours. Both families visited together frequently, and the men were friends. They also did a considerable amount of cooking and cleaning. Both, however, insisted that their wives not let the other couple know of the extent to which the men did domestic labour. The fear of public ridicule may reflect a deeper fear. When wives insist that men move into an area that has traditionally been defined as 'women's work', men face a challenge to their conventional notions of femininity and masculinity. This may arouse deep psychological and emotional resistances, and stimulate anxiety and fear.

Because most couples are unable to negotiate openly a redistribution of labour, they often get locked into tension-producing manipulations. This was illustrated rather graphically by the story one woman told about how she 'got' her husband to do the laundry.

She began by explaining that she felt it was only right that he do some of the domestic labour once she started working full-time outside the home. She asked him to help her and he agreed in principle, but he did not do anything. When she asked him to do things like cook supper or wash the dishes he would regularly say that he was going to, but then he would put it off indefinitely so that she ended up doing it all. She decided that she needed to teach him to do one specific task on a regular basis. Laundry, she estimated, would be an appropriate job for him, so she figured out what the discrete tasks involved in doing the laundry were.

The first day she left the laundry basket of sorted clothes sitting at the top of the basement stairs. As he was going down to his workroom she asked him to take the laundry down and put it on top of the machine. She repeated this several times until he automatically took the basket down without being asked. 'Once he had done that a few times I knew he'd taken it on regular so I was ready to move on to the next step.' She then asked him, as he went down with the basket, to put the laundry into the machine. Once that was learned, she asked him to put in the soap and turn the machine on.

> Finally it got so he would regularly carry the laundry down, put it in and turn it on. I never even had to ask him. So then I began getting him to pick up the dirty clothes.

Eventually, after more than six months of careful, though unstated strategizing on her part, the man was doing all the work involved in laundry. 'Now he does it all regular. I think I will train him to do the dishes next.'

While neither of them discussed what was going on, the husband by participating in the process gave his tacit acceptance of the new division of labour. However, because the work was being redistributed by manipulation rather than negotiation, the process only served to exacerbate the already existing tensions between the spouses. It did not engender greater respect or affection between the two. By 'tricking' her spouse, the woman had relieved some of the burden of her work but she was contemptuous of him for the way he took it over:

> What a fool. If I'd have asked him, he would have refused. If I'd begged and pleaded he would have said he'd do it if he knew how, but

would have said he didn't know how and so couldn't. So I fooled him and now he does it. But the whole thing's really stupid.

For his part the husband refused to discuss what was occurring. The wife's interpretation was better:

> Things are changing in our life. My job has forced us to do things differently. But he will not talk about it. So I play tricks and hate him and I think he must resent me – but I don't know because he won't tell me. So things change but I don't know what it means. Sometimes I think men are really stupid, or they hate women or at least there's no point trying with them.

Conclusion

This case study suggests that changing patterns of paid employment are creating a crisis in the way labour is currently distributed and accomplished in the family household. It illustrates the ambiguities reflected in the Gallup poll findings and shows that these ambiguities arise from serious problems in the way domestic labour is changing. It also suggests that ideologies of 'family' are very strong and play a central part in the way most people organize their interpersonal relationships and their domestic lives.

Because people tend to evaluate their experiences in light of existing social explanations and ideologies, the response of Flin Flon women can be set in a broader context. The three perspectives expressed reflect ideologies which are currently prominent.

Those women who put forward a 'separate spheres and hierarchical relations' position were defending the traditional conservative view which locates women inside the family, subordinates women's interests to men's, and places priority above all on the preservation of the breadwinner husband/dependent wife/nuclear family.

Because the beliefs these Flin Flon women held conflicted directly with the activities they engaged in, they were compelled to mediate the contradiction. Their attempts to defend a strict gendered division of labour forced them deeper into the hardship of the double day. Their actual experiences highlight the conditions under which support for right-wing 'pro-family' reform movements is generated, for in their opinion it is their paid work that creates the problem.

Those women who argued for 'separate spheres and co-operative relations' were expressing a classic liberal view of appropriate female/male relations in the family. This 'different but equal' perspective echoes the maternal feminism of some early twentieth-century theorists. It is also found in many sociologists of the family such as Young and Wilmott, who argue that marriages are now symmetrical or companionate.[10]

Those women who argued for 'shared spheres and changing relations' were expressing contemporary feminist views which hold that the existing gendered division of labour is a major factor in women's oppression. In challenging the way work is divided in the home, they are questioning the existing relationships between women and men, and between children and adults. Discussing existing family relationships, Hartmann has argued that 'Because of the division of labour among family members, disunity is thus inherent in the "unity" of the family.'[11]

This study suggests that a large-scale social transformation is occurring as traditional patterns are eroding and new ones are emerging, but to date the change has been acted out on the level of the individual household, and may, in the short run, be intensifying family disunity. What emerged from these interviews was the total isolation both women and men felt. Women involved in active, collective organizing to change the division of labour in the paid workforce have the women's liberation movement, the trade union movement, Status of Women committees, and sometimes the law and other organizations or institutions such as the Human Rights Commissions, to back them up. In contrast, women challenging the gendered division of labour in the home do so on an individual basis. Similarly, there is a complete lack of social and material support for men with regard to domestic labour. Very few unions have won paternity leave, for example, so it is very difficult for new fathers to get time off work to be with their new children. This makes it very difficult for men actually to take equal responsibility for their infants.[12] Accordingly, any man who takes on domestic labour places himself at odds with current social practices. It takes a certain amount of self-confidence and courage to do so.

As a result, the majority of respondents implied that they considered that the changes in their domestic division of labour were specific to their individual households. They perceived these changes not as part of a large-scale transformation in the patterns of work and family life, but as a personal struggle between them and their spouse. Such a perception only exacerbated the tensions between women and men.

As material conditions change and new ideologies emerge, many individuals and families are floundering, trying to decide what they want, how to get it, and most problematically, how to resolve conflicts between various possibilities and needs. There are currently no social policies or clear-cut, developing social norms to provide a context in which individuals can evaluate their own actions. Instead, there are several contending ideologies and related social movements, such as the 'pro-family' movement and the women's liberation movement.[13] While these movements articulate positions on what female/male relations should entail, they rarely organize to provide support for women to achieve the desired end. The current situation is thereby generating a great deal of confusion and often pain and interpersonal conflict, especially between women and men.

Finally, this study demonstrates that until the exclusive identification of women with domestic labour is broken, there is no possibility of achieving any kind of equality between women and men. If the necessary labour is not redistributed, women end up with a dramatically increased work-load. Unlike earlier studies, the findings of this research suggest, that despite all the problems, some working-class women are contesting male power and challenging male privilege and some men are responding by assuming more responsibility for domestic labour.

Women's Work:
Domestic and Wage Labour in a
Nova Scotia Community

Patricia Connelly and Martha MacDonald

There is little argument about the fact that it is still primarily women who are responsible for work done in the home. Unlike most men, women in Canada spend a large portion of their lives doing housework. In addition, at present over 50 per cent of women are in the work-force and account for 40 per cent of the labour force. The clear implication of these facts is that many women contribute to their families both through household and labour-force activities.

In recent years there has been an increasing amount of research and debate around the relationship between women's domestic and wage work and the family wage.[1] A major issue within the literature centres around the role of women as a reserve army of labour which can be called out of and returned to the home as economic conditions change.[2] In the Canadian context it has been argued that women meet the conditions of cheapness, availability and competition, which are the defining characteristics of a reserve army of labour. Some women have always been part of the active reserve, that is, the unemployed, and in addition married women have been held in an inactive reserve position within the home. Since the mid-twentieth century this reserve of married women has been active on a more or less permanent basis. Changes in capitalist production have led to an expansion of traditional female jobs, creating a demand for female labour. Changes in household production have led to commodities once considered luxuries becoming necessities, creating a demand for increased household income. It is under these conditions that married women have entered the labour force in Canada.[3]

In this paper we contribute to this research by examining at the national, regional and community levels economic changes and their effect on women's work and the family household. In historical terms we outline the changes from petty commodity production, when all family members contributed to a household economy, to a wage labour economy and a new family form based on a conception of male breadwinners and women as dependent homemakers. The questions we raise concern the existence of the male family wage and the contribution of women's work to the maintenance of the family household.

We argue that working-class households have always required more than the male wage and that women have always contributed to the maintenance of the family household either by intensifying their domestic labour in the home, by earning money through an informal economy, or by participating in the labour force and earning a wage themselves. The combination of ways in which they contribute depends on specific economic conditions. For example, participating in the labour force is not always an option for women since other labour reserves are available and may be preferred; the informal economy is available to some women but not others, and in some places but not others; intensification of domestic labour is sufficient in some periods of time, but in some periods and in some areas substitution of domestic labour for money income is not possible.

An examination at the national level allows us to get a general picture of the trends affecting women's work and the family household. By working at this level, however, crucial differences between groups of women usually are lost – groups such as older and younger women, urban and rural women, women from different classes, and women at the centre and periphery of the national economy.[4] For this reason, we conduct a case study of a Nova Scotia fishing village. By doing so we are able to see how these trends operate under more concrete, specific historical conditions.

The paper is organized into three sections. The first provides a general historical picture of women's work, the family household and the Canadian economy. The second section briefly describes the nature of underdevelopment in the Nova Scotia economy and the implications of this underdevelopment for the role of women's work. The third section is a detailed case study of a Nova Scotia fishing community using a parallel historical analysis.

The research methodology involves the use of interviews and secondary data to examine changes in the fishing industry as they relate to this particular community. Since the major employer of women is the fish plant, interviews were conducted with managers and workers concerning changes in the sex distribution of jobs within the plant, wage rates, working conditions and sources of labour. In addition, women were interviewed concerning their work patterns and the contributions of family members to childcare, housework and the family wage.

The Canadian Economy and Women's Work: A Historical Overview

In the early nineteenth century, before Confederation, Canada was a rural society. Almost everyone was involved in primary production, ranging from farming to lumbering, to fishing, to fur trading, depending on the locality. In areas where fishing predominated the family fishing operation was the main economic unit. The majority of families, however, lived on farms. Farm families usually built their own homes, constructed their own furnishings, made their own clothes and produced their own food. If goods were produced for exchange, either the money or the goods received in return were used for the family's maintenance.[5]

Within this kind of organization of production, that is, within independent commodity production, men, women and children worked together as an economic unit to produce their livelihood. Internally there was a division of labour by sex and age; tasks were allocated with the aim of meeting the shared needs and interests of the family. For women the bearing and rearing of children, as well as the production of goods and services, were integrated aspects of their work role.

At the time of Confederation in 1867, 85 per cent of Canada's population still lived on farms or in small villages.[6] However, industrial capitalism and urbanization were clearly on the horizon. Once it had begun, industrial capitalism progressed relatively rapidly in Canada, though its impact was uneven by region.

As the British had before them, Canadian capitalists looking for a labour supply drew on families whose small farms had gone bankrupt and on tradespeople and artisans who had been forced out of their independent work by competition from large-scale production. Machinery and capital equipment introduced into agricultural production 'freed' many farm workers who had no choice but to become wage labourers. In other words, the capitalist labour market was fueled by the erosion of independent commodity production.

While there were clear regional differences in this development, it is safe to say that the family as a productive unit was beginning to disappear. A new family structure was coming into existence – a structure based on women's labour as wives and mothers and on the notion of men as breadwinners or family wage earners. The new structure meant a greater economic dependence of women on men and an almost total dependence of the family on the wage.

Once the family household was no longer self-sufficient, it became necessary for working-class men and women to combine some amount of wage and domestic labour to support the family. Although the ways in which they are combined depend on specific economic conditions, the evidence is clear that women's labour has been a major flexible component of the working-class family unit under capitalism in Canada.

In the first quarter of the twentieth century the expectation was that men should be able to support their family, that is, earn a 'living' or 'family' wage. Trade unions fought for higher wages for men on these grounds, yet working-class men's wages were very low and most families needed a second income earner.[7] In most cases it was children and unmarried women who contributed this second wage. Some married women worked for a wage, but women were segregated into 'female' jobs and these jobs were limited in number. For example, the supply of women workers for jobs in shops, offices and factories exceeded the demand.[8] Although quite likely an underestimate, evidence indicates that only 3 or 4 per cent of all married women in Canada worked outside their homes before the Second World War.[9] For the most part, married women during this period remained in the home, stretching their husbands' wage by intensifying their labour and by bringing in extra money whenever possible. For example, rural women did market gardening and raised chickens to sell eggs. Urban women did laundry, took in boarders or did dressmaking in their homes.

One reason why jobs remained limited for women was that men saw cheap female labour as a major threat to their wages and even their jobs. Some unions openly attempted to exclude women not only from membership but from the labour force itself. Unsuccessful at excluding them, men supported their segregation into low-paying female jobs. In fact, the segregation of women in this way solved major problems for both employers and male workers. For employers it meant a continued source of cheap female labour. For men it meant the removal of women from direct competition for their jobs.[10] For women, of course, it meant that the jobs open to them in the first part of the twentieth century were severely limited.

Another reason there was not a great demand for women workers was that there was a more desirable reserve labour source in the form of predominantly male immigrants. Between 1900 and 1920 there was unprecedented immigration and both the labour force and the population grew more rapidly than ever before in the history of Canada. Immigrants were more desirable than women already in Canada because like these women they were cheap labour, but unlike women they added to the small Canadian population, thereby increasing the consumer market. Furthermore, occupational growth took place in areas such as construction, mining, and heavy industry, where the demand was for unskilled male labourers. Women immigrants generally found jobs as domestic servants – one area where there was a demand for female labour.[11] Between 1901 and 1914, 2.9 million immigrants were added to a Canadian population of less than 5.5 million; the vast majority of these were men.[12]

When the Second World War began, there were a great many people unemployed in Canada. However, the supply of male labour quickly diminished as a result of recruitment for the armed services and the expansion of war production at home. Labour demand was high and employers and the government had no choice but to turn to women. At first they did not call on married women. However, as time went on it became necessary to activate the reserve army of married women.[13] Incentives such as free government nurseries and income tax concessions were provided to attract married women into the labour force. Married women responded to the call, which was put in terms of doing one's patriotic duty. Evidence shows, however, that many women entered the labour force out of economic need rather than patriotic duty.[14]

When the war ended, the incentives were withdrawn in an attempt to move married women back into the home. Married women were forced out of government jobs through regulations and legislation.[15] Single women were strongly encouraged to return to their former 'female' jobs. Many married women left the labour force, but others remained to fill the growing number of 'female' positions in the clerical, retail trade, and service areas.

The 1950s was a period of rapid economic expansion in Canada. It brought a higher standard of living and increased government services. Increased technology and changes in the organization of labour power brought higher productivity and greater amounts of goods which had to be consumed in order for the economy to continue. A psychological need for these goods was created through advertising, and a material need was created through the failure to develop alternatives and through the erosion of existing alternative ways of doing things.

There was a shift in the industrial and occupational structure and it generated a need for a more highly skilled and better-educated labour force. As in earlier times immigrants were one important source of labour for the expanding economy. In addition, unlike the earlier part of the century, married women became an important source of labour power. Whereas earlier on the segregation of women into low paying 'female' jobs had the effect of limiting the number of jobs open to them, by the middle of the century it had just the opposite effect. 'Female' jobs were on the increase and this created a demand for female labour.

By the 1950s, then, the Canadian family faced the need to consume more goods as well as the need to produce better-educated workers. This had to be done by means of the wage since by mid-century 77 per cent of Canadians in the labour force were dependent on the wage.[16] Trade unions fought the battle for higher wages and a higher standard of living – successfully to some extent. Between 1951 and 1971 real wages did increase, but the disparity between higher and lower paid income earners also increased.[17] The reality was that a large number of working-class families needed an additional income in order to achieve the new standard of living. It was becoming less possible to intensify labour in the home to meet these needs. This was the case at the same time that there was a demand for female labour to fill the growing number of 'female' jobs in the service sector of the economy.

With two members of the family working for a wage, the new standard of living could be met by the majority of families (although many could do it only through the use of credit). The result was that dependence on consumer goods and services increased and young people, particularly young men, stayed in school for longer periods of time, thereby 'improving the quality of the labour force'.

Because men's real wages did increase, the standard of living did rise, and young people did stay in school longer, married women appeared to be working for 'extras'. In fact, had women not gone into the labour force, men's wages, despite the increase, would not have been sufficient to meet the new standard of living.

By the mid-1970s, real wages had begun to decline. Two incomes were necessary just to maintain the standard of living achieved in the previous three decades. As we move into the 1980s with the high rates of inflation and unemployment and declining government support for health, welfare and education, household members will once again have to rearrange their resources in an effort to prevent the standard of living from dropping drastically.

In summary, then, we have argued that the economic activity of family household members – especially women – changes as the economy changes. When we move to the provincial level, the same general trends are evident. We want to situate these changes in the specific context of the nature and development of the Nova Scotia economy, in keeping with our theoretical focus on the relationship between the needs of the economy and the needs of the family household in particular times and places. This will set the stage for the community case study.

Nova Scotian Underdevelopment

In the previous section, we discussed the general history of the Canadian labour market. 'Canada' is, however, by no means homogeneous in its economic character. It is characterized by a high degree of uneven development relative to other advanced industrial countries. This is one symptom of the economic disarticulation and non-self-centred nature of its development,[18] which stems from its role as a resource hinterland and from the dominance of foreign capital in its development. The Canadian economy as a whole is characterized by dependent development,[19] and has within it severe and persistent regional disparities. One area where this uneven development is most evident is the Maritimes, which includes Nova Scotia.

Nova Scotia can thus be considered an underdeveloped or dependent economy in its relation to North American capitalism. A growing literature uses models developed in a Third World context to analyse this regional underdevelopment. The process of underdevelopment is the subject of considerable debate,[20] and it is not within the scope of this paper to elaborate on this important issue. For the purpose of our study, however, we adopt a structural rather than a market or institutional failure approach.[21] We intend to examine the work of women in the context of underdevelopment and in this way contribute to the body of work aimed at clarifying the nature and process of underdevelopment.

The Nova Scotia economy has a weak manufacturing base oriented towards the export of semi-processed raw materials (fish, pulp, lumber) and characterized by extensive foreign ownership. Major employment sources are service industries, including government, and primary industry, especially fishing, forestry and mining. The province has high unemployment and subemployment and acts as a labour reserve for the rest of Canada. When labour demand is high elsewhere, there is a large out-migration, but to some extent it is a revolving door.[22] The labour force is thus mobile, even within the province, commuting great distances and for long periods of time to gain employment. This mobility is masked by the high unemployment rate and the strong attachment to community which tend to generate an image of a stagnant labour pool.

For the purposes of this study, certain features of the Nova Scotian economy are particularly relevant. One is the rural economy – its importance and characteristics. Related to this is the prolonged survival and gradual transformation of independent commodity production. The second is the composition of the large labour reserve in the province and its relationship to the development process.

In 1976, 56 per cent of the Nova Scotian population was 'urban', compared with 75.5 per cent for Canada. A further 42.7 per cent of the population was 'rural non-farm', which is twice the Canadian average of 20 per cent. Understanding changes in the rural economy is thus of central importance in the case of this province. Most studies of economic change and the role of women in industrialized countries have an implicit urban bias and may not be relevant to Nova Scotia. When the rural economy is examined, we find that communities were traditionally based on subsistence agriculture, inshore fishing and/or small woodlot operations. In some communities all three activities were combined, whereas in others one activity predominated. In each of these activities, the mode of production was independent commodity production. There is a growing literature on the relationship of this mode of production to the dominant capitalist mode, and the nature of the transformation process.[23] Underdevelopment – whether of regions or of countries – is generally characterized by a prolonged survival of the independent mode, alongside a capitalist mode, and integrated into a world economy *dominated* by the capitalist mode.

In Nova Scotia, the present relationship of independent producers to capitalism can quickly be summarised. Small woodlot owners sell to a dominant multi-national pulp company which controls the market. Woodlot owners must also compete with company pulp subcontractors who use wage-labour crews and advanced technology to cut company-owned or leased land.[24] Farming is dichotomized between subsistence family farms and medium-sized modern farms. Inshore fisherman, decreasing in number, sell to vertically integrated fish companies in an industry which has become increasingly concentrated in recent decades. In fishing, the days of merchant domination and the 'Codfish Aristocracy' have given way to domination by industrial capital.[25] There has been rapidly changing technology; a reduction in inshore independently owned boats; an increase in the offshore, high-technology, company-owned fleet; and a growing regulation and subsidization by government of the industry. In each of these primary production areas, underdevelopment has meant the depletion and distortion of the resource base in the interest of securing cheap raw materials for the world market and surplus extraction and export by the corporations. The erosion of independent primary production and of rural communities, however, has been only partial. In attempting to understand this underdevelopment process, it is the stubborn persistence, rather than demise of this mode of production – independent in name only – which is the essential concern of critical analysis.

Insights into this process have been gained from writers on colonialism and neo-colonialism. For example, writing on the process of underdevelopment in Latin America, Laclau[26] argues that with the establishment of capitalism as the dominant mode of production in Western Europe, there arose a world capitalist system linking social formations dominated by pre-capitalist modes of production to those dominated by capitalist modes.[27] The effect was to *consolidate* the pre-capitalist modes, not to destroy them. However, as other writers have pointed out, the *nature* of the independent commodity production was changed by the dominance of capitalism. Capitalism thus needs to conserve the pre-capitalist modes at the same time that it needs to dissolve them. Gradually they become transformed into a subordinate form of the capitalist mode.

Several writers have analysed the rural Maritimes from this point of view. Veltmeyer argues that the survival of the pre-capitalist relations kept labour in reserve – in other words the latent reserve labour force – is very large and is able to fuel, at low wages, both industries which locate there and labour demand elsewhere in Canada.[28] As capital has become concentrated and centralized at one pole, reserve labour has become concentrated at another. The base of rural independent commodity production has been *slowly* eroded and attenuated, rather than abruptly transformed, so that the labour pool function remains.

Veltmeyer points out that when accumulation reduces the economic base of subsistence farming and inshore fishing in peripheral areas like Nova Scotia, creating the latent surplus population, there is

> no counter-movement of attraction to offset the repulsion of those freed by the capitalist development of production. . . . As a result the latent form of surplus population not only produces a dramatic emigration of workers, but it forms the basis of a sizeable semi-proletariat and a large under-class of dispossessed farmers and poor inshore fishermen . . . on the fringe of a capitalist labour market.[29]

Sacouman discusses this same development:

> What, then, is at issue is not the long-term decline of petty primary production activities in the Maritimes (though this long-term decline is demonstrable), but the stubborn persistence of petty production activities as the basis for surplus labour power. What is at issue is the capitalist underdevelopment of these activities through the truncation, yet maintenance of the domestic mode of production.[30]

There are several manifestations of this latent labour reserve and the partial transformation of independent commodity production in rural Nova Scotia.

1. Much of the unemployment from wage labour is seasonal, for example in tourism, construction and fish processing. In the off-season this population is 'forced back into self-subsistent or independent commodity production, where, with the support of UI [Unemployment Insurance] their labour power is held in reserve'.[31] Nowadays UI has eliminated much of the male pattern of multi-occupational work by season; however, the rural community still absorbs this labour pool while on UI at a cost of living considerably subsidized by the persistence of independent production.

2. *Families* combine the wage labour of some members, such as women in fish plants, with independent commodity production by other members. The effect of this, as Sacouman points out, is to enable these workers to be paid 'less than their subsistence for their labour'.[32] The primary producers, concomitantly, receive less for their product than its cost of production, through relations of unequal exchange.

3. The 'independence' of the inshore fishermen has been increasingly undermined by the concentration and centralization of capital in the fishing industry. Large national and multinational companies dominate the processing of fish and the selling of gear. They have a near monopoly on the purchase of fish, and in addition they catch a sizeable portion of the supply in their own offshore boats, giving them additional leverage in price. In this context, the number of inshore fishermen has decreased, and though those remaining have legal title to their boats, the price they receive from the monopolies for their fish is virtually a wage. They are caught between a consciousness as 'workers' and one as small businessmen.[33]

4. Fishermen themselves tend to develop multiple relations to the means of production, doing some independent commodity production, some wage work in the community, and often some wage work 'away' to earn money for a boat and gear.[34]

It is argued elsewhere that the inshore fishery is maintained in this distorted way because of the quality of the products;[35] the role it plays in supplying cheap labour to fish plants;[36] the general effect it has on depressing wage rates in the whole region;[37] the value of preserving a rural population base for reserve labour purposes; and contradictory government policy regarding the inshore fishery.

It is in the context of this semi-tranformation of primary production that we conduct our case study to examine the changing economic role of women. The life cycle pattern and seasonal patterns of work for women in these rural communities is not well documented. Nor is it well understood when *men* in the community worked in the fish plant, for example, rather than as inshore fishermen. Furthermore, the *family* employment patterns are unstudied. Sacouman's analysis suggests that the wives and children of fishermen became wage labourers as did men who were forced out of independent fishing by the gradual contraction of numbers. However, in the modern context one has to consider a more elaborate configuration of male 'jobs' than fisherman/plant worker. A man may be a boat owner, inshore crew, offshore crew, captain of a company boat, seasonal government worker, or commuter to an industrial job. Futhermore, he may fulfil more than one of these roles. The economic role of women in this current configuration is theoretically less clear.

The jobs for women in the rural areas have not dramatically increased in recent years. Therefore we do not expect to find the same strong 'pull' from the economy on the female reserve labour force that characterizes the aggregate economy. However, the composition of the available reserve (male and female) is changing and we expect capital to make adaptations to this. The question becomes how the *allocation* of the jobs changes when changing economic conditions affect the supply of reserve labour. Clearly the most dramatic changes in conditions have occurred in traditional *male* jobs in the primary sector, and this affects the extent to which married women are an available reserve. We expect that as the community becomes more variegated in its male job and income structure, the pattern of women's work and family income will become more complex.

The Community Case Study

The fishing community we studied, which we will call Big Harbour, has a population of approximately three hundred. It is in a fairly remote part of the province, four hours' drive from the main city of Halifax. The nearest centre is a town of about eight thousand – an hour's drive away – whose major employers are a university, a hospital, a dairy and a trade sector. The community is located in one of the poorest rural areas in the province, and one of the poorer fishing areas. It is the major fishing port and has the only fish plant for at least fifty miles in either direction. There are a few neighbouring fishing villages, but the majority of villages within a twenty-mile radius are non-farm, non-fishing communities.

Five miles to the east of Big Harbour is a large inlet which until recently cut off access to communities on the other side, unless one drove for an hour around the inlet. In 1977 a ferry was put in, a development which integrated the area, particularly the labour market. The communities on 'the other side of the river', as it is called, are predominantly based on pulp cutting, under contract, for a multinational company with a pulp plant fifty miles away. These communities are noticeably poorer than Big Harbour. When one drives into Big Harbour, one is struck by how well kept the houses and properties are, and there is an impression that the residents are for the most part comfortable, though certainly not affluent. There are none of the signs of rural poverty so evident in some surrounding villages – rusting cars in yards, mobile homes, unpainted and half-finished houses. Many of the homes are new, suburban-looking bungalows. There is almost no sign of subsistence farming activity in the community.

Big Harbour stands in contrast to many other key fishing ports in the province in that the fish plant is not owned by one of the two big companies which are gaining a virtual monopoly in the industry. The plant,[38] which is of medium size for the province, is owned by a small company which owns two other fish plants, along with several offshore draggers. It is one of the more prosperous fishing communities in the province.

In our study of this community we trace the process and extent of transformation of independent commodity production and the way it altered family work patterns. We consider the following questions: When did women intensify domestic labour to make ends meet, and when did they turn to wage labour? How have family incomes and standards of living changed and how does this reflect/affect women's labour-force activity? How has reserve labour, including women, been created, maintained and reabsorbed in this community though time?

The Early Days

Big Harbour, founded in the late 1800s, has always been based on the inshore fishery. In the early days, the family was the production unit. There was a gradual change from almost total self-sufficiency to an ever-increasing dependence on the cash or market economy. Throughout this time, until the building of the fish plant, women's economic role was centred on the family production unit. Women assisted directly in the business by keeping the books for their husbands' boats. Their domestic labour involved stretching dollars and lowering the money-cost of subsistence. Women kept cows, sewed clothes, made quilts, and canned and preserved food. They exchanged services with each other: nursing care, babysitting and quilting together. The non-market economy also included men. They joined together to lay foundations for each other's homes, to build and clear roads, and to hunt. Children also participated, and as soon as they were old enough, boys joined their fathers in fishing. Life was hard and the standard of living was barely above subsistence. Incomes fluctuated throughout the year and from year to year. Sacouman notes that, as late as 1933, average annual incomes in the inshore fisheries in this part of the province ranged from $100 to $200, and that men regularly worked seventy-two hours at a stretch and in treacherous conditions to earn these amounts.[39]

The 1920s and 1930s in Nova Scotia were a time of extreme hardship and accelerated rural depopulation.[40] Fish companies bought cheap and sold dear. They controlled the communities by selling boats, gear and bait – thereby keeping the fishermen continually in debt – and by competing through a growing off-shore fleet. In response to this hardship and exploitation, the Antigonish Movement developed.[41] It was one of the initiators of the world-wide co-operative movement and the effort by small producers to gain more control over production and over the market. A co-operative among fishermen was formed in Big Harbour in 1942. At first the Co-op acted solely as a buyer and sold the fish to other plants, or trucked fresh fish directly to market. At that time lobster was important, along with ground-fish and swordfish.

These were still difficult times for the inshore fishing families. There was no government support such as unemployment insurance to fall back on. The government, however, expected their share of the incomes. Incomes were so low and so variable that families found great difficulty in putting aside enough cash to pay income taxes and therefore were always behind in their taxes and permanently in debt. There was never enough employment within the community and each generation saw many people leaving to find work in Upper Canada or the eastern United States. Some left for good but others left only to return home later. The rural economy absorbed those whom the industrial labour markets could not.

Wage Work and Independent Production: 1950-70

The Co-op built a groundfish processing plant in 1950, and the extent of reserve labour in the community was revealed by how eagerly the plant jobs were filled. For the first time there were many jobs open to women. Given the fishermen's financial situation, which as indicated was one of permanent cash shortage and debt to the government for taxes, wives eagerly took some of the jobs. The rest were filled by young single women, students who worked part-time, and men who might otherwise have left the community.

A small lobster factory also existed for several years during this period. The Co-op prospered during the 1950s and 1960s, and the fishing was relatively stable compared to earlier and later years, and in terms of the number of boats. The Co-op was profitable for twenty years. During that time there were as many as seventeen 45 foot by 60 foot boats[42] fishing out of Big Habour, many of which were initially financed by the Co-op. There were also fifteen or so 20 foot by 35 foot boats used mainly for lobsters. The Co-op also built two draggers, which complemented the inshore supply, particularly in the winter. The industry was doing relatively well in the early 1960s and some young people who had left the community for jobs elsewhere came back and got into fishing.

This was a period of relative stability in the community in terms of family work patterns. The hierarchy of male work went from inshore boat owners, to crew, to offshore crew, and to plant worker. Almost all men were still directly involved in the fishery, although more were wage earners than in the early period. The small boat owners had to supplement their incomes with crew work on bigger boats, or part-time wage work of other kinds. Women in the community worked in the plant, in the home, or both. Wage work by family members subsidized the continuance of 'independent' commodity production – simultaneously keeping the price of the product and the wages low. Married women found it necessary to substitute wage labour for domestic labour in order to achieve family subsistence, since only money would satisfy the tax people and meet the growing necessity to participate in the market economy. There is some evidence that the labour force activity of women increased when the fishing was bad, and vice versa. The extent of this trade-off, however, was limited because plant work varied directly with fish supplies. However, the offshore fleet often provided fish for the plant when the inshore catch was down and fishermen were in trouble. The pattern seemed to be that all women worked when single, and in the early years of their marriage, and then worked intermittently after the children were born. There were no day-care facilities in the community and working outside the home with small children was extremely costly and difficult. Women who worked full-time were those whose husbands were least well off. One pattern among inshore fishing families was that women worked in the plant in the winter when the men were fishing less and could look after the children. In the summer when the children were out of school, women stayed at home and high school students worked in the plant. Even in families where the wives did not work in the plant, the children usually did. No one in the community was earning a 'family wage'.

The standard of living during this period was still very low. Unemployment insurance existed, but was minimal, and someone in the family had to be economically active at all times of the year. Families managed by building their own homes – often one room at a time – with the help of neighbours. Most of the houses built in the 1950s were built for less than $3,000 and no mortgages were held. People still worked together for mutual economic and social support. During this time women's economic role involved both wage and domestic work. Their wage labour was performed at less than subsistence wages and under poor working conditions. Their domestic labour was necessary in order to produce the goods and services that they were unable to purchase, either because such items were unavailable or because they were too costly. Although the plant was a co-operative, the wage and price levels reflected the overall industry rates and these were controlled by the large companies. The only benefit of the Co-op was that it kept some of the surpluses in the community.

Early 1970s: Crisis in the Inshore Fishery

During the 1960s the lobster supply diminished and men switched to groundfish. This was a sign of things to come, for by the late 1960s there was a general crisis in the fishing industry due to dwindling stocks. The government became very involved in regulating the fishery through quotas and licensing schemes in the early 1970s. This also coincided with a rapid trend towards concentration of ownership in the processing industry, rapid development of the offshore fleet, rapidly changing technology, and heavy competition from the foreign fleets.[43]

When the fishing went bad in the early 1970s, there was a forced exodus from the industry. Boats and licences were sold, and the fleet dropped from seventeen in 1970 to only eight boats (45 foot by 60 foot) by 1977, two of which were company owned. Only six of the fifteen smaller boats remained by the end of the decade. At least four families left the community. Others took jobs at a new Coast Guard station which had been established, or became crew on company boats, or did some other seasonal government job, or commuted to wage work as far away as Halifax.

In 1973–4 there was a bit of a turnaround, but due to the licensing system those who had left could not get back in. The Co-op decided to expand the plant at that time, and did so out of retained earnings rather than through borrowing. That was a fatal mistake, for when the fishery went bad again in 1975–6, they had no back-up resources, and they went into receivership. The government did not help them over the hump; rather it ran the plant for one year and then sold it to a private company in 1977. Many individual fishermen lost significant amounts of money in this transaction. The community was very bitter about losing the plant which they had built up over the years.

During this time of crisis and transition, as independent commodity production was further eroded, the availability of plant work for women was constant. The women who worked outside the home continued to do so, and others took jobs for the first time. Many wives worked sporadically through that time, either in the plant, or selling cosmetic products from their homes, or babysitting or selling crafts. Many of the men who were forced out of fishing spent several years moving from job to job before settling into a new occupation. In general, during this time more family members, and more families, became dependent on a wage. The proportion of independent commodity producers in the community dropped dramatically.

A further development during this time contributed to changes in family employment patterns. The unemployment insurance programme was reformed in the early 1970s so that payments were more generous, and fishermen were supported through the winter. Before this, fishermen fished through most of the winter and the plant also kept operating, processing the inshore and offshore catch. For both fishermen and plant workers, unemployment insurance became a major variable in decisions concerning the household economy and the supply of labour. One effect was that women plant workers could not afford to take the summers off because they needed those hours to qualify for unemployment insurance. This affected the employment opportunities for students and changed the seasonal work pattern for women. Women's importance as wage earners overshadows their role as domestic labour in this time of crisis. It is evident that *more* women would have worked if there had been jobs available.

Late 1970s: Regulation and Recovery

The fortunes of the fishery have improved again since the mid-1970s. In 1977 the 200-mile limit was declared, benefiting the Canadian industry. Quotas were created for inshore, offshore and foreign boats, and licences became even stricter in order to limit the fishery and control the number of vessels in any one area. In this community, those who remained in the inshore fisheries are now earning as much as $40,000 per year, although the small-boat marginal fishermen still make as little as $6,000 and there are still dramatic year-to-year fluctuctions.[44] However, there is great concern in the community over what will happen when the present generation of fishermen, now in their mid-forties, retires. Young people are not entering, because there are no licenses available and the cost of boats is very high – $200,000 for a 45-foot boat.

The new company has made several changes which have affected employment in the community. The two draggers have been moved to the company's other port, severely restricting the amount of plant work in the winter. Work at the plant has become more sporadic, even though numbers employed have increased slightly. There has been some expansion, but also some mechanization which has reduced employment of skilled cutters. For the past year, the company has run a 240-foot shrimp dragger out of this port, which employs eighteen men. This job entails being at sea for forty-nine days at a stretch. These men were home only twenty-seven days last year. However, earnings are as high as $50,000 per year on the shrimp boat. The company also owns two of the remaining eight inshore boats, so men crewing on these boats are wage earners rather than independent producers.

Before examining the changes which have occurred in the family work patterns in this period, we summarize the jobs now available for men and women in the community.

In terms of male jobs, there are eight inshore boats (45 foot by 60 foot) with three to four crew each. Incomes here are good, although crew make considerably less than owners once the boat is paid for. There are eighteen men on the shrimp dragger, where incomes are high but the conditions intolerable and the future uncertain. There are also five or six men with small lobster boats who make $5,000–6,000 fishing and supplement their wage with unemployment insurance and part-time wage work. In addition, 35 per cent of the approximately 120 employees (peak season) in the fish plant are men. However, less than twenty of these men are from Big Harbour. Men in the plant earn $4.55 per hour, or approximately $9,000–10,000 per year (plus unemployment insurance). There is also a small boat-building operation which employs seven men. About 10 per cent of the men in the community commute (weekly) to jobs in the major city of Halifax. The only other male jobs are seasonal road work and construction. There is almost no male unemployment in the community other than that reflecting the seasonal nature of most jobs.

For women, the wage opportunities are even more limited. There is one postmistress, one bookkeeper for the boatbuilders, two school teachers, two store workers, and of course the fish plant. Other options include commuting to the nearest centre (twenty miles) to work in the nursing home or the tourist industry there, selling handicrafts, or commuting sixty miles to the nearest town for clerical and sales jobs. All of these jobs are low paying. The fish plant pays women $4.15 per hour, and the work is not steady. In the past two years women have averaged $5,000–7,000 per year, plus unemployment insurance. Jobs in the tourist industry or other service jobs pay the minimum wage,which has just been raised from $2.75 to $3.30 per hour.

The number of women working in Big Harbour is lower than in the previous period. Only ten to fifteen of the more than sixty women in the fish plant are from the community. One explanation of this may be that very few young people are staying in the area, so that there is an over-representation of middle-aged, financially established families in the community. Many long-term women employees have recently retired. The main explanation, however, is that male incomes in the fisheries have improved substantially in this recent period, as noted above. The fishermen who kept their boats through the bad times, while still far from wealthy, have higher incomes in absolute terms than ever before. With this increase in income it no longer makes economic sense for wives of fishermen to work in the plant. One woman explains why:

> If I can't get a job where I can make $9,000 minimum then it doesn't pay me to work, in terms of lost income tax deductions, extra income tax and extra costs due to working . . . It's more profitable if I just stay home.

Most of the women in this position indicated that they would work in the plant if they could earn some money by doing so. Only one woman now in the plant is the wife of a boat owner.

The recovery and rationalization of the fishery had a positive effect on the incomes of the crews also, both inshore and offshore. Those who did *not* benefit were the plant workers; families in which both husband and wife work in the plant make less than one fisherman earns alone.

By the late 1970s, the plant was feeling the effects of this withdrawal of fishermen's wives from the plant and was complaining of a labour shortage. The option was to raise wages which, according to the women, would have been sufficient to draw them back to the plant. This would also have likely led to capital/labour substitution and technological change. Instead, however, the plant was able to make use of a new, more marginalized and therefore cheaper labour supply. This became possible with the opening of the government-sponsored ferry service which opened up access between Big Harbour and an area we shall call Pleasant Bay.[45] People in Pleasant Bay had to drive over an hour to reach Big Harbour before the ferry; after, it could be done in twenty minutes.

Few women from Pleasant Bay had worked outside the home before this period, because there were no jobs. The nearest job opportunities – sales clerk, waitress, clerical work – had been sixty miles away. For the most part, they paid minimum wages and entailed expenses for clothes and travelling which did not make it economically worthwhile. One woman, a secretary, told us: 'I figured the pay wouldn't be that high in town, and I'd have to have another car, and then meeting the public you have to go dressed up, so I figure I'd be just as well off to be where I am.'

Pleasant Bay is based on forest work. Most men work cutting wood for subcontractors to the multinational pulp company mentioned earlier. There are six subcontractors, each with fifteen or so men. Incomes are not nearly as high as for fishermen, although one woman said 'pulp workers make more in a day than in the fish plant in a week'. The work is seasonal and is also subject to cyclical fluctuations. The income is supplemented by unemployment insurance, or sometimes by other odd jobs. Other men in the community do such jobs as carpentry, running an ambulance, driving a school bus, salvaging car parts, and road work, or they commute long distances to industrial jobs.

The standard of living in this community is noticeably lower than in Big Harbour. Thus, when job opportunities appeared the women from this community took them immediately – as had the Big Harbour women thirty years earlier. Employment at the fish plant provided a relatively dependable year-round income that made it possible for families to do some planning for the future. Although there were no benefits and working conditions were far from ideal, the plant did pay slightly higher than minimum wage and the women were happy to have the jobs. In fact the access to this new labour reserve has meant that the plant now has a waiting list of workers rather than a labour shortage.

With the influx of women from Pleasant Bay, a new division between workers within the plant was created. A division by sex had always existed. Men traditionally worked as cutters and machine operators and in maintenance, boat preparation and fish freezing. Women worked as trimmers and packers, and recently have become cutters. The women's work is on an assembly line, whereas the men move about the plant, working (and 'hanging around') in groups. The women perceive that they work harder than the men. In addition, there are two 'lines' of women so that at slow times of the year only one line is called in at a time; by contrast there is only one crew of men so their work is steadier. Superimposed on this sexual division is now a division by community. These divisions are reinforced by plant policy on who works when fish supplies are low – the Big Harbour 'line' or the Pleasant Bay 'line'. The two lines are supposed to rotate, but there is still constant bickering about whether the work equalizes. The fact that the Pleasant Bay women need the jobs, combined with this split in the workforce has meant that there has been no concerted effort to improve working conditions or wages within the plant, and never any talk of unionization. Another effect of this change to 'outside' plant workers is that there is no longer any common interest perceived or put forward between the fishermen and the plant workers in their relationship to the company.

Our case study provides an illuminating contrast between fishing-based and forestry-based communities. When both communities were based mainly on independent commodity production, women contributed significantly to this process through activities such as bookkeeping, as well as through lowering the money cost of subsistence by keeping gardens, sewing, preserving and so on. In the fishing communities, as fish processing became capitalized and separated from family production, women were an obvious supply of labour for the new production process. Communities with fish plants were able to achieve a higher standard of living than those other fishing villages where only intensified domestic labour could supplement the price of fish. The opportunities for wives of independent woods workers were never so great. Processing in sawmills and pulp plants has traditionally been male work. As mentioned in the overview of underdevelopment in Nova Scotia, in the present day when 'independent' woods workers have become subcontractors for the multinational pulp companies, the rural communities dependent on forestry for their livelihood are among the poorest in the province. This partly reflects the lack of complementary economic roles for women in forestry communities and the erosion of traditional roles in family subsistence production.

At the present stage in the transformation of the fishing industry, fishing families in this community are no longer dependent on the wage labour of women to make ends meet.[46] The pulp-cutting communities are at a different stage of development and do require multi-earner families. Depletion of the resource is also creating particularly difficult times in forestry communities.

In our study the women in the fishing community provided a labour reserve until economic conditions changed. Under these new conditions it did not make economic sense for them to work outside the home because wages were too low. The plant would have had to raise wages to keep this supply of women or else find a new, cheaper labour supply. Underdevelopment of the whole area ensured that the latter course could be followed. The introduction of the government ferry opened up the more marginalized forestry-based area and allowed the plant to take advantage of a new labour reserve.

Life Cycle Considerations

The previous sections have illustrated the flexibility of the family household, and particularly women, in adapting to changing economic conditions. In this section we want to look at women over their life cycle, and at what happens to their lives as these economic changes occur. How are housework and child rearing integrated with wage work? Under what conditions do women enter wage work? What have been the life-patterns of women of different ages? Most of the women have worked in the plant at sometime during their life, although some held other jobs, or were full-time homemakers, at the time of the interview.We begin by discussing women who are now under thirty – those who comprise the majority of plant workers at the present time.

Women marry and have children at a young age in these communities. Most of the women we interviewed had children. Of the younger women only a few required full-time babysitters. The others had children of school age. There were a number of women who had recently left high school, and were unmarried, and had no children. There were also ten women who were single parents.

In the case of the single parents, grandmothers usually provided childcare. However, contrary to our expectations, these were almost the only cases of grandmothers providing this function. Women told us that their own mothers no longer wanted to, nor felt compelled to, look after grandchildren. In two cases both mother and daughters worked in the plant. Childcare is definitely a problem for young mothers in this area. Most of them stay home for lack of babysitters.

The young women took jobs because they needed the money. Their husbands earned low incomes and they did not have the kind of household technology that today most people find necessary. One woman went to work to get a washing machine and stayed in order to replace the refrigerator that had broken down. Most of these women said their family was dependent on their wage. Most of these young plant workers are from Pleasant Bay rather than Big Harbour. In Pleasant Bay the youth are not encouraged to stay in school. They leave school early and the majority of them stay in the area, taking jobs in the woods or in the plant. Those who have gone to Western Canada for work are generally expected to return. This, they say, is always what happens.

This is in contrast to Big Harbour, where the dwindling opportunities in fishing and the rising incomes and aspirations of parents have combined to lead young people to stay in school. Most young people leave the community to further their education and then find jobs outside the community, since there are no jobs for their new skills in Big Harbour. Thus, there are few young families in the community, and the school population has dropped from one hundred and fifty to fifty in the last ten years.

When young women work outside the home, they still have to contend with their domestic responsibilities. Most of the young husbands 'helped' by 'starting supper', drying dishes, and hanging out clothes. With young children the work load is still hard, and thus even though the women need the income, they say they are happy that the work at the plant is irregular, particularly in winter.

The older women we interviewed – those who work outside the home generally – have grown-up children. Many entered the plant when their children were young teenagers, and some only started after their children left home. Most of them had worked full-time for wages when they were single and intermittently during the time they were raising families. Like the young women of Pleasant Bay, many of them had left school early. Some, however, had clerical skills or accounting training, which were unusable in Big Harbour. These women thus tended to be underemployed, even when they were working full-time. Many of these women and their husbands had lived outside of the community at one time or another, usually in an urban area. While away, their husbands did jobs ranging from merchant seaman, to construction, to equipment operator, to Royal Canadian

Mounted Police officer, to manufacturing work. Some later became independent fishermen, but had had this early experiment of wage labour and sometimes financed their investment as a result. This is a life-cycle aspect of the term 'semi-proletarianized' rural workers. Many of the women had jobs while away that required skills for which there was no market upon returning to Big Harbour.

Unlike the younger women, these women had homes that were quite comfortable after twenty years of marriage. The Big Harbour women in this age group clearly had higher family incomes than the Pleasant Bay women. When asked why they worked, most women in this age group said they worked for 'extras', or that they did not have to work. Some took the jobs at a time when they 'had to work', such as when the fishing was bad, but stayed at it even after the male income got to be 'enough to get by on'. Their definitions of extras reveal that for many anything above a very minimal standard of living is 'extra'. Extras included replacing furniture that had withstood twenty years of marriage, sending children to school, or buying a first car.[47]

Some women said they were 'bored' at home, and worked for something to do, for social contact, and for independence. Their explanations for boredom reflected the fact that children had left home, the contraction of housework compared to earlier times, and also the breakdown of 'community' which has accompanied the integration of this area into the modern market economy. Thus it does not pay to bake or sew; people watch (and therefore buy) television rather than put on community entertainment; quilting bees are becoming an anachronism and in general the non-market aspects of the rural economy have been eroded.

These women were extremely diligent at their housework, trying to maintain the same standards as they had when they were full-time homemakers. Most of them still 'run the cleaner every day', and many wash a load of clothes every night. Their husbands are less likely to help them than those of the younger women, for they were used to full-time wives and had to be 'shaped up'.

Both younger and older women tend to express surprise at the length of time they have been working. They did not start with the idea of staying, yet most now expect to continue working. Their enthusiasm for a job which is cold, wet, low-paying and monotonous is matched by the sense of isolation they express when speaking of 'staying home'. Women whose husbands are 'well off', or who disdain work in the fish plant, still crave a chance to be active outside the home. Contraction of the domestic labour required in the rural community has made women eager for wage work. Enough domestic work remains, however, that wage work still involves a 'double shift' for women. For most women in the area, however, there is an economic imperative to work in terms of achieving a 'family wage'.

Conclusion

We have analysed the historical development of the Canadian economy in terms of the changing balance between women's role as domestic labour and as wage labour. We have traced the broad transformations which have occurred in the economy, from independent commodity production to capitalist product and labour markets, from rural to urban, and from goods production to service production. We argue that women have always constituted an available cheap labour reserve and that they have consistently responded to any and every wage-labour opportunity opened to them. They have not been the only source of reserve labour, however, and for much of the heavy-industry/goods-production stage of Canadian development they were not the reserve which was absorbed by the labour demand. We argue that women have consistently worked for less than their subsistence and that their domestic labour has meant that total family wages have been less than the true cost of family subsistence. The economic development of Canada has meant the development of a universal market, which has progressively undermined non-wage alternatives to subsistence. This has eroded women's base in domestic labour in the same way that independent commodity production was eroded as an alternative to wage labour. However, just as independent commodity production survives in limited form and retains labour not able to be absorbed in the market, so women's domestic role continues to hold reserve labour and underwrite the costs of reproduction of labour.

These themes have been extended by looking at women in the context of the process of underdevelopment in one region of Canada. Whereas the general Canadian historical patterns are similar to those of other advanced Western industrial nations of the world, the patterns in our case study may be more similar to those of the less-developed economies in the international capitalist system.

In our case study of the rural community, we trace the partial change from independent commodity production to capitalist production, drawing on literature which analyses the process of underdevelopment in terms of this truncated, distorted development of primary production. We found evidence that women's wage labour has been crucial in maintaing this form of production and that this has been profitable for the corporate sector of the industry, keeping wages and the price of the raw material low. It has also preserved rural communities as general holding tanks for reserve labour, and kept wage rates low in the whole regional economy.

In the fishing community, there was a complementarity between inshore fishing for men and plant work for women. The female labour reserve was activated and was a major element in the survival of the 'independent' producer and the underdevelopment of the industry. In the forestry-based community, wage opportunities for women were scarce and women relied on domestic subsistence activity and the informal economy to help maintain the family. When these women finally had access to jobs, they eagerly entered the labour market, at wage rates which were no longer attractive to women in the fishing community. In both communities women's wage activity has been inversely related to men's income. Thus, more women in Big Harbour worked in the plant during hard times than during good times, and at any time the women in poorer families were most likely to be working.

The history of both communities has been one of increasing reliance on wage labour, and recently on unemployment insurance, to complement the distorted remains of independent commodity production. Recent developments in the fishing industry have created 'family' incomes for a few large-boat inshore fishermen, and for some offshore crews. However the small-boat fishermen have become more marginalized and many people have been forced out of the industry altogether. The community we studied fared well in this process, causing women to have higher reservation wages for their labour. This might have led to wage increases in the plant or technological change (that is real development of the industry). However, in the context of underdevelopment, a new labour reserve willing to work at subsistence wages can always be found. In this case, it was the women from the woods-based area who took the jobs and perpetuated the poor working conditions. In both communities women were underemployed in terms of their skills and their desire to work.

Essentially, this study has shown that in historical terms the allocation of women's work between the home and the labour force has occurred as a response by the family household to changes in the needs of the economy. It reveals the heavy burden placed on women as both domestic and wage workers in an economy where full employment and adequate wages for every individual are not possible.

Women's Responses to Economic Restructuring: Changing Gender, Changing Space

Suzanne Mackenzie

Five years ago, I had such a normal life. I mean I never thought about it. You got married and had kids and went out on Saturday nights. Now, I mean, look. My husband's job is gone. And most of the time, he's gone. And all this stuff is going on here, in my house, all these people coming and going. I go out nearly every day, sometimes with the kids, to pick up stuff for the sewing and to deliver the dresses. I go to places I never went to before. I don't know what's going to happen to my life, but it sure isn't going to be normal for a while.

> (Thirty-one-year-old seamstress operating a co-operative business with four other women out of her home in an Eastern Ontario city)

I'm not a chauvinist. I always thought that what women did was important, especially with the kids and all, but it had nothing to do with me. But now the mill's closed, see, they still have jobs. It's funny, my wife she has twice as much to do now because she's doing the job she had before, looking after the kids and the house and then she's earning money too, at home you see, looking after some other kids. I'm at home a lot more now. I don't see the guys I used to work with a lot, we haven't got money to go out much now. But my wife and her friends now, they spend all their time together.

> (Twenty-five-year-old unemployed sawmill worker in a small city in the interior of British Columbia).[1]

Both the people quoted above were talking about the implications of economic restructuring; the decreasing availability and reliability of wage employment outside the home, the increasing reliance on resources and strategies inside the home.

Their experience suggests two things about the nature of these implications. It suggests that economic restructuring is altering the way in which people use the places where they live and work. It also suggests that these new uses of the environment are bound up with changes in the relations between women and men.

This article argues that changes in the use of environments and changes in gender relations are inextricably connected and cannot be fully understood in isolation from each other. Feminists have argued that economic restructuring has changed the kinds of activities women and men are carrying out, and thus changed the nature of gender relations. Recent feminist-informed work in the environmental disciplines – geography, architecture, urban and regional planning – has argued that this process of changing activities proceeds through adjustments in the way women and men use space and time, an adjustment which not only responds to existing environmental forms but which redesignates and redesigns these forms.[2] The constitution and change of gender proceeds in interaction with the constitution and change of environments.

The history of the industrial city can be seen as a history of increasing spatial, temporal and functional separation between home and work, on a continuum which runs from the early industrial home workshop to the suburban home, separated from industrial commercial firms. This has been a separation correlated, in many respects, with an increasing differentiation between the gender categories woman and man. Yet this separation and the form of this differentiation appear to be in the process of fundamental alteration, potentially moving toward a convergence.

The following article examines this relation between environmental change and gender change, carrying out a reading of the changing urban landscape from the perspective of its implications for gender roles and relations. This is a reading which begins by looking at some aspects of the feminist analysis of gender constitution and alteration as a basis for outlining a gender-sensitive concept of environment. It will then look at the relation between gender and environment in Canadian cities in the past century, especially at how women working from home in the current period of economic restructuring are altering the form and meaning of home and community and thereby contributing to a new kind of socio-economy, which opens up new possibilities for gender relations.

Feminism and Environment

Feminism is concerned with the social processes whereby the two genders – women and men – which make up the category human, are constituted, reproduced and changed.[3] The feminist model of 'human' is an explicitly historical as well as an androgynous one. To be human is not a static thing. It is a changeful process, altering as women and men alter their activities and thereby alter the attributes considered appropriate to each gender. The constitution of humanity is an active, sometimes conscious, frequently politically contested process.

The exploration of this relation has made it clear that women's activities have contributed to altering the content and the context of gender relations, thereby constantly constituting and reconstituting gender categories. While women have not done this in conditions of their own making, a good deal of feminist exploration has been devoted to identifying the conditions which allow women to extend control over their lives, and a good deal of feminist strategy to extending and building upon these conditions.

Both socialist and radical feminists have defined, albeit in very different ways, the essential parameters of gender constitution as the relations between the production of society's goods and services and the reproduction of people as biological and social beings. And while radical feminists concentrated on the 'politics of reproduction', socialist feminists attempted to articulate this understanding to broader theories of social change, primarily, although not exclusively, historical materialism.

In so doing, socialist feminists have not just adopted, but also adapted, historical materialism. 'Including gender' is not just a matter of an empirical addition at the historical level. It involves, or more accurately makes evident the need for, a shift in our analytic focal point.

Women in capitalist society (and by implication men) are defined from, live and work in, and analyse themselves from an inherently contradictory material position. Women are defined as responsible for essential social work – mothering and caring for adults – what is commonly called reproductive work. They do this in a society where power and analytic categories derive primarily from the productive sphere. Like class relations, but in a more obvious way, gender relations are constituted not only by relations of production, but also by the relations involved in the reproduction of people.

As a consequence, socialist-feminist analysis focuses not primarily on production, not primarily on reproduction, but on the relations between the two. The nature of this intersection is seen to define gender relations. These are the essential social parameters which analytically encompass women's (and men's) activities, those activities which constitute and change gender.

These are also the activities which constitute and change environmental forms. Just as gender is a category which alters through alterations in the activities of production and reproduction, so the environment is a historically mutable set of forms and patterns, which has constantly altered as women and men altered their activities in time and space.

Environments are not 'just there'. They are a significant part of who we are and what we do, of how we change and how we understand ourselves and direct change. Environments are human creations, storehouses of past and present human creativity. They are sets of resources which are appropriated in historically variable ways, these modes of appropriation altering through alterations in women's and men's space and time patterns. An environment is a set of concrete forms: buildings, rooms, roads, and patterns: bus routes, the routines through which one assembles raw materials and prepares meals or political resistance. These are forms and patterns which we have created, which we use, reproduce and alter in the process of producing goods and services and reproducing ourselves as biological and social beings.[4]

The fact that environments are human creations means that a sensitive reading of the environment can give us an often unique insight into social history. Concrete forms and routine patterns incorporate a good deal of life's 'taken for granted'. Like gender relations, many environmental forms are so deeply and ubiquitously embedded in the social fabric and in daily experience that they are virtually invisible. A critical reading of the environment, of the forms and patterns our social lives have created, can provide critical understandings of the social processes and the assumptions they reflect and reinforce. Learning how to read the environment is especially important in reconstructing women's past and present creativity. Women often leave a meagre verbal or written history of how they carry out the 'petty' and 'mundane' details of reproducing life in capitalist or other societies. However, they leave a rich record on the landscape. A reading of the social environment is also, unlike a reading of many documentary sources which have been selectively produced and preserved, necessarily a reading of gender change.

But environments are not just records. They are integral to the process of carrying out daily life. Environments are the source of material and social resources utilized in carrying out daily activity. Specific environments provide specific sets of resources: particular forms of buildings and rooms, particular patterns of access to other resources. These will facilitate some forms of activity and restrict others. A given arrangement of rooms within a household, especially the relation between kitchens and other areas, will structure family interaction and influence the allocation of tasks, as will relative access to communal resources such as shops and launderettes.[5] Similarly, as illustrated below, any set of resources will open up some forms of political and social change, and will restrict or close others, curbing and confounding not only responses but also imagination.

Changing the environment is not just a process of rearranging space. It is also a process of facilitating new activities, creating new resources, opening up new possibilities. The historical discussion below documents that environments were once different and that they are being fundamentally altered now.

Redesignating the Home and Community

Creating the separated city

The activities involved in production and reproduction have varied over history, and this variation has been accompanied by variation in the environments in which they go on, as well as the resource bases that these environments provide. The establishment of industrial society, in shattering the unity of production and reproduction which had characterized the pre-industrial home workshop, also laid the basis for the creation of a new form of city and new forms of gender differentiation.

The spatial and functional separation of production – socialized in industrial commercial firms – from reproduction, retained largely by the private family, faced late nineteenth century Canadian urban dwellers with a historically new problem: co-ordinating the needs of these new industrial firms for labour with the ability of the family to produce this labour.[6] While such problems were common to all industrializing societies, they were especially acute in Canada, where industrialization was largely a process of the rapid and wholesale introduction of American branch plants. Canada's colonial status thus telescoped the problem of 'inadequate' reproduction – insufficient or inappropriately skilled labour, growing numbers of family breakdowns, declining fertility and marriage rates, disease, malnutrition, crowding.[7]

These problems were further exacerbated by women's response to these new industrial conditions. Many aspects of production and of labour force reproduction became increasingly socialized. In response to problems of public health and the need for universal education, social institutions took on a share of responsibility for training and health care. The expansion of industry filled the home with manufactured substitutes for domestically produced goods. As many elements of family service and household manufacture were transferred from the home or family firm to the factory or state sector, women followed. Women entered the sectors of office work, the 'caring professions' and consumer goods manufacture in growing numbers. They came to numerically dominate these expanding, highly visible sectors, doing in a new locale and in new conditions many of the same things they had formerly done in the household. This adjustment in women's labour process did not substantially increase the number of women who worked to help maintain their families. But it did make women's work visible in transferring large portions of it to the 'public' wage sector.

Women's visibility was magnified by the fact that women were numerically dominant in the sectors which were displacing traditional craft manufacture and service, and therefore displacing male workers. Their labour force participation was often seen as a cause rather than a symptom of the changes generated by the transition to an industrial society. The adjustments women made to new labour processes appeared to threaten the whole structure of the economy.

Women's responses to new conditions also appeared to threaten the family as an agent of reproduction. Marriage and fertility rate decline, in conjuction with the campaigns of bourgeois women for higher education and the vote, raised the spectre of the total disintegration of the family.

It appeared that what was required was a strengthened family, carrying out some aspects of the reproduction of an appropriately socialized and healthy labour force, a family which was complemented rather than undermined by the expansion of the consumer goods sector and the new sectors of public health and education.

The solution to the problem of co-ordinating production and reproduction in the industrial city was an extension and spatial rationalization of their separation. Throughout the late nineteenth and early twentieth century, the local state, within the context of the urban reform movement, acted to co-ordinate the creation of the 'separate city'. The local state underwrote the extension, by private developers, of residential suburbs where single-family homes were complemented by appropriate commercial and social services, thus leaving the centre of the city free for efficient productive work. The city became a 'patchwork' of specialised reproductive complexes and specialised productive complexes.

The suburban reproductive complex was not only a healthy place to raise children and facilitate the recuperation of adult wage earners, it removed women and children from the temptation of the central city, especially the temptation to take on wage employment. It provided the basis for a new kind of family, concerned with personal life and the reproducing of an industrial labour force. And it provided the basis for a new role, the hard working full-time housewife, dedicated to the adequate reproduction of her family with the assistance of the new 'science' of home economics and a range of new consumer goods.

The nineteenth-century 'woman question' was thus resolved by confining most women's persons and defining all women's natures in terms of the home and community. The newly separated residential suburb had collected together all requisites of social reproduction and really distanced them and the women who carried out domestic work from production.

Throughout the twentieth century, women lived and worked within the bounds of the gender-typed, separated city, invisibly organizing to improve their working conditions.[8] The bounds extended spatially into more extensive and ever more far-flung suburbs. The suburbs 'worked' for the brief historical period between the 1930s and 1950s when some men (it was assumed all men) had secure, renumerative jobs, and most women (it was assumed all women) could devote all their time to planning around and caring for the home and family. But as maintenance of this form of home came to rely increasingly on two incomes, and women took on dual roles, the bundle began to unravel. The activities appropriate to women came to include earning money as well as providing goods and services in the home.[9]

Just as the suburban solution depended upon and reinforced one set of gender roles – the full-time domestic worker-mother and the full-time breadwinner – so the maintenance of temporally and spatially separated home and workplaces depends upon another set, primarily women's dual roles (and to some extent companionate marriages). But women's dual roles are themselves problematic.

While the nineteenth-century 'urban question' had been primarily focused around inadequate conditions for reproduction in the central cities, the solution to these problems – the extensive, distant and expensive suburb separated from wage workplaces – becomes the mid-twentieth century 'urban problem', a problem which is especially acute for that growing proportion of the labour force who are also domestic community workers. Work in the home, the place associated with leisure, is not seen as real work, nor are the home and neighbourhood designed as workplaces. What women do in these places is invisible in the public sector, as it was meant to be. Employers make few concessions to the fact that women have other jobs. As it is assumed that someone is looking after the children in the private home, childcare is not a public priority. And at the end of a long day, after having got her family off to school, to childcare, to work, travelled to a wage job herself, to shop, to see a child's doctor or teacher, a woman comes home again to a domestic workplace which requires hours of hard work and complex planning to keep running.[10]

In response to the fact that women are working at the intersection of home and work, providing not only resources in kind in the home and community but also monetary resources, they are creating services at the intersection of home and work, services which bridge the two spheres and fill the formerly invisible gaps in the separated city. As employment opportunities and flexibility decreased as part of economic restructuring, and as government restraint programmes cut back the already inadequate social services available to families, especially to wage-earning mothers, these small and socially unacknowledged services at the intersection are becoming increasingly important to the economic and social survival of households.

A growing number of women, or at least an increasingly obvious group of women, begin to extend their home roles to earning money at home.[11] Homeworkers are a heterogeneous group. They are doing a wide variety of work; a recent American study identified over two hundred types of home-based businesses.[12] These range from international import-export businesses and internationally renowned artists working from home studios to the woman 'down the street' who crochets dolls for sale at local craft shows or minds her friend's children a few hours a day. But whatever their differences, all these women have one thing in common. They are attempting to use the resources available in the home and community to carry out a new set of activities. They have all adjusted their organization of time to include work in the home for pay as well as providing goods and services to their families.

The rigid, spatially reinforced separation between production and reproduction – the concomitant basis of clearly demarcated gender roles – was severely weakened by women's dual roles. It is being further dissolved by the adaption strategy homeworkers are developing in response to economic restructuring and to the problems of maintaining dual roles. While homework is not a radically new strategy, its implications are potentially significant for restructuring the whole basis of separated production and reproduction.[13]

Homeworkers: Creating New Urban Resources

In an attempt to ascertain some of these implications, I interviewed groups of homeworkers in the Trail-Nelson area of the interior of British Columbia and in the Kingston area of eastern Ontario, asking them not only what they did and how, but also about the implications of their homework for their relations to the resource base of the home and community, including their networks of family and friends (Table 1 provides some information on the women to whom I spoke).

Table 1. Characteristics of Homeworkers[a]

	Kingston	Trail–Nelson	Total
Total sample	59	63	122
Child-care-givers	27	23	
Craftworkers[b]	32	40	
Number who had children at home	32	38	70
Average age (in years)	38	36	
Average family income ('000s of $ Canadian)	28	24	

Notes:
[a] Interviews took place between January and June 1985.
[b] This group ranged from artists with international reputations to people who produced 'in their spare time' for local sales.
Source: Questionnaire survey.

In general, I found that homeworkers were utilizing existing local resources, primarily their homes and communities, and their given networks and skills. They were doing so in the context of specific environmental constraints. Many lacked viable employment alternatives, either because of their domestic responsibilities or lack of available jobs. And while most earned relatively little from their homework, the job often provided a substantial part of family income (see Table 2).

Table 2. Homeworker's Gross Earnings as a Percentage Contribution to Total Family Income

	Total number	%	Cumulative %
Less than 10	7	5.7	100
11–25	36	29.5	94
26–50	40	32.9	65
51–75	13	10.7	32
76–99	12	9.8	21
100	14	11.5	12
Total sample	122	100	

Source: Questionnaire survey

Within these constraints, however, the social relations involved in attempts to utilize a limited set of resources designed for one purpose – private family life and individual consumption – in order to carry out a related but different purpose – the provision of a public service and the gaining of a livelihood – are causing homeworkers to alter the environments in which they work. They are using their 'given', limited environments and skills in new ways, principally by converting or redesignating resources formerly seen as private into public or collective productive resources. In the process, they are extending these resources, and often creating new resources.

This process of extending and creating resources at the interface of home and work has three implications for women's activities and for domestic community life. First, these women are developing new sources of employment, providing new social areas for 'work' and thus contributing to redefining the nature of work. Secondly, they are providing services to other members of the community, thus contributing to restructuring domestic-community working conditions, and to altering the nature of reproductive activities which go on there. Thirdly, they are altering the balance of resources in kind and monetary resources which households need to survive, and thus changing the relations between home and wage workplace. In the following, each of these is examined in turn.

Women, caring for each other's children, sewing each other's clothing, are creating their own jobs. In the process, they are redefining and extending the sets of skills which are considered worthy of payment. These women are taking their 'natural' parenting skills, their homemaking skills or their experience in home manufacture and crafts and redefining them as marketable skills. The experience they have gained as 'private' mothers and housewives has been converted into a set of defined and valued skills with which to make a living. And the majority are attempting to extend their personal skills. Most have had some 'outside' training, or at least collective sharing, of these skills immediately prior or subsequent to starting homework. This training has varied from professional qualifications to informal drop-in or self-organized collective work sessions (see Table 3).[14]

Most of these homeworkers have also redesignated networks among friends and neighbours as 'working' networks. This takes a variety of forms, based around formal or self-created organizations, or around informal meetings of homeworkers with similar

Table 3. Homeworker's Training

	Child care-givers	Craft-workers	Total
Total sample	50	72	122
None[a]	12	9	21
Seminars, drop-in courses	21	16	37
Courses in their area of homework	30	61	91
Other, related courses	17	14	31
Professional qualifications	21	20	41

Note: [a] With the exception of 'none', categories are not mutually exclusive.
Source: Questionnaire survey.

interests. These networks were not only sources of contact, advice and assistance, but also often referral and, in some cases, monitoring agencies. These networks acted to self-regulate and to disseminate information about the quality of goods or services provided by the homeworkers. In developing and utilizing these networks, homeworkers are providing themselves with some of the protection and services of a combined trade union and professional association. In addition, they are often attempting to increase the social recognition of their skills through lobbying, publicity and education.[15]

Homeworkers have also altered and extended pre-existing networks with family. Most indicated that family members often helped with their work, either through directly working on the money-earning activities or in taking over other domestic tasks.

Secondly, homeworkers are providing direct 'public' services to other members of the community. These services are, as noted above, becoming increasingly central to domestic community life, and are often the only form in which some services are available. This has the effect of altering the conditions and the environment in which domestic community work goes on.

For homeworkers, both the household and the neighbourhood become workplace as well as living space, simultaneously public and private space. In fact, the division into public and private becomes an increasingly meaningless one. For homeworkers, the formerly separate activities involved in maintaining the household become increasingly incorporated into the activities involved in earning money, and their content merges. A childminder cooking lunch for her own children as well as those she is paid to care for is simultaneously doing a 'labour of love' and a wage-earning labour. In many cases, the places where these two sets of activities go on are the same, or parts of the home are set aside primarily or exclusively for money-earning work. Women working at home are in fact redesignating, and in some cases redesigning their homes as places to earn a living as well as to 'live'.[16]

Similarly, homeworkers are redesignating their neighbour-hoods as workplaces, assessing the local and wider communities in terms of demand for their product or service and in terms of facilities to assist their work.[17] Women using their neighbour-hoods as workplaces are also actively redesigning these environments. Not only do the houses of many homeworkers include spaces set aside for the activities of homework, but these women are creating, in concrete terms, new public spaces: milieux where both 'private' domestic-community work and homework go on collectively. Such spaces include the sites of playgroups and drop-in centres, attended by both mothers and homeworkers, the crafts guilds which include both 'hobbyists' and home-workers, co-operative craft shows, stores and networks which purchase materials and equipment for both homeworkers and 'private' domestic workers.

Therefore, these networks and spaces not only provide ser-vices to homeworkers, but they are also restructuring the con-ditions under which women with dual roles or no paid jobs are carrying out their 'private' domestic-community work. A regular part of parenting increasingly includes attendance and some organizational work at a co-operative playgroup. A regular part of maintaining the home may include attending informal classes on craft manufacture and the purchase of materials from co-operative networks.

Thirdly, women earning money at home are restructuring the balance between domestic work – producing free services and goods in kind – and wage work – producing money for the pur-chase of services and goods. This alters both the value of labour power and the conditions of its reproduction.

Wages have never been sufficient for most people's sub-sistence. Subsistence has always required some form of domestic work and, for most, some form of family and community-based mutual aid. Women in the community have a long tradition of organising community mutual aid, based in attempts to com-pensate for the quantitative and qualitative differences between the male wage and the needs of the family. But such organization has necessarily become more dense and more formal as an increasing number of women, especially mothers, entered the wage labour force. The loose network of extended family and friends could meet the needs of a community of full-time house-wives-mothers on an *ad hoc* basis. However, more regular assistance, more often co-ordinated by exchange value relations rather that use value relations, became necessary to meet the needs of a community of dual-role women. The forms of mutual aid provided in the community thus become more central to the exchange process between labour power and capital as a growing percentage of the labour force defines themselves as domestic workers as well as wage workers.

Wage work patterns are also influenced by the homework sector. A socio-economy where the maintenance of family life requires that both adults be economically active tends to break down the barriers, real and analytic, between wage work and consumption on a number of levels. And this breaking down is extended as the services necessary to maintain the labour force include more and more aspects of the social wage, and issues such as childcare become workplace issues.[18] Formerly 'private' activities like childcare become workplace issues not only in a formal sense of being union bargaining matters or incentives to attract labour, but also in the sense that the availability, affordability and accessibility of childcare helps determine the availability of parents for wage work. The location and accessibility of childcare influences the range of places parents (especially mothers) are able and willing to work. And as the majority of childcare is provided by home care-givers, the size, location, cost and quality of this sector becomes intimately bound up with both the availability and the satisfaction of the wage labour force, especially that of mothers.[19]

The homework sector, as a community resource, also influences the amount of money a family needs in order to reproduce itself; that is, it influences the balance between use values and exchange values in the household budget. The homework sector often provides alternatives to formal market services, not only in the case of services like childcare, typing or household maintenance, but also in the form of alternative sources of household goods. Not only do homeworkers manufacture goods for sale, the networks of all homeworkers are supplemented by lively barter relations. This includes both barter in kind (for example, pottery for clothing), and also services for goods (for example, babysitting for paintings, craft lessons for garden produce). In addition, the co-operative networks set up to purchase materials for craft manufacture, utilized by both hobbyists and professionals provide alternative sources of raw materials for household manufacture.

Homeworkers are thus involved in altering the nature and content of exchange relations, sometimes on a small scale, as with most craft manufacture, sometimes, as in the case of the home childcare sector, dominating the field. In some respects this takes the form of an alternative economy. In most respects however, it is an alternative intimately bound up with and changing the nature of the mainstream socio-economy.

Women's dual roles can thus take a multitude of forms. Women can work in two separate and functionally disparate places, attempting to bridge constant discontinuity in their daily lives, largely through individual effort and the use of a range of use and exchange values available in their communities. Alternatively, they can obtain a variety of resources in a variety of ways within the home and community, and thus alter not their location, but the social meaning and function of home and work. However they carry them out, women's dual roles are not a radical break with the past, but another adjustment of their use of space and time in order to maximize access to resources.

In their daily activities, women make multitudes of small, daily decisions and choices, attempting to adjust the time and space for care of children, for domestic community work, for money-earning work. All of these arrangements must take account of the fluid constraints imposed by a specific balance of resources and family needs. Women's allocation of space and time must attempt to balance the resources the family requires to achieve a desired lifestyle – the amount of money, the number of commodities and services, the amount of time from the mother, the wife, the cook, the wage earner. All of these adjustments have had specific effects upon the nature of capitalist society and, more immediately but less obviously, upon the nature of both the home and community and of gender relations within this society.

This recent change is thus part of a radical, rooted continuity which stretches both across time into the social history of pre-industrial society and across space into the economies of contemporary Third World countries.[20] But saying it is not new does not imply that the social space it creates cannot be the source of new social and gender relations. The implications can be both exciting and horrific; they are certainly worthy of serious analysis. The potential of the social milieu which homeworkers are creating for the alteration of gender relations and, more generally, for the conditions under which gender relations are constituted, is the subject of the final section of this paper.

Restructuring Space and Gender

It was stated at the outset that gender and environment alter simultaneously, in a process of interaction, and that the link between androgynous humans and their environments is the activities of women and men in producing society's goods and services and reproducing people as biological and social beings. In this context, the home and community were seen as a set of fluid but structured resources which existed in relation to a wider set of resources. The adjustments which women have made in utilizing these resources have constantly defined and redefined the home, just as the concrete form of home and community, the resources it provides and the restrictions it imposes have defined and redefined the activities appropriate to women and men and thus the gender categories 'woman' and 'man' and the content of 'human'.

Gender is influenced not only by the activities women and men perform, but also by their locationally reinforced differential valuation. The creation of a separated city was the basis for the creation of new gender relations and definitions. Women's re-entry into the labour force as workers with dual roles reinforced their confinement to female-dominated occupational ghettos. In these ghettos women did, in public and for a small amount of pay, the same kinds of things which they did privately, unpaid, in the household. This reinforced the social definition of these activities not only as women's work, done by women whatever its location, but also the social definition of these activities as of relatively low economic value, either unpaid or badly paid, depending upon their location. Women were also excluded, by their dual roles, from engaging in much labour organization, of the traditional kind, to improve their labour force position.

They were not however, excluded from organizing in the community, and the motivation to organize at the interface of home and wage workplace was more pressing. In response to declining family resources and employment opportunities, women organized from their 'traditional' economic base, the home and community. And in the process they altered the base, changed it from an arena of unwaged and invisible private domestic work to a resource base capable of sustaining the production of both money earning and use-value goods and services. They are thereby altering simultaneously the nature of wage work, the nature of domestic community work and the nature of the relations between them. They are altering, in short, the nature of production and reproduction upon which both gender and class relations have been based.

The implications for gender relations of the most recent adjustment women have made – the extension of homework – are contradictory. On a superficial level, it may seem that homeworkers are not only isolating themselves from the economic centre stage and confining themselves to the private home and community, but that by so doing their activities are being increasingly confined to and typecast as reproductive work. Yet this appearance belies the nature of social *change.* The economic 'centre' is not static. The economic centre can alter location, as it appears to be doing in a period where rising unemployment has forced a growing number of households to rely increasingly on resources in the home and community.

This change in location is both an outcome of and reinforces alterations in the content of the economy. Homeworkers, in redefining their 'natural' domestic-community based skills as marketable skills, are commodifying a new set of use values, converting them into exchange values. But this is not a simple (nor even a complex) extension of commodification, nor is it the obverse, the 'privatisation' of public services. It is indeed a concomitant, if not an outcome, of these processes. The general extension of commodities into the home and the consequent raising of the cost of reproducing labour power have indeed been factors impelling women to extend their activities into earning money as well as providing services at home. Similarly, the restraint programmes 'rolling back' state services are creating an increasing need for the services home workers provided. But homeworkers' conversion of 'natural', unvalued skills into the collective arena is the extension of a new content, a reincorporation of those excluded values which Raymond Williams sees as an essential contradiction of capitalist society. Williams says:

> there is something fundamentally contradictory in the capitalist mode of production which is not only to do with its internal economic laws. What capitalism produces in commodity form excludes certain crucial kinds of production which are permanent human needs. ... All the essential human needs that could not be co-ordinated by commodity production – health, habitation, family, education, what it calls leisure – have been repressed or specialized by the development of capitalism. The deepening of the division of labour, and the radical reduction of the notions of humanity and sociality that these processes have involved, have produced profound contradictions – more impossible for capitalism to solve than those which are generated within the market.[21]

To some extent, women's creating of 'jobs' out of the formerly 'natural' skills involved in meeting some of these 'permanent human needs' is thus an alteration of the content, the nature and the site of this exclusion and therefore of this contradiction. And this is extended by the concomitant effects of this work: the restructuring of domestic community working conditions through the provision of new services in new ways, and the alteration of exchange-value relations between labour power and the wage sector.

In effect, the focus on the intersection, and therefore the content of productive and reproductive activities in the discussion above, suggests that it is perhaps more useful to see these 'permanent human needs' not as excluded, but as met in historically variable and different ways. Seeing them as excluded implies an analytic focal point based in the 'included'. Alternatively, a focus on the permeable intersection implies, as Williams himself notes, the basing of analytic categories on the ahistorical human content of social life.

We cannot focus long on the relation between production and reproduction without moving a considerable way from both the 'bad old days' of economic determinism and from the seductive 'Althusserian moment' – the theoretically comfortable but politically irresponsible view of people as 'bearers of social relations'. In part this is because such a focus breaks down the neat conceptual divisions between production and reproduction; between work and non-work or life; between wage workplace and home-community, even between class and gender. It forces us instead to see people's activities anew, conceptually unclad and undisguised. In fact, looking at reproduction as analytically important, as politically pertinent, makes a focus on content unavoidable. There is little else to see apart from the small, 'insignificant', common-sense details of keeping people alive and socially integrated in a capitalist society. And as these become evident, they mingle with or even crowd out the abstract questions of tendencies and structures which formed the basis of positivist social science and which still dominate in some contemporary non-positivist work.

So a focus on the intersection of productive and reproductive activities tends to create an analysis which is full of content, which is concerned with the kinds of interpersonal relations through which we get by day by day, and which is concerned with how we can change these. It suggests that we recentre our attention on the taken-for-granted details, the small human actions which constitute and change our categories, our tendencies, our structures, that we look for social change at the level where they are created, in human lives and in the small-scale environments of the home and community, as well as at the higher levels of abstraction with which many of us have become so expert at conjuring. In short, this focus is one of the major analytic bases for the emphasis, in feminist political actions, on prefigurative politics, on building a new society from the bottom up.[22]

One of the implications of women's concern, both practically and analytically, with content, has been the idea that they can control and change their own lives. Women have experienced tremendous alterations in their daily lives, and in the conditions under which resources for these lives are provided. They have also seen the image of woman change radically, from someone who was naturally guided to cook, clean, bear and care for an uncontrollable number of children, all within the home, to an energetic and efficient organizer, combining a career with raising an agreed upon number of clever children in a companionate family. Partly in response to the changes underlying these stereotypes, women have seen and experienced feminism redefine 'woman' from a biological determined state of being to a self-conscious and articulate political force. Feminism remains an analysis directed towards providing understandings which allow us to actively and consciously overcome the oppressive aspects of gender relations, a process which will involve profound and far-reaching social, interpersonal and environmental change. In attempts to develop understanding necessary for this change, feminists in the last few generations have extended the area over which we have, and know ourselves to have, some control – interpersonal relations, sexual relations, family life – from a 'natural' area to an arena for articulate, international politics. Simultaneously, feminists are utilizing the forms of analysis designed to delineate 'grand theory' in discussion of and action around daily life and thus imbuing this analysis with concrete content.

The potential implications of the restructuring of the productive and reproductive work, which homeworkers are creating, are profound, not only for our environments and gender relations, but for the content of our analysis. Yet it is perhaps fair to suggest that this most audacious crossing of the boundaries – the intergration of personal politics and theory – may be the most profound result of such restructuring.

Women's Emancipation and the Recruitment of Women into the War Effort

Ruth Roach Pierson

It is often assumed that the employment of women in the labour force during the Second World War greatly advanced the emancipation of women, at least in the sense of women's struggle to achieve equal status with men in Canadian society.[1] Building on that assumption, feminists have lamented the ease with which many of the gains were lost at the war's end. One famous account, concerned with US society but considered to have relevance for Canadian society as well, postulated the propagation of a 'feminine mystique' to account for the post-war reverses suffered by women's struggle for equality.[2]

Both the assumption of great gains made by women during the Second World War and the bewilderment over the post-war reversals rest on an inadequate examination of the context of women's wartime employment and an inaccurate assessment of the degree to which attitudes towards women's proper role in society changed during the war. Canada's war effort, rather than any consideration of women's right to work, determined the recruitment of women into the labour force. The recruitment of women was part of a large-scale intervention by government into the labour market to control allocation of labour for effective prosecution of the war.

Four factors are crucial to an understanding of women's increased participation in the work force. 1. National Selective Service (NSS) and the federal Department of Labour, in their wartime mobilization of the work force, regarded women as constituting a large labour reserve, to be dipped into more and more deeply as the labour pool dried up. The recruitment would first seek young 'girls' and single women and then childless married women for full-time employment, next women with home responsibilities for part-time employment, and finally women with children for full-time employment. Starting with the most mobile, NSS pulled in these groups successively as the war effort intensified. Government officials publicly expressed a reluctance to draw upon those women in the female labour reserve whose mobilization would disrupt the traditional family system. 2. It was the traditional labour of women, their unpaid labour in the home and their volunteer labour that was mobilized on the grandest scale during the war. 3. The government recruitment agencies viewed their task as service to Canada's war effort. Accordingly, the paramount appeal of recruitment campaigns was to patriotic duty and the necessity to make sacrifices for the nation at war. Women's obligation to work in wartime was the major theme, not women's right to work. 4. Accommodations to the particular needs of working women were made within the context of the war effort. These were generally introduced as temporary measures, to remain in effect only so long as the nation was at war.

I

Canada was not out of the depression when the Second World War began. There were about 900,000 registered unemployed in a work-force of approximately 3.8 million. In the following two years these unemployed persons largely met the increased demands for workers created by military recruitment and wartime production. By 1942 the slack in the labour market had been taken up. With war industry geared for full production and the armed forces drawing large numbers of male workers from the labour force, the labour market had changed from one of labour surplus and unemployment to one of shortage. 'To meet the pressure of war needs attention, therefore, became focused on the reserve of potential women workers who had not yet been drawn into employment.'[3]

By thirteen Orders-in-Council, the NSS programme was established in March 1942, under the jurisdiction of the Minister of Labour.[4] When Prime Minister Mackenzie King in the House of Commons on 24 March 1942 announced the establishment of National Selective Service to co-ordinate and direct the near total mobilization of Canada's labour power for the war effort, he declared that 'recruitment of women for employment was "the most important single feature of the programme" '.[5] He went on to outline a ten-point plan for drawing women into industry.[6] In May 1942, a division of NSS was created to deal with employment of women and related services. Mrs Rex (Fraudena) Eaton of Vancouver was appointed assistant (later associate) director of NSS in charge of the Women's Division.

One of NSS's first steps was to measure the top layer of the female labour reserve. 'It was decided to conduct a compulsory registration of *younger* women in order to ascertain more definitely what resources of woman power were available.'[7] On 8 September 1942, Labour Minister Humphrey Mitchell ordered the registration of all females aged twenty to twenty-four, with the exception of members of religious orders, hospital patients, prison inmates, and women currently in insurable employment.[8] The registration was held from 14 September to 19 September 1942. Although both married and unmarried women were required to register, the main objective of this initial inventory of Canada's womanpower was to determine the size of the labour reserve of young single women. The twenty-to-twenty-four age group had been chosen because 'Single women would compose a higher percentage of the total than would be found in older age groups.'[9]

On 20 August 1942, Mrs Eaton had met in Ottawa with executive representatives of twenty-one national women's organizations to enlist their support for NSS and the September Registration of Canadian Women. She explained that the registration

> will show us exactly how many single women we have available to meet the increasing shortage of workers in our war industries. Then we will have a pool of single workers from which to draw when an employer asks for additional staff, and single women can be supplied immediately.[10]

The policy was not merely to mobilize single women, but to render unnecessary the employment of married women with children. Mrs Eaton stated emphatically: 'We shall not urge married women with children to go into industry.' Married women had been drifting into work in war industries because 'no known reservoir of single workers existed'. It was hoped that the registration would enable NSS 'to direct single women into essential war industries rather than to have employers building up huge staffs of married women with children'.[11]

On 15 December 1942, A. Chapman of the Research and Statistics Branch of the Department of Labour submitted a report on the 'Female Labour Supply Situation'. From the results of the women's registration, interviews by local Employment and Selective Service Offices, and detailed analyses by local offices of the relation of unfilled vacancies to unplaced applicants, she concluded: 'Study of the available information regarding the supply and demand for female labour clearly indicates the existence of a large reserve of female labour throughout the country.'[12] Beyond 'the overall surplus of female labour', the figures showed 'that the bulk of the readily available surplus of female labour is concentrated in those areas where war industry is least developed'. While allowing for regional variation of response to the registration, Chapman insisted that the figures 'do emphasize the tremendous reservoir of female labour in areas such as the Maritimes and the Prairies where development of war industry has been slight'.[13] The information from the registration and follow-up interviews led to the adoption of a programme for transferring young unmarried women workers from areas of surplus to areas of labour scarcity.

In May 1942, a survey of the anticipated demand for female labour had shown 'that at least 75,000 additional women would be required in war industries before the end of the year'.[14] The registration itself stimulated young women to apply for employment.[15] In addition, NSS launched a nation-wide publicity campaign to urge upon women 'the need to engage in some phase of the war effort'.[16] Editors agreed to give space in their publications to pictures of women working in war production and to stories of accomplishments by individual women. Papers published news releases on NSS and the problems it was facing. The Canadian Broadcasting Corporation presented over the national network 'a series of dramatic plays, written expressly for NSS around the theme of women war workers'.[17] The campaign paid off. By January 1943, the additional 75,000 women required for war industries had been recruited. Indeed, between January 1942 and June 1943 158,000 women had joined the industrial war effort, bringing the number of women engaged in war industries to 255,000. During the same period, several thousand women had volunteered for service in the women's divisions of the three armed forces.[18] The 'readily available surplus of female labour'[19] had evaporated.

By the summer of 1943 serious labour shortages had developed in areas of the service sector long dependent on female labour. Women were leaving low-paid service jobs for higher-paying employment in war industries. Service businesses were clamouring for help. Women were needed as ward aides in hospitals, as waitresses and kitchen help in restaurants, as chambermaids and waitresses in hotels, and for various subordinate positions in laundries and dry-cleaning establishments.[20] The labour pool of single women available for full-time employment was exhausted. 'It became necessary to appeal to housewives and those groups who would not ordinarily appear in the labour market.'[21] While the first recruitment had sought young unmarried women and then childless married women for full-time employment, in mid-1943, NSS (Women's Division) decided to launch a campaign to recruit women with home responsibilities for part-time work.

The need for part-time workers had been foreseen as early as November 1942.[22] Supervisors of the women's divisions of local Employment and Selective Service Offices were instructed to persuade employers to make plans for employing women on a part-time basis. At first employers resisted the idea. In a 7 May 1943 memorandum, Mary Eadie, Women's Division Supervisor, Toronto, reported that, although some had 'undertaken to use it with success ... the employer as a whole "will not be bothered" ... with part-time help'.[23] Employers cited higher administrative costs and a feared rise in absenteeism and turnover as reasons for their opposition. But when firms producing non-essentials, such as candy, tobacco, soft drinks, and luxury items, were informed that NSS would make no effort to send them 'full-time workers while essential services and war industries were short of labour'[24] and when by the spring of 1943 even firms providing essential civilian services were short of labour, many employers became more willing to employ women part-time.

The first campaign for part-time women workers was mounted in Toronto from 12 July to 26 July 1943. To prepare for it, Toronto Selective Service first sought the co-operation of employers. 'Several conferences were called' with employers in hospitals, restaurants, hotels, laundries, and dry-cleaning establishments 'to discuss the possibility of [their] using part-time' women workers.[25] On 22 May 1943, Mary Eadie reported to

Mrs Eaton that 'the Ontario Restaurant Association, the Laundry and Dry Cleaning Association of Toronto and the Hospital Association of Toronto will co-operate with us because they are in such dire straits for help these days'.[26] The Toronto Selective Service also won for the campaign the sponsorship of the Local Council of Women.[27] According to Mrs Eaton, it was 'with great courage' that Mrs Norman C. Stephens, president of the Toronto Council of Women, 'offered to promote a publicity campaign inviting Toronto women to accept part-time work in these occupations which no one will claim to be glamorous or highly paid'.[28]

The campaign was 'particularly directed to housewives'.[29] At the same time, 'no women with important home responsibilities were unduly urged to register'. Furthermore, 'no appeal was made for women to work part-time in addition to a full-time job'. However, 'many women without children and with few home responsibilities consented, under pressure of the campaign, to accept full-time work'.[30]

In her report of 28 July 1943 to the NSS Advisory Board, Mrs Eaton applauded the results of the campaign: 2,267 women had responded to the call. Of these, 1,518 had been placed in essential services, 643 in part-time, and 875 in full-time positions. Another 599 had accepted part-time employment in war industries. The remainder (150) were yet to be placed. For Mrs Eaton, 'the success of the campaign offered some assurance that there is still a pool of women ready and willing to fill a breach when emergencies arise'.[31]

The Toronto campaign served as a model for similar campaigns in other Canadian cities. NSS Circular No. 270–71 (18 August 1943) outlined the operation. Its goal was to relieve a labour shortage in 'essential services such as hospitals, restaurants, hotels, laundries and dry cleaning establishments'. Targeted would be 'a new type of recruit', namely 'the housewife or others *who will do a Part-time Paid Job* for six days per week, perhaps only four hours per day, or perhaps three full days each week'. Not only was the campaign aimed at housewives, but the work they were being asked to do was also seen as an extension of housework outside the home. As the circular stated: 'It is possible for many women to streamline their housekeeping at home to do the housekeeping in the community for standard wages.' Local offices were first to secure the willingness of employers to provide definite orders for part-time workers, then to secure the sponsorship 'of an organization of women who have the high confidence of the community'. The Local Council of Women was specifically recommended. The publicity campaign would engage the combined efforts of the employers, the sponsors, and the staff of the local Employment and Selective Service Office. The expenses of the campaign were to be borne by the benefiting employers and the Dominion government on a fifty–fifty cost-sharing basis. Women of the sponsoring organization could help in the local office with registration of applicants, but all referrals to jobs would remain the responsibility of the local Employment and Selective Service Office staff.[32]

The president of the National Council of Women, Mrs Edgar Hardy, agreed to endorse these campaigns. A letter signed on 31 August 1943 by A. MacNamara and Mrs Rex Eaton was sent to all Local Councils of Women enlisting their support, stating: 'There is no reserve of men in Canada today. In fact there is little reserve of either men or women.'[33]

Working in close co-operation with the Local Council of Women, NSS launched special recruiting campaigns for part-time women workers in autumn of 1943 in Edmonton, Saskatoon, Regina, Brandon, Ottawa, Moncton, and Halifax. Appeals to women to take part-time jobs in commercial laundries, dry-cleaning establishments, restaurants, and bakeries made explicit reference to the double burden borne by many women war workers and presented these businesses as serving to ease that burden. A radio address for the Halifax campaign, for instance, reminded listeners that 'many women who are engaged in essential war jobs have no time for doing the family laundry' or preparing meals.[34]

The drives also sought part-time workers in some centres, such as Edmonton, for jobs in the garment industry. In some places, such as Brandon and Edmonton, the part-time campaign was combined with a campaign for full-time women workers. In Ottawa, the campaign aimed exclusively at encouraging former female employees of the civil service, now married, to return to part-time or full-time work to alleviate the serious shortage of workers in war departments of government.[35]

Although for as long as possible only full-time women workers were sought for war industries, by the end of 1943 and throughout 1944 women were hired for certain war jobs on a part-time basis. In some areas 'housewives' shifts' came into existence, so named because they were made up primarily or entirely of 'housewives who could work only in the evenings' from 6 or 7 to 10 or 11 p.m.[36]

Even before the end of the part-time campaign in Toronto on 26 July 1943, NSS faced an acute labour shortage in war industries there. An estimated 3,500 women were needed to fill full-time high-priority jobs in war production.[37] The urgency of the need ruled out transferring women workers from other parts of Canada.[38] At the suggestion of the War Council of the Artists' Guild, the Toronto Selective Service proposed that management 'recruit women for employment in war industries for full-time work for a period of not less than three months'. Although employers thought they needed long-term full-time workers, they saw advantages to a special appeal for three-month service: it would give the media 'a new publicity angle to emphasize the need of war industries for more workers'; women once hired might remain in employment; and it would counteract 'the fear of being frozen to the job', which seemed to deter many women from 'employment full time in essential industry'.[39]

The key note of this special Toronto campaign was 'three months' service'.[40] Although the call went out to all women, special appeal was made to housewives, with the promise of a counselling service for mothers and endeavours to place women in war plants near their homes.[41] Preceded in early August by radio publicity on the need for women in war industry, the campaign ran from 30 August to 11 September. During the first week a 'war industrual show' was put on at the T. Eaton Company Auditorium. 'Girls' from war plants demonstrated operations they performed 'in their ordinary work at the plant' and 'a fashion show was given in which the girls wore their plant uniforms'.[42] In her final account of the campaign, Mrs Eaton reported that 4,330 women had been referred to war industries, 168 were awaiting referral until day nursery care for their children had been arranged, and 300 who had applied for part-time work were yet to be placed.[43]

Through the autumn of 1943 NSS continued its recruitment campaigns for full-time women workers as labour demands dictated. Both the garment and textile industries, traditional employers of women in Ontario and Quebec, were feeling the pinch as female workers moved to better-paying jobs in munitions plants. In early October 1943, an extensive campaign was mounted in Peterborough for 550 new women workers for full-time jobs in textile factories and other high-priority manufacturing firms.[44] Similarly, in November 1943, special drives to recruit female textile workers for full-time jobs were carried out in the textile centres of Hamilton, Welland, St Catharines, and Dunville.[45]

In Montreal, NSS officials began planning in late September a massive recruitment campaign to alleviate a recorded labour shortage of 19,000. But on 2 November 1943 a meeting of Montreal employers with the NSS regional superintendent for Quebec decided to postpone indefinitely the large-scale campaign. As opposition to women's employment still persisted in Quebec, it was felt that the public would be more receptive to a series of small, separate drives specifically for 'hotels, laundries, hospitals, textiles, etc'.[46]   In December 1943, the urgency for recruitment campaigns subsided[47] and the first months of 1944 saw a 'slow but noticeable reduction in war industry'.[48] The number of women in the labour force actually declined by 10,000–15,000 in the first three months of the year. Although the end of the war was in sight, NSS would not allow any slackening of the war effort until victory was secured. There was some concern that women might leave the war industry in greater numbers than the slowdown in production warranted.[49] Married women might want to return to their homes 'and a less strenuous life'; single women might want to secure post-war jobs NSS countered with publicity asking 'women [to] remain steadily on their jobs throughout the year' and instructed women's divisions of local Employment and Selective Service Offices to persuade women requesting separation notices to stay at their posts. To the reluctant they were to suggest a brief holiday, or transfer to a more convenient shift, or 'a part-time job in essential work near their homes'. These efforts were successful: 'there was no general exodus [of women] from war industries and essential services'.[50]

Then in June 1944 came a new emergency. The invasion of France, the Department of Munitions and Supply informed NSS, required ammunition plants in Ontario and Quebec to operate at peak production. An estimated 10,000 additional women workers were required. This made necessary a last large-scale recruitment campaign. It was organized by the Public Relations Office of the Department of Labour[51] and 'promoted co-operatively by the plants concerned'[52] with every assistance from NSS. Local Employment and Selective Service Offices 'redoubled their efforts to persuade women to accept jobs' in nearby ammunition plants,[35] and, working with recruiting agents of the munition firms, NSS resumed the transfer of women from the east and west to central Canada. For example, some 350 Alberta women, including many school teachers, were persuaded to forgo their summer vacations for munitions jobs on the agreement they would be back in Alberta for school opening, 2 October.[54]

In addition to the wartime recruitment of women into industries and services, there was also recruitment of women into agriculture 'to fill some of the gaps in farm man power with female labour'.[55] In all provinces formers' wives and daughters took over farm work in the absence of male relatives and farm workers who had left the land to join the Armed Forces or work in industry. In two provinces, however, special programmes were organized to recruit farm labour on the basis of the Dominion-Provincial Farm Labour Agreement, entered into by Ontario in 1941 and by British Columbia in 1943. The Ontario Farm Service Force divided female labour volunteers into three brigades: the Farmerette Brigade for female students (over fifteen) and teachers during their summer holidays; the Women's Land Brigade for housewives and business and professional women on a day-to-day basis; and the Farm Girls' Brigade for farm women (under twenty-six) to lend a hand where necessary. The work was hard, usually nine to ten hours a day, and the wage rate low, 25 cents per hour. In 1943, '12,793 girls in addition to a considerable number of teachers' were enrolled in the Farmerette Brigade, approximately 4,200 women in the Women's Land Brigade, and about 1,000 in the Farm Girls' Brigade. After its creation, NSS helped to publicize the appeals for Farm Labour Service.[56]

II

Far and away the largest contribution made by Canadian women to the war effort was through their unpaid labour in the home and through 'volunteer' work. Women's unpaid domestic work was as crucial to family maintenance in wartime as in peace.[57] The difference, however, was that the war effort brought public acclaim to that everyday labour women perform as housewives and mothers. The mobilization of Canadian society for efficient prosecution of the war called upon the co-operation of women as preparers of food, clothes makers, consumers, and managers of family budgets. Women as homemakers helped the war effort by respecting the limitations that rationing imposed, by preventing waste, and by saving and collecting materials that could be recycled for use in war production. After 1942, urban homemakers in particular had to learn to cook with limited supplies of almost everything from milk to molasses.[58]

To increase Canada's food production women cultivated victory gardens and canned the produce. While many housewives and mothers had been forced to practise severe economies during the depression, wealthier women learned for the first time during the war to remake old clothes into new outfits and to curtail their buying of consumer products in the face of cutbacks in production of everything from brooms to baby carriages. Homemakers saved fat scraps and oils for the ammunition industry and pennies to buy war stamps. As one poster put it, women were to 'Dig In and Dig Out the Scrap' and save metals, rags, paper, bones, rubber, glass.[59]

Someone had to collect the salvage and the contributions to Victory Loans and to pass out information on how to practise domestic economies necessary for the war effort. Almost all of that work at the neighbourhood level was performed voluntarily by women. Indeed, at the local level the voluntary labour of women, who worked in or outside the home or both, sustained a vast network of wartime services and activities. The Department of National War Services established a Women's Voluntary Services Division in the autumn of 1941 to co-ordinate these efforts. Mrs W. E. (Nell) West was appointed director of WVS. While the Ottawa office served to direct and advise, and to supply government information, the main burden of the programme was carried by Women's Voluntary Services Centres set up, eventually, in forty-four Canadian cities from Sydney, Nova Scotia, to Victoria, BC. These centres kept a roster of the local societies and clubs performing war services, recruited volunteers and placed them according to interest and ability, and acted as a clearing house for information from the war departments of the federal government.[60]

Women's voluntary contribution to the war effort, however, did not have to wait for action from the federal government. Women themselves took the initiative. Immediately after the declaration of war, established women's organizations of all kinds turned their attention to war work and new organizations sprang into being for that express purpose. Even co-ordination of women's voluntary efforts did not have to wait until the Department of National War Services established its WVS Division. In Winnipeg, for instance, a group of women founded a Central Volunteer Bureau for the city early in the war, which registered volunteers and directed them according to skill and interest to the appropriate club or agency. It encouraged the formation of new organizations where need existed and discouraged potential redundancies.[61] This bureau smoothly turned itself into the Women's Voluntary Services Centre of Winnipeg in October 1941.

In contrast, the private Ontario organization for co-ordinating women's volunteer war work resisted encroachment by the Dominion government. A group of Toronto women had founded it only one month before the creation of Women's Voluntary Services Division in the federal government, and it was their intention, once they got Ontario organized, to spread into other provinces and develop into a national organization. They called themselves the 'Canadian Women's Voluntary Services (Ontario Division)' after the British Women's Voluntary Services, which was, however, a government body. Once the Canadian federal government decided to get into the act, it notified the CWVS (Ontario Division) that as of September 1942 their work would be superseded and, to avoid confusion, they would have to relinquish their name. This touched off a minor furore among members of the Ontario organization. They pelted the Department of National War Services with letters protesting that unsalaried, charitable work was women's domain and questioning the right of the government to barge in and pre-empt a women's voluntary organization. Some letters even demanded to know why anyone should be getting paid to co-ordinate voluntary work and, more particularly, why the government should be paying the director and one of the assistant directors of its Women's Voluntary Services Division when both women were married to men with good incomes. In the end, having appeased the leaders of the CWVS, Ontario Division (one, for instance, was sent on a trip to England to observe the work of the British WVS), Ottawa negotiated a *modus vivendi* with the organization that involved the absorption of its already functioning network into the federal system.[62]

The core of Canada's volunteer war work remained the millions of Canadian women organized into hundreds of local societies and clubs, orchestrated by the local Women's Voluntary

Services Centres under the direction of Ottawa's WVS. Most of the centres were staffed voluntarily, although a few of the bigger ones had paid executive secretaries or directors. Fifteen of the centres used a Block Plan to organize the community for house-to-house canvassing and collection, with a hierarchy of responsibility stretching from block leaders through section leaders and zone leaders to director of the Block Plan in the WVS Centre.

The WVS Block Plan was one of the cornerstones of salvage collection. Take, for example, the collection of waste fats and bones. By 1942 Canada's supplies of oils and fats were down to 50 per cent of normal. Phyllis Turner, Administrator of Oils and Fats under the Wartime Prices and Trade Board, took action to save unreplenishable stocks of oil for glycerine, a necessary ingredient in explosives: she set rigid restrictions on the civilian use of oils and fats, such as limiting the number of colours of paints and of shades in lipsticks and rouges and the amount of coconut oil in shampoo and chocolate bars.[63] She also encouraged the Department of National War Services to launch a waste fats and bones salvage campaign and, through its Women's Voluntary Services Division, to have women mobilize women and children to carry this out. For the fats and bones and other salvage campaigns, a WVS block captain first made door-to-door visits to all the women on her block urging their co-operation, then once a week rallied the block's children to make the rounds and collect what had been saved, and finally arranged for its delivery to the local offices of the National Salvage Committee. Women also served voluntarily in those offices, helping to sort through the piles of material that came pouring in each week.[64]

Centres participated directly in other national programmes, such as distributing rationing cards, carrying out a fact-finding survey on the size and productivity of victory gardens, recruiting and training volunteer staff for wartime day nurseries, and promoting the sale of war savings stamps. Ottawa's WVS Division developed the idea of using attractive young women as 'Miss Canada Girls' to advertise the sale of war savings stamps as well as other patriotic events in support of the war. Local women's organizations were given the task of making 'warsages', boutonnières with war savings stamps attached.[65] The Women's Voluntary Services held a 'Volunteer Week', 12–20 September 1943, to publicize the importance of voluntary work. The CBC broadcast two programmes on the national network in its honour and centres across Canada put on special exhibits, strung WVS banners, gave outdoor concerts, and set up registration booths in the shops of local merchants in an all-out drive to register more volunteers.[66] Recognizing that 'a very large proportion of mail to the Troops is sent by women', the Women's Voluntary Services Division threw its centres behind the 1944 drive of the Postmaster General to get more letters written to members of the armed forces.[67] On a regular basis the volunteers mobilized through local WVS centres distributed ration cards, canvassed for blood donors and staffed blood donor booths, gave information to householders on the disposal of books and magazines for the armed services and to apartment dwellers on the cultivation of window box victory gardens, distributed wool to the various 'ladies' organizations' for the knitting of socks and other garments, and arranged hospitality and entertainment for servicewomen and servicemen on leave and far from home. In 1944 and 1945 WVS centres sponsored lectures and the showing of films to members of women's organizations in co-operation with the Canadian Women's Army Corps anti-VD campaign. Meanwhile, at the level of the individual club, women sewed and knitted and quilted and packed parcels and put together 'ditty bags' for the servicemen and women overseas. They also made jam, collected bundles, and raised money for milk for Britain.

In the countryside the Women's Institutes, all across Canada, carried the burden of women's voluntary war work. The Women's Institute of Burton, British Columbia, for example, held 'Military Whist Drives' to raise money for soldiers' parcels.[68] Women's Institutes on the Gaspé gave aid to survivors of torpedoed vessels. In the words of the Convenor of War Services of the Federated Women's Institutes of Canada, speaking of the war work of Canadian rural women:

> They have worked harder at farm work than ever before. They have driven tractors, made hay, picked fruit, raised wonderful gardens and increased the poultry and egg production of all Canada. Yet they have found time to make tons of jam for overseas, clothing for refugees and thousands of articles for the Red Cross.

In the period 1943–5, the Women's Institutes of Canada had raised 'over half a million dollars in cash' and made 'nearly the same number of garments . . . for the Red Cross and others'.[69] After the war, Women's Institutes and Voluntary Services

Centres organized committees to welcome returning veterans and to help foreign 'war brides' of Canadian servicemen feel at home in their new country.[70] In October 1945, these volunteer women helped the National Clothing Collection reach its total of 12 million pounds of used clothing for distribution in war-devastated countries.

Another way in which women voluntarily contributed to the war effort was to help monitor inflation. After the Wartime Prices and Trade Board set price and production ceilings on many consumer items in 1941–2, women's clubs across Canada appointed committees to keep an eye on the movement of prices and availability of goods essential to housekeeping and family care. Women took pad and pencil to food and clothing and hardware stores and made notes of price infractions or commodity scarcities. Once again the initiative of women suggested the establishment of a federal body to co-ordinate their activities and the Consumer Branch of the Wartime Prices and Trade Board was brought into being under the directorship of Byrne Hope Sanders, editor of *Châtelaine*. Canada was divided into fourteen administrative areas, each with a Women's Regional Advisory Committee. Working with these committees at the local level were subcommittees in urban centres with a population 5,000 or more and corresponding members in smaller communities. In addition, every individual women's organization in towns with more than one was asked to appoint a liaison officer to keep in touch with the local subcommittee. Through this network one million of Canada's three million adult women were mobilized to keep a close watch on the behaviour of price and production restrictions across the country and to report to Ottawa.[71] Women thus played an indispensable role in the Canadian government's wartime fight against inflation.

Despite women's massive voluntary contribution to Canada's war effort, as well as the increased reliance on women's paid labour, women had to struggle to make their voices heard even to a limited extent on any of the various reconstruction committees that emerged during the war to plan Canada's post-war future. One of the most influential, the federal Advisory Committee on Reconstruction, convened in 1941 by the Minister of Pensions and National Health and chaired by Dr F. Cyril James, principal of McGill University, had no woman among its six initial members. Nor were women or women's issues to be found on the subcommittees subsequently created to explore specific post-war problems: agricultural policy, conservation and development of resources, post-war construction projects, housing and community planning, and employment opportunities. It took repeated lobbying from women's organizations, particularly the Canadian Federation of Business and Professional Women's Clubs and the Québec-based League for Women's Rights/Ligue pour les droits de la femme, before a sixth subcommittee was finally created in January 1943, the Subcommittee on the Post-War Problems on Women, composed of ten women.[72] But this concession remained inadequate in the eyes of many women. In the spring of 1943 the Local Council of Women of Toronto voiced its dissatisfaction that the James committee itself still had '*no* women members', and that all post-war problems affecting women had been hived off for separate consideration by one subcommittee, instead of the appointment of women to the existing subcommittees investigating issues every bit as important to women as to men, especially those on housing and community planning and employment.[73] Throughout 1944 the National Council of Women repeatedly pressed on the federal government the policy 'That on all boards and committees dealing with reconstruction and rehabilitation well qualified women shall be appointed.' Their efforts met with less than perfect success. The reply from the Prime Minister's Office, for example, regarding the request that a woman be appointed to the Wartime Labour Relations Board in March 1944, was that neither the labour organizations nor the employers' organizations had been able to suggest a suitable woman.[74]

III

It was in the name of patriotic duty that women's voluntary services were at first spontaneously offered and later, once government became involved, officially recruited for the war effort. It was also in the spirit of near-total mobilization for war that women's traditional domestic services received new recognition as socially necessary labour, as an examination of wartime advertisements reveals.

Wartime advertising was a complex business, as advertisers competed for customers and sought to protect their trade names for post-war markets while demonstrating a patriotic spirit. The manufacturers of commodities such as guns, planes, and tanks had the least difficulty appearing patriotic, for they could easily show how their product was helping to win the war. Those who manufactured products for use in the home had a somewhat harder time; but, once they took up the theme of how important efforts on the 'home front' were to winning the war, they could argue for the contribution, albeit indirect, of the work performed in the kitchens and laundry rooms of homes across Canada to the battles overseas.[75] One finds advertisements celebrating the important war work housewives performed when they kept their families on healthy diets and in clean clothes. One imaginative example was the 1942 advertisement by the Canada Starch Company of Montreal and Toronto. 'All honour,' it said, 'to those mothers and wives who are exerting every effort to keep the workers of Canada fit, vigorous, and keyed to "victory through production". *They are Canada's Housoldiers.'*[76]

This 'militarization' of women's housework was not limited to commercial advertisers. War departments of government also played on this theme, as when the National Finance Committee advertised to 'Invest in the best – buy victory bonds' with the slogan 'She's in there fighting, too' and pictured a mother in an apron drying dishes with the help of her young daughter.[77] Contributors to the women's pages of magazines and newspapers also got into the spirit, as when the director of the Châtelaine Institute entitled a 1943 article on the proper care of woollens 'Blitz on Moths'.[78] Did women accept this 'militarization' of the domestic sphere? The poem 'Kitchen Brigade', submitted by May Richstone to the August 1943 issue of the *National Home Monthly* on the subject of women's work in saving fats and oils, indicates that some may have:

> Behind each gallant fighting man,
> Loyal we stand, the kitchen brigade.
> Our weapon is the frying pan –
> We'll see that glycerine is made.
>
> Out of the frying pan, fat flows,
> Not one drop wasted, if you please;
> Out of the frying pan it goes
> Into the fire – at our enemies![79]

Building on the belief that women's social role was to be emotionally supportive of men, to smooth over difficulties, and to make the home a genuine refuge from the stresses of the larger world, the government actively reminded Canadian women of their duty as morale boosters as well as cooks and housekeepers. In 1942 the Department of Munitions and Supply issued a series of full-page advertisements with this message to be published in Canadian magazines. One bore the title 'A Lot Depends on You!' and, in small print, beneath a picture of a woman in whose shadow stand a munitions manufacturer and a soldier:

> These are trying times for your men folk. Some of them are on the firing line; others on the production line.
>
> The men of your household are probably working longer hours these days. Whether in office or factory, they are under a greater strain. For they are striving to get vital equipment to our fighting forces before it is too late.
>
> It's up to you to keep your men folk fit and happy. Men produce more when their minds are at ease, when they are not worried by domestic problems. If you shoulder these worries and help your men to relax, you are playing a real part in winning the war.
>
> Perhaps your husband is irritable when he comes home tired from his work. Perhaps he must be away from home weeks at a time or longer. Be sympathetic and understanding under these circumstances.
>
> Remember, this is an emergency. The more each of us helps, the sooner we can get back to the happy days of peace-time living. So do your part cheerfully for your country's sake. Keep that man of yours fit and happy for his job.

The final motto carried the self-admonition: 'Brave Men Shall Not Die Because *I* Faltered.'[80]

This wartime mobilization of women's domestic and volunteer labour also capitalized on the traditional housewifely virtue of thrift. 'Thrift . . . Is Practical Patriotism' was the headline of a victory loan campaign poster, designed by the National War Finance Committee for placement in rural weekly newspapers. The question 'How many ways can you save . . . to lend to Canada?' was posed in big letters beneath two drawings of housewives at work in their homes.[81] Another advertisement issued by the National War Finance Committee pictured a sinister, shadowy Hitler whispering into the ear of a woman just reaching into her handbag to extract a five-dollar bill, 'Go on, spend it . . . What's the difference?'[82]

Patriotism was also the main motif in the propaganda used to recruit women for paid employment related to the war effort. Labour Department officials, NSS officers, and Farm Service officials, charged with recruiting women into the labour force during the Second World War, viewed their task as service to the war effort. Accordingly, in their recruitment campaigns, they appealed primarily to patriotic duty and the necessity to make sacrifices for the nation in wartime.

This note was struck in the NSS General Report on the Employment of Women of 1 November 1943. Next to determining the size of the existing labour reserve of women, the NSS's main task was 'to outline to all Canadian women the part they would be expected to play in the anticipated expansion of all war demands'.[83] It was NSS's job to convince women 'that it was their duty to go to work' and to persuade women 'that work in war industries offered the most direct contribution which could be made to the prosecution of the war, apart from enlistment in the Armed Forces'.[84] The overalls and bandana of the woman war worker 'became a symbol of service'.[85] The 'vigorous publicity campaigns' of the Ontario Farm Labour Service laid 'considerable stress on patriotic service'.[86]

'There must be no let up in the supply of vital arms and equipment – no let up in food production – no let up in essential services,' stated the letter sent by the director of NSS and Mrs Eaton to the Local Councils of Women enlisting their help for the campaigns in the autumn of 1943 to recruit women workers. The letter made two suggestions:

> Arrange for an inspirational address in which the prestige and importance of any work essential to the war or to the home front is stressed, as well as a tribute to women now so employed.
> Stress the need of women for the armed services but point out essential employment as an opportunity for women not of military age to serve with equal effect.[87]

The NSS circular of 18 August 1943, outlining the Campaign for Part-time Women Workers in hospitals, laundries, dry-cleaning establishments, restaurants, and hotels, ended with this ringing declaration: 'The health and wellbeing of the Canadian people must be maintained while they participate in the March to Victory. The civilian essential services in the community are of vital importance.'[88]

'Roll Up Your Sleeves for Victory!' was the headline of the December 1943 design prepared by the Information Division of the Dominion Department of Labour for a full-page newspaper

advertisement to recruit women for war industry. In the centre of
the advertisement was a drawing of a woman, shoulders squared,
rolling up her sleeves. Behind her, a montage of photographs of
women working, one a taxi driver, another a nurse, and the rest
on production lines in war industry. The caption read:

> The women of Canada are doing a magnificent job . . . in the Muni-
> tions factories, making the tools of war, in the nursing services . . . in
> the women's active service units, on the land, and in many other
> essential industries. But the tempo of war is increasing, and will
> continue to increase until Victory is won. We need more and more
> women to take full- or part-time war work. . . . Even if you can only
> spare an hour or two a day, you will be making an important con-
> tribution to the war effort.[89]

In May 1944, when it was feared that women were wearying
of war work and might be leaving the labour force altogether or
changing to jobs promising more of a future, Mrs Eaton drafted a
letter to the local Employment and Selective Service Offices. It
contained this directive:

> Try to change the attitude of mind represented in the words: 'I want
> to get a post-war job' or 'I am tired of making munitions.' We need to
> remind ourselves and others that the war has yet to be won and
> completed. It is too early to express other ideas. Service and sacrifice
> are yet the key words.[90]

Finally, in the massive campaign of July 1944 to recruit
women for labour in the Ontario ammunition plants, the slogan
was: 'Women! Back Them Up – To Bring Them Back.' This
slogan appeared on advertisements placed in the major newspapers, reprints of which were delivered to thousands of homes
in the neighbourhoods of the war plants, and on posters attached
to the fronts and backs of street cars and displayed in store
windows, outside movie theatres, and in theatre lobbies. The
press release prepared for Moffats Ltd, manufacturer of
ammunition boxes for the 25-pounder gun, quoted this appeal:
'Only by the single and married women coming forward and
offering their help will it be possible to get these ammunition
boxes out in the required time and thus keep faith with the boys
at the front.'[91] The call to patriotism, to sacrifice for the nation at
war, to loyalty and service to the troops fighting overseas – that
appeal dominated the recruitment of women workers from
beginning to end.

At the same time Labour Department and NSS officials were aware that many women were in the labour force, or applying to enter it, out of economic rather than patriotic motives. In a 5 March 1943 memorandum to Mrs Eaton, Renée Morin of the Montreal NSS reported the observation of a personnel officer for the Dominion Rubber Company:

> Most of the married women with children who seek work in our factory are in need of money to help their family. Those who are working merely to buy luxuries have not the courage to stick to their work. Very few have in mind a contribution to the war effort.[92]

On 30 March 1943, the Women's Division of the Toronto Employment and Selective Service Office ran a questionnaire on married female applicants over thirty-five years of age. The fifth question asked: 'What is the prime object in your securing employment?' Of the women questioned, 9 per cent indicated patriotic motives, 59 per cent wanted 'to supplement family income', and 32 per cent stated 'personal needs'.[93] *Relations* in May 1943 disclosed the results of an investigation carried out by the Quebec *Jeunesse ouvrière catholique* into the working experience of 700 of its gainfully employed female members: 31.4 per cent of the women had given 'as their reason for working economic necessity – no other source of revenue'.[94] Although the representativeness of these studies is not established, some discrepancy clearly existed between the official emphasis on patriotism and the actual motivation of women workers.

Not all reports to NSS on the motivation of female workers cast doubt on their patriotism. On 30 April 1943, the director of technical education of Nova Scotia sent this account of the motivation of women workers in a munitions plant in his province: 'Their general attitude showed that they felt their effort was directly connected with war activity and based on a keen feeling of patriotism.'[95]

Advertisements for women workers did include mention of appeals to economic incentives. The caption on the 'Roll Up Your Sleeves for Victory' advertisement ended: 'By taking up some form of war work you will not only be showing your patriotism in a practical way, but you will also be adding to the family income.'[96] Besides the slogan 'Back Them Up – To Bring Them Back', the advertisements in July 1944 spoke of 'Opportunity for Women in Modern War Plant ... [for] doing an important job and at the same time making that extra money which you can use to plan your future.'[97] None the less, patriotic service to the war effort was the main motif of campaigns to recruit women workers.

IV

From the start of attempts to bring increasing numbers of women into the labour force, it was realized that the needs of working women, especially married women and women with young children, would have to be accommodated. By and large, however, such accommodation was justified by the war emergency and would not outlast it.

One accommodation, an economic incentive to married women, was the Amendment to the Income War Tax Act of July 1942. Before that date, a married woman whose husband also received an income could earn up to $750 without her husband losing his claim to the full married status exemption. The July 1942 revision of the tax law granted the husband whose wife was working the full married status exemption 'regardless of how large his wife's earned income might be'.[98] The 'special concession' was a 'wartime provision'[99] designed 'to keep married women from quitting employment'[100] and to 'encourage the entry of married women into gainful employment'.[101] Through 1946, the husband paid no tax on any income up to $1,200, regardless of his wife's earnings. The wife paid tax on income exceeding $660.[102]

The incentive came to an end after the war. As of 1 January 1947, once a wife's income exceeded $250 the married status exemption of her husband would be reduced by the amount of her income in excess of $250. This post-war change did not simply return the income tax regulations for married couples to the status quo *ante bellum*. On the contrary, it introduced a disincentive to married women's working for pay outside the home that was more penalizing than that of the depression years. Many married working women figured that the tax change would seriously diminish their actual contribution to the family income after taxes. Many employers of married women feared the change would deplete their skilled female labour force. Representations poured into the Departments of Labour, Finance, and National Revenue. Fruit-packing and canning firms complained that their most skilled female packers and sorters were leaving once their earnings reached $250.[103] Textile firms complained that they were losing many of their most experienced power sewing machine operators, silk cutters, winders, and carders.[104] Similarly, business offices reported losing stenographer-typists;[105] hospitals, married nurses;[106] school boards, married women teachers;[107] department stores, married female employees.[108] The Deputy Minister of Labour, Arthur MacNamara, denied that his department had intended the tax change 'to drive married women out of employment', and certainly not 'out of nursing, teaching and any other line of employment where their services are so seriously needed'.[109] But as the spokesman for the Primary Textile Institute, Toronto, reasoned: since the 1942 revision had been designed to draw married women into industry, its cancellation would have the opposite effect.[110] And the federal government admitted as much: the tax concession of 1942 had been a war measure, 'justified only by the extreme state of emergency which then existed'.[111]

Perhaps the major wartime accommodation to the needs of working women was the establishment of childcare facilities in Ontario and Québec on the basis of the Dominion-Provincial Wartime Day Nurseries Agreement. But this, too, was made in the context of the war emergency and viewed as right only so long as that emergency lasted.

In 1942, when it was realized that the Canadian economy would have to draw more extensively on women's labour, it was also recognized that government provision of childcare facilities for working mothers might become necessary. The Prime Minister's address to Parliament on 24 March 1942, explaining NSS and outlining a programme for bringing women into industry had called for 'The provision of nurseries and other means of caring for children.'[112]

Although the Women's Division of NSS did not begin in 1942 to campaign for the employment of mothers, women with young children had been in the labour force before the outbreak of war and had continued to enter it as production quickened.[113] As Mrs Eaton wrote in June 1942, 'without any urging on the part of Government, married women, usually on the basis of need of further income, have already gone into industry and are doing a good job'.[114] The mothers among these married women had to make their own arrangements for the care of their children, with the help of relatives and neighbours.[115] 'But these unorganized arrangements do not always work out so well and break down for days and weeks at a time.'[116] The number of existing private nurseries, run by churches and charitable organizations, was inadequate. In 1942, in Ontario, especially in the Toronto area, public pressure for government provision of nurseries and after-school supervision of children increased. There was mounting concern over 'latch-key' children and the possible connection between working mothers and the rising rate of juvenile delinquency.[117] Asked by the Minister of Labour for ideas on child-care for his upcoming meeting with Ontario and Québec Ministers, Mrs Eaton replied that:

> Consistent and well-founded reports lead one to believe that children are neglected – thus becoming unhappy, undernourished and delinquent. Such a situation must be accepted as a responsibility of government in these days, when it has become a burden too heavy for private agencies.[118]

Before the end of April 1942, the director of NSS was in contact with the government of Ontario concerning 'the setting-up of nurseries in co-operation with the provinces as needed'.[119] In May, Mrs Eaton conferred with the Minister and Deputy Minister of Public Welfare in Ontario and with the Minister of Health and Social Welfare in Québec.[120] Experts in childcare, such as George F. Davidson, executive director of the Canadian Welfare Council,[121] and Dr W. E. Blatz, director of the Institute of Child Study of the University of Toronto,[122] were consulted.

On the basis of these preliminary talks, a draft for a Dominion-Provincial agreement on childcare was drawn up. On 16 June 1942, the federal Minister of Labour called a conference in Ottawa to discuss the proposed agreement with the Minister and Deputy Minister of Public Welfare of Ontario and the Minister of Health and Social Welfare of Québec. After clause by clause consideration of the draft agreement, it was approved.[123]

Then on 20 July 1942, through Order-in-Council PC 6242, the federal Minister of Labour was authorized to enter into agreements with any of the provinces to establish day-care facilities for children of mothers employed in war industries, in accordance with the draft agreement. A copy of the agreement and a letter inviting participation in the plan were sent to every province. The two most industrialized provinces signed that summer: Ontario on 29 July 1942; Québec on 3 August.[124] The only other province to sign was Alberta, in September 1943.[125] But the Alberta Provincial Advisory Committee on Day Nurseries, set up to assess the need in that province, voted on 26 April 1944 that there was none,[126] despite considerable pressure from groups in Edmonton and Calgary for day nurseries in those two cities.[127]

In the meantime, Ontario and Québec, the only two provinces to make use of the agreement, began to implement it. The agreement provided that capital and operating costs were to be shared equally between the Dominion and the province.[128] The initiative for establishing particular day nurseries rested with the provinces.[129] Ontario and Québec each created an Advisory Committee on Day Nurseries and local committees in urban centres to determine where need existed. Provincial directors were appointed, and in Toronto a director for the city.[130] At the federal level, Miss Margaret Grier was appointed in October 1942 as assistant associate director of NSS, under Mrs Eaton, to administer the Dominion-Provincial Wartime Day Nurseries Agreement.[131] Local Employment and Selective Service Offices were to interview applicants on need for childcare, determine their eligibility, make referrals to operating childcare facilities, and keep records of the numbers of applicants and referrals.[132]

The programme was slow in getting off the ground. In fact, the first day nursery to open, at 95 Bellevue Avenue in Toronto on 6 October 1942, was initially a provincial project and only later brought under the terms of the Dominion-Provincial Agreement.[133] A second day nursery in Ontario, the first under the agreement, was opened in Brantford on 4 January 1943. February brought the opening of Ontario's third, fourth, and fifth day nursery units in St Catharines, Oshawa, and Toronto; March, the sixth and seventh, also in Toronto.[134] To accommodate the increasing number of married women entering the labour force in the spring and summer of 1943, six more day nurseries were opened in Ontario between April and September.[135]

Initially Women's Voluntary Services volunteers assisted at the nurseries one whole day or two half-days a week and in preparation for this were given a twelve-lecture WVS training course in childcare. But it was soon found that day nurseries had to be fully staffed by paid workers. In Ontario these received an intensive course in the psychology and care of the child at the Institute of Child Study in Toronto. The Bellevue Avenue centre gave demonstrations in practical administration of a day nursery to those who would later take charge of other units. The Women's Division of NSS sponsored radio dramas to convince mothers working in war industry that day nursery care would benefit their young children. Journalists also sang the praises of the new childcare programme. For instance, in an optimistic article for *Saturday Night* entitled 'Nursery Schools in Canada Have Come to Stay', Mary Weeks wrote approvingly of the personnel and sound principles in child development that the Institute of Child Study had imparted to the programme. And Marjorie Winspear in the *National Home Monthly* applauded the gentle but firm discipline used to get the two- to six-year-olds to eat everything on their plates and to take afternoon naps without fuss.[136]

The nurseries were open Monday through Friday, from 7 or 7.30 a.m. to 6.30 or 7 p.m., and Saturday mornings until noon. Children were given two full meals a day, dinner at noon and supper at five, plus a morning snack. A few day nurseries were set up in houses, but more often church, Sunday school, or community halls were converted for the purpose. Independently of the Dominion-Provincial Wartime Day Nurseries Agreement, some companies, such as the Canada Rubber Company in Galt, Ontario, built day nurseries near their factories and operated them exclusively for their own employees.

In addition to day nursery care, the Dominion-Provincial Wartime Day Nurseries Agreement also provided for foster home care for children under two and school day-care for children between six and sixteen. The latter included supervision of school-age children during vacations as well as provision of a hot noon meal and supervision before and after school during the regular school term.[137]

By September 1945, there were twenty-eight day nurseries in operation in Ontario: nineteen in Toronto, three in Hamilton, two in Brantford, and one each in St Catharines, Oshawa, Galt, and Sarnia, caring for about 900 children in all. In addition there were forty-four school units, thirty-nine in the Greater Toronto area; Hamilton had two, and Windsor, Oshawa, and Sarnia each had one. The Wartime Day Care Programme for School Children accommodated aproximately 2,500 children.[138]

The childcare programme was even slower getting off the ground in Québec and never developed there to the extent it did in Ontario. The first wartime day nursery in Québec opened on

1 March 1943 in Montreal. The site chosen for it was in the Maissonneuve district close to the station where women left for work in the Cherrier shell-filling plant of Defence Industries Limited. In 1943 five others opened in Montreal, four on 1 May and one on 1 October. As the latter closed on 31 December 1944, there were in September 1945 only five wartime day nurseries operating in Québec, all in Montreal, and accommodating on the average between 115 and 120 children.[139] There was no development of school-age day care in Québec.[140]

From the outset, the federal agencies involved viewed the establishment of childcare facilities as a war emergency measure designed 'to secure the labour of women with young children' for 'war industry'.[141] One of the principles drawn up to govern federal aid for day nurseries stated: 'That any such service should be strictly limited to provision for the children of women employees in war industries.'[142]

The actual Dominion-Provincial Day Nurseries Agreement departed somewhat from that original intention.[143] Clause 11 provided that up to 25 per cent of any facility could be opened to children of mothers employed in other than war industrial occupations. Furthermore, Clause 1(d) gave a broad definition to 'war industries'.[144] In practice, however, only firms with an A (very high) or B (high) labour priority rating were considered to be 'war industries'.[145] The federal government's position was that childcare was 'normally the *responsibility* of the Province, in co-operation with its local groups'. Only the additional burden on the provinces 'caused by war conditions' justified the federal government's sharing that responsibility. Therefore the programme should 'relate *chiefly* to war industries'.[146]

In 1943 strong objections arose to Clause 11 of the Day Nurseries Agreement, particularly from the Toronto Welfare Council and the Toronto Board of Education. Officials of the Toronto Board of Education wrote to Humphrey Mitchell, Minister of Labour, and to Prime Minister Mackenzie King.[147] They asked that 'war work' be broadly defined as 'anything essential to the community at war' so that the children of all working mothers would be eligible. The quota, they pointed out put the principals administering the school day-care programme in the difficult position of having to refuse some children while accepting others. Limiting eligibility discriminated against mothers working in firms with a low labour priority rating. This

was unfair, they argued, as all working mothers were contributing to the war effort, if only indirectly. In many cases, the
woman doing the 'non-essential' job was freeing a man or
another women for work in war industry.

On 10 June 1943, Mrs Eaton chaired a meeting in Ottawa of
NSS, Labour Department, and Québec and Ontario officials to
assess the Wartime Day Nurseries programme. Heading the
agenda was criticism of Clause 11. The meeting agreed that 'the
ratio of 75 and 25 for mothers employed in war industry' should
continue and that the interpretation of 'war industry' as firms
with A and B labour priority ratings should still hold. Labour
Minister Humphrey Mitchell approved this decision.[148] To Mrs
Eaton's mind, 'If the Agreement is extended to include the children of all mothers who work, there is a further case that could be
made out quite logically for the children of the woman who is ill
or who is doing essential voluntary work.'[149]

But objection to Clause 11 persisted. Newspaper editorials
took up the criticism.

> We are now into the fifth year of war. For at least three years the
> pressure has been heavy to get more women into the industry. In the
> last year Government agencies have urged women with children to
> fill the gaps so that the nation's economy could continue to function.
>
> If mothers are to follow the advice of those agencies, then surely
> this division of children of working mothers into two classes is
> beyond common reason.[150]

So editorialized *The Globe and Mail* on 28 October 1943. 'It is a
sort of crusade taken up by the papers, churches and women's
organizations to get the children admitted regardless of any
other consideration,' Mrs Eaton observed in a memorandum to
NSS Director MacNamara on 1 December 1943.[151]

Under this mounting pressure, the Ontario Minister of Public
Welfare 'gave way publicly' in November 1943, and NSS officals
began to reassess their stand.[152] Mary Eadie, Women's Division
Supervisor of the Toronto local office, was asked to estimate the
consequences of increased enrolments if the Day Nurseries
Agreement were extended 'to cover the children of all employed
mothers'.[153] By 1 December 1943 Mrs Eaton had concluded
that 'It is now apparent the 25 percent [quota] does not
altogether suffice.'[154] Negotiations with Ontario and Québec to
revise Clause 11 were begun.

By Order-in-Council, on 6 April 1944, for Ontario, and on 18 May 1944, for Québec, Clause 11 was amended to extend the Wartime Day Nurseries Agreement to include children of all working mothers. None the less the amendment stipulated that 'children of mothers working in war industry shall have priority at all times in admission' to any childcare facility established under the agreement.[155]

That the Dominion-Provincial Day Nurseries Agreement was construed as a wartime emergency measure is underscored by the relative swiftness of the programme's discontinuance. On 23 August 1945, J. A. Paquette, Québec's Minister of Health and Social Welfare, informed Labour Minister Mitchell that he planned to close the day nurseries in Québec on 1 October. His argument read:

> Article 23 of the Agreement, signed by the Federal Government and the Province of Québec on the 3rd of August 1942, provides that the Agreement shall continue in force for the duration of the war.
>
> Now that the war is over, I would be inclined to close these Day Nurseries immediately, but I feel that a month's notice to the parents would only be fair.[156]

Although W. S. Boyd of National Registration argued that Canada was still legally at war since no final peace treaty had been signed and neither His Majesty nor the Governor in Council had proclaimed that the war had ended (as Section 2 of the War Measures Act required),[157] none the less on 1 September 1945, Mitchell wrote Paquette that he, 'as chief administrator of the scheme', had the right to close the nurseries when he chose and 'upon such notice as is deemed advisable'.[158]

The closing of the Dominion-Provincial Wartime Day Nurseries in Québec was set for 15 October 1945. In mid-September day nursery staffs were sent a letter from the Deputy Minister of Health and Social Welfare that their services would no longer be required after that date.[159]

Margaret Grier, the NSS official in charge of day nurseries, received appeals to keep open the five Montreal day nurseries from the Montreal Council of Social Agencies,[160] from officials of the Welfare Federation and the Federation of Catholic charities, and from the Montreal Association of Protestant Women Teachers.[161] As early as 20 April 1945, mothers of children attending the first wartime day nursery established in Montreal had drawn up a letter urging the government to continue the day nurseries after the close of the war.[162] In October these women gathered signatures on a petition to be sent to Dr G. L. LaPierre, Director of Wartime Day Nurseries for Québec.[163] A major reason the mothers gave for continuance of the programme was that the mothers who placed their children in the nurseries were working out of economic necessity, because of separation from, or the death, war injuries, sickness, or inadequate income of the husband. Further, the mothers argued that, compelled as they were to work outside the home, they could do so, thanks to the day nurseries, relieved of anxiety over the well-being of their children. In fact, their children were receiving better day-care in the day nurseries than they would have under any other circumstances: better health care, training, and diet. The day nurseries were actually helping the mothers keep their families together.

These appeals were of no avail. The Québec government's position remained firm: the Dominion-Provincial Day Nurseries programme had been a war measure; the war was now over, and therefore the agreement was no longer in force.

The situation was different in Ontario where more wartime childcare facilities had been established and there was correspondingly greater pressure to keep them open after the war. It was the federal, not the provincial, government that opened discussions to end the Dominion-Provincial Wartime Day Nurseries Agreement in Ontario in the autumn of 1945.

On 11 September, Fraudena Eaton reported to Arthur MacNamara that applications for day-care in Toronto had 'increased rather than diminished during the past two months'. She was having Miss Grier investigate 'this seemingly unreasonable situation'.[164] Although the Wartime Day Nursery and School Day Care Centre in Oshawa were closed on 21 October 1945, due to decreasing enrolment,[165] elsewhere in Ontario reports from local employment offices showed in November 'a continuing high demand for day-care of children of working mothers'.[166]

Mrs Eaton's reaction was to give a gentle nudge to Mac-Namara:

> The time will come fairly shortly when the employment of mothers will not necessarily be related to production for war purposes or for highly essential civilian goods. It brings the matter of providing day-care for children back to the point where it may be reasonably looked upon as a responsibility of the Provincial Government.[167]

MacNamara took the hint and instructed Mrs Eaton to draft a letter to the appropriate Ontario minister asking his views on when to end the agreement on day-care of children.[168] In his letter of 22 November, MacNamara wrote:

> You understand that the financing of these and similar plans by the Dominion Government has been done as a war measure and our Treasury Board naturally takes the position 'now that the war is over why do you need money?'[169]

He suggested as the termination date of the agreement 'the end of the Dominion Government fiscal year or soon thereafter'.[170]

Investigations indicated that the mothers using the childcare facilities in Toronto were, in fact, in desperate need of full-time day-care. Fifty per cent of the women were working full-time out of economic need: some were widows without, or with very small, pensions; others were deserted and un-married mothers; still others had husbands who were unem-ployed or ill or earning inadequate wages. In 5 per cent of the cases husbands had been 'apprehended because of conduct'. Thirty per cent of the mothers were working full-time to help husbands pay off debts, purchase homes, or get re-established in business. Fifteen per cent were working part-time to sup-plement family incomes.[171]

Hope was growing in Ontario that, after the Dominion government pulled out of the agreement, the provincial govern-ment might pick up the whole tab. Margaret Grier informed Arthur MacNamara on 15 February 1946 that Deputy Minister of Public Welfare B. M. Heise himself had told her 'he now had every hope that the Province would continue to maintain the day nurseries'.[172] In early February deputations went to Toronto City Hall, the Board of Education, and the provincial Depart-ments of Education and Public Welfare to press for the continu-ation of day-care in Ontario.

Meanwhile, four months had elapsed since the Dominion government's proposal to end its participation in the day nursery project. On 18 February 1946 Mrs Eaton wrote to MacNamara suggesting that, as Ontario might continue the operation of day nurseries, provincial authorities were in no hurry to see federal funds cut off. The time, however, had come. 'No suggestion could be made now or even four months ago, that the employ-ment of those women whose children are in day-care centres is essential for work of national importance.'[173] Humphrey Mitchell took up this argument in his letter of 26 February 1946, to W. A. Goodfellow, Ontario Minister of Public Welfare. 'As you know,' Mitchell wrote, 'the Dominion share in financing this project was undertaken as *a war measure* for the reason that women whose children were in day-care centres were engaged in *work of national importance.'* Implying that the employed mothers of Ontario were no longer doing work of national importance, he announced his department's decision to stop Dominion participation on 1 April.[174]

Now a three-way passing of the buck began. Goodfellow informed the federal minister that enabling legislation was before the Ontario legislature to make day nurseries a municipal concern, with the provincial government sharing costs. The end of federal contributions on 1 April, together with the planned transfer of day nurseries from the Department of Public Welfare to municipalities, threatened to disrupt the running of existing childcare facilities before the end of the school year. In view of that, Goodfellow asked Mitchell to consider extension of the Dominion-Provincial Wartime Day Nurseries Agreement to 30 June 1946.[175]

Humphrey Mitchell approved the extension to 30 June, although this information got lost in the shuffle of intradepartmental memoranda and did not reach the Ontario Minister of Public Welfare until 2 April 1946.[176] In the interim, the Ontario legislature had given first and second reading to Bill 124 authorizing municipalities to 'provide for the establishment of day nurseries for the care and feeding of young children' and the provincial government to contribute one-half of the operating costs. The bill passed third reading on 4 April and became law as the Day Nurseries Act, 1946.[177] The day-care programme for school-age children was to be dropped altogether.

On 17 May 1946, Goodfellow wrote to Mitchell with a new request. Some of the municipalities had indicated that, as their budgets for 1946 had already been passed, they had no funds to pay 50 per cent of the operating costs of day nurseries for the last half of 1946. Toronto, for example, the city in which most of Ontario's wartime nurseries and day-care centres for school children were located, had made no provision in its 1946 budget for assuming the day nursery costs. Therefore, Goodfellow asked Mitchell to consider the following proposition:

For those municipalities which indicate a desire to have the [day nursery] programme continued and which are prepared to assume the administrative responsibilities from July 1, would you consider continuing the 50 percent net cost of operation until December 31, 1946?[178]

On the same day Mrs G. D. Kirkpatrick, chairman of the board of directors of the Welfare Council of Greater Toronto, forwarded to Mitchell the board's resolution not only that the Dominion government continue to contribute 50 per cent of the funding for Ontario's day nurseries until 31 December 1946, but also that the provincial and Dominion governments continue their support of the day-care for school-age children.[179] A second letter from Mrs Kirkpatrick to the Minister on 29 May 1946 reiterated the concern of the Toronto Welfare Council's board of directors that the day-care programme for school-age children not be eliminated.[180]

On 21 May 1946, Humphrey Mitchell wrote to Brooke Claxton, Minister of National Health and Welfare. In Mitchell's view, the current pressure on the federal government was the result of 'the Ontario Government's endeavouring to arrange for municipalities to pay the fifty percent heretofore paid by the Dominion Government and the municipalities are objecting'.[181]

Claxton replied on 7 June that he could 'see no reason why the Dominion Government should continue in peacetime to share in the costs of a program, the interest in which is apparently centred almost entirely within one province, and indeed largely within one large city in that province'. Claxton had learned from his deputy that Hamilton had agreed to pay its share of the day nursery costs from its 1946 budget. In Claxton's opinion, if Hamilton could do that, 'even after the municipal tax rate has been struck and the budget set for the year', certainly other cities, such as Toronto and London, 'should have been able to do likewise'.[182]

On 12 June 1946, Mitchell conveyed to W. A. Goodfellow the government's decision not to grant Ontario a further extension.[183] On 30 June 1946, the Dominion-Provincial Wartime Day Nurseries Agreement with Ontario came to an end. All the day-care facilities for school children ceased to operate in Ontario on that date, though eight were eventually re-opened. By the end of November 1946 nine out of the twenty-eight day nurseries were closed and by 1948 the total number had been reduced to sixteen.[184]

V

The post-war abrogation of government-supported day nurseries in Quebec and most of the day-care for school children in Ontario, the post-war reduction of government support to day nurseries in Ontario, as well as the post-war cancellation of the tax concessions to employed married women, were all in keeping with the official attitudes towards working women that prevailed during the war itself. As labour shortages developed in 1942, women were regarded as a large labour reserve that Canadian industry could draw on in the war emergency. But women's place was in the home, and so initial recruitment was directed at young unmarried women and then married women without children. To meet increased labour shortages in 1943, however, government had to dip deeper into the female labour reserve, down to women with home responsibilities, even to mothers of young children. In deference to 'majority opinion' that tended 'to favour mothers remaining in the home, rather than working, where at all possible', NSS and Labour Department officials appealed to the fact of war conditions to justify their having to encourage mothers with young children 'to accept industrial employment, as an aid to our national effort'.[185] Even after the establishment of childcare facilities in Ontario and Québec, the Department of Labour insisted that its policy was 'to put emphasis on single or married women without children accepting employment in the first instance'.[186] As only war service justified a mother's leaving home for the public workplace, the Dominion-Provincial Wartime Day Nurseries Agreement was intended to provide daycare primarily for the children of mothers working in war industries. According to Mrs Eaton, the Women's Division of NSS had 'found that women with children were unwisely deciding to look for employment' and had therefore in October 1943 advised the counselling service of local employment and Selective Service Offices 'to hold back from employment those who seem to be neglecting their home and family'.[187]

Where there was opposition to the employment of women in industry, as there strongly was from certain quarters in Québec,[188] the Women's Division of NSS did not respond with arguments of women's equal right to work but instead invoked the necessity of sacrifice for the nation at war and stressed the temporary nature of that sacrifice. Where women accepted jobs previously held only by men, they were generally regarded as replacing men temporarily. The large-scale part-time employment of women was not supposed to last. The very increase in numbers of women in the labour force, from approximately 638,000 in 1939 to an estimated 1,077,000 by 1 October 1944,[189] was regarded as a temporary phenomenon. Therefore, it is not surprising that, faced with problems of women's unemployment and economic dislocation in the post-war period, the Women's Division of NSS sought to return married women to the home and to channel young unmarried women into traditionally female occupations: domestic service, nursing, and teaching.

But even the wartime recognition of women's crucial domestic contribution to society and women's centrality in the wartime anti-inflation and conservation drives did not translate into an equal place for women on the post-war councils of the nation. Women were not represented on the post-war reconstruction and rehabilitation committees in any way commensurate with their proportion of the population or the socially necessary nature of their labour.

Towards Feminist
Marxism?

Working At Home

Roberta Hamilton

In this article I shall discuss two recent Canadian publications from the Women's Press, *Hidden in the Household*, edited by Bonnie Fox and *More than a Labour of Love* by Meg Luxton.[1] What sort of contribution is made to the description, understanding and interpretation of women's oppression? And to what extent do these studies reflect a diversity of contributions from others seeking similar objectives? For it is certain that in the development of effective strategies for change we will require an understanding of how the relations of domination and subordination are reproduced and perpetuated at every level, and in every nook and cranny of our social life.

The authors of both books situate their work within the framework of what has been called 'the domestic labour debate'. The roots of this debate can be found in an article in that first anthology *Women Unite!*[2] Peggy Morton in 'Women's Work Is Never Done'[3] discussed both how women's work in the home is shaped by capitalist relations of production, and how women make sense of their lives as mothers, consumers and housewives within these parameters. Writing in 1968, Morton had little systematic evidence upon which to draw. Yet as an insightful observer with a set of sharp questions she raised many of the issues which were investigated in the next decade by writers here and elsewhere. Studies on motherhood, sexuality, the historical interconnections between women's work at home and in the market-place have informed, and been informed by, political struggles for daycare, free abortion on demand, refuge centres, equal pay for work of equal value, challenges to female job ghettos and countless unpublishable (and unpublished) struggles within the home. This is indeed a partial list.

From Specialization to Closure

One aspect of Morton's interest – how Marxist categories can be used to encompass women's work in the home – became the central focus of the 'domestic labour debate'.[4] Here the concern shifted from providing an understanding of the many facets of women's oppression towards an interest in demonstrating that Marxism is an internally consistent theory into which an understanding of women and their work can fit; a theory which can be appealed to for answers without having to engage in the untidy and painstaking process of encountering the social world. The body of evidence interrogated is those theoretical writings held *a priori* to be correct; the evidence accumulated by historians, sociologists, economists, psychoanalysts, the first-hand accounts of mothers and wives, and the literary contributions occasionally receive ritual salute but are most often ignored. In this sense the contributers to the debate go beyond the specialization shaping much of the work of the last decade towards the systematic invocation of closure. (A crude but revealing confirmation of this for those who do not wish to tackle the literature itself is provided by a perusal of its footnotes.)[5]

By closing off discussion that does not fit into preconceived formulations, the debate has provided some Marxists with a neat and tidy way to suppose that they are dealing with 'the woman question' even as they studiously avoid such an encounter. The concern with understanding and struggling against women's oppression takes a back seat; a harsher judgement has been that it is no longer even taken along for the ride. Eva Kaluzynska in an article irreverently titled 'Wiping the Floor with Theory – a Survey of Writings on Housework' declares, 'The shift was from investigating the usefulness of Marxist categories for potential women's movement strategy to categorizing women in a prefabricated framework, addressing "Marxists" rather than "women".'[6]

Both Fox and Luxton initially define their tasks within the parameters of that debate. The intention of the authors of *Hidden in the Household* was 'to write a book that would carry forward the discussion of domestic labour that began with such promise in the 1960s'. Luxton's goal was 'to locate domestic labour within the development of industrial capitalism in North America to show how it has changed throughout the period'. Yet there was reason to expect that both books would break out of the self-enclosed system of that debate, and pick up and expand the full range of Morton's ideas in light of the large body of work that has been undertaken since. On the one hand some of the writers have been active in the women's liberation movement: on the other hand, *Women Unite!* was the Women's Press first publication. How then do they fare?

Judging a Book by Its Cover

Hidden in the Household is a collection of six original articles. While the authors share a common objective, namely to demonstrate how domestic labour in capitalist society can be perceived within a Marxist theoretical framework, each writer takes up the questions that he/she believes are most pertinent. Yet although there are substantial disagreements between them, which Fox discusses in brief introductions to each article, they refrain from encountering each other's arguments directly. The reader is left mainly on her/his own to decide how the articles relate, who has scored what point against whom, and whether it matters; this is the shadowboxing mode of debate, where if nothing is clarified, at least no one gets hurt.

The problem is magnified by the book's language and style: it is written by and for those Marxists who are particularly concerned with the applicability of Marxist theory to an understanding of domestic labour. Since no concessions have been made in language or style to those outside the circle, the book's accessibility is limited. Nowhere is the contrast between this book and Luxton's more striking. *More than a Labour of Love* could be read by interested high school students (and hopefully they will read it as an antidote to everything they probably believe about love and marriage). Never patronizing, always clear, Luxton wants to communicate to as many as possible, and does not appear concerned that in so doing she will fail as an academic or a Marxist. Indeed Luxton's study of three generations of married women in the northern Manitoba one-company town of Flin Flon was critically read by some of her local informants prior to publication.

Earlier I stated that whatever the domestic labour debate, as it has evolved, is about, it is not primarily about women's oppression. Yet with a kind of sleight-of-hand Fox collapses the categories of domestic labour and women's oppression into one: 'this analysis must clarify the particular nature of domestic labour and thus women's oppression under capitalism' (p. 11). The implicit claim is that the subject of women's oppression can be subsumed under a consideration of the particular nature of domestic labour. Through making such a claim, a whole range of historical, sociological, psychological and literary evidence is cut off prior to its interrogation. This is surgery, not research, with the scalpel replacing 'tools of analysis'.

That crucial issue aside, what are the contributions that these articles make to an understanding of women's oppression, to an understanding of our social life. Because of the many different arguments presented in these articles I will look closely at one of the central themes running through each: what is the relationship of non-waged members of the working class, in particular wives and children' to the wage? This question has surfaced as a contemporary political issue in discussions about the 'family wage'.

Women, the Family and the Wage

The starting point is Marx's insight that the wage appears as payment for work done, but is not. Rather the worker exchanges his labour power for a wage to cover his subsistence. This represents only part of the value that he creates while working; the rest is appropriated by the capitalist and becomes after other expenses are met, the profits or capital available to him for reinvestment and expansion. Alice Clark's work in seventeenth-century England shows that in the early days of capitalist agriculture the wage represented very precisely that needed for the worker's subsistence – enough to cover his food and drink as supplied by the farmer.[7]

It is within this relationship between labour and capital that the Marxist understanding of exploitation and alienation under capitalism is found. But its usefulness in such stark form is primarily to be found in comparisons *between* modes of production, this means of extracting surplus value being peculiar to capitalism. Within capitalist societies the way in which subsistence is defined and agreed upon, and, therefore, the price realized in exchange for labour power, arises from particular historical, national and local conditions. But in these articles the emphasis is on how this understanding about the extraction of surplus forms part of the 'law of value' or the 'laws of commodity production' or 'the laws of motion of capital'. These laws come complete with a set of categories into which social reality must then be pummelled and squeezed.

With that predilection the authors approach the question of the relationship between the wage and non-waged family members. Marx wrote that the value of labour power was determined by that needed to provide not just for the wage earner but for his dependents as well.[8] This assertion becomes an albatross around the necks of these writers; like the ancient mariner they struggle to get it off their backs but attain only varying degrees of success. Starting from the premise that all commodities (including labour power) are exchanged for those of similar value, and that Marx must have been right both about that, and about what has come to be called the family wage, they then turn to confront (some confront, others taste) the historical record which refutes both. The result is an often honest but tortuous attempt to interrogate the evidence while retaining the theory: the goal is nothing less than to reconcile the irreconcilable.

Seccombe argues that there is no point in 'theological arguments about the "real meaning" of sacred texts' (p. 236). His recognition that historically there has not been a 'family wage' most of the time for most of the people leads him to argue that it is the working-class family that adjusts to the wage; the wage does not appear as a pre-packaged family deal. Yet despite his clear moves (from previous papers) towards more historical and dialectical understandings he never replaces his initial question, 'How does the law of value shape the reproduction cycle of labour power?' with those he formulates more historically. His statement that 'there is a permanent disjunction between the function of the wage and its form under capitalism' encapsulates both his unwillingness to discard his model and his recognition that it does not work. If there is a 'function' of the wage under capitalism it is undoubtedly what it has always been – to get people to come and work for you. Everything after that is up for grabs in the ensuing individual and collective struggles.

Seccombe's dilemma lies in the way he perceives historical study. While giving it more importance than any other contributer except Curtis, he is none the less not sure how far to go. His drawing upon the historical record is sketchy, his formulations are schematic, treated as fact when they are actually issues of controversy among working historians, many of them Marxist.[9] His history knows no national boundaries; he ignores most Canadian research which he would find reflects the 'peculi-arities' of the Canadians.[10] On the one hand, his citing of Luxton's evidence for Flin Flon indicates he must know some of these specificities; on the other hand, they are not deemed worthy of being drawn out. If he had taken more seriously his important insight that the labouring masses in capitalist society have 'an historically unprecedented leeway' (p. 38) to arrange their means of subsistence and seen it as an occasion to concen-trate upon the specificities of class and sex struggle, history would not be the poor cousin to abstract theory that it remains in his work.

Fox approaches the question of the relationship between the wage, the wage earner and his family through asking an impor-tant question. Why have women been drawn into the labour force in increasing numbers since 1940, given that men's real wages have risen in this period? Her answer is useful, if partial. Earlier in this century children's wages or women's unrecorded wage work at home supplemented the main wage. There has been no guarantee she suggests, throughout the twentieth cen-tury that the price of the individual's labour power has equalled the commodities needed by a family. Yet a little more digging – Alice Clark in seventeenth-century England, Bettina Bradbury and Suzanne Cross in nineteenth-century Montreal would have led her to ask, 'And how is this century different from all other centuries?'[11]

Fox recognizes a central contradiction in capitalism: capital relies upon continual reproduction of the working class from one day and one generation to the next, but only pays wages to cover the subsistence of the individual worker. But this does not lead her to re-examine her theory. She argues that the housewife does not contribute to the value of labour power because that would skyrocket its value beyond that which the worker could produce for the capitalist. And 'their equivalence is one instance of the general assumption, in *Capital*, that exchange involves things of equal value' (p. 183). How can such argument by fiat help us understand the relationship between domestic labour and the wage? How can it help us understand anything except that tautologies are useful for tidying up the world?

Linda Brisken approaches the relationship between the wage and the family by arguing that while the household exists within capitalist social relations, it falls outside the laws governing the inner dynamic of capital. She accepts, quite rightly I think, that essentially the wage (whatever its size) is an individual, not a family wage. Yet she too wants to maintain that it is always commodities of equal value that are exchanged in the market-place. Individual labour power is exchanged for a wage which will purchase commodities sufficient for that individual to reproduce himself or herself and turn up again the next day at work. For these commodities to be equivalent, Brisken, like the Queen of Hearts argues that language will mean what she wants it to mean. The housewife does not help reproduce labour power for that only becomes a commodity at the moment of the exchange. Rather she contributes to the development of the wage labourer, to potential labour power; similarly the housewife does not produce use values – she only transforms commodities into things that can be used.

Underlying this kind of semantic argument is Brisken's understanding of the antagonism between *a priori* laws and the actual processes of history. For her history is a sneaky devil, always gumming up the works. 'The development of the capitalist mode of production illustrates that the laws of motion of capital are systematically distorted by historical events' (p. 168). Similarly, 'domestic labour can in specific historical instances, provide substitutes for commodities . . . however, this must be explained at a conjunctural/historical level, not as a general effect of the laws of motion' (p. 159).

Are these laws of motion outside historical processes? And if they are, and if they cannot hold their own in the face of the onslaught are they worth counting upon?[12]

Blumenfeld and Mann approach the question of a family wage by assuming its existence, thus avoiding that particular argument altogether. Their view of capitalism as a well-oiled machine would not permit them presumably to imagine that it would leave such an important issue unattended. In language functionalist enough to make Talcott Parsons blush, they choose to examine the barriers to the socialization of domestic labour within a capitalist social formation by asking, 'Why does capital leave the production and reproduction of its most vital commodity (labour power) in the hands of non-capitalists'? (p. 273). Basically, they answer, because it would cost too much to do it any other way. But, since they assume that capital pays a family wage now, it is not clear why this would be prohibitive.

Alone among the contributers Curtis argues that the existence of a family wage must be seen primarily as an outcome of the class struggle. It exists because working men and women mounted a collective struggle for a wage large enough to cover family subsistence so that the wife-mother could remain at home and the children receive an education. In advancing his argument, he turns to the history of the struggle in England for protective legislation regulating the wage labour of women and children. While a thoroughly historical approach to this question is surely what is needed, Curtis's interest is not in illuminating the complexity and many contradictions of that history. Rather, to put it crudely, his aim is to let working-class men off the hook. To do this he skims over the historical record without considering evidence that some working-class men wanted women out of the industrial work force for more than just humanitarian reasons. More importantly the research on this question is just beginning and there is a range of contradictory evidence and interpretations which he does not discuss.[13]

He also remains hamstrung by his insistence that the price of labour power cannot fall below its value. As a result, while he acknowledges that the housewife helps to reproduce labour power he cannot give this point its due; like Fox he cannot deal with the skyrocketing cost of reproducing labour power beyond the price it can actually realize in the market-place.

I do not wish to belabour the point that the priorities of the domestic labour debate, its commitment to explaining how the world fits the theory and its lack of a thoroughly historical approach, limit the contribution it makes to describing and understanding the housewife's work and its relationship to the wage, let alone to the question of women's oppression. Rather I will outline the nature of Luxton's book on women's work and then consider it in light of the debates in *Hidden in the Household.*

More than a Labour of Love

More than a Labour of Love is a study of three generations of married women in Flin Flon. It is based on participant observation, extensive interviewing and historical research. As a result Luxton is not the only one speaking to us; the housewives of Flin Flon speak movingly and clearly on their own behalf about the subjects that intertwine themselves in their lives: love, marriage, husbands, sexuality, violence, children, mothering, cooking and housework. Permeating these discussions is a central theme: keeping their families physically and emotionally intact at often great cost to themselves.

But Luxton does not present the women as simply buffeted by pressures of the company, husbands and children. While they live within certain parameters, even these can be broken through if their lines are too unyielding. A husband who reacts violently to suggestions that he participate in domestic chores is left; a woman who really wants to work convinces her husband to move to another town. And less dramatically, on a day-to-day basis, women plan and work, scheme and compromise, to create satisfying lives for themselves and their families.

Luxton's graphic portrayal of family life lived around, through and despite of, the gruelling eight-hour shift-work (the husband's necessary lot in Flin Flon) does more to demonstrate the need for a class analysis of male–female relations than all the polemics that could be marshalled. She shows how 'the long arm of the job' affects people's most intimate experiences even as they seek to love and to make (or to avoid making) love.

Can the arguments of the domestic labour debate help Luxton, or us, in understanding her subject?

The Domestic Labour Debate Encounters the Housewives of Flin Flon

Most of Luxton's families live on one wage. Does this mean that they live on a family wage? Or that capital has taken this into account in some *a priori* fashion? Well it seems that these men who run the Hudson Bay Mining and Smelting Company Limited play it a bit by ear. They wanted a stable work force and decided that that meant primarily one of married men. So the wages offered were enough to entice such workers to town. On the other hand, many more women would like to work for wages than actually do, mainly due to the company's spurious use of nepotism regulations.

Are these women who want waged work being greedy, liberated or are they hoping to make ends meet? Clearly the historical specificity of what constitutes subsistence is more central to understanding the behaviour, needs and values of these Flin Flon women than some abstract or base-line notion of subsistence. These arguments are made in another way in *The Double*

Ghetto, a Canadian study that the authors of *Hidden in the Household* could have profitably drawn upon.[14]

But there is more to women working for wages than the question of how the kingdom of necessity is defined historically, as a casual perusal through some of the literature of the women's liberation movement would have suggested.[15] This is clear in Luxton's account.

'The best part about working is having my own money. I don't have to ask for everything. I feel more like my own person,' declared one of her respondents (p. 190). In the drawing out of these questions Luxton does not resort to 'laws of motion'. Rather her account seeks to lay bare the particular, often contradictory, interests between capitalists and workers, husbands and wives, and capitalists and wives.

Similarly the entire convoluted argument about whether women in capitalist society produce use values seems irrelevent in the face of Luxton's careful descriptions of women's work in the home. While that work probably could be classifiable into the production of use values, the transformation of commodities into use values or the purchase of immediately usable commodities, there seems little point. Instead she describes how all these activities constitute work, how women structure their time to accommodate them, and how the tasks and their meanings generate tensions within the household. It is work for a woman to anticipate that the family needs new sheets, to painstakingly save the money to purchase them, wait for the annual sale at the department store, make a careful purchase and return home with the merchandise. But it is something else to be told by your husband upon returning home that he is furious and that you have wasted his money (p. 173). In the way that the authors of *Hidden in the Household* ask their questions and define and set about their tasks, it is not surprising that the conflict between real men and women, husbands and wives even over something as clearly material as the disposition of the wage does not surface.

Sex, Struggle and Children: Still Hidden in the Household

Missing then from the articles in *Hidden in the Household* and emerging many times in Luxton's account is the struggle within the working-class family between the sexes, a struggle clearly based on male domination and female subordination. While each author laments women's double day, for example, none of them discusses it as an arena of intense daily struggle in individual households – a struggle that may work towards a breakdown of the sexual division of labour, or result in rape and battering, or end in separation, divorce or desertion, and hence to a breakdown of the nuclear family itself. Nor is the question of the distribution of resources *within* households raised.[16]

This absence has two important causes. First, the units of analysis – labour, capital, commodities, value – are not used in the service of explicating the social relationships between men and women but appear as entities in themselves. Blumenfeld and Mann write,

> the contradictions between home responsibilities and work demands that comprise the 'double burden' are just concrete manifestations of a larger contradiction that exists within every capitalist system between the capitalist production of commodities in general and the non-capitalist production of the commodity labour power (p. 271).

The women and men of Flin Flon do not have a prayer of getting even a footnote in this kind of analysis. And while this article errs the most disastrously in this direction, it is only an exaggeration, not a departure, from the book's tone.

Secondly, *Hidden in the Household* leaves more hidden there than it brings to light. Specifically there is no sex and hardly any children. And as the Catholics at least still insist there is a direct relationship between these two subjects. First, children. There is no proper discussion of the central role played by children – their bearing and rearing – in the maintenance of the sexual division of labour. When children are mentioned it is in the way a housewife might discuss them while she is actually washing the kitchen floor – that they 'interfere' with her work. Which is true. But an analysis should get behind this description to the underlying reality: that children are a primary cause both of domestic labour and of the sexual division of labour. It is not an historical accident that women are the domestic labourers; indeed it would have been a miracle if they were not. And it will require a major and sustained struggle accompanied by a collective and planned effort to go about changing it. Think how different it would be if the stork brought babies to people who put out baskets the night before.

While none of these authors probably believes that men and women have children in order to provide wage earners for capitalism, they do not reveal what they do think. For that would mean getting into that whole messy and controversial area of the psychological underpinnings of both the economic system and of the 'monogamous' nuclear family. Blumenfeld and Mann do take a paragraph to refute the entire Frankfurt School, including Herbert Marcuse. Other than this dismissal the entire domestic labour debate gets carried on without any reference to the relationship between male dominance and female subordination, and sexuality, and socialization.[17]

The advantage here is that none of those quintessentially feminist struggles around abortion, rape, birth control, battering, control over sexuality, the sharing of housework, and childcare need disturb the landscape. However, as Luxton's study of Flin Flon shows, it is through these issues that the contradictions, the pain and the joy of these women's lives are most poignantly experienced.

In the drawing out of this experience, in her treatment of it as crucially important, Luxton moves, I would argue, as social historian, as anthropologist and as feminist beyond the explicit theoretical framework in which she situates her study. Despite these moves, her theory occasionally cramps her. At times she resorts to squeezing her interpretations into preconceived formulations. If wife-beating 'is a phenomenon that occurs with equal frequency among families of all classes' (p. 69) why does she explain its presence in these families primarily through the particular work experiences of working-class men? Equally it is hard to tie her sensitive descriptions of the totally different expectations and experiences of sexuality that men and women (including teenagers) have, to the exigencies of waged work under capitalism.

What might have happened to these interpretations in the presence of a theoretical consideration of the underpinnings of patriarchal relations as discussed in very different ways in Chodorow, Dinnerstein, Mitchell, Rubin or Horowitz?[18] The absence of such a theoretical consideration means that certain aspects of working-class life are glossed over, and the deep internal division in the working class between men and women is painted in rosier hues than is warranted. It seems to me that different interests between men and women, the ways they see themselves, and each other, will mean that the struggle between the sexes will intensify in Flin Flon, and things will get a lot worse before they have a chance of getting better. If the men had been given more space to tell us what they feel about women, and about forthcoming changes in sex roles, that might have become more evident. The absence also of discussion on monogamy and heterosexuality leads one to believe that both are alive and unchallenged in Flin Flon. Perhaps the northern, isolated clime encourages both; but, if so, will the contemporary challenge to them be long in arriving?

The Domestic Labour Debate: Out of the Tunnel into the Dark

My objective has been to evaluate these books with specific criteria in mind: to what extent do they contribute to the description, understanding and interpretation of women's oppression? And to what extent do they draw upon a wide range of evidence in their work? Not surprisingly, the answers to these questions vary at least in part with the author's conception of that oppression.

For Blumenfeld and Mann, women's oppression in the bour- geoisie is reducible to the need to transmit property to one's legitimate heirs. (Would not Engels be disappointed to think that he had had the last word on the subject?) In the working class there is no intrinsic basis to sexism: its existence is due to the privatization of domestic labour which seems to be essentially maintained by the bourgeois state.

Curtis joins them in ignoring all evidence of women's oppres- sion. Making a gigantic and thoroughly unjustified leap from his (at best premature) conclusion about protective legislation, he claims, 'it is the state that reproduces labour power in the com- modity form and that reproduces the oppression to which the domestic labourer is subject'. Husbands and other house-mates, bow out.

While Fox used the term, 'women's oppression' in her intro- duction, her own article does not attempt to draw out its nature. She feels the double day of work will increase class conscious- ness among women but fails to discuss its possibility for raising consciousness among women of their own oppression. Evidence from Flin Flon alone suggests that it does.[19] Her recommen- dation for action centres around the organization of consumer co-operatives, a valid enough strategy but one equally relevant to both sexes.

Linda Briskin's argument that the household exists within capitalist social relations but outside of the laws governing the inner dynamic of capital, is, in fact, intended to justify the need for an autonomous women's movement. There are a lot of good reasons for such a movement that relate to male domination and female subordination at every level in society. But Briskin's attempt to justify it on those grounds is both convoluted and unconvincing, resting as it does on a law/history dichotomy, which, if valid, would truncate severely the potential efficacy of such struggle.

While feminists will not be happy with Seccombe's discussion of the underpinnings of patriarchy, he does begin from a useful assumption: 'that patriarchal family relations cannot be established solely at the level of the capitalist mode of production' (p. 60). But that insight is not elaborated upon and the absence of any discussion on monogamy, control over sexuality and the psychological underpinnings of the relations of domination and subordination is critical. His discussion of 'breadwinner power' and the importance of the ownership by the working-class man of the means of subsistence is very useful, providing both a good critique of Engels and a decisive move away from other formulations in this book.

Despite moments of insight and a formidable array of sophisticated argumentation, the authors of *Hidden in the Household* limit its usefulness through employing closure at many levels. Their theory and methods lead them to consider only a narrow range of the literature that could have informed their discussions. When discussing feudalism, the transition to capitalism and industrial capitalism, and the differences between the two modes of production, they ignore the rich historical literature. When looking at domestic labour they pass over national difference. Most dismaying, they scarcely touch upon the Canadian research. While there is a dearth of such material compared to England and the United States, there is a growing historical, economic and sociological literature which could have profitably informed their work. The feminist literature is either ignored or treated summarily.

Hidden in the Household is a book then that appears to float along with the most tenuous connection to other scholarly and political work. As a result the struggle for women's liberation when it appears at all, is a truncated and boxed-in sort of affair.

Women's Liberation: A Many-Sided Struggle

The many issues and kinds of experience that Luxton draws from life in Flin Flon are linked to a range of strategies and kinds of struggle. Since her focus is clearly upon the people of Flin Flon, we see them as shaping and creating their own lives: therefore, the idea of struggle is not superimposed upon an analysis that seems to preclude it.

Neither is capital disembodied. The directors of the company made decisions about how to attract and keep workers, while their current decisions are clearly influenced by the nature and intensity of worker resistance. And Luxton draws upon historical evidence to show how women as wives and mothers *have* contributed to that resistance. Her drawing out of the ways in which their lives are shaped by capitalist relations illustrate that it is in their interests to continue and accelerate that activity.

But as Luxton makes clear, this is not the only front for struggle. A strong impression with which I am left about life in Flin Flon is that of the mother-wife and her children tiptoeing both physically and psychologically around the father-husband. While the physical tiptoe is a consideration for one who has to work shifts, the psychological tiptoe is more than that. Luxton draws out the relations of domination and subordination within the household that give rise to the psychological tiptoe. While I do think that both her theoretical choices and the decision to mainly interview women led her to underestimate the breadth and depth of the struggle required at this level, her understanding of it is, none the less, open-ended.

Luxton truly does make the housewives of Flin Flon (and herself) both the subjects and objects of their own lives. As such she allows full weight to the subjective experience of oppression, and to the risky, tortuous and exhilerating process of consciousness raising through which women see their lives both in individual terms and as shaped by pressures that make their personal problems 'political'.

It would have been useful to see a discussion of how Luxton's own presence in Flin Flon affected that process. As a 'long-time activist' in the women's movement can we believe that she would have laid aside Marx's admonition that the task is not just to understand the world but to change it? Certainly her book should become part of the literature of the women's liberation movement in Canada and, therefore, a contribution in the struggle to do just that.

Rejecting Working at Home

Bruce Curtis

In 'Working at Home' Roberta Hamilton reviews Meg Luxton's *More than a Labour of Love* and the essays edited by Bonnie Fox in *Hidden in the Household*. As a contributor to *Hidden in the Household*, and as a teacher who has used Meg Luxton's book in two courses on the sociology of women, I am compelled to reply. My task is made difficult by the lack of agreement amongst the contributors to *Hidden in the Household* and also by the nature of Hamilton's review.

The contributors to *Hidden in the Household* shared only two general positions. First, the socialist feminist attempt to locate women's oppression under capitalism in the household, in the responsibility of women for domestic labour in the broad sense and in the separation of household and industry, was an attempt we all took more or less as a point of departure. Secondly, we all agreed that Marxism was a useful theoretical framework from within which to pose questions about the nature of women's oppression. The lack of a broader agreement amongst the contributors limits me in my response to Hamilton to a general defence of our collective project. I happen to disagree with many of the positions taken by my fellow contributors. However, since Hamilton tars us all with the same brush, I will respond to her general criticism by reference to my work.

The second problem I confront is constituted *by the internal* weaknesses of Hamilton's review. Hamilton seems to feel herself exempt from the requirement to support her key propositions with that intellectual nicety known as evidence, preferring rather broad assurances seasoned with calumny and innuendo. Because of this she fails ever to address squarely or satisfactorily the two main issues her review raises: the relation between and relative merits of theory and description, on the one hand, and the role of class and gender in women's oppression, on the other.

Hamilton begins her review by pointing to the guilty associations of the two works in question. These works, we are told, were produced in the context of the domestic labour debate. This debate is not about combating or even understanding women's oppression. On the contrary, the domestic labour debate is an attempt on the part of dogmatic Marxists to preserve the sanctity of the gospels of St Karl from criticism by forcing women into Marxist categories. Contributors to the domestic labour debate are infamous for their predilection to eschew 'the untidy and painstaking process of encountering the social world', finding it rather more pleasant to cram the world into the prefabricated theoretical boxes which the gospels provide. Dirty work at the theoretical crossroads!

Hidden in the Household, in Hamilton's view, is guilty of all the theoretical sins of the debate: it uses the 'laws of motion' of capital, it assumes Marx was correct in his social analysis, its contributors falsify or ignore the historical record to preserve their conceptions and categories, and the book is full of tortuous reasoning.

Fortunately, *More than a Labour of Love* seems to have remained more or less unsullied, despite the fall of its sibling. Here we get the real stuff, uncluttered with arguments or theoretical boxes (most of the time): women talking, struggling, fighting and compromising in their lives, hampered only by a few 'parameters', and even these are broken down if they get too much in the way. Hamilton sees Luxton's accomplishment as that of giving us real grade-A gritty oppression without having to go beyond description. Here the world is easy to understand. Here women always win. Here 'careful descriptions' make 'convoluted arguments' unnecessary.

In effect, Hamilton confronts what she has learned to identify as the poverty of theory with the romance of the empirical. In so doing she does both the theoretical and the empirical a disservice and does not help us in our attempt to come to grips with women's oppression under capitalism.

Hamilton rejects the *legitimacy* of the theoretical in the case of *Hidden in the Household* and apparently on three main grounds. First, Hamilton rejects the book's attempt (and, I think, the general attempt) to understand the basis of women's oppression in a socialist-feminist way. Locating the roots of oppression in capitalist class relations and in the separation of production and reproduction, according to Hamilton, means that 'a whole range of historical, sociological, psychological and literary evidence is cut off prior to its interrogation'.

In my opinion, quite correctly the contributors to *Hidden in the Household* made no apology for their theoretical orientation. We did not consider it practicable or necessary to retrace the particular processes whereby we had come to this theoretical orientation. Hamilton assumes in her review, on the basis of no evidence that she shares with her readers, that we took this position because we ignored or wanted to ignore a whole host of other positions. We are accused from the outset of being unscientific merely because of our theoretical orientation. This tells us more about Hamilton's intellectual prejudices than it does about the book in question. Further, if Hamilton indeed claims that socialist feminists by definition ignore lots of other perspectives on their problems, she has only to pose to us a more satisfactory theoretical position. However, in her review, the alternative to the supposedly precut theoretical boxes of Marxism is no boxes at all. I, for one, do not find the lure of the empirical quite so seductive.

Clearly, if we are not to spend all of our time describing the world or, as seems more common in anti-theoretical circles, celebrating the world of the oppressed while ignoring their defeats, we must pose theoretical questions. This means, inescapably, abstracting and selecting from the real. This process of abstraction can proceed incorrectly or in the wrong direction, but to understand the world one must do it. I would be pleased to be convinced that the theoretical project of *Hidden in the Household* proceeds incorrectly, and if there is a better way of proceeding I would be happy to learn of it. Hamilton claims that this is the case, but why this is so and what other possibilities exist she does not deign to share with us.

Hamilton's second ground for rejecting *Hidden in the Household* is the slavish dogmatism of Marxists. Using Marxism means setting in motion a 'set of categories into which social reality must then be pummelled and squeezed'. The authors of *Hidden in the Household* are charged with believing that 'Marx must have been right'; not, mind you, that Marx might have been right, could have been right or might allow us to pose an important question. Oh no! 'Marx *must* have been right'; slavish and snivelling dogmatism of the worst kind. One can only counter such charges, I think, by inviting Hamilton to demonstrate that the authors have neglected evidence which any reasonable person would see as convincing out of an intention to preserve their theoretical position. In the absence of such a demonstration, Hamilton is merely making unfounded but not inoffensive allegations.

The third ground upon which Hamilton rejects the general project of *Hidden in the Household* is potentially the most serious. Not only do we, the Marxist marionettes, dance to Marx's (?) statement that 'all commodities (including labour power) are exchanged for those of a similar [sic] value', but also, 'the historical record . . . refutes both' this proposition and the notion of a family wage. I'm sure everyone breathed a sigh of relief upon learning that these troublesome debates had been solved once and for all by the historical record. Hamilton seems to have forgotten to mention where we could find this historical record. Really, though, this seems rather unfortunate, for had she been so kind as to indicate, perhaps just by a hint or an oblique reference, where the records are kept we could all finally get rid of those old copies of *Capital* which take up so much space.

I cannot conclude my remarks on Hamilton's treatment of *Hidden in the Household* without responding briefly to the comments she makes on my own article. I make the argument that the origins of the domestic sphere under capitalism may be understood through examining the struggles of working-class women and men for a domestic life. I attempt to refute the argument, quite common at the time I was writing, that men or men of all classes had incarcerated women in the household. This position seemed to me to underplay the significance of the role of class divisions in the development of women's oppression. Using the English case, I examined the ways in which capitalist development had produced changes in the organization of domestic life, and I pointed to the existence in mid-nineteenth century England of a socialist struggle. This struggle was quite broad in its objectives, seeking among other things a domestic sphere for workers, political rights for women, universal education, and the abolition of what its partisans called 'domestic slavery'. Hamilton claims that I made this argument purely *with the aim*(!) 'to let working-class men off the hook' and that to do so I skimmed over the historical evidence, ignoring the crucial parts which show working-class men trying to get women out of the labour force for sexist reasons. I am also castigated for not being familiar with literature published after my article had gone to press.

When my article in *Hidden in the Household* was written, the recent explosion of research into the history of the household and its origins was just beginning. Given that many people were arguing in print that the household arose out of a plot on the part of men, I think that my attempt to consider the possibility of class differences between women and of a class alliance between working-class men and women was a useful contribution. It is one whose limitations will increasingly become apparent as the literature on family history continues to blossom, and perhaps I will be shown to be wrong or misguided. That is as it should be. But what is the state of criticism, I wonder, when attempts to discuss class in historical development are regarded by feminist critics as motivated simply by sexism?

To one charge of Hamilton's I must plead guilty. It is true that my article neglects the role of the trade unions (most of them, mind you, not in existence until after the period I treated), which were male-dominated, in excluding women from industrial production. Hamilton does not mention that my article also fails to discuss the role of the maternal feminists, concerned to get their sisters under the patriarchal thumb so that race purity and good domestic servants would continue. I wonder which of Hamilton's prejudices is revealed by the fact that I am charged with aiming to let working-class men, rather than bourgeois women, off the hook?

In so far as Hamilton points to the accessibility and lucidity of *More than a Labour of Love*, I am in more or less complete agreement with her. I suspect that anyone who has used this as an undergraduate coursebook will have had experiences similar to my own: students quickly and often delightedly make contact with the book. It dispels much of the romantic claptrap about domesticity that people who have not experienced it as adults carry about in their heads. It presents a clear picture of the day-to-day struggles women encounter and sets these struggles in a context of social class. As an instrument of political education Luxton's book is quite remarkable.

However, Hamilton's concern to romanticize the empirical mystifies Luxton's accomplishments. Luxton's book isn't a good book because it makes theory unnecessary, or because it makes convoluted arguments clear. It is not a substitute for theory! It is a good book because it presents reality in a light which contains all the political forcefulness of its truth. It is a good book not because people can do away with theory if they have got Luxton, but because the book and the truth it contains force people to reflect on social reality, on the reality of women's oppression and on the reality of class exploitation. This is a good book because it is a path for people into the dialectic of theory and description, of struggle and reflection on struggle, which alone (if we are able to do both) has the potential to lead us to the destruction of exploitation and oppression.

In my view, Hamilton's review does not further that possibility by vilifying the theoretical while glorifying reality. I call on Hamilton, if she wishes to reject the legitimacy of *Hidden in the Household* while glorifying *More than a Labour of Love* to present us with the solutions to the problems with which we have tried to grapple. What is the role of theory in the struggle against women's oppression? What theory (or theories) should we use for our guide? What is the relation between, and relative importance of, gender and class? How can you claim that empirical description absolves us from theory? Shall we then describe the heroic day-to-day struggles of American women to make abortion murder while selling Amway's products? Tell us!

Reply to Curtis

Roberta Hamilton

Curtis's reply to my review (*Atlantis*, vol. 7, no. 1, pp. 114–26) has bolstered my original criticisms of *Hidden in the Household*. Rather than using the review as a take-off for a genuine debate, he has chosen to erect fences, proclaim absolutes and construct false polarities. I take exception to almost everything he says, and how he says it. My response is organized under five subjects. (1) language; (2) uncovering differences; (3) the theoretical and the empirical; (4) naive empiricism; and (5) Curtis's research.

Language: A Contemporary Morality Play

Those readers who are upset by the words that Curtis attributes to me should turn to the original review. Certainly my analysis was intended to be direct and critical, an attempt to convince people, including the authors, to reconsider arguments and expand the range of questions considered important. But *I* did not use such unbecoming phrases as 'slavish and snivelling dogmatism', 'Marxist marionettes', 'guilty associations', 'the gospels of St Karl' or 'dirty work at the theoretical crossroads'. These are Curtis's epithets and I wonder why he chose to put into circulation language that purports to describe himself and his colleagues in such disrespectful tones. He may think that we are engaged in a struggle between good and evil, but for my part I do not wish to confuse the writing of criticism with the production of a morality play. As to charges that my review was seasoned with calumny and innuendo, I can only (in this one instance and in keeping within the terms of that play) plead innocent. 'Innuendo: an oblique hint or suggestion.' Hardly. 'Calumny: false and malicious misrepresentation.' Not really.

Uncovering Differences

The second issue refers to Curtis's decision to defend the whole book 'despite the lack of agreement amongst the contributors' because I 'tar them all with the same brush'. To the extent that the book was presented as a collective endeavour I did make general comments about its self-proclaimed task. Yet with little help from them or the editor I attempted to tease out some of the differences among them in a way that few readers would have the patience or will to do. These differences, while not trivial, are rarely considered by authors or editor. I am, therefore, disappointed that Curtis did not use his reply as an opportunity to explicate and draw them out. In a review of *Hidden in the Household*, Lise Vogel concluded that 'as it stands readers . . . must expect to thread their way as best they can through material that is often insightful and sometimes significant, even as it is by turns repetitive, dense or internally contradictory'.[1] That is the kindest way possible of putting it. Why didn't the authors have a good go at each other? That might have produced a genuinely critical debate. And, in any case, what do we have here? An extension of the ideology that families should not wash their dirty linen in public? If so, the real question then becomes: are Curtis's collaborators grateful for his defence of them? Or do they feel a certain hesitation, like the old man the two boy scouts took so long to help across the road 'because he did not want to go'?

The Theoretical and the Empirical: The Mystification of Marx

Let us examine the validity of Curtis's assumption that the theoretical and the empirical are two distinct (almost opposing) practices. Raymond Williams in *Keywords* defines theory as an 'explanatory scheme'.[2] Theory is 'always in active relation to practice: an interaction between things done, things observed and (systematic) explanation of these'. There is no moment when the observation ceases and the explanation begins: indeed when that happens the explanation is cut off from that which it is called upon to explain. Marx wrote that 'economic categories are only the theoretical expressions, the abstractions of the social relations of production'.[3] He criticizes Proudhon for sharing 'the illusions of speculative philosophy' by transforming such categories through 'his twaddle into pre-existing eternal ideas'.[4] There seems little point in emulating Proudhon.

To turn to the empirical. Williams defines it this way: 'The simplest general modern senses indicate a reliance on observed experience, but almost everything depends on how experience is understood.'[5] As we live our lives we constantly seek to make sense of them. Luxton's respondents in Flin Flon do not furnish her with simple observations but with explanations, interpretations, questions and speculation about themselves and their relationships with others. Indeed the very process of developing language, of using symbols to represent things, feelings, ideas, events, of having to constantly make selections among words, stands in contradiction to some notion of 'mere' description or simple observation.

The important area of convergence between the theoretical and the empirical emerging from these definitions is clear: both involve the continuing quest for understanding and explanation; both seek to make sense of the world as it has been received and as it is experienced. What we call Marx's theory actually involves a great range of overlapping practices from observations on the factory system through complex philosophical discussions. It was through an ongoing dialectical analysis that included critiques of previously offered explanations, historical analysis and continuing observations/interpretations that he was able to strip away the apparent naturalness from the developing relations of capitalism.

Why then do the theoretical and the empirical so often seem to be, as they do to Curtis, two distinct practices? Most importantly because the processes through which the theory developed are forgotten. Marx's dialectical method is left to lie fallow; his historical analysis is frozen; his observations on the world are shunted off, leaving the concepts and categories which he derived *through* the analysis and observations to stand alone. Given this historical amnesia the theory appears as a reified and closed system of ideas, concepts and interpretations. Curtis states candidly that this was the starting point of the authors of *Hidden in the Household*: 'We did not consider it practicable or necessary to retrace the particular processes whereby we had come to this theoretical orientation.' This decision is especially ironical because however much we can learn from *what* Marx found out, we can learn more from *how* he found it. For the processes he elaborated and used are transferable and continue to be creatively developed. On the other hand, the march of history has produced ever changing situations which, in his absence, we must observe and interpret for ourselves.

In this task no realm of knowledge should be privileged; there can be no sanctuaries where systems of ideas and concepts rest safe from scrutiny. By Curtis's admission the authors *did* protect their theoretical orientation (the received system of ideas and concepts) in precisely this way. The consequences are clear. By virtue of this decision the historically specific analysis, when it was engaged in at all, was put primarily at the service of fleshing out the theory rather than of revealing the particular nature of women's oppression in capitalist society. Furthermore, the 'theory' that was intended to help unravel the way things work, itself became part of the mystification process as the memory of its own historical development was blocked. Instead of being used to help explore and prise out the meaning and implications of our social relationships, instead of being called upon to help formulate questions and in the process being reformulated itself, it is required to produce ready-made answers. It is the equivalent of only talking to oneself. Or to quote Marx: 'Criticism with a completely uncritical attitude to itself.'[6]

Naive Empiricism: Curtis's Mystification of Luxton

This leads to a discussion of a fourth issue advanced by Curtis: his assertion that I liked *More than a Labour of Love* because it was a literate version of a coffee klatch. Curtis's burlesque account of my comments about this book illustrates the nonsense of his theory/empirical division. To understand the world he argued one must 'pose theoretical questions'. To do this we must abstract and select from the real. The conclusion he draws is bizarre at best. 'This process of abstraction can proceed incorrectly or in the wrong direction but to understand the world one must do it.' I assume that he does not mean what he seems to be saying: that to understand the world we must proceed in the wrong direction! More fundamentally, however, selecting out from the 'real' is not just a theoretical prerogative in the way Curtis suggests. All our comments on the world are selective emerging from the ongoing accumulation of experiences, interests and previous understandings.

Now Luxton went to Flin Flon with a particular set of interests, ideas and questions that overlapped with those shared by many others, including me. If most of her book had described the clothing and manners of the people she would have reached a different audience:

Gregory B., personnel manager [she might have written], was wearing a double-breasted suit, a pretty print tie and a lovely pale yellow shirt. His warm handshake and admiring eyes told me that he approved of my slightly faded but well-cut blue jeans and the plaid shirt I had picked up on sale just the week before.

This account too is based on selection, but the criteria are different. Furthermore there is little attempt to provide any context for, or interpretation of this encounter in terms of class or gender relations.

But in my review of *More than a Labour of Love* I made it clear that Luxton's challenge was to prise out the nature, meaning and implications of the social relationships she studied: she seeks 'to lay bare the particular, often the contradictory interests between capitalists and workers, husbands and wives, capitalists and wives'. I did not imply that this was an a-theoretical undertaking. Luxton did not parachute herself into Flin Flon with an empty head and a few pencils in her pocket. Nor, despite Curtis's sarcasm about anti-abortion and Amway products, did I suggest she should have. Somewhere between Curtis's theoreticism and the naive empiricism which he offers as its only alternative is surely another way. In his discussion of the sociology of culture Raymond Williams suggests the broad outlines of such a path:

An adequate sociology of culture ... cannot avoid the informing presence of existing empirical studies and existing theoretical and quasi-theoretical positions. But it must be prepared to rework and reconsider all received material and concepts and to present its own contributions within the open interaction of evidence and interpretation which is the true condition of its adequacy.[7]

In my review I suggested that Luxton had worked in this way: that as social historian, anthropologist and feminist she had broached a far broader area of questions and concerns than she would have had she remained within the framework of her express theoretical commitment. Still, my one stated criticism of her work, ironically enough considering Curtis's charge, was that she did not allow the feminist literature on patriarchal relations to sufficiently inform her analysis. That criticism alone contradicts Curtis's assertion that I applauded her for arriving in Flin Flon as a blank slate. But despite this important absence in what she *took* to Flin Flon she was able, through a process of moving from developed concepts to observations and back again, to weave together a detailed understanding of some of the ways in which capitalist and patriarchal relations intersect in the lives of working-class men and women. This was scarcely an attempt (nor did I suggest that it was) to celebrate 'the world of the oppressed while ignoring their defeats'. What Luxton's study did offer, which Curtis perhaps finds objectionable, was an interpretation of how men and women, as subjects, create their own lives within a particular historical and social setting. This included the complex reasons why women choose to remain within, and how they handle, the family relations that socialist-feminists identify as oppressive.

From this Luxton drew out some of the contradictions in the lives of the women which might lead to struggle and change. On the other hand, the only implication we can draw for the future from the Curtis account of 'domestic slavery' is that there will be more of the same: 'we can see that the domestic worker is repro-duced under conditions of domestic slavery . . . She in incar-cerated in an isolated, technically backwards and stagnant unit.'

Curtis could profit from Thompson's admonition to those who evaluate life solely in terms of the inevitable and eventual attainment of working-class power:

> history cannot be compared to a tunnel through which an express races until it brings its freight of passengers out into sunlit plains. Or, if it can be, then generation upon generation of passengers are born, live in the dark, and die while the train is still within the tunnel. An historian must surely be more interested than the teleologists allow him to be in the quality of life, the sufferings and satisfactions, of those who live and die in unredeemed time.[8]

To Curtis this may smack of romanticism; furthermore, for him, the romantic and the empirical appear as equivalent. Never-theless, before writing such prose again, laboured in tone and content, perhaps he will pause, with us, to remember that Luxton's housewives have only one life to live; we should not, therefore, be surprised to find that each is prepared to give it what she's got, despite its unfortunately premature timing.

History as Done by Curtis: How to Reach Foregone Conclusions

Finally let us look at Curtis's defence of his own historical analy-sis. I am especially puzzled about his insistence that theoretical knowledge be privileged in light of his own assumption that *if* there was a family wage it was because it had developed through struggles mediated by the state, between the working class and the capitalist class. This, I think, can be demonstrated through a wide-ranging historical analysis, and this is not a point of contention between us. My quarrel with him is not this starting point. It is rather with the partial and distorted way in which he proceeded, on the one hand, and with his conclusions, on the other.

First, he developed a one-sided case: 'that the struggle of the worker's movement for the possibility of domestic life must be seen as a progressive one'. At the very least the struggle was far more contradictory. Even Jane Humphries who made a similar argument to Curtis in 1977 produced some conflicting evidence.[9] While he complains that he did the best job he could, given the available evidence, this plea can scarcely be sustained. Sheila Lewenhak and Sheila Rowbotham have discussed this question. Dorothy Thompson's article, 'Women and Nineteenth-century Radical Politics: A Lost Dimension', is extremely suggestive, while Sally Alexander provides a broader context for looking at women's work in this period.[10] But it was Curtis's task to ferret out the evidence, to have done the research, not mine. The point is that Curtis raises a complex historical question and deals with it in a cavalier fashion. His hit-and-miss method is reminiscent of what Thompson described as the Kangeroo Factor. This is a method of 'theoretical practice' which

> prohibits any actual empirical engagements with social reality . . . Hence the theoretical practitioner proceeds in gigantic bounds through the conceptual elements . . . But every so often (since the law of gravity cannot be disregarded forever) he comes down: *bump!* What he comes down upon is an assumption about the world. But he does not linger on this assumption, sniff it, taste the grass. *Hop!* He is off into the air again.[11]

While some of the evidence I cited in my review was only available in unpublished form before *Hidden in the Household* went to press, this did not prevent Seccombe, who had a far more sophisticated understanding of this question, from using it to advantage.

However, I faulted Curtis not just for having constructed a shaky case about this particular historical process, but also for insisting it support his pre-existing prejudices. The 'progressive nature of the struggle for a domestic life' proves for him that:

> The separation of household and industry under capitalism and the sex-based division of labour which it involves forms the basis of the division of the working class along sex lines . . . working class men and women share a common position of opposition to the capitalist state.

This leap earned him my charge that his object was to let working-class men off the hook. I do not, however, attribute his desire to sexism, but rather to his *a priori* decision to sustain his theory. This can be seen clearly because he states his conclusion before he presents his historical research: asking rhetorically 'is the source of the barbarity to which many housewives are subject to be found in the figure of the working class husband?', he responds 'surely the ultimate source of this barbarity is capitalist exploitation!' What happens to the overwhelming evidence that women are subject to their husbands in precapitalist and in socialist countries, albeit in very different forms? He ignores it. Curtis's theoretical blinkers (can we demystify this and call it prejudice: 'an unreasoning predilection'?) save him from many time-comsuming historical excursions.

In the end Curtis simply cannot expect feminists to appreciate his work when he so categorically rejects their concerns. His ossified rendition of Marxism permits him to remain blissfully unhampered and untouched by fifteen years of socialist-feminist inquiry.

Economism and Feminism: A Comment on the Domestic Labour Debate

Angela Miles

What has come to be called the domestic labour debate originated in Marxist critiques of the political analysis of housework that Selma James and Mariarosa Dalla Costa developed in the early 1970s.[1] James and Dalla Costa followed Italian social capital theory[2] in arguing that today the working class is no longer the nineteenth-century proletariat defined by Marx; it now encompasses white- as well as blue-collar workers, and the wageless as well as the waged worker. This theory holds: (1) that the massification of labour and the sheer volume of production in advanced capitalism is breaking down occupational divisions within the working class; (2) that the new level of productive forces in advanced capitalism has broken the traditional capitalist connection between hours of labour time and the amount of surplus value created; (3) that these developments, and the resulting massive increase in wealth, are opening the way for a qualitatively new level of workers' struggle built on the refusal of labour (and thus refusal of an alienated existence as labour power); and (4) that this struggle challenges the core of capitalist relations more directly and decisively than earlier forms of workers' struggle based on the right to work (and to exist as labour power).

Dalla Costa and James drew out the implications of this perspective, not just for the wageless male worker in developed industrial societies, but for the wageless in the home and in the Third World.[3] They argued that the best way to articulate the struggle against labour was for the wageless to demand wages. They developed their position most fully within the women's movement in respect to housewives, arguing that their demand for wages would aggravate the contradictions of a society that had outgrown the material base of capitalist social relations and social control organized around the wage.

The revision of Marx's analysis of the role of labour in the creation of surplus value in earlier capitalist economies throws into question the analytical and strategic importance of his distinction between productive and unproductive labour. It is this, and not a misunderstanding of these concepts or of the significance that Marx assigned to them, that underlies the willingness of Dalla Costa and James to argue that it is no longer *politically* relevant to distinguish housework from waged work on the grounds that it is 'unproductive'. In this they echo Marx's own critical method: the analysis of existing society entails an essential political moment and the necessary direction of liberatory struggle is contained/revealed in the social critique itself.

Neither of the two main Marxist responses to the 'wages for housework' analysis has addressed the perspective at a theoretical/political level. One set of critical literature has focused on the immediate practical and tactical implications of the demand for wages for housework. It raises such questions as 'Who will pay the wages?' and 'Will payment for housework institutionalize this degrading labour?' But it does not recognize or refute the general analysis of late capitalism on the basis of which this strategic demand is posited.[4] The other main critique took issue, not with the general analysis of capitalism or the call for a struggle against labour, but with the claim of James and Dalla Costa that housework produces surplus value.[5] By focusing on this question without addressing the wider questions which underlie it, this critique tended to limit a potentially important political debate to questions of textual exegesis. It assessed the wages for housework analysis in relation to established Marxist categories rather than in relation to the world and the possibilities for liberatory struggle.

Marxist categories were not originally developed to deal with labour in the home. There is, in any case, room for debate about such conceptions as 'productive labour' even in reference to the sphere of waged labour.[6] So it is not surprising that wide differences emerged even among those who agreed that this textual exercise was important. It is around these differences that the domestic labour debate has developed. The genesis of the debate thus lies in the reduction of such large theoretical and political questions as the nature of class in advanced capitalism, and the relationship of class and gender oppression to a narrow economic analysis of domestic labour under capitalism.

The book, *Hidden in the Household: Women's Domestic Labour Under Capitalism*, ably edited by Bonnie Fox, brings together many recent Canadian contributions to the domestic labour debate. Its recent appearance provides a good opportunity for me to substantiate my charge of this literature's economism and to examine the limitations inherent in it.[7]

In his two articles, Wally Seccombe critiques and extends Marxist categories in an attempt to develop a general analysis of the capitalist mode of production that can encompass areas of capitalist reality with which Marx and Marxists have not dealt. Bruce Curtis, Linda Briskin, Bonnie Fox, Emily Blumenfeld and Susan Mann take a less dynamic approach. They focus on more specific moments of that reproduction, and are more concerned to preserve than to develop Marxist categories. Nevertheless, they take widely different positions on such 'classical' questions of the debate as whether this labour can or cannot be analysed in terms of Marx's labour theory of value, whether it creates surplus value, and whether its privatization is necessary to capitalism.

Wally Seccombe's articles are a major development of his own earlier work and an original contribution to the debate. He distinguishes 'four interrelated facets of the mode of production: (a) the mode of appropriation of the producers' product by the producers; (b) the mode of its distribution among producers; (c) the mode of its consumption in the domestic group; and (d) the mode of labour power's production, both on a daily and on a generational basis'.[8] He then asks, 'What becomes of the categories, "forces" and "relations" of production under the foregoing treatment of the mode of subsistence?' and answers: 'In each case these categories must be stretched to incorporate the subsistence dimension. Productive forces must include both the technological means of production and the capacities of the producers.'[9] The bulk of his two articles reflects his attempts to do this 'stretching' and, in the process, to 'salvage the essential categories of Marx's political economy from a reductionist tendency'.[10]

Many of the other articles in the book express scepticism about whether this is salvage or sabotage. The domestic labour debate consists in large part of varying positions on this question of the admissibility of stretching Marx's categories and on the correct way to apply stretched or unstretched categories. The narrow economic and textual limits of these questions are not in themselves a significant political problem. However, these limits go unrecognized by most of the contributors to the domestic labour literature who tend to mistake their essentially economic analysis for political analysis. In the rest of this article I want to document the presumed identity between economic analysis and political theory in this literature and to outline its grave consequences for the development of radical theory and practice.

The most obvious instance of economist confusion is the general tendency to present an analysis of domestic labour as if it were a theoretical examination of the oppression of women. All the authors in *Hidden in the Household* write as if patriarchal power and gender domination were a central concern of their work: Bonnie Fox's introduction identifies 'the issue of the relation between capitalism and patriarchy' as 'crucial'[11] and calls the 'structural determinants of women's oppression' a 'key question'.[12] Bruce Curtis's main aim is to rebut the argument 'that the domestic sphere emerges as a plot on the part of male workers and capitalists to oppress women and children'.[13] Linda Briskin investigates domestic labour in order to achieve a 'better understanding of women's oppression (and to clarify) the strategic political questions facing the women's movement'.[14] Emily Blumenfeld and Susan Mann claim to 'illuminate the intersection of sexual oppression and class oppression'.[15]

In fact the authors *describe* women's oppression. They do not *analyse* it. They all acknowledge, in varying degrees, the specific 'dependence' and 'oppression' of women under capitalism. Curtis says 'her dependency and isolation separate her position from his'.[16] Briskin describes oppression as opposed to exploitation, as a 'condition that takes many forms, including racism and sexism'.[17] Fox says that 'within the working class, women have special interests. They occupy a unique position because of their sex. Domestic labourers are dependent on a *man's* wage (or on state subsidies).'[18] Seccombe develops a finely observed and original description of 'the prerogatives that accrue to the primary breadwinner, by virtue of his personal appropriation of the bulk of the family's income'.[19] These, he argues, form 'a powerful basis for petty male dominance in the proletarian household'.[20] But, with the exception of Curtis's article,[21] these observations lead to no theoretical questions about *why* this might be and how one can explain the fact that capitalist relations (and not only capitalist relations) have developed in such a way as to ensure men's power over women.

The kinds of questions the domestic labour debate is built around do not address the causes or significance of women's oppression. Rather, they presume it and seek to understand the mechanisms of its institutionalization in capitalist society – a very different level of analysis that is reflected in the following sample questions from the book: 'Is the socialization of domestic labour in fact possible under capitalism?' 'Is the relationship between the household and capitalist production changing?'[22] 'How does the law of value shape the reproduction cycle of labour power?'[23] 'What is the effect on the socialization of domestic labour and the increased participation of women in the labour force? Under what conditions is domestic labour intensified? What is the effect of domestic technology and the expansion of consumer goods production on the household? What happens with large families, single workers? What influences the level of wages? What is the developmental dynamic of the "family wage"? When does childcare change in form? Under what impetus does the state socialize services or remove them? How do women participate in the class struggle? What is the role of the family in the class struggle?'[24]

The authors all explicitly recognize that the analysis of capitalism as such can throw no light on the vexed question of why it is invariably women who do the labour in the home. Curtis notes that 'while an examination of the structural features of capitalism reveals the structural bases of domestic labour and the working family, it does not explain the sex-based division of labour between working class men and women'.[25] Blumenfeld and Mann note that the sexual division of labour is not theoretically necessary to capitalism: 'Equally obvious (although of no necessity) is the fact that it is generally the woman who prepares the food and feeds the family within the context of the privatized household.'[26] Briskin remarks that 'The question why women traditionally do domestic labour requires a separate investigation.'[27] Seccombe explains that the 'unequal value (of men and women's) respective labour powers on the market . . . impresses an unequal division of labour on them',[28] but this does not (and I doubt that he would claim that it does) explain that unequal value.

The failure to tackle questions of gender domination at a theoretical level leaves these articles in the strange position of both acknowledging (descriptively) and denying (theoretically) women's oppression. Bonnie Fox notices that 'domestic labourers are dependent on a *man's* wage' only to say, at the same time, that 'the domestic labourer owns her own means of production'.[29] Blumenfeld and Mann deny the fact of men's power over women even as they recognize its results: 'As the "sanctity" of privacy allows the household to close its doors to public scrutiny and supervision it is not surprising that the household in modern society remains the major arena of personal violence: wife battering and child abuse are the very products of privatization.'[30] Women's economic dependence goes a lot further to explain their vulnerability to these attacks than the privatization of the home. But women's economic position alone cannot account for the attacks. How is it that Blumenfeld and Mann feel no need to ask why 'unsupervised' men routinely attack women and children in our culture? To ask this question breaches the economic limits of the domestic labour debate. But surely it is a question that must disturb those attempting to build a new and better world, and one that must have some place in our development of theory.

Wally Seccombe, in examining the 'core condition of women's oppression under capitalism', is more careful than others in the book to avoid any suggestion that he is examining the causes of women's oppression in general. Nevertheless the schizophrenia involved in noticing that oppression, while at the same time avoiding the question of its causes and meaning, is more pronounced in his work because his descriptive treatment is fuller. He notices that 'In the confines of [the] rationality [of the household budget] women's needs and interests are normally subordinated.'[31] But he chooses not to examine the ways and degree to which men and women's interests differ individually and collectively, and whether that difference is reflected in the operation of the law of value. Instead he focuses, like the other authors in the book, on the shared interests of men and women in the household in 'securing subsistence' within the constraints of the capitalist mode of production. He argues that taking 'the family unit and not the individual wage labourer' as the starting point is 'an exemplary methodological premise for the contemporary study not only of women's labour but the whole question of the allocation of the working class's total labour time between the sexes and between the two production sites'.[32] Clearly, however, taking the household as the basic analytical unit specifically precludes consideration of the allocation of total labour time *between* the sexes. It means necessarily presenting such questions as whether to 'intensify domestic labour, shift its focus or seek a second wage'[33] as if the optimum choice were the same for the man and woman. In describing the tensions involved in the 'household' attempts to maximize the standard of living and minimize the labour effort, he writes as if there were only one standard of living and labour effort in a household. In fact there are two and the trade-offs between them are direct. Less leisure for the woman means more for the man.[34] More important, the trade-offs involve not only material goods and physical effort, but power as well. A paid job for the woman may bring more money into the household but threaten the man's power. The documentation of actual working-class family interaction in such books as *Coal Is Our Life* by Fernando Henriques and *Worlds of Pain* by Lillian Breslow Ruben shows clearly that power considerations such as these play a big part in 'household' decisions.

The unequal value of male and female labour on the market makes it 'rational' in household economic terms for the woman to stay at home if one of the adults must do so. But it cannot account for the fact that it is the woman who is responsible for domestic labour even when she is in the paid labour force. It is clearly not in her interest that this should be so. Although the greater economic power of the male might explain his ability to impose this situation, it does not explain why he does so.

If it is true that even the most original and far-reaching of contributions to the domestic labour debate throws no theoretical light on the substance and causes of gender domination, how can all these authors make this claim for their work? Their claim rests on the mistaken belief that to show the significance of capitalism in shaping women's oppression is to adequately explain this oppression in class terms.

These articles all demonstrate the unexceptionable, even obvious (though partial), truth that women's responsibility for domestic labour performed in the privatized household is the specific form in which women's oppression is institutionalized under capitalism. But to document this is not to deal with the question of *why* capitalist relations have developed in such a way as to ensure women's subordination to men. To illustrate that women's oppression takes specific forms under capitalism is *not* to prove that it is derivative. The authors' belief that it is leads them to pose a false dichotomy between gender and class domination. Therefore they read any serious theoretical attention to gender oppression as a domination that is not, or may not be, derivative of class, as a denial of the influence and even the existence of class exploitation.

Over and over again the authors describe feminist attempts to understand the universality of gender oppression as if such attempts necessarily involve a denial of its historical and cultural specificity in different times and places, and specifically under capitalism:

> Those attempts at an analysis of women's oppression that begin with the assumption of women's universal subordination are inherently limited. In ignoring the marked historical and cross-cultural variations in women's position, these analyses abandon the search for causally related material and social factors before it has really begun.[35]

The attempts of feminist radicals of all stripes (Marxist, socialist, radical and lesbian) to move towards a new, more universal analysis of domination that can encompass both class and gender oppression[36] are presented as a simple substitution of gender for class:

> This analysis presents capitalists and male workers as sharing a common interest in the oppression of women. The exploitation of labour power by capital, which itself structures the oppression of working class women, is *replaced* by a conception in which men in general oppress women in general.[37]

The reductionist presumption that one must deal theoretically *either* with class *or* gender domination limits the development of dialogue around the question of the relationship and genesis of the two. We have seen how in this volume it leads to the mistaken belief that studies of the shape of women's oppression under capitalism are analyses of its causes. It also reduces all feminism to reformism and renders invisible the attempts of feminist radicalism to tackle both class and gender domination.

Emily Blumenfeld and Susan Mann make this reduction explicitly when they move from the fact that feminists 'maintain that the oppression of women is the most fundamental and deep-rooted form of oppression, and that the struggle for sexual liberation must not be subordinated to any other' to the presumption that this means that for feminists 'the transcendence of

women's oppression [is] separate from the question of the abolition of private property' and 'sexual oppression and class
oppression [are] two distinct issues'.[38] There are reformist
feminists who seek women's equality within capitalism. But the
hallmark of feminist radicalism is a commitment to explore what
we believe are the deep and common roots of *all* forms of
oppression. This becomes essential when the defining value of
the struggle is the end of domination and alienation rather than
the end of private property and the equality of material distribution. It is not to ignore the specificity of the changing shape of
different dominations or their relationship, but to develop,
through an analysis of their specificity, an understanding that can
guide our struggle for the freedom of all.

Many of us have come to this through Marxism. Whether we
call ourselves Marxist, socialist, radical or lesbian feminists, our
heritage from that tradition is to demand of ourselves a theoretical understanding of the totality of our society that goes beyond
appearances. We retain a commitment to a dialectical, historical
and materialist methodology. In fact, the complexity of a project
that seeks to understand both patriarchal and class power has
meant that we cannot so easily slip into the economist reductionism that bedevils Marxism and that is evident in the domestic
labour debate's presumption to explain women's oppression.

The psychological and economic, personal and political, individual and social components of life and analysis have to be
brought together to begin to tackle the questions feminists raise.
How is it, for instance, that the abolition of private property fails
to secure women's freedom and, indeed, workers' freedom?
Marxism has shown that the existence of relative surplus is a
necessary precondition to the emergence of private property in
goods and the means of production (though not, apparently, in
women) and to class power based on it. Relative surplus however, is surely not a sufficient condition. It does not, alone,
explain why men's (the term is used advisedly here) response to
surplus was private appropriation.

Feminism, dealing as it does with oppression by fathers of
sons and daughters, husbands of wives, and lovers of 'loved'
ones, is forced to face such difficult questions. And they arise,
too, around the origins of class in ways they have not yet done
within Marxism.

Feminists would want to ask of this volume such questions as:
How is it that self-interest is often experienced by men, even in

personal life and even in the common struggle of working-class households for subsistence, in terms of individual and collective *male* power and advantage? Can this really be explained as a survival requirement of the capitalist mode of production;[39] a result of the unequal law of value for male and female labour;[40] the product of the privatization of the household;[41] or pollution by 'the patriarchal institutions and practices of the ruling class and state'?[42]

Is an analysis of the capitalist family 'as an integral part of the capitalist reality' sufficient to end the 'mystification of the relations in the home' in which the 'focus of tension becomes the relation between the domestic labourer and the wage labourer'?[43]

Can the relations between men and women, and men's oppression of women – even in their capitalist forms – be encompassed by the respective terms 'wage labourer' and 'domestic labourer'? How can one deal in this framework with such systematic male violence against women as rape, prostitution (including child prostitution and the large international trade in women), pornography, incest, wife-beating and sexual harassment (to leave aside such non-capitalist practices as *sutti*, witch-burning, clitoridectomy and foot-binding)?

Is the feminist contention that male workers as well as male capitalists protect patriarchal power adequately refuted by showing, as Curtis does, that the 'domestic sphere [did not emerge] as a plot on the part of male workers and capitalists to oppress women and children in industrial labour' because the working class was 'forced to fight the battle' on the sexist grounds established by the English bourgeoisie's exclusion of women from the 'rights of freeborn Englishmen . . . to sell their labour as they saw fit'?[44] Did the working class use bourgeois sexism to gain a point? Or did the bourgeoisie use working-class sexism to limit the struggle? Was it a bit of both and might this help explain the persistence of patriarchal power without a cross-class conspiracy thesis?

Can the political case for an autonomous women's movement be made adequately without reference to the power and interest differences between men and women, on the purely economic grounds that 'women's oppression is rooted in the capitalist family, which exists outside the sphere of commodity production'?[45]

The presumption that these kinds of questions can only arise from a position that denies or trivializes class exploitation is the basis of traditional Marxists' confusion of feminist radicalism with feminist reformism, and their dismissal of both as 'bourgeois feminism'. The political costs of this are high because it insulates Marxist theory and practice from the creative challenge of recent work by feminists. It has meant that the theoretical debate around class and gender is developing within feminist radicalism rather than also within Marxism.

The domestic labour debate, focused as it is on women's work, with its claims to analyse women's oppression, is well placed to acknowledge these questions and to open the dialogue between feminists and Marxists. Unfortunately, the false identity posed between women's oppression and domestic labour under capitalism leads to an acceptance of, rather than a challenge to, Marxist definitions which render feminist *radicalism* invisible and exclude its questions from Marxist dialogue.

This explains how it is that all but one of the authors in this volume can claim to deal theoretically with patriarchy and class without referring to the existing, well-developed feminist literature on the question. Seccombe, who is least guilty of claims to be analysing women's oppression in general, cites recent feminist historical, anthropological and philosophical work. Curtis joins him in referring to the recent Marxist-feminist collection of writings in political economy, *Feminism and Materialism: Women and Modes of Production*, edited by Annette Kuhn and AnnMarie Wolpe. Apart from this, reference to socialist and Marxist-feminist analysis is restricted to extremely early work: Margaret Benston's *The Political Economy of Women's Liberation* (1969); Mariarosa Dalla Costa's *Women, Subversion and the Community* (1972) and Sheila Rowbotham's *Women's Consciousness, Man's World* (1973). The *only* radical feminist work cited is Shulamith Firestone's *Dialectic of Sex* (1970). Even the classical article, 'Housework: Slavery or Labour of Love' (1970), in which the radical feminist, Betsy Warrior, developed the first analysis of domestic labour as producer of the commodity labour power, is overlooked.[46]

All the early articles cited are seminal works and deserve attention. But ten further years of theoretical writing in anthropology, history, psychology, sociology, philosophy as well as political economy have passed unacknowledged. There is no requirement for analysts of domestic labour to cite this literature, but when they claim to analyse gender oppression, its absence becomes a grave weakness. The weakness is especially evident in the Curtis and Blumenfeld and Mann articles which attempt a direct critique of feminist theory.

Many people, among them, I am sure, some of the contributors to this volume, would argue that any Marxist analysis must aim to be historical, dialectical and material and to bring together the political and the economic. This may, in fact, explain the persistent, unfounded claims to do this, made in the domestic labour debate by its participants. My purpose here, however, has not been to argue that writing on domestic labour *must* deal with the theoretical questions raised by the oppression of women and feminist analysis of that oppression. It is not the debate's economic analysis of domestic labour, but the fact that it presents the analysis as a theoretical treatment of gender and class, that dooms it to economism. Therefore, I would urge one of two courses on those working in the area: *either* they should develop a definition of their project which recognizes more realistically limited economic parameters and breaks with the claim to encompass the gender/class debate, *or* they should open the debate beyond its economic limits by defining parameters in ways that recognize the questions that feminists are raising. The debate would then move beyond itself to the extent that it could no longer be called 'the domestic labour debate'. It would be a major contribution to the initiation of an already too long delayed Marxist/feminist dialogue.

Never Done: The Struggle to Understand Domestic Labour and Women's Oppression

Bonnie Fox

I hesitate to write another word in 'the domestic labour debate'.[1] This hesitancy comes from a gut-level impatience with scholastic debates. The observable differences between women and men in terms of life circumstances (for example, position in the labour market, responsibilities in the home), privileges and personal power are blatant and large, and our collective understanding of their causes sufficient to make clear what must be fought for and against. So I wonder why we are writing: writing takes energy and time, which might better be used in the course of more concrete action.

Nevertheless, I write out of a conviction about the importance of theory. More specifically, I write out of a sense that there was merit in the domestic labour debate. On the one hand, I think that many of the powerful insights in that early writing are now part of feminist consciousness – and those early theorists never credited. All that we remember now is the theoretical errors of which the debaters were guilty. On the other hand (and this is important), there exists the tendency to dismiss all of the debate's insights as 'economist', and in so doing to avoid any structural analysis. Virtually the only theoretical analysis that escapes the sin of 'economism' is idealist in nature.[2]

What I have to say, then, is written with a desire not so much to take issue with the arguments of others, and thus sharpen the differences among positions, as to highlight some assessments that we might share as socialist-feminists, and thus to contribute to a collective understanding of women's oppression. Surely, radical feminists and Marxist-feminists seem to be converging towards that collective understanding – the former recognizing the importance of the capitalist context and the latter realizing the significance to women of issues of sexuality and other aspects of intimate male–female relations.

The Domestic Labour Debate

It seems to me that there were several minimal assumptions made by those who contributed to the domestic labour debate. While there were other assumptions – more specific and stringent – made by each contributor, it is these common assumptions that might yet be salvaged. First, it was assumed that in order to understand women's oppression it was essential initially to develop *theory*. It was assumed that appearances can mystify, and certainly confuse. It was assumed that, without theory, empirical study of the social relations and dynamics of family life, the processes at work in the labour market, the economic forces affecting the household, and changes over time in all of these areas of life would be directionless. (Most of us had worked through critiques of 'barefoot empiricism', otherwise known as 'positivism', which holds that social 'facts' speak for themselves.) That individuals are often not cognizant of , or at least understanding of, social structure and social forces was assumed, and this assumption contributed to the sense that there was a role to be played by theorists in the struggle for women's liberation.[3]

Secondly, there was the assumption that the family was the site of women's oppression. More specifically, though, the debate was premised on the materialist assumption that to understand women's oppression it was necessary – though (most knew) not sufficient – to understand women's household work. The debate endorsed Marx's assumption that work represents a basic form of self-expression, constituting a major part of people's lived experience and influences their psyches.

Thirdly, capitalism – the social and economic context in which we live – was assumed to be significant in structuring women's oppression. Marxists began their discussions of women with their theoretical understanding of capitalism not only because it provided a clear, well-worked-out analysis of exploitation and the dynamics of inequality, but also because they assumed that capitalism provided the structural context in which personal life was lived. Although 'patriarchy' became a popular concept only after much of the work on domestic labour was completed, most of the domestic-labour theorists might have agreed more specifically with the argument that the form that male dominance (or, more specifically, men's control over women's sexuality, fertility and labour) assumes is dependent upon the historical period, and current social structure – and thus that it assumes a particular form under capitalism.[4]

Despite the limitations of the domestic labour debate, some of its insights might be remembered. First, the importance of women's household work – the other half of the work done in this society – came to light (in terms of theoretical analysis and public discussion) with the early writers in this debate. The oppressiveness of household work was proclaimed by other feminist writers like Betty Friedan, but its significance – and the way in which it is significant – was pointed out by the Marxists and the radical feminists who attempted an analysis of domestic labour.

Secondly, the explicit aim of the domestic labour debate, and its most important contribution, was to come to an understanding of the relationship of the private household to capitalist commodity production. From Peggy Morton's argument that women's household work reproduced labour power, and Wally Seccombe's later formulations of the household's location between the commodity market (for the means of subsistence) and the labour market, came insights about the ways in which the larger economy acted upon the household.[5] And while the sexist dynamic characterizing the relationship between women and men in the family was not dealt with in the debate, the elaboration of the particular nature of women's household work implicitly and sometimes explicitly highlighted the fact that women are in a different material position than men, have different interests, and thus need autonomous political organization.

Indeed, the tendency towards scholasticism in the domestic labour debate (which we all remember) was offset, to some extent, by the fact that the political and strategic implications of an argument were always spelled out – a fact that distinguishes this debate from the more recent debate on 'sex and class'. Finally, one of the rewards of the domestic labour debate, though one that most of its contributors did not anticipate, was precisely to make clear the limits of a class analysis for understanding issues about gender. Without using the framework, we otherwise might not have known.

The limitations of the debate are more salient to us now than its contributions. In assessing women's oppression to be largely economic in nature, the debate turned attention away from the personal relations of sexuality and fertility, and away from the social construction of peoples' gendered psyches. In fact, because writers were concerned with the relationship of the household to the large economy, the interpersonal relations between women and men in the family were not typically discussed (although Margaret Coulson's, Branka Magas's, Hilary Wainwright's and Jean Gardiner's critiques of Seccombe raise this issue). Yet, it is often through these relationships that structural forces make themselves felt at the level of the individual. Thus, the implications of the positions being argued, in terms of stresses, constraints and general influences on personal relations, should have been better elaborated. At minimum, it would seem, the debate might have turned to the ways in which capitalism structures male–female relations in the home (for example, the effects of the privatization of personal life). But such discussion awaited empirical and descriptive studies, such as Luxton's (which makes some sense).

A related shortcoming of the domestic labour debate, it seems to me, was its scholastic nature – not in the sense that it was *abstract* so much as that it tended to confine itself to definitional matters, often without even clearly seeing the *theoretical* significance of a question being addressed. For example, the question whether women's household work is 'productive' or 'unproductive' of surplus value was often discussed for very confused reasons (for example, to determine whether or not the work was important, whether or not it primarily benefited capital). In fact, the answer to that question has implications in terms of the nature of the relationship of the household to capitalist production, the ways in which household work is shaped by forces coming from the larger economy, etc. Yet, little of the energy directed towards determining the answer to the question went to elaborating the implications of the different answers.

Finally, most of the early theorists argued that 'the family' exists because of the *functions* it performs for capital,[6] an assumption especially problematic in the implication that those functions are responsible for the origins of the family. Functionalist answers were thus provided to the following crucial questions. Is the privatized reproduction of labour power and consumption necessary for capitalist society? Why is privatized

domestic labour retained in an economy that normally com-
modifies work? Who benefits from this privatized work done by
women? Functionalist answers resulted from the method of
inquiry, which involved tracing the logic of the relation of the
household to the larger economy, without simultaneously tracing the lived history of this relation. That is, although questions
were raised that theory alone could not address, there was little
'testing' of the arguments against empirical reality.[7]

Of the domestic labour debate, Angela Miles writes that

> women's responsibility for domestic labour performed in the priva-
> tized household is the specific form in which women's oppression is
> institutionalized under capitalism. But to document this is not to deal
> with the question of *why* capitalist relations have developed in such a
> way as to ensure women's subordination to men. To illustrate that
> women's oppression takes specific forms under capitalism is not to
> prove that it is derivative.[8]

Most of the later contributors to the debate assumed only that
they were examining a key aspect of women's oppression –
though they can be accused of sloppiness (I include myself) in
implying that privatized domestic labour represented the sum
total of women's oppression. However, with only a few exceptions, for example, Bruce Curtis in *Hidden in the Household,* no
claims were made about investigating the *causes* of women's
oppression – why *women* do domestic labour, how the work
came to be both feminized and privatized, etc. The present form
of female subordination and its causes are clearly different
issues. The object of the domestic labour debate, surely, was to
understand a significant aspect of the total configuration of
forces and factors oppressing women today. This concern gave
rise to questions about the functional nature of household work
and whom it benefits. Answers to such questions are necessary in
order to approach the question of strategies for change. In fact, it
is to some extent irrelevant to the issue of change whether gender
inequality began with capitalism or not.

The Debate on Sex and Class

Aside from its economism, the major fault of the domestic
labour debate, according to most reviewers, was its failure to
question why *women* do domestic labour and, more broadly,

why women are oppressed. The more recent debate on 'sex and class' addresses those questions, by seeking the historical origins of the gender division of labour and the inequality associated with it, and also by questioning as Johanna Brenner and Marie Ramas put it, how 'capitalism perpetuates rather than under-mines gender divisions'. Both are central questions for feminists. Unfortunately, the reader is presented with an odd choice: Michèle Barrett's argument, on the one hand, underplays the importance of capitalism in bringing about gender inequality and also (problematically) presents an analysis of the daily perpetu-ation of women's oppression that is often idealist;[9] Brenner's and Ramas's argument, on the other hand, attempts a materialist analysis by arguing that biology determines social position.[10].

This too is a scholastic debate: the object, especially of Barrett's book, seems to be theoretical purity. While *Women's Oppression Today* stands as a very useful literature review, which takes on a range of difficult questions and deals with them in a considered way, its aim nevertheless seems to be to list all extant theoretical errors without offering an alternative argument. Having labelled as 'reductionist' arguments that emphasize the importance of one factor relative to others, Barrett avoids this sin by not presenting a very clear argument of her own. And while Brenner's and Ramas's advocacy of biological deter-minism can easily be refuted, some of their historical arguments are not only devoid of biological determinism, they also are quite convincing. I come away from this debate wondering if common ground cannot be found.

Barrett correctly distinguishes the privatization of the domestic sphere brought about in the development of capitalism from its perpetuation in capitalist societies today. In addressing the question of the origins of women's oppression, she argues that the gender division of labour took the form it did as capi-talism developed because of a prior ideology of gender which identified childcare as women's work. In turn, women's position in the labour market reflected the priority of their domestic responsibilities and also precapitalist ideological assumptions about wage levels appropriate to women and men (which dif-fered because of the perceived differences in the consumption requirements of the two sexes).

There is some question about the accuracy of Barrett's separation of the varied changes brought about as capitalism developed from the ideology of gender. The 'separate spheres'

ideology which attached women to domesticity, and also changing conceptions of childhood, seem to be related historically to
the privatization of the household as it lost its role as the chief
unit of production.[11] Moreover, if indeed the ideology about
gender pre-dated capitalism, then the question of its origins must
be addressed.

The point Barrett seems to be making is an important one,
however: the 'laws of motion' of capitalism are not 'sex blind'.
Consequently, it is no accident that women are systematically
paid less than men in the labour market and therefore represent a competitive threat to men. Aside from prior divisions
of labour by sex, the separation of home and workplace provides a structural context that puts women and men in different bargaining positions in the labour market. As well, at the
level of the individual actor, women and men had and have
different subjectivities and identities. Gender divisions were
and are thus structured into society, and the salience of gender
was and is etched into our psyches. Such an argument is hard
to dispute.

With respect to the current reprodiction of gender divisions
and inequalities, Barrett seeks to redress an economist emphasis
by arguing that 'ideology' plays a considerable role. In fact, she
gives ideology tremendous weight. But by 'ideology' she does not
appear to mean ideas, much less ideas that justify the status quo
(as is usually meant); she seems to mean people's psyches, their
subjectivity:

> The concept of ideology refers to those processes which have to do
> with consciousness, motive, emotionality; it can best be located in the
> category of *meaning*. Ideology is a generic term for the processes by
> which meaning is produced, challenged, reproduced, transformed.

At this point in the book, I expected a discussion of the
process of socialization, and the social construction of gendered
subjectivity, which involves the creation of the 'object of desire'
and is thus the site of the deployment of power (as Michel
Foucault has written). While Barrett mentions the production of
'gendered subjectivity that . . . can account for the desires of
women as well as men to reproduce the very familial structures
by which we are oppressed', her chapter on 'ideology and the
cultural production of gender' is about gender stereotyping in
the schools, the media and literature. She does not discuss the

consequences of these things for the personalities of women and men. Is Barrett, in the end, referring to *ideas* when she refers to 'ideology'?

Where Barrett is clearly idealist is in her brief mention of the socialization process:

> The point I am emphasizing here is that we can make a distinction between the construction of gender within *families*, and the social construction of gender within an *ideology of familialism*, and we can conclude that the latter formulation is the more accurate one . . . It is, therefore, in an *ideology* of family life, as distinct from concrete families, that gender identity and its meaning is reproduced. (My emphasis)[12]

While Brenner and Ramas purport to be attempting a biological-determinist argument, their discussion of the effects of capitalist development can easily be restated – and even in their own words often does not rely on biology. They point out that childrearing was women's work prior to capitalism (though they neglect the extent to which childrearing was 'socialized' in the sense that women often sent their babies to 'wet nurses' and their older children 'into service' in the households of other families).[13] In precapitalist households, motherwork accommodated itself to the demands of women's other work. When work moved out of the household with the growth of larger capitalist workplaces, and workers increasingly neither worked at home nor had control over their work, childcare assumed a different nature.

If Brenner and Ramas could have developed a different general argument, without altering their historical analysis, their work would not as easily be dismissed as it was in Barrett's reply. Specifically, their historical analysis follows from the argument that the social consequences of biological givens depend upon the social formation, or social context. So, for example, being female need not entail less privilege, greater handicap and less power in a society without class divisions and thus without barriers to access to the means of subsistence, as in foraging societies. Female sexuality will be subject to control by men (personally) or a male-dominated social order (via legislation, etc.) only if it represents a capacity that is valuable in some way to individual men or that is of concern to society. Childrearing is a burden when the work of acquiring subsistence is time-consuming, or when it precludes other activities, and when childrearing is privatized and becomes the responsibility of the individual woman.[14] Surely, it is social structure and not biology directly that ultimately is relevant.

Conclusion

At present, we have the beginnings of an understanding of women's oppression. Brenner and Ramas remind us that we must start to explain the position of women by assessing the social consequences of women's capacity to bear children. Certainly, the extent of, and forms of, control of women's sexuality and their fertility are major determinants of women's relative autonomy in any society. The domestic labour debate began a political-economic analysis of women's basic work in capitalist society. Hopefully, the critiques of that debate have not served to negate the significance of the economic and structural factors shaping women's lives. Barrett's book serves to prod us in the direction of considering as well the ideological processes affecting gender relations.

It seems to me that in terms of understanding women's oppression, questions both of social structure and of individual psychology (or 'ideology', as Barrett uses the word) await theoretical analysis and empirical investigation. In pursuing questions of social structure, whether they are historical and about the source of women's oppression, or political-economic and about factors perpetuating this oppression, the source, significance, and necessity of the privatization of the domestic sphere must be further analysed. Indeed, the history of the social construction of housework is not fully understood. We still do not know why so much of the labour involving the reproduction of daily life is privatized. We do not even fully understand why women so completely immersed themselves in domesticity in the 1950s and 1960s. And finally, we still do not know whether capitalism requires the privatization of personal life and the work that reproduces it.

At the level of the individual, however, there is another key issue. In several places in her book, Barrett refers to 'gendered subjectivity'. It seems to me that what is most lacking in our theorizing on women's oppression is an analysis of the very subtle processes through which our gendered sense of self is constructed. Social psychologists have outlined the different ways in which girls and boys are treated, from birth and by 'significant others'. They have been less clear about the effects on personality of sex-differentiated upbringing, perhaps because standard behaviourist research strategies and measures are not appropriate for discerning such subtle differences.[15]

Far more suggestive has been Nancy Chodorow's reinterpretation of the Freudian understanding of personality formation. That, fairly sociological, analysis has generated Lillian Rubin's insightful interpretation of female–male differences with respect to fears about and experiences of intimate relations, and has also produced explanations of men's hatred of women, leading to pornography and rape. Similarly Carol Gilligan's work on gender differences in reasoning about ethical problems is interesting and provocative.[16]

What requires analysis are the ways in which the construction of gendered subjectivity, and more precisely sexual desire for the opposite sex, build into people's psyches differential power in the form of personality characteristics.[17] We need to understand the emotional dynamics within intimate, and even casual, relationships and exchanges between women and men. We need to understand all of the implications of the fact that our identity, and subjectivity itself, are *gendered*. We need a feminist psychology, to complement our structural analysis of women's oppression.

Reflections on the Domestic Labour Debate and Prospects for Marxist-feminist Synthesis

Wally Seccombe

The domestic labour debate was, in its essentials, an attempt to generate Marxist answers to feminist questions.[1] The central feminist question concerned the unequal division of labour in modern marriage, where domestic labour remained stubbornly women's work, despite a massive increase in their work load outside the home. The Marxist answer attempted to specify the relation of domestic labour to wage labour for working-class households under capitalism.

Clearly, these problems are closely bound up with one another. But they are by no means interchangeable analytically, which was the basic problem with the answers we developed. To our credit, we went some way towards comprehending the special character of housework as a labour process, the reasons for its obscurity under capitalism, its indirect effects on patterns of capital accumulation (via its role in the daily and generational reproduction of labour power) and, most importantly, the forces shifting the proportions of paid and unpaid labour which house-hold members, as a group, perform in making ends meet. These were pertinent issues; they retain all of their relevance today. In this sense, the discussion is by no means surpassed, though it is now more empirically based, and the specific theoretical fixations of the initial phase are behind us, fortunately.

But the central question – why women continue to do the great bulk of domestic work, even as their involvement in wage labour increases – could not be answered within the discourse of value theory as constituted at the time. While we were highly critical (and rightly so) of the neo-classical model of the house-hold, with its unitary utility function, our own model of the household was not qualitatively superior. In both paradigms, the household was essentially a black box, responding to price trends in consumer and labour markets: a pooling-sharing unit with a single living standard, its adult members making joint decisions on how best to deploy their labour power to make ends meet. While the overall labour burden of the household was amenable to Marxist explanation, its unequal allocation between spouses was not.

The argument of this paper is that these two problematics need to be integrated. We cannot adequately grasp the dynamics of one without comprehending the other. I first want to reflect on the particular place of the domestic labour debate in Marxist-feminist discourse. With all of its weaknesses, our discussion countered tendencies to conceptual dualism embodied in *both* feminism and Marxism, pointing the way towards a more wholistic analysis. I shall then proceed to survey, very selectively, some interesting recent work in mainstream sociology and neo-classical economics which is of direct relevance to the project of synthesis outlined above. The first round of the domestic labour discussion suffered from the imperviousness of most contributors to pertinent bourgeois scholarship, an ignorance which was fully reciprocated by mainstream academics. There is simply no excuse for such intellectual parochialism; I should like to take this opportunity to rectify my own past omissions in this regard, by critically evaluating some empirical findings and alternative paradigms. Finally, I shall offer some tentative suggestions for integrating both sides of the labour market in a unified analysis of gender hierarchy.

I

Many feminists have accused contributors to the domestic labour debate of trying to cram women's reality into sex-blind Marxist categories. There was a certain validity to the charge, to the extent that authors endeavoured simply to apply pre-existing categories of Marxist political economy to private domestic labour without seriously rethinking these concepts from a feminist standpoint. A great deal of effort was devoted to establishing the complete fidelity of one's position to the value categories of *Capital*. Talmudic references were repeatedly made to 'what Marx really meant' in certain passages. The pivotal questions became taxonomic: did domestic labour create value; was it productive, unproductive, indirectly productive, or were these categories simply inapplicable to domestic labour? Huge quantities of ink were spilled over definitional issues. At least one contributor, Lise Vogel, is still convinced the debate was 'resolved' on this level: 'as it turned out, it was relatively easy to demonstrate that domestic labour in capitalist societies does not take the form of value-producing labour'.[2]

Surely the substantive issue is how such designations illuminate or obscure the concrete analysis of domestic labour. If the definition adopted, following Vogel's lead, insists on the disconnection of the domestic labour process from the value equilibration of wage labour, one wants to know at what level the analyst posits their connection and interaction. Do consumer goods and services purchased with a second wage eliminate some work from the home and raise the productivity of housework, thereby reducing the unpaid labour time necessary for subsistence? How far can this substitution proceed? Obversely, how far can an intensification of domestic labour compensate for a temporary decline in household income, maintaining living standards in a recession? Because these kinds of empirical questions, concerning trends in the distribution of paid and unpaid labour, were submerged as the taxonomic debate raged, the analytical utility of various schemes offered was not adequately scrutinized or tested. I am not denigrating the requisites of theoretical coherence or definitional precision, but when these considerations remain remote from the decisive test of concrete analysis, the discussion suffers from theoretical abstraction and dogmatism. These tendencies were all too evident in most contributions (including my own).

There was a second implication, however, in the common feminist assertion that women's domestic labour could not be adequately understood through the categories of Marxist value analysis. Many postulated, in effect, a family/economy dichotomy. Marxism was presumed to furnish an insightful analysis of the capitalist economy, while feminism shed a penetrating light on familial relations in private households. In this way, the conceptual tension of the Marxist-feminist encounter was 'resolved' by specialization in a division of labour – different theories and expertise for distinct spheres. But this strategy was a theoretical cul-de-sac, reinforcing the breach which the spatial separation of households from places of employment fosters under capitalism, instead of disclosing their underlying connections. The family/economy dichotomy hinders an analysis of the unequal sexual division of labour which occurs on both sides of the labour market.

In order to account adequately for male/female pay differentials and the sex segregation of occupations, for example, we require a theory of domestic patriarchy which can explain why the labour force participation of wives is subordinated to their husbands, disrupting their employment careers and weakening their bargaining power in the labour market. Conversely, in order to explain the peculiar power and persistence of the male breadwinner wage norm, we require Marxist insight into the fetishism of the wage form, and the property prerogatives accruing to proletarian men as its primary possessors.[3]

From a theoretical standpoint, households should be included in a conceptualization of the capitalist economy; not merely as sites of consumption, but also as production units generating labour power from one day and from one generation to the next. Secondly, households as economic units and families as kin groups should not be theoretically disjoined. Distinguished, yes; separated, not. The household/family distinction, now commonplace, was not systematically employed in the domestic labour discussion, to our detriment. This imprecision permitted the persistent conflation of the two problematics mentioned at the outset, since feminists were primarily concerned with family relations while Marxists focused on households as economic units. In treating households as part of the economy, and taking their unpaid labour contribution seriously, we at least bridged the divide between paid and unpaid work, conceiving of their interaction in a wholistic framework. It was much more important to grapple seriously with their interaction than it was to insist endlessly on their 'specificity' and 'relative autonomy'.

Readers will recognize here the Althusserian terminology which gave rise to a parallel pressure towards conceptual dualism from the Marxist side, by means of the base/superstructure metaphor. In Althusser's paradigm, the antidote for economic determinism (by common consent, the original sin of classical Marxism), became an insistence on the relative autonomy of superstructures.[4] While emphasizing the endogenous dynamics of other realms, this conception left intact the old tunnel vision of the capitalist economy, riveted narrowly on private firms and their markets. Households were peripheral in this perspective, of marginal concern. Neither their internal labour process nor their influence in economic change (above all, in shaping labour supply) had been addressed by Marxists. Althusser's response was to treat the family as a superstructural institution −'an ideological state apparatus'.[5]

Since the Althusserian paradigm is now *passé*, it is easy to forget the pervasive influence of these conceptions in western Marxism in the early 1970s, as the domestic labour debate unfolded. Yet our discussion entailed, even if we were not fully aware of it, a major challenge to the entire base/superstructure framework as it was then conceived. The paradox of our rather laboured attempt to eleborate positions with strict fidelity to Marx's *Capital* was that we obscured the far-reaching challenge the entire discussion presented to Marxist orthodoxy. I confidently asserted, for example, that it was simply a matter of filling in an area of Marx's original canvas that had been left blank: 'in *Capital* Marx laid out a framework within which domestic labour clearly fits'. But the fit was not so clear cut, as we were to discover.[6]

In addition to stretching the value categories of Marxist economics, we were also challenging the standard view of capitalism as a mode of production. It took me some time to realize this. Were the private households of the bourgeoisie and the proletariat an integral part of the capitalist mode itself? Was it necessary for proletarians to live apart from capital, performing an unpaid labour of daily maintenance, for the commodity form of labour power to fully develop, and monetary wages to become the general means of funding subsistence? My answer to these questions was yes, and so I went on to rework and expand the mode of production concept to include the social relations of labour power's production as an integral facet of all modes.[7] Other contributors opted for a subsidiary domestic mode of production under capitalism.[8] In either case, these theoretical innovations promised to redraw the Marxist map of capitalist social formations in fundamental ways.

By striving to integrate the analysis of private households with capitalist production, paid and unpaid labour, the discourses of kinship and political economy, we were challenging dualist conceptions on either side of the Marxist-feminist hyphen. In my view, this was the most positive consequence of the entire debate. It helped open the way toward a more integrated perspective, where the real divide which capitalism fosters between private households and the sphere of employment would be analytically bridged.

But even where the connection was made, two distinct problematics remained. While there have not been decisive breakthroughs on either front in the past decade, advances have none the less been considerable. Much of it has been descriptive and empirical (a dimension sadly lacking in the debate itself), but there has also been progress in the theoretical modelling of casual dynamics. I want now to consider some of the most promising developments. I shall then conclude this survey by making some provisional proposals for integrating these two perspectives.

II

The dogmatic form of most contributions to the domestic labour discussion was manifest in their sectarian insularity. Throughout the 1970s, in the same years that the debate raged, progress was being made by scholars in at least three areas of relevance to our concerns.

1. There was a spate of empirical studies by sociologists on the marital division of labour and on the daily time allocations of family members. Through surveys conducted in several developed capitalist countries, this research shed international light on strikingly similar patterns of spousal inequality in the context of joint subsistence.

2. Heretics in neo-classical micro-economics were revising standard models of household dynamics, of consumption 'tastes' and labour supply 'preferences', proposing alterations which made them much more realistic and interesting. Labour supply was now conceived from the standpoint of human capital theory, which mirrored many concerns of Marxist discussion of the valorization of labour power, despite vast conceptual differences.

3. A wide-ranging discussion burgeoned on persistent male/female pay differentials and the sex segregation of the labour force, on dual labour markets and the rationality or irrationality of employer discrimination, challenging standard neo-classical conceptions of the labour market. What is particularly relevant to a materialist theory of patriarchy and the reproduction of gender inequality, is the ongoing attempt to sort out cause and effect relations between supply side factors (this is, domestic

division of labour) and employer demand (segregated hiring and promotion). Let us consider each of these areas in turn.

What we take to be the 'traditional' male breadwinner/female homemaker division of labour within marriage was not simply a residual product of our pre-industrial past. It assumed its modern proletarian form in the nineteenth century, as industrial capitalism matured. In the eighteenth century, as wage work became the dominant form of labour, employment for married women was welcome. In Britain, for example, it was widely remarked that no working man would consider marrying a woman who was economically dependent.[9] But by the late Victorian era, the family wage norm had been decisively reversed. A woman's place was in the home; her husband was something of a disgrace as a breadwinner if she had to go out to work.[10] In the typical working-class home, a husband's principal duty was to hold his job on a steady basis and bring his pay home reliably. Having done that, he claimed general exemption from housework, meal preparation and childcare. His wife managed the household day-to-day finances and did virtually all of the unpaid work, with the help of an elder daughter if she were lucky. A husband's domestic participation was exceptional: he might 'help out' when she was sick or confined to be with a new-born, or 'fill in' if she were unavoidably absent from the home. Beyond that, he regarded his home as a place of rest and relaxation.

In modern households, whenever women remain exclusively homemakers, this traditional division of labour prevails. Men typically do very little regular work around the house except for a few 'masculine' jobs – garden work, house and car repairs, perhaps removing the garbage and occasionally washing some dishes. They may also do light childminding for short periods where their spouses are absent, and some shopping. But that is it; they do, on average, around one and a half hours of unpaid work a day. What is remarkable is the *consistency* of this finding in developed capitalist countries with vastly different cultures and welfare state structures.[11] Wives do virtually all the rest, working on average seven hours a day. The contribution of children, both around the house and through regular employment and wage remission, has steadily declined in the twentieth century.

The total time homemakers spend in all facets of domestic work does not appear to have diminished much, if at all, in this century. As particular tasks eased, standards were raised. Wash time was cut in half, but now the linen 'needed cleaning' twice as often.[12] But two changes have made a world of difference, enabling married women *en masse* to increase their participation in paid work. First, vast improvements in urban residential infrastructure, together with new household technologies, have made various domestic jobs – clothes washing, cooking, house cleaning – much less physically arduous and hazardous than they were a century ago. Secondly, the steep decline in fertility, beginning late in the nineteenth century, has shortened women's reproductive years by about two-thirds, dramatically abbreviating the phase of infant care and early childrearing. In addition, childbearing has become much safer, and women's health has improved. Longer life expectancy has extended the empty-nest life-phase, making it possible for women to resume employment who had ceased paid work to remain at home when their children were young. The maternal investment in each child's care has increased considerably in the child-centred modern family. But viewed across the life-course, women's overall burden in childbearing, infant care and childrearing has undoubtedly been alleviated very considerably in this century.

It is perhaps not surprising that modern men do very little work around the house when their wives remain full-time homemakers. But what happens when the latter go out to work, as they increasingly have in the past forty years? The finding of study upon study, in one western country after another, is that husbands do not increase their domestic contribution at all, or do so very marginally, around the edges of women's core tasks.[13] In the meantime, women's total work load increases as they take jobs and extend their hours in employment. Their domestic work does decline quite considerably on workdays, cutting unpaid labour time almost in half, though some of this is made up on the weekends.[14] But this very real reduction (facilitated by the goods and services a second wage can purchase, some of which will raise domestic productivity) does not nearly offset the time consumed in employment. The double day of labour, with its scheduling conflicts and harried travel back and forth from home to work, adds additional stress to the increase in women's necessary labour time. In addition to these domestic inequalities, the increase in women's paid work has been accompanied by a decrease in the labour force participation rate of adult men, particularly those over fifty years.

Considering all of the above mentioned factors, we arrive at a disconcerting but inescapable conclusion: the overall distribution of labour in marriage has become *more unequal* in the post-war period. Whether we calculate this distribution on a daily or weekly basis (where the shift is modest), or more adequately on a lifetime basis (where the deterioration is apparently severe), the evidence is umambiguous. Despite the rise of feminism and positive changes in mass consciousness concerning women's rights, women's position has nevertheless regressed in this *fundamental* aspect of gender relations.

Most of the studies cited above were conducted in the 1970s. Is it possible that matters have improved since them? Perhaps as women's independent incomes and employment experience strengthen their marital bargaining power, the traditional patriarchal exemption from housework and childcare will erode, as the rest of the male breadwinner edifice crumbles. There is encouraging evidence from a 1983 study of steelworker families in Hamilton, Ontario of a trend to increased male participation in childcare and meal preparation, as wives obtain outside jobs.[15] This shift is interesting, particularly since blue-collar men are often reputed to be relatively backward on gender issues by comparison with their white-collar brethren. But the change is none the less modest.

I would venture to guess that the measurable deterioration in the marital division of labour in the post-war years may have been halted in the eighties and perhaps even marginally reversed. But this could easily be the wishful thinking of an eternal optimist. We *do* know that married women are now less stigmatized as wage workers than they formerly were, and feel less guilty about 'abandoning the family'.[16] These ideological shifts should enable women to put more pressure on their spouses to do more work, and take more responsibility, around the house.[17]

III

Neo-classical modelling of the household is based on a set of premises which are axiomatic in standard micro-economic analysis: that people are interested in defending and advancing their own well-being (utility maximization); they have stable preferences in this regard and make rational choices in the pursuit of their interests within a set of externally imposed constraints. In the case of households, these assumptions are normally applied to the unit (which therefore has a single utility function), implying that the household's members have common interests and make joint decisions as an income-pooling, goods-sharing group.

Since I am here concerned with recent work which radically revises this set of premises, I should perhaps begin by identifying what I regard as the valid kernel of the entire approach. This core must be extracted and reworked if a Marxist-feminist alternative is to be fashioned. In doing so, I part company with many contributors to the domestic labour debate.

The premise of utility maximizing behaviour can, and must, be accepted, *provided* we differentiate (as most neo-classical analysts do not) profit maximizing drives and accumulative behaviour from subsistence optimizing objectives and comfort and security related activities. Proletarian households possess no income generating property, subsist almost entirely by means of wage income, and are normally in no position to accumulate capital. They work to subsist, however comfortably, and are in a fundamentally different position than bourgeois households, with a different set of drives and constraints. It is therefore fallacious to speak of the value of labour power in terms of 'human capital', since the terminology effaces this difference. But we may none the less appreciate powerful insights which have been developed within the latter paradigm.[18] We make an analogous statement in asserting that proletarian households strive to maximize the aggregate exchange value of their labour power on the market and its use value in unpaid household production. This imperative operates at the level of bedrock subsistence, but also above that, as Marx recognized when he wrote that 'the number and extent of [the labourer's] so-called necessary wants, as also the modes of satisfying them, are themselves the product of historical development and depend to a great degree on . . . the habits and degrees of comfort in which the class of free labourers has been formed'. Hence he included a 'historical and moral element' in the value of labour power.[19] We may wish to relax the assumption that cultural preferences hold stable in the constitution of proletarian living standards; but this will depend on the time frame of the analysis. As long as the development of new needs occurs in a predictable fashion as living standards rise, the problem of evolving preferences will not be an insurmountable one for household modelling.

The persistent operation of rational choice among a limited set of options (with time and income constraints) is also a valid and necessary premise in comprehending the never-ending struggle of working-class households to make ends meet. We need not assume, as most neo-classical analysts do, perfect certainty and perfect information at the service of rational decision-making. Risk and incomplete information can be introduced; rational expectation models of market behaviour would seem to hold promise in this regard.

The informal decision-making process of domestic optimizers cannot be adequately conceived in frameworks developed to reflect profit maximizing firms, where executives are guided by market research, cost accounting, measures of productivity and the unambiguous verdict of the bottom line – profit and loss. On the other hand, households are much smaller units than firms, the results of their market decisions and labour practices are often immediately apparent, and living standards are a reasonably sensitive barometer of the results of their efforts under a given set of conditions. Working-class households are under fairly continuous pressure to secure a stable wage income and to stretch it as far as possible by means of careful budgeting, comparative shopping and diligent housework. Furthermore, they are in a competitive position in relation to one another as sellers of labour power in what is normally a buyers' market; they are subject to an implacable market discipline. Relatively inefficient practices at home or at the workplace redound to the material detriment of the coresident group. Those contributors to the domestic labour debate who insisted that value theory did not apply to household production were, in effect, denying the reality of competitive market discipline.

IV

There are two massive deficiencies in standard neo-classical models of the household. Both have been addressed in the past decade and alternatives proposed. These revised models are much more attractive from a Marxist-feminist standpoint. First, in orthodox models employment trades off against leisure time, generating an indifference curve, where the attractions of extra income and leisure balance out. (Leisure is here being treated as a 'normal good', with 'opportunity costs' for foregone income.) All waking hours outside market work are treated as leisure time; unpaid domestic labour simply disappears. Neo-classical theorists insist that 'for most purposes, this neglect will not harm the end-result', which only demonstrates how remote their analytical purposes are from women's interests![20]

While the problem of lumping together 'non-market work' and leisure has long been recognized, domestic labour was initially treated, in a fairly trivial way, as an indirect consumption cost (making goods requiring additional labour to consume, less desirable than a fully furnished service, all else being equal). In the past decade however, unpaid work has begun to be conceived as integral to a 'household production function', recasting the utility paradigm from the consumption to the production side.[21] Since the same domestic activities constitute *both* consumption (of wage goods) *and* production (of labour power), it is valid to conceive of them either way. Yet the foregrounding of the production perspective is particularly valuable for our purposes, in addressing domestic labour and the supply of family labour power to the market.

With this conceptual innovation came the capacity to model alternative uses of non-market time allocated to leisure and to *different kinds* of household tasks and responsibilities.[22] This permits an engagement with empirical studies which subdivide the total domestic burden into distinct areas, analysing its redistribution with changes in household technology and the prevailing mix of consumer goods and services. Most importantly, it enables us identify strongly sex-typed preferences in men's and women's unpaid work.

The second deficiency in standard neo-classical models is the way a unitary utility function is conceived for the household. The assumption that family households (leaving aside more temporary cohabitants) are income-pooling work-sharing and joint consumption groups remains a valid and important one. Subsistence optimizing and joint decision-making *do* occur at the level of the household. It is precisely 'for the sake of the family' *as a group* that women's interests are typically subordinated. But this unity must not be taken to imply internal harmony, completely aligned interests, nor an equality between spouses of workload and benefits.[23] As mentioned, the evidence points to persistent inequalities in labour burden, leisure, property ownership, pension provision and decision-making prerogative – all to the wife's detriment. Any paradigm of the family economy which is both realistic and feminist must surely register this power disparity and divergent interest in its basic premises. The trick is to do this without abandoning the unitary household in favour of two independent utility functions.

The most interesting models advanced thus far accomplish this integration by conceiving of unequal bargaining power between spouses within a framework of joint decision-making.[24] A couple's decision for the wife to seek employment will raise their household's living standard, while increasing her total work load. It becomes rational from her standpoint, as well as her household's, in so far as her own income will strengthen her bargaining power with her husband. Anticipating precisely this result, he may oppose the move, even though additional income would raise his living standard. Bargaining power becomes a sought after 'good', to be valued, weighed and traded off against other goods in the overall disposition of the household's resources. Where other goods may be shared, power is individuated, a zero-sum equation. This innovation moves household models beyond the pursuit of goods and services narrowly conceived. Power, as we know, has its uses and material benefits. People are prepared to make sacrifices to obtain and retain it in the intimate confines of the nuclear family, just as they are elsewhere. With bargaining models, we can speak of a *political* economy of the household. Patriarchy comes in from the ideological cold, finding a material home.

V

There is now a massive literature documenting the pervasive sex segregation of the labour force in the developed capitalist world.[25] Despite considerable variation in the overall rate of women's labour force participation, in every Western country they are crowded into certain occupations, while being virtually absent or grossly underrepresented in most others. The sex-typing of this distribution is evident; women are concentrated in jobs which replicate some aspect of their traditional domestic labour (as teachers, nurses, waitresses, secretaries, cleaners, textile and dressmakers and so on).[26] In a minority of occupations, women and men are represented in rough proportion to their overall numbers in the labour force. On closer inspection, however, we find, almost invariably, that they are strongly clustered within the occupation according to sex-typed job descriptions and hierarchies of authority. The finer grained our analysis becomes, the higher level of segregation we find. Men and women rarely work side by side as co-workers of equal status in the same unit.

De facto employment segregation has proven to be remarkably resistant to legal initiative prohibiting ascriptive discrimination in hiring and promotion. The market concept of equal opportunity is juridically toothless. Statistical measures of segregation (that is, the index of dissimilarity) when calculated over time reveal flux and gender switching in particular sectors, while in aggregate terms the general pattern remains stubbornly intact. The index of dissimilarity has declined only marginally in the last three decades, despite the entry of women into the labour force in massive numbers. The stability of pay differentials over the same period is also notable; clearly the two phenomena are intimately linked. It appears that the only way to reduce the wage gap is to break down the sex segregation of better paying occupations. Affirmative action holds the key to equal pay.

In endeavouring to account for the persistence of these patterns, many economists have argued for the existence of a dual labour market.[27] Primary markets group desirable jobs with relatively high pay, reasonably safe and comfortable working conditions, on-the-job training and opportunities for advancement. These jobs are overwhelmingly attained by men (whites, long-time residents, etc.), through selective hiring in the first place, but even more importantly through subsequent processes internal to the firm, involving job reclassification, personnel allocation and promotion. Secondary labour markets group noxious dead-end jobs at low pay, with little or no on-the-job training nor opportunities for advancement. Not surprisingly, secondary labour markets, where women, blacks, immigrants, etc., tend to cluster, experience much more rapid labour turnover, due to frequent lay-offs and high leaving rates. The proponents of the dual labour market thesis argue that high turnover is due to the dead-end nature of the jobs, not to the personal characteristics of their incumbents.[28] Human capital theorists, by contrast, maintain that women have a lesser attachment to the labour force than men, due to the primacy of their family duties, and thus end up in inferior sectors of the labour force.

Evidence of pervasive sex segregation in the labour force establishes a solid case that separation or streaming is fostered and sustained through hiring selection, job allocation and promotion procedures. Certainly there is evidence that women apply for desirable high paying jobs, and increasingly they have comparable educational qualifications to men. The real question then is *why* this stratification occurs.

VI

With this question we have come full circle, returning to the original issue of the interplay between the domestic division of labour and sex segregation in the labour force. Consider two polar explanations, a labour supply and an employer demand thesis, where the cause and effect relation between the two sites is reversed. The argument will be formally similar in each case: an endogenous rationale for women's subordination within a particular division of labour is developed, involving a fundamental power drive as what is taken to be the primary site. Once this inequality is established, gender hierarchy at the second site is postulated as an effect of the first, mediated by the labour market.

The *labour supply thesis* argues that the patriarchal assertion of men as primary breadwinners and women as homemakers is decisive. This domestic arrangement undermines women's participation in the labour force, they become second class participants in it. The argument proceeds by identifying a male power interest within marriage in maintaining men's primacy as wage earners. A bundle of prerogatives accrues to the possessor of the family's main pay cheque: an independent source of spending money, homeownership, pension security in old age, exemption from domestic labour and thus greater leisure time, and (the bottom line in cases of severe conflict) a more plausible threat to leave, on the basis of the spouse's economic vulnerability. As long as women remain financially dependent within marriage, their bargaining power is bound to be weak, as they will be impoverished by separation and divorce.

In this perspective, women's inferior position in the labour force is basically derived from their domestic subordination, their specialization as unpaid homemakers and family caregivers. Their disadvantage works in several ways: women's labour market range is circumscribed by residential location, based on spouses' workplace; women's working hours must fit with their husbands' and childrens' schedules, so they can prepare meals, care for the children, etc. For these reasons, women are more inclined to take part-time work at places of employment close to home, in order to cope with the double day of labour. During their childbearing years, when their earning power would otherwise be at its peak, childcare responsibilities often remove women from the labour force altogether, though this has diminished in the 1980s. At the very least, childcare duties curtail women's availability for many kinds of employment. These constraints result in a much more discontinous employment experience than men. Each interruption proves costly to women's life-time earning curve (loss of seniority, lesser opportunities for retraining programmes, skill upgrading and on-the-job training). Subsidized in part by their husbands' wage, married women have lower wage thresholds than men; they will accept jobs the latter refuse, for their wages are supplementary in family budgets. (This is not to say that wives work for 'pin money', or for purely discretionary income. Yet the effects of a husband's income in lowering his wife's 'reservation wage' (minimum threshold) must be openly acknowledged.[29])

Recognizing these patterns, employers take advantage of them. They 'statistically discriminate', slotting both single and married women into inferior jobs, without bothering to learn more about their individual family circumstances. Most single women, they reason, will soon marry, quitting to become mothers and homemakers. There is nothing to be gained by training or promoting them. In the anonymity of the labour market, such gross generalizations are valid as probabilities. Personnel officers rely on aggregate trends in forming hiring and promotion guidelines: the practice is certainly sexist, but it is not irrational. Women's labour supply patterns still remain substantially different than men's, due primarily to the division of labour in marriage.

Having moved from the household to the labour market, we now reverse the optic, considering an employer demand model, where causal forces flow the other way. The fundamental thesis here is that discrimination is profitable under most circumstances, and hence is rational conduct for profit maximizers. They may or may not be sexists, but if they pursue their primary interest in cost cutting and raising labour productivity, they will segregate their labour force, and discriminate by paying women, crowded into predominantly female occupations, as little as the market will bear. By sex streaming in hiring, promotion and in the organization of work teams, managers capitalize on gender hierarchy at large , building it into the authority relations of their firms. Segregating co-workers by sex, reduces sexual diversions and tension, while promoting the age-old tactic of divide and conquer, making it unlikely that the workers will be able to set aside petty hierarchies to unite against management. Placing men in authority over women, managers take advantage of prevailing patterns of deference in society, and by ensuring a 'natural' chain of command, raise the overall productivity of their workforces. Since men do not take direction well from women, nor work with enthusiasm under their supervision, an employer who promoted women in a non-discriminatory way would be acting against his interest as a profit maximizer. Fairness simply does not pay; *all* the basic social divisions and hierarchies which society fosters must be exploited to the hilt. Horizontal segmentation sponsors a calmer, more docile workforce; vertical lines of authority work best when they run along paths of least cultural resistance.

Once pervasive inequality is concealed in the labour force, it conditions the division of labour in wage-earning households.[30] Male/female pay differentials make it rational from a couple's standpoint to prioritize his employment career over hers. When childcare is required at home, it is more economical for the household *as a unit* if the wife quits work while he retains his present job and seniority, seeks a raise and promotion, or elects to move so that he may pursue better employment opportunities elsewhere. As an optimizing subsistence strategy at the household level, it makes economic sense (however inequitable it is from the woman's independant standpoint), for the wife to specialize in homemaking and childcare, while the husband, with a much higher earning power, specializes in wage work. If wage discrimination profits capitalists in employment, then it is bound to engender a market recognition of this reality among proletarian couples who must manage the awkward combination of paid and unpaid work in the allocation of their labour power.

The foregoing are two apparently polar explanations for the interrelation of gender inequality at home and in the paid labour force. The first (supply side) model identifies domestic patriarchy as the lynchpin of gender inequality, operating in the interest of male breadwinners. The second (demand side) model identifies the profit drive, having harnessed gender divisions historically, perpetuating domestic inequality.

I see no compelling reason to choose, once and for all, between these models. Elements of both of them may be combined by postulating forms of reciprocal reinforcement. Thus far, the statistical evidence is mixed; it is often difficult with the synchronic data sets employed in most studies to move with assurance beyond noting correlations to disentangling complex cause and effect patterns. Certainly Marxist-feminists will be ideologically disposed to postulate the synthetic combination of these models. But dispositions and untested grand theories are not enough; nor is there any *a priori* reason why social forces must be 'balanced' in a multicausal model. Both of these simpler unicausal models should be experimentally pushed as far as possible, in engagement with empirical materials, in order to discern what patterns each explains well, and where they fall down. These kinds of investigations can lay the groundwork for the construction of more complex, multi-dimensional models. There is a great deal to be gained in this regard, by extracting and reworking insights from 'malestream' sociology and neo-classical economics.

Beyond Sexless Class and Classless Sex: Towards Feminist Marxism

Pat Armstrong and Hugh Armstrong

There can be little doubt that Marxism has been and continues to be, as Heidi Hartmann puts it,[1] sex-blind. But this paper is not an attack on discrimination in political economy or an appeal to pay more attention to women's issues. Rather it argues that Marxism must recognize that sex differences are integral to all levels of theory and analysis. The issue is not 'women's questions' or 'the question of women' but the efficacy of an analytical framework which fails to recognize or explain how and why sex differences pervade every aspect of human activity.

Building on and profiting from a wide range of feminist and Marxist analysis, the paper suggests ways to move beyond the classless sex of much feminist writing, and sexless class of most Marxist work, to a political economy that recognizes sexual divisions as integral to theoretical development. Sex differences were hardly a central concern for the 'fathers' of political economy, yet the analytical tools developed by Marx and Engels can help us explore the social construction of the fundamental divisions between men and women.

The domestic labour debate, out of fashion in recent years, did attempt to extend Marxist analysis, in order to apply it to the question of women. Not surprisingly, given their pioneering nature, these early efforts were fraught with difficulties. Often mechanical, functionalist and undialectical in trying to relate women to the capitalist production process, these applications sometimes distorted Marxist categories to the point of uselessness. Biological differences were rarely discussed; resistance seldom recognized; ideology frequently ignored. Nevertheless, by focusing on the historical development of the work which takes place outside the market and on the contribution of this labour to the accumulation process, the debate has exposed many of the mechanisms which divide the sexes and subordinate women. It has established the pervasiveness of sex segregation in all kinds of labour and the significance of work in the home for the daily and generational reproduction of free wage labourers. It has shown how market conditions to a large extent shape and are in turn shaped by domestic work. Unfortunately this crucial theoretical work seems to be largely invisible to much of political economy.

This paper suggests ways to move towards a political economy that is sex conscious as well as class conscious – towards a feminism that is class conscious as well as sex conscious. Our purpose is to argue that sex divisions should be considered at all levels of analysis and to suggest that theoretical efforts should focus on developing an analysis of class that recognizes the fundamental cleavages based on sex and on an analysis of biology that is historical, materialist and dialectical.

Marxist Analytical Tools

Our starting point is – to use C. Wright Mills's term – that of plain Marxists.[2] We seek to work within Marx's own tradition, which requires that we avoid treating his writing as a holy writ through which to search for the correct answers. The danger of creating a vulgar or dogmatic Marxism is nowhere more apparent than in analysing the position of women. Marx and Engels, most Marxists would agree, did not say much about women, and what they did say is not always useful or illuminating both because they concentrated on explaining capitalist production and because they reflected the particular male bias of their historical period. As Juliet Mitchell puts it,[3] 'Raking around in the texts of the master under the heading "women" is enough to convince the most loyal Marxist that the founder was a male chauvinist *par excellence*'. But Mitchell goes on to say that it is a ridiculous task to search through Marx for a complete explanation of the situation of women, ridiculous because historical materialism is an approach, a method of analysis.

For us, it is a method that is materialist, dialectical and historical. By materialist, we understand an approach that posits the existence of a real material world, one which conditions the social, political and intellectual processes in general. At the same time, we seek to distance ourselves from the economic determinism that pervades so much of orthodox Marxism and that has so frequently and justifiably been attacked by (among others) feminists of all persuasions. The ways people co-operate to provide for their daily and future needs, combined with the techniques and materials at their disposal, establish the framework within which all human activity takes place. This does not mean that everything can be reduced to or is determined by matter; nor does it imply that ideas are irrelevant, false or the mere products of material conditions. Central to dialectical materialism is the rejection of a false dichotomy between ideas and reality; indeed, of all such separations. Their very relatedness is central to the framework.

Marx of course went far beyond the call to begin with an analysis of material conditions. He exposed how capitalism became dominant, and isolated its motivating force, accumulation. In the insatiable drive for capitalist accumulation, more and more goods and services are bought and sold. Labour power, or the capacity to work, is itself increasingly transformed into a commodity, as more and more people are separated from alternative means of providing for their basic needs and have to rely increasingly on the purchase of wage goods. Because Marx understood that the commodity production process establishes the broad framework for any capitalist society, he initially focused on how this production process works. He, like the capitalists, left the reproduction of workers largely to themselves. But free wage labour, which is essential to the very definition of capitalism, entails the reproduction of labour power primarily at another location. This separation under capitalism between commodity production and human reproduction (including the reproduction of the commodity labour power) in turn implies a particular division of labour between the sexes, and thus a division within classes. It is a division that pervades all work, whether productive of surplus or not, and one which is fundamental to the understanding of how the capitalist production system operates at all levels of abstraction and of how and under what conditions people will rebel.

Two related points following from this line of argumentation need to be underlined. First, by agreeing with Marx to assign pride of place under capitalism to the commodity production process – to the process by which surplus value is produced and appropriated – we distinguish ourselves from those who advocate a dual-systems approach, with structures of patriarchy assuming a weight equal to, or at least an independence from, those of capitalism. While acknowledging that the subordination of women predates capitalism, we find that the term patriarchy tends to conceal more than it reveals about the many forms of this subordination. More light can be shed on the subordination of women by understanding it as inherent to the capitalist mode.

This leads to the second point, which is that we are able to use Marx's approach in moving beyond his sex-blind position. It is precisely by accepting his argument on the primacy of commodity production that we gain further insight into the subordination of women in capitalist society. We are not being reductionist or more specifically economistic to insist that wage labour is distinct from domestic labour. The logic of the capitalist accumulation process has made them distinct. Furthermore, it is capital, not (faulty) Marxist analysis, that has devalued the domestic labour which is performed normally by women, and which in turn conditions their participation in wage labour.

At the same time, we should of course avoid being carried away by the apparently compelling logic of the system. Marxist analysis is not simply materialist; it is dialectical and historical as well. Just as 'materialism' has a double meaning – that there is a real world and that material conditions establish the framework for any society – so too is 'dialectical' used in two senses. For Marx, every system produces contradictions at all levels. Not only are capital and labour in constant conflict, but in the process of attempting to cope with this conflict, new contradictions are constantly being created, combated and partially resolved, generating even more contradictions. At the same time, the term dialectical can also mean that social processes and social relations are in themselves contradictory. Seccombe provides an example by arguing that 'Although the proletarian condition is formally an open one, the great mass of the class cannot escape its class position even though, as individuals, they are free to try.'[4] Similarly, wage labourers are freely compelled under capitalism to sell their ability to work to an employer. So too are women freely compelled to marry and to have children, and thus to do domestic work and, under certain conditions and within certain limits, labour force work as well.

With his eyes fixed too firmly on the commodity production process, Marx was unable to incorporate the conflicts between women and men, and between households and capital, into his dialectical analysis. Nor was he able to perceive the contradictions facing women, who often cannot be full participants in capitalist society unless they are wives and mothers, and cannot often be full participants if they are. His view of contradiction, and thus of struggle, was partial and flawed. While the working class may or may not be differentiated by race, ethnicity, religion, occupation, industry or whatever, it is invariably differentiated by sex. It is perhaps not accidental that for Marx, it is *men* who make their own history, albeit not under conditions of their own choosing. The standard worker was for him at best sexless, at worst always male. As a result, the orthodox Marxist view of class struggle is vitiated by the failure to recognize that the working class has two sexes, a failure which hinders the understanding of men, much less of women.

The recognition that the working class has two sexes need not be the grounds for pessimism about the working class as revolutionary agent. After all, the working-class household can be an expression of unity as well as of tension between the sexes. More importantly, the seeds of pessimism are sown above all by failure, and an aspect of any successful working-class struggle to create itself is that it must become conscious of itself – a development which entails taking into account its own contradictions. Ignorance is not bliss, at least not for long. So the fact that sex differences cannot be eliminated by an effort of will is of tremendous strategic importance. We can agree with Marxism that the subordination of women is certain to continue as long as capitalism continues. We would add that the demise of the capitalist accumulation process will not necessarily mean an end to the subordination of women, and further that, if the revolutionary project is limited to the elimination of this process, it is unlikely to attract many women to its banner. Nor should it. The strategic point then, is to stretch dialectical analysis to make it a better tool for understanding and changing reality, for men as well as for women, for women as well as for men.

All these material conditions, contradictions and struggles have a history. In insisting on historical development, Marx was emphasizing the social construction of reality at the same time as he was drawing attention to the wide range of possibilities that exist within any particular mode of production and within any social formation. Where the capitalist mode is dominant, it transforms all aspects of society. Money, class differences, the sexual division of labour – they all predate capitalism, but all acquire a different significance and form under this mode. None, however, remains untouched by the logic of the dominant mode. There are necessary conditions for capitalism, but these can be satisfied in a number of ways. Yet the very workings of capitalism are modified by the struggles both to impose certain capitalist possibilities as against others and to transcend (or to maintain) the capitalist mode itself. Indeed, many of the practices and ideas that develop under capitalism are contrary to the interests of capital. So analysis must be historical as well as dialectical and materialist. It must sort out the historical variations between modes of production and within them. More concretely, it must distinguish what is central to the logic of the capitalist mode of production from what is within the range of possible capitalist variations. It is in this spirit that we reject both the ahistorical usage of the concept of patriarchy and assumptions about the unchanging nature of human biology.

The Domestic Labour Debate

With the rebirth of feminism in the late 1960s, it is not surprising that, in attempting to provide a material explanation for women's subordination – in trying to counter those who understood women's oppression primarily in terms of the ideas in their heads or the hormones in their bodies – theorists concentrated on women's work and its usefulness to capitalism. Nor is it surprising given the centrality of class both to Marxist analysis in general and to the struggle for change in particular, that Marxists asking feminist questions began by trying to fit women into the class concept.

Engels's statements in *The Origin of the Family, Private Property and the State* were ambiguous enough to form the basis for diametrically opposed approaches to understanding women and class. Shulamith Firestone, in what has stood up as a clear and comprehensive statement of the radical feminist position, commends Engels for observing that 'the original division of labour was between men and women for the purposes of childbearing'. Using what she terms a 'materialist view of history based on sex itself', she argues that women form a class by virtue of their shared biology. For Firestone, sex is class: 'The natural reproductive difference between the sexes led directly to the first division of labor at the origins of class.'[5] Like the productive technology which will lay the basis for equality in productive relations, scientific developments will free women from the tyranny of reproduction and childrearing, eliminating the physical differences between men and women and, not incidentally, the basis of all other differences amongst people as well. Such an approach is clearly ahistorical, denying that women's procreative and childbearing activities take place within a social context – one that is dominated, although not determined, by decisions and actions taking place in the market. Consequently, it also ignores the class differences amongst women, differences which have an important influence on the timing, experience and consequences for women of childbirth and childbearing. It fails to consider the way women have fought for, and gained, some control over their bodies. And the implication that the elimination of the biological differences between men and women will cause all other differences to wither away is difficult to consider seriously. Moreover, technology is not an independent force but one that is developed, introduced and sustained within a social context.

But the importance of women's procreative possibilities and childbearing responsibilities cannot be so easily dismissed. In searching through the cross-cultural and historical research, amongst the enormous variety in social formations and practices, only childbearing and infant care appear as common factors for women, suggesting that these realities play a significant role in women's subordination. While the historical and class variations in the process of childbearing, birth, and caring indicate that the productive factors alter the conditions for the meaning, consequences and experience of the procreative process, and that sex does not therefore make women a class, women's bodies clearly set them apart from men. The implications of these differences too have a history, and also vary with class, but they cannot be ignored in any class analysis.

Nevertheless, sex differences have seldom been acknowledged in Marxist analysis that is not also feminist. Instead of classless sex, or sex as class, we have sexless class. When sex divisions are considered, they often appear as a kind of epiphenomenon, a result of the exclusion of women from capitalist production. For Charnie Guettel, 'Women are oppressed by men because of the form their lives have had to take in a class society, in which men and women are both oppressed by the

ruling class.' Like Engels, she sees women's labour force participation and the collectivization of domestic labour as the
prerequisites of women's liberation because 'women's position
within the contending classes determines her role in the
struggle'.[6] Since women's subordination is the result of capitalist
organization, women must become wage labourers, become
members of the proletarian class, and, as members of that class,
struggle for change. By implication, sex differences will
eventually wither away.

This approach is also ahistorical in failing to acknowledge the
male dominance that predates capitalism. To be sure, under
capitalism all relationships are transformed, but in understanding their current nature it is important to examine the
factors contributing to their precapitalist existence. Because she
fails to examine the persistence of female subordination, blaming
it solely on capitalism, she also ignores what women have in
common – their bodies and their childbearing possibilities – and
underestimates the significance of domestic labour. Thus the
difficulties of overcoming the sex divisions within classes are
minimized and reduced to equal pay for work of equal value,
organizing the unorganized, and taxing corporations to pay for
universal, democratically controlled day-care. The relationship
between men and women within capitalism is developed in a
mechanical, undialectical fashion. Only sexless classes resist.
Women's control over their bodies and their sexuality is not part
of the project, nor is their procreative work integrated into the
structure of capitalism. Although women's work in the labour
force is the primary, almost exclusive focus of this analysis, thus
at best giving a distant second place to sex divisions, at worst
denying their fundamental existence, this approach does draw
our attention to the importance of women's entry into wage
labour – work that cannot be ignored in explaining what divides
women from women and from men.

For radical feminists like Firestone, women's biologically
determined shared work experience in childbearing and childrearing makes them a class. For Marxists like Guettel, women's
capitalist-determined oppression melts into their future work in
the labour force, work that will integrate them into an undiffer-
entiated proletarian class. Neither of these approaches pays
much attention to the household labour that has become the
focus of the domestic labour debate and of other attempts to fit
women into the class concept on the basis of this work.

Margaret Benston argues that women are already workers and thus a class in the objective Marxist sense of the term under the historically specific conditions of advanced captialism. Using the Marxist distinction between use value and exchange value, she maintains that women can be defined as the group of people who are responsible for the production of simple use values associated with home and family. Unlike the paid work of men, which produces exchange value as well as use value, the unpaid work of women, which produces only use value, is valueless from the standpoint of capital. Although women might also participate in wage labour, such participation is transient and unrelated to the group definition. They form a reserve army of labour who can be called on when needed for capitalist production, and sent home when no longer required. This women's work is functional for capitalism because it fulfils 'the needs for closeness, community, and warm secure relationships', and thus stabilizes the entire economy by maintaining the ideal consumption unit for capitalism -- one in which the wages of the man purchase the necessary labour of two people, while allowing for the low-paid labour force work of the woman as required. For Benston,[7] there are two related material conditions for changing women's position. These are true equality in job opportunities outside the home, and the transfer of work now done in the home to the public economy.

The argument is provocative, confusing and internally contradictory, yet it raises most of the issues that must be dealt with if we are to make the position of women understandable. She does suggest that capitalism has transformed the content and meaning of work, although she does not develop the argument. Cut off from the means of subsistence, money has become increasingly necessary to purchase what is needed for survival, but, increasingly, can be acquired only by selling the ability to work for a wage. More and more goods and services are commodified, although much of domestic labour is not. The source of power and control is the market and it is this production for the market which relegates unpaid work to a secondary status that creates not only the definition of work but much of domestic work itself. Indeed, domestic work as a separate form of work does not pre-date capitalism. Yet Benston maintains both that capitalism defines women's work and that this work is precapitalist and preindustrial. She cannot have it both ways. While her distinction between use value and exchange value does expose the dominance of capitalism and does emphasize the fact that women too do work that is both useful and necessary, it does not establish domestic labour as a precapitalist form that will wither away.

The distinction does, however, allow her to introduce the concept of the reserve army of labour, although her definition of women's labour force work as transient, with no structural relation to capital, limits the usefulness of this approach for her. Nevertheless, the concept can be used, as Patricia Connelly has so clearly shown in *Last Hired, First Fired*, in order to 'emphasize women's permanent connection to the production process', and to provide 'a link between their labour force participation and their work in the home'. According to Connelly's expansion of the analysis, 'under advanced capitalist forms of production, not only does female domestic labour have no exchange value, but female wage labour receives less than its exchange value'.[8] Since women do necessary work in the home which does not have exchange value, they form a cheap, available labour supply, competing with each other for women's segregated labour force jobs in a way that not only keeps down their wages but those of men as well.

The distinction between use value and exchange value thus indicates how capitalism transforms work primarily into wage labour and domestic labour (making the latter invisible in the process), and allows an exploration of the relationship between the two through the concept of the reserve army of labour; it does not, however, solve the problem of how to fit women into the class concept. While Benston argues that women are now a class on the basis of their production of use values in the home, her conclusions suggest that women are to become part of another class by eliminating their household labour and joining the labour force on equal terms. What, then, is the use of declaring them a class by virtue of their household labour? And how can class differences amongst women be explained? Like Guettel, she seems to assume that sex distinctions will disappear when women join the working class.

While she does offer a material base for women's oppression, focusing exclusively on women's work and its uses to capitalism, Benston does not understand this work in dialectical terms nor does she see the structure as a result in part of struggles between men and women and between workers of both sexes and owners. Freely compelled to marry, freely compelled to mother, and now freely compelled to undertake labour force work, the essence of womanhood can be contradictory. The home is not simply a stablizing force. The family is not simply created by capitalism. The home is filled with tensions that also result from developments within capitalism. Its existence depends to some extent on the efforts of male workers to obtain a family wage, on their struggles both to prevent women from competing for their jobs and to protect 'the weaker sex', on women's attempts to decrease their work-load and to maintain what is sometimes a haven, and on the nature of women's work itself, especially their procreative work.

But perhaps the most controversial legacy Benston bequeathed to the domestic labour debate was her statement that domestic labour is valueless from the standpoint of capital. Does domestic labour produce value? Is it subject to the law of value? What does this mean for the women's struggle and for the possibility of eliminating sex divisions within a capitalist society? Concern with these questions gradually shifted the debate away from the class issue towards a focus on the reproduction of labour power and the connection of women's work to capitalist production.

For Peggy Morton,[9] women do not simply produce use values; they produce something that connects them much more directly to capitalism – labour power. While she does not draw out the implications of this argument, and does not raise the question of value that was to become central to the later debate, she does develop a much more dynamic and dialectical approach to women's work, connecting women's domestic and wage labour, placing them within the contexts of capitalism and ideas about male supremacy, thus illustrating the contradictions that are inherent in this duality of domestic and wage labour. Recognizing the two workplaces of women and the class inequalities amongst women, she rejects the notion that women form a class. Not addressing directly women's shared procreative capacities, she raises, but does not explore, questions of women's control over their bodies and the class differences in access to birth control and abortion.

The argument that women, in providing the care and feeding of men and children, are performing work that produces surplus value shifted the focus of the debate from questions of class to questions of value, sparking a theoretical struggle waged to a large extent in the pages of *New Left Review*. Essentially the criticisms of the argument that housework creates value boil down to the fact that domestic labour is not equivalent to wage labour. By claiming that housework creates value, theorists such as Wally Seccombe and Jean Gardiner[10] must be suggesting that housework is itself a commodity that is exchanged for part of the husband's wage. Yet as Margaret Coulson *et al.* in particular point out, the housewife as housewife does not sell her labour power as a commodity to her husband.[11] Although she does contribute to the maintenance and reproduction of labour power, her participation in the social process is mediated by the marriage contract rather than the labour contract. She is not paid a wage: the exchange between husband and wife is variable and arbitrary, and subject to interpersonal bargaining. This has fundamental consequences in terms of the difference between wage labour and domestic labour. Wage labour is free labour in the sense that the wage labourer sells his labour power to an employer of his choice for a definite period of time in return for a wage. Time not at work is his own and he is free to change employers when he wishes (and conditions permit). The employer constantly attempts to decrease the necessary labour time, which is paid for in the form of a wage, in order to increase surplus value.

Domestic labour, on the other hand, is not free labour. For the housewife, there is little distinction, in terms of either time or space, between her work and her leisure. Since she is not paid a wage and thus does not produce surplus value directly, there is little interest on the part of the capitalist in reducing the necessary labour time by increasing her productivity. Since her work is based on social and emotional as well as economic commitments, it is difficult for her to change 'employers' freely. And the relationship between husband and wife is different from that between employer and employee both because it is seldom a strictly economic relationship and because it involves all, rather than part of, the housewife's daily life. Finally, because the relationship is a binding one, there is no tendency towards the equalization of labour that occurs in capitalist commodity production.

Domestic labour and wage labour are not equivalent; they are not interchangeable. Marx revealed the mechanisms that affect a specific form of work – wage labour. These mechanisms do not, however, apply in the same way to domestic labour, precisely because it is not wage labour. As Paul Smith points out, domestic labour is not directly responsive to the price of labour.[12] It is performed even when its product cannot be sold. Because it is not subject to the law of value, there is no social mechanism to define the necessary tasks, no measure of value, and it is not equivalent to other forms of labour. To argue, as Seccombe does, that domestic labour 'contributes directly to the creation of the commodity labour power while having no direct relation with capital',[13] does little to expose the nature of the relationship between domestic labour and wage labour. According to Gardiner, 'there appears to be no mechanism for the terms of sale of labour power to be determined by the domestic labour performed in its maintenance and reproduction'.[14] Better housework is unlikely to result in a better wage.

But to argue, as Gardiner later does, that domestic labour lowers the value of labour power, does not make this relationship any more transparent.[15] Because wage labour and domestic labour are not comparable, 'there is no basis for the calculation of the transfer of surplus labour-time between the two spheres unless the law of value is redefined'.[16] Men married to women who are full-time housewives do not receive lower wages than men married to women who work full-time in the labour force, or men of similar age with no wives at all. In fact, the reverse relationship is more likely; women married to men who receive low wages are more likely to work for pay and thus do less housework. It would make more sense to argue that women entering the labour force who obtain wage work, lower the value of labour power by covering at least some of the costs of their own reproduction rather than having all these costs met out of the husband's wage. Even if the cost of domestic labour is hidden, it is still a cost, making it difficult to understand why, in value terms alone, capital would have an interest in maintaining domestic labour – especially when some of its goods and services could be transformed into commodities, thereby producing surplus value.

The early value debate virtually ignored women's wage labour, concentrating as it did on the reproduction of workers, all of whom seemed to be male. In responding to his critics, Seccombe argued that there is an average domestic labour time which can be defined as 'that labour time necessary to convert the average wage into the average proletarian household, at the average price of wage goods'. From this base, he argues that when real male wages fall, women can compensate for the decrease by either intensifying their housework or by entering the labour force to 'supplement the family income'.[17] The woman makes a 'value trade-off' when she enters the market, compensating for the increased cost of the replacement of her domestic labour with her additional income. But the argument that domestic labour creates value does not, as Seccombe claims, explain movement from one form of labour to the other. If they are equivalent, why would a woman take on the other job? Wage labour and domestic labour are not equivalent. It is precisely because domestic labour is not wage labour that they are not interchangeable. Women cannot decide today that they will stop being pregnant so they can go out to work, but they can decide to stop washing the floor once a week and do it only once a month. There is no 'exchangeability of labour time embodied in wage goods for domestic labour time',[18] as Seccombe argues. While clearly some housework can be replaced by purchasing goods previously processed at home, most women do not replace their domestic chores with McDonald burgers and substitutes hired to clean the toilets and make the beds. They simply leave some work undone, do some work less often, and lower the quality of other labour – none of which suggests that there is necessary labour time involved or that this work constitutes average domestic labour time. Indeed, it is precisely because women are not creating value and are not directly subject to the law of value (because they do not produce surplus value) that they can form a reserve army of labour. It is because floors can go unscrubbed and beds unmade, and because they can vacuum less often, that they can in many cases enter the labour force. And it is because they cannot easily transform infant care and childcare into purchasable items that many women with small children provide a less flexible supply of labour.

But to argue that domestic labour does not create value or surplus value and is not directly subject to the law of value is not to argue that the law of value does not influence this work. Under capitalism, all labour is transformed, since the law of value impinges on most aspects of human activity. As Seccombe points out in a later article, the household is influenced by both the labour market and the retail market.[19] The household varies in response to wages and the demand for labour, as well as in response to the prices and availability of goods and services, by varying family size and the spacing of children; by varying the wage labour of men, women and children; by adjusting purchases; and by going into debt. Further, women do base their 'decision' to take on a second job to a large extent on female wages, male wages, and the prices of the commodities their families need.

The debate over the law of value has not shown that women's domestic labour creates value, although it has made clear the fact that women do necessary work at home – work that is useful to capitalism in many ways. While it has not shown that the law of value directly governs the allocation of domestic labour, it has opened the door to an analysis which explores how the operation of the law of value in the market impinges on the household, influencing but not determining domestic labour time and content. In struggling through the implications of applying the law of value to domestic labour, the participants in the debate have revealed the opposite of what was initially intended. They have shown how domestic labour differs from wage labour. They have thus led the way to the argument presented here: that it is the different nature of domestic labour – its existence outside the law of value and the production of surplus value – that creates the flexibility and thus the possibility of domestic workers becoming a reserve army.

It should not be assumed, however, that domestic labour is completely flexible – that there is no minimum necessary labour in specific households. Toilets may go uncleaned but infants do have to be fed. Nor should it be assumed that women's movement in and out of the labour force is completely flexible and/or simply a matter of choice. Instead of arguing that women were forced out of the labour force in early capitalism and later pulled in and out at the whim of capital, it is necessary to examine, in an historically specific way, which women were entering and leaving, and under what conditions. Patricia Connelly's work indicates that in Canada married men and single women were the first to be forced into wage labour, the first to lose access to the means of directly producing for their needs, the first to have no alternative but to sell their ability to work for a wage.[20] As well, some married women, probably more than official statistics indicate, also worked for a wage from the earliest period, because they too had no alternative way to acquire food and clothes. However, it seems likely that in Canada at least, many married women had access to the means of producing directly for their own survival or of gaining income without entering the labour market. Not only did they have considerable necessary labour in the home which prevented them from searching for wage work, but they could also directly produce food, sew clothes, do laundry, take on boarders or do other domestic chores, without selling their ability to work for a wage. Such alternatives do not mean that most men earned a family wage, nor do they mean that women were completely or even primarily dependent on a male wage. What they do mean is that women were supporting their own reproduction in a way that allowed them to combine this work with the labour they had little chance of escaping – childbearing and caring responsibilities. More recently, married women have been losing access to the means of production and to alternatives to wage labour. Darning more socks, even if polyester socks could be darned, does not greatly affect family maintenance. The point in this – a recital which may seem very familiar – is that we have been looking at women's work upside down.

Instead of seeing women's domestic work as substituting for the wage, we should be seeing the wage as what becomes necessary when, like men, they have no alternative means of providing for their own needs. We should question whether women have ever been dependent on a male wage and if so, which women – women from which classes? By analysing domestic labour from this perspective, we will not only expose the class differences amongst domestic workers – not only trace the transformation and commodification of much domestic work – but also perceive the reduction in women's access to means of support. For larger and larger groups of women, the intensification of domestic labour is not an alternative.

Moreover, women's movement in and out of the labour force should not be understood as being simply functional for capital or as a passive response by women to labour market requirements. By drawing women into the labour force, capital may lower the value of labour power through competition and decrease the costs of reproducing workers by spreading them over more workers, but it also may create a crisis because not all people can be absorbed into paid employment. Capital also encourages tension in the home, for women and men, between women and men. In addition some groups of women, especially those with higher education and training, are fighting to enter the labour force and to abandon their domestic chores; others, especially those with small children, are struggling to escape the compulsion to work at those dull, low paid, monotonous jobs that create for them the double day. Of course, the alternatives are structured by capitalism itself. Resistance is seldom powerful enough to win, but it does have an influence that cannot be ignored. Women do not passively respond to family or market demands. None of this is to deny that women form a reserve army of labour, especially as part-time and seasonal workers. However, it is to argue that from this perspective, married women are becoming less and less flexible as their alternatives to wage labour are reduced. It is also to argue that some classes of women are more flexible than others and that women are active in directing their labour. And, it must not be forgotten that all of this happens within the context of a society that encourages ideas about male dominance and that values independence and competition, although these values themselves vary from class to class.

Because domestic labour is not wage labour, women form a reserve army for the capitalist productive system. Because wage labour has become dominant and necessary – either directly or indirectly – to the survival of most people, other work and other workers have been devalued. Because domestic work is centered on the reproduction of the next generation of workers, as well as on the daily maintenance of all workers, it is women's work. Finally, this critical summary provides a basis for the next sections of this paper – sections which suggest ways to go forward in developing a political economy that comprehends the fundamental importance of sex divisions at all levels of analysis. The focus is on class, on the separation of domestic and wage labour, and on biological questions as central, but not the only, questions for a sex-conscious theory.

Sex Is a Marxist Issue

Although feminists have focused on domestic labour, or the split between the public and the private, Marxists who are not feminists have concentrated on the production process. If justified at all, this concentration on production is explained either in terms of the dominance of this process or in terms of the level of abstraction. At the highest level of abstraction, it is argued, sex divisions are irrelevant.

But, at the highest level, capitalism is defined as a system which separates capital from labour, with labour power typically bought and sold as a commodity. As Seccombe has so clearly explained, capitalism is premised on the existence of free wage labour.[21] The split between the public and the private is the very essence of capitalism. The sale of labour power as a commodity seems to assume reproduction at home, away from labour force work. It does not, of course, necessitate a particular kind of home or a particular kind of family. The nature and conditions of workers' reproduction are matters for historical investigation at another level of analysis. This does not, however, seem to be the case for the existence of the sexual division of labour itself, which necessarily accompanies the separation of the reproduction of labour power in some kind of home from the production of goods and services in some kind of market. Women, not men, have the babies. If producing the next generation of workers is separated from the commodity production of goods and services, then this split implies a division of labour by sex. The particular duties that are associated with procreation are matters of history, but the division is central to capitalism itself. It is no accident of history that the everyday tasks of maintaining and reproducing the next generation of workers have in fact been disproportionately performed by women.

There is a tendency within capitalism towards commodification; much of domestic labour has already been commodified. But it seems likely that there are real limits to this process if capitalism, and the free wage labourer, are to continue to exist. Some childcare work can be, indeed has been, integrated into the market economy. This labour can be equalized and abstracted. But babies can be produced only by fertile women. Such labour, at least given present circumstances, cannot therefore be equalized and abstracted. If all aspects of the reproduction of workers could be commodified, the process would require either the private production of workers with its consequent tendency towards monopoly (a circumstance inimical to the production of a free wage labourer), or an enormous expansion of the state (an eventuality counter to the existence of capitalism). Furthermore, the ideology of the free wage labourer, so important to the capitalist status quo, would be difficult to maintain if people were entirely produced through capitalist production processes or the state. A capitalist society, with its concomitant free wage labourer, seems to imply a separation, in some form, between the reproduction of workers and the production of goods and services. The separation seems also to imply a segregation, and denigration, of women.

Therefore, to insist on distinguishing a highest level of abstraction that entirely excludes consideration of sexual division of labour is to be sexist – to reinforce the notion of women being hidden from history or, more accurately, from theory. It is also to guarantee an inadequate understanding of capitalism, given that the split between the public and the private, and thus a sexual division of labour, is essential to this mode of production, at the highest level of abstraction. In summary, the existence of a sexual division of labour, although not its form or extent, is crucial to capitalism and therefore to its theorization.

Class Is a Feminist Issue

Few would deny that capitalist societies are class societies or that women as a group are oppressed. But the questions of whether or not there is a material basis to that oppression and of whether or not that basis is shared bodies or shared work is still a matter of debate. Are the fundamental divisions those between owners of the means of production and owners of labour power, those between men and women, or those between women and their bodies? Is the main enemy, to use Christine Delphy's terminology, capitalism, men or female anatomy?[22]

While it is essential for a class analysis to locate women in relation to class, the answer cannot be one of these alternatives alone. Women are simultaneously subject to capitalism, male dominance and their bodies. To pose the question in the form of alternatives is like asking whether ideas or material conditions structure women's subordination. They are inseparable. They act together. Patriarchy and capitalism are not autonomous, nor even interconnected systems, but the same system. As integrated forms, they must be examined together.

This is not to argue that women constitute a class. Although it is clear that most of those who own and control the means of production are male, most men own only their ability to work. There are also class differences amongst women. Lady Astor is not oppressed by her chauffeur and it is questionable whether her cleaning-woman is more oppressed by her husband than her employer.[23] The consequences, nature and responses to male dominance vary from class to class.

To argue that there are class differences amongst women and that they do not form a class on the basis of their bodies or their work is not to solve the problem of fitting women into classes. Locating women through their domestic labour either puts most women into the same class or places them automatically in the same class as their husbands. For those women with direct involvement in the labour market, the alternatives are independent class membership, the same class membership as their husbands, or a common membership with other women because of the domestic labour they also perform. Gardiner's alternative of expanding the definition of the working class to include all those not directly involved in but dependent on the sale of labour power does expose the broad class cleavages but fails to take into account the fundamental divisions between men and women in the working class.[24] Surely having an indirect, rather than a direct relationship to production has important consequences for women's class sympathies – sympathies which cannot easily be equated with those of the young and unemployed whose dependency is temporary and transient. Furthermore, such an approach ignores the double work of women, their position as a particular kind of reserve army, their segregation into separate labour force jobs, and the ideology that reinforces and is reinforced by these divisions.

The problem here is more than one of counting, of figuring out how to classify women. Both bourgeois and Marxist categories treat sex differences as irrelevant to stratification and class systems. As Delphy points out, both approaches imply that 'wider inequalities have no influence on the (assumed) "equality" of the couple, and on the other hand that relationships within the couple because they are seen as equal cannot be the cause of wider inequalities'.[25] Theories that lump all women together as a class ignore class differences amongst women. Theories that attach women to their husbands or families ignore women's subordination, their domestic labour and their labour force work. Theories which locate women in terms of their own paid employment forget both the segregation of the labour force, and the domestic labour that most women perform. Theories that are blind to sex differences obscure not only divisions fundamental to all classes, but also the structure of capitalism. The working class, as well as the ruling class, has two sexes. Without acknowledging these divisions – without integrating them into a class analysis – neither capitalism nor households can be understood. This is not a plea to add women back in, but a challenge to a theory that has not made the system transparent, has not developed an analysis of class which accounts for a bifurcation of classes – a division which is central to an understanding of how capitalism itself works.

The domestic labour debate does lay the basis for a revision of theory based on an expansion of the class concept. Without denying that the most basic divisions are between those who own and control the means of production and those who own only their labour power – a primacy implied by the dominance of the wage system in capitalist society – it is possible to comprehend the antagonisms between the sexes, and amongst those of the same sex, by including all labour in our analysis. Those dependent directly or indirectly on the wage are objectively and subjectively divided by their material conditions, by their lived experiences, and by the work they do. If work for a wage (or the absence of work for a wage) and work required to transform that wage into consumable form, as well as work necessary to provide the next generation of workers, are included in our approach to class, then divisions between men and women and amongst women may be better understood. Such an approach would permit the domestic and wage labour of both men and women to be taken into account. Domestic labour would thus form an integral part of the explanation for men's interests just as wage labour would be a basic component in comprehending women's class position and relations. Connecting domestic and wage labour within classes would also extend the analysis to the relationship between domestic and wage labour – to the sex segregation in both areas of work. In this way, it would be possible to develop a theory which exposes the material basis of the subjective and objective antagonisms between sexes. The domestic labour debate suggests a movement in this direction; Marxism provides the tools; political economy should continue the work.

Bodies in History

For Marx, analysis at all levels should begin with the way people provide for their daily and generational needs – with the production and reproduction of goods, services and people. These production and reproduction processes are inseparable aspects of the same whole. They are social processes requiring co-operation, and are subject to historical change. They do however have physical components which set limits on possible variations. A minimum of food is necessary, some protection from the elements is essential, and some ejaculation, insemination and gestation must take place for babies to be born. While there are enormous variations in how physiological and socially constructed needs are satisfied, in all societies and throughout history, women have the babies.

That women have babies is not a matter which has relevance only at the level of a particular social formation. How women have babies, and the conditions and consequences of childbearing, are relative to particular social formations. So is the sexual division of labour related to childrearing. But the fact that women, not men, have babies is not. To theorize production and reproduction at the highest level of abstraction involves a recognition of the differences in female and male reproductive capacities. Any other approach fails to comprehend the nature of production and reproduction.

Here, we are distinguishing ourselves from much of Marxist analysis. Those Marxists who fail to discuss the sexual division of labour at all must be assuming, like Guettel, that it is a mere by-product of the capitalist system and thus will wither away with the end of the system – that it is a minor factor in the functioning of capitalism. Those who discuss the sexual division of labour without acknowledging the biological component seem to point in a similar direction. Or perhaps they are assuming that pro-creative capacities are not amenable to Marxist analysis. But this analysis must be extended to include sexuality, childbearing and childbirth if the realities of production and reproduction are to be understood and changed in a way that would benefit both women and men.

To recognize that women have the babies is not, however, to resort to a biological explanation of women's subordination, nor to call for the elimination of women's childbearing responsibilities. Unlike many feminists, we do not see biology as fixed and immutable. We do not see childbearing as the same for all women in the same society or in different historical periods. We do not see biological factors as primary or even separate factors. Physical capacities do not exist outside – autonomously from – power structures and productive processes. Nor are they beyond human control and manipulation. Procreation is itself to a large extent socially constructed. It has a history. Its process, its consequences, and its meanings also vary from class to class.

Capitalism has transformed the productive and reproductive processes. Contradictions are created, resolved, and transformed. And women, on the basis of these contradictions, struggle to resist, to gain some control over their biological capacities. What follows is an indication of the direction a Marxist analysis should take if it is to include women's particular reproduction in general.

It may be readily agreed that inequality results not from the different biological capacities, but from the social mechanisms which ensure that these capacities become a weakness rather than a resource. To suggest, however, that the very 'biology' of the procreation process has varied historically with the economic system may be more a matter of debate. According to Gayle Rubin, 'The needs of sexuality and procreation must be satisfied as much as the need to eat, and one of the most obvious deductions which can be made from the data of anthropology is that these needs are hardly ever satisfied in any "natural form", any more than are the needs for food.'[27] Or as Richard Wertz and Dorothy Wertz put it in their history of 'lying in' in the United States: 'Because people have understood and shaped birth in changing ways, both the means and the meaning of childbirth have a history, an extraordinary one because childbirth is at once a creative act, a biological happening, and a social event.'[27] Research on the history of women's role in procreation clearly indicates that the general economic situation, the class structure, the development of technology, women's other work, health care and standards and available food supplies – in short, the economic system – affect the kind of pregnancies women go through, the number of pregnancies they have and their chance of survival.

For example, Louise Tilly and Joan Scott[28] show how low standards of nutrition and health in early modern England inhibited conception, promoted miscarriage, affected the milk supply of mothers and made women infertile by the age of forty or forty-five. Wertz and Wertz report that, in the colonies, as in France, 'there was a seasonal periodicy to the arrival of children' which 'may correlate not only with work demands and consequent exhaustion but also with nutritional variation'.[29] In the introduction to her moving collection of English working-class women's testimonials on their experiences with maternity, Margaret Davies argues that the high infant mortality rate and the extensive maternal suffering at the turn of the century were attributable to: inadequate wages; lack of knowledge regarding maternity and of skilled advice and treatment; and the personal relation of husband and wife.[30] Similarly Neil Sutherland, referring to a 1910 report prepared for the Ontario government, lists the following as agents of high infant mortality rates:

> poverty, ignorance, poor housing, overcrowded slums, low wages and other social conditions that forced mothers of young children to work outside their homes, impure water and milk, loose controls over the spread of communicable diseases, poor prenatal care, inadequate medical attendance at birth, tardy registration of births, and the lack of clinics and nursing services helping mothers care for their babies properly.[31]

These factors, which also affect the process of pregnancy and childbearing, result primarily from the existing material conditions. And the very 'biology' of menstruation also varies with these conditions over time. According to Janice Delaney, Mary Jane Lupton and Emily Toth, 'the fact is, the age at menarche (first menstruation) depends greatly on good food and good health. Those who eat well mature earlier. Today, the average American girl first menstruates when she is twelve and a half years old. Figures from Norway, where the oldest such records are kept, show that in 1850 the average girl had her first period at seventeen; by 1950, at thirteen and a half. For each generation since 1850, then, a girl's period has come about a year earlier than her mother's.[32] Furthermore, as Joyce Leeson and Judith Gray point out, changes in economic and social arrangements have meant that 'thirty-five years or more of virtually uninterrupted menstruation is thus a recent phenomenon.'[33] Bodies are not independent of their economic and social surroundings. The conditions are set by the productive system.

Yet changes in the productive system, and more specifically in women's work, do not automatically produce changes in women's experiences with sex and with childbearing. To quote Stella Browne, a socialist-feminist writing in 1922, 'No economic changes would give equality or self-determination to any woman unable to choose or refuse motherhood of her own free will.' As she so eloquently explained: 'Birth control for women is no less essential than workshop control and determination of the conditions of labour for men . . . Birth control is woman's crucial effort at self-determination and at control of her own person and her own environment.'[34] The development of, and the conditions of access to, birth control and abortion technology are clearly of central importance to women.

Some form of birth control has been known since hunting and gathering societies. Yet even the early forms were suppressed if and when this suited the interests of the productive system. As Linda Gordon argues, the coincidence of the suppression of birth control with the development of agriculture is attributable to the need for more labour power and the desire to control inheritance of the accumulating private property.[35] While new technology has been developed in the productive sector, religious and state laws have limited access to, and information on, both old and new methods of birth control and abortion.[36] The research carried out by Wertz and Wertz indicates that the technology and its regulation have had both positive and negative consequences for women.[37] The point is that the interests of women have seldom been taken into account in decisions to develop and to allow access to the technology; consequently, women have had difficulty in asserting control over their bodies through contraception and abortion technology.

Important as this technology and its regulation are to women, there are other ways in which their procreative experiences are conditioned by the productive and state sectors. Procreation is influenced by labour force demands, by state policies and regulations, and by economic requirements and resources. For instance, Tilly and Scott argue that 'young populations and job opportunities for young workers kept birth rates from falling' in some French industrial cities during the mid-nineteenth century.[38] According to Angus McLaren, 'Factory work often prevented the young mother from being able to nurse her child' in nineteenth-century England, thus reducing even the limited contraceptive protection provided by breastfeeding and consequently encouraging women to seek methods of abortion to prevent birth.[39] The 'combination of large-scale immigration from Southern Europe and the casualties of the First World War stimulate[d] widespread alarm over birth and mortality rates',[40] and resulted in government and private programmes designed to change the conditions of childbirth and childrearing. In 1937, when depression conditions had dramatically increased unemployment, the Canadian rate of natural increase dropped to a record low of 9.7 (per 1,000 population) in spite of the restrictions in access to birth control techniques and information.

During and immediately after the Second World War, the rate rose steadily from 10.9 in 1939 to a record high of 20.3 in 1954.[41]

In addition, these rates are affected, as many social policy researchers indicate, by existing laws and regulations which

> touch on the ability to more effectively plan the number and timing of children by Canadian families (which will bring into consideration abortion and sterilization and contraception), the ability to determine the grounds on which individuals can decide to form or dissolve families (which will involve divorce laws and regulations), and the legal implications of the formation or dissolution of a family unit.[42]

Today in Canada it is evident that the demand for women as workers in the labour force and the concomitant decline in the economic resources of the family have encouraged women both to participate in the labour force and to reduce the number of children they produce. This reduction itself has been made possible both by the development of birth control technology and by changes in state intervention – especially in the laws that relate to birth control and abortion, but also more generally in the provision of health care services and information.

Like the concept of the virgin mother, procreation has internal contradictions for women. Adrienne Rich has described in eloquent detail the contradictions inherent in mothering within an advanced capitalist society.[43] It is at one and the same time a joyful and painful experience. Women can see the possibility for control over their reproductive capacities, but the control is denied by abortion laws, poor technical development, medical practices and limited information, not to mention the ideology of male superiority. They have 'free choice' in marrying and bearing children, but like the wage worker who is freely compelled to sell labour power, women are compelled by conditions of pregnancy, wage work, medical techniques and legal restrictions to marry and have babies in particular ways. Labour force work interferes with pregnancy and birth; pregnancy and birth interfere with labour force jobs.

And while capitalists seek to pursue their interests, the results are frequently contradictory here too. The process is dialectical. Barbara Ehrenreich and Deirdre English explain that Margaret Sanger's campaign for birth control in the United States was aimed at preventing the problems created by 'overbreeding' in the working class.[44] But the consequence of her victory was a greater decline in the birth rate amongst those Sanger would have described as fit. In Canada, a crown attorney claimed in 1901, 'that employment opportunities permitted women to avoid marriage or to fall back on "crime" which led to a "low birth rate"'.[45] Women have more recently responded to the growth in demand for women workers and the rising costs of rearing children by reducing the number of children they have and by demanding childcare facilities. Now that the demand for female workers is falling off, there are few children to draw women back into the home, although decreasing support for existing childcare service increases the pressure on women to go back home.

More generally, the contradiction between the technical possibility for women to control their bodies and the lack of control which results from policies designed for other interests has formed the basis of women's protests for centuries. As Gordon points out in her history of birth control in America, 'In no area of life have women ever accepted unchallenged the terms of service offered by men. Sexuality and reproduction were no exception.'[46] There are many instances of such rebellion. McLaren argues that in nineteenth-century England, 'the workers, and in particular the women workers of the textile areas, should be seen, not as waiting passively for the knowledge to trickle down from their superiors which would permit them to emulate the middle class, but as taking independent action, which might well violate bourgeois morality, in an attempt to achieve their own desired family size'.[47] In Canada, 'A contributor to the *Canadian Churchman* (1900) went so far as to assert that the pressures of existing society encouraged ". . . to put it bluntly, in nine cases of ten, women to murder their unborn children".'[48]

The entire history of abortion indicates women's resistance to both the law and their procreative capacities. And similar patterns appear in breastfeeding practices. Reporting to the Ontario government in the early part of this century, Dr Helen Mac-Murchy argued that women should be convinced to breastfeed their infants in order to prevent high infant mortality rates. 'In order to encourage women to breastfeed, a mother's qualms about the cost of such a procedure had to be overcome. A working mother who could not adjust her schedule to a breastfeeding schedule should have a pension, if necessary, to take care of the family.'[49] Women have not passively accepted the dictates of the state, the church, or men. Indeed, childbearing itself may be a form of resistance against imposed standards and against powerless conditions. Women may gain power from bearing children – power over children and over men. It should not be seen only as a passive response. Women are not merely vessels. They are active in making their own history.

In various historical periods, women's bodies, and their lack of control over their bodies, have provided the basis for the organized opposition of some women. But, while shared physiology has brought some women together, the variation created by existing material conditions has divided women – has encouraged women in different classes and in different marital situations to experience their bodies in different ways. Women differ in terms of the healthcare they receive during pregnancy, in terms of their access to information on birth control and on the way their bodies function, and in terms of the ease of gestation as it is related to nutrition, information and exercise. They also differ in the consequences of childbearing – whether it will cause financial or emotional strain, and whether it will limit free movement and/or labour force participation. Lady Astor and her maid may both give birth, but the treatment they receive and the consequences of childbirth for them vary greatly. This is clearly indicated by the research on women of different class positions. For instance, Ehrenreich and English show that, in nineteenth-century America,

> It was as if there were two different species of females. Affluent women were seen as inherently sick, too weak and delicate for anything but the mildest pastimes, while working class women were believed to be inherently healthy and robust. The reality was very different. Working class women, who put in long hours of work and received inadequate rest and nutrition, suffered far more than healthy women from contagious diseases and complications of childbirth.[50]

Wertz and Wertz[51] describe how poor women were encouraged to deliver in hospitals so that doctors in training could practise on them. On the other hand, in Canada during the latter half of the nineteenth century, 'one of the main reasons for the incidence of puerperal insanity [the 'insanity of childbirth'] in the Victorian era was, ironically, a consequence of medical practitioners delivering babies – a service which the well-to-do were more likely to be able to afford . . . Today, it is evident that puerperal insanity has less to do with the nature of women than it has to do with the nature of medical treatment.'[52] The letters from working-class English women collected by Davies at the turn of the century clearly indicate the 'different conditions under which the middle-class and the working-class woman becomes a mother'.[53] These examples suggest that there is not one procreative process for all women but different procreative processes for women in different classes and in different historical periods.

The alternative analytical approaches are not limited to ignoring sex differences, assuming they are mere social constructs, or concluding that they represent fixed, primary differences which create their own relations – ones which are beyond Marxist analysis. An historical materialist approach not only allows us to situate female sexuality and childbearing within capitalism but also to show how these processes are conditioned within particular social formations – in different ways for women of different classes. It permits the integration of biological factors as limiting but not determining. Any alternative to capitalist organization must recognize that women, not men, have babies. Like other aspects of the material conditions which human beings face, the goal is to bring procreation under human control, to shape the conditions under which it happens. Theory in political economy should help us understand what these conditions are and how they can be changed; it should direct us towards a strategy to ensure that female bodies, like the ability to do work, are a resource rather than a liability.

That women have the babies, albeit under a variety of conditions, does not necessarily mean that they will rear the children or clean the toilets. Nor does it mean that they must live in nuclear families. However, because capitalism is premised on the separation of most aspects of workers' reproduction from the commodity production process, and because women have the babies, women will at times be limited in their access to the production process. Such limitations permit the elaboration of the sexual division of labour (itself not without contradictions) just as they encourage women's dependence on men for financial support and the dependence of higher-paid, wage-earning men on women for domestic services. Access to wage labour is value laden, given the primacy of productive processes and the centrality of the wage. Of course, precisely how this division comes about is a matter of historical investigation, beyond the scope of this paper.[54] But the domestic labour debate and other research suggest that such an approach can expose the mechanisms at work which ensure women's subordination.

Conclusion

The domestic labour debate has honed the analytical tools, has exposed the dual nature of women's work, has shown how this work is useful to capitalism and in the process has laid the basis for an analysis that is more dialectical, more historical, more conscious of active resistance, more conscious of sex divisions. Feminist analysis has shown that bodies and their procreative capacities also condition possibilities, although Marxist analysis helps us to place these bodies in history, in classes, in relationships that are themselves best understood within the context of existing material conditions. This paper attempts to create a platform on which to build a critique of political economy and a sex-conscious analytical framework.

We have argued that there is a sexual division of labour particular to capitalist society (although many aspects clearly predate capitalism), that this division and the concomitant subordination of women are integral parts of capitalist production and reproduction and that this division has a biological component which cannot be ignored. Moreover, we argue that because capitalism is premised on free wage labour – on the separation of most aspects of workers' reproduction from the production process – women's reproductive capacities separate them out of the production process for childbearing work. This establishes the basis for an elaboration of sex differences, a sexual division of labour which subordinates women and pervades all levels of human activity under capitalism. Such segregation also fundamentally divides classes.

Any theory of capitalism must be conscious of and provide explanation not only for the separation between home and work but also for that between women and men. It must put women and men back into their history at all levels of analysis. The domestic labour debate suggests that Marxist analytical tools can be applied to the task. That political economy has been sex-blind is a challenge, not an indictment.

On Marxism and Feminism

Patricia Connelly

Recently the issue of class and gender has been raised in the pages of *Studies in Political Economy* – by Angela Miles in 'Economism and Feminism; Hidden in the Household: A Comment on the Domestic Labour Debate',[1] and by Pat Armstrong and Hugh Armstrong in 'Beyond Sexless Class and Classless Sex: Towards Feminist Marxism'.[2] These authors argue that we need more dialogue around this issue to develop a framework appropriate for the explanation of women's oppression under capitalism. In the spirit of such a dialogue, I would like to comment on several of their points. In addition, I will draw on some arguments made by Michèle Barrett in *Women's Oppression Today: Problems in Marxist Feminist Analysis.*[3]

In her review of Canadian contributions to the domestic labour debate, Angela Miles argues that the authors claim to be providing a theoretical analysis of gender and class but that the questions posed and the concepts used in the debate do not address the causes or significance of women's oppression. Moreover, radical feminist attempts to 'move towards a new more universal analysis of domination that can encompass both class and gender oppression' are presented by the authors as a substitution of gender for class and then dismissed. She concludes that since the debate ignores feminist questions and thus reduces women's oppression to a narrow economic focus, even the most original and far-reaching contribution has no theoretical insight into the substance and origins of gender domination. Moreover, their claim to do so stands in the way of initiating an 'already too long delayed Marxist/feminist dialogue'.

It is true, as Miles points out, that the contributors to *Hidden in the Household* do not explain the causes of women's oppression, but in her review she reproduces quotes which clearly state that they are not trying to explain the historical causes of gender inequality; they are trying rather to reveal the structural basis of domestic labour and by so doing uncover some mechanisms by which women have been subordinated under capitalism. With regard to the issue of patriarchy, some of the authors may have overstated their case, but my sense is that their discussion was not meant as a dismissal of gender relations but rather as a reference to the fact that in general, radical feminist analyses have given primacy to patriarchy over the capitalist mode of production. Earlier feminist works such as those by Kate Millett and by Shulamith Firestone, for example, use patriarchy to mean a universal trans-historical category of male dominance grounded in the logic of biological reproduction, while more recent feminist works such as Christine Delphy's use patriarchy to focus on social rather than biological relations. Delphy argues that since men appropriate the unpaid labour of women through the institution of marriage, the material oppression of women lies in patriarchal relations of production within the family. Although the emphasis is different, these authors all give patriarchy analytic independence and analytic primacy over the capitalist mode of production.[4]

In a short review essay, Angela Miles cannot be expected to have presented fully her own position on this issue. She alludes to it, however, when discussing what she considers the basis for a Marxist and feminist dialogue. She says that 'the defining value of the struggle is the end of domination and alienation rather than the end of private property and equality of material distribution'.[5] There is no doubt that she means class as well as gender domination, but if the struggle is defined in terms of domination in general rather than class or property relations, it seems fair to ask what would then be the central contradiction – the basis for social change – in capitalist society?

While these first points raised by Miles refer specifically to the contributions in *Hidden in the Household*, her conclusions refer more generally to the entire domestic labour debate. In general, it is true to say that the domestic labour debate has focused narrowly on structural categories and has not addressed the totality of women's oppression. It is not true, however, to say that the domestic labour debate has made no theoretical contribution to an understanding of the significance of this oppression. Nor is it correct to say that the domestic labour debate has stood in the way of initiating a dialogue over gender and class. Indeed, I would argue that the domestic labour debate has advanced our understanding by demonstrating that women's oppression has a material basis and is linked to the political economy of capitalist society through their domestic and wage labour. It has also contributed to the debate that is well underway between Marxists and feminists and among Marxist feminists in such works as Eisenstein's *Capitalist Patriarchy and the Case for Socialist Feminism*; Kuhn and Wolpe's *Feminism and Materialism*; Sargent's *The Unhappy Marriage of Marxism and Feminism*; Barrett's *Women's Oppression Today*; and closer to home, in the pages of *Atlantis*.[5]

Within this dialogue the issue has emerged as follows: in very general and simplistic terms, Marxist analysis focuses on the relations of production without distinguishing between women's and men's experiences under capitalism. Radical feminist analysis focuses on the relations of gender without considering the specific historical and economic context of these relations. Marxist feminists are trying to develop an analysis of how unequal gender relations which preceded capitalism have been affected historically by capitalist relations of production – by class domination and class struggle. As the attempt to integrate both class and gender progresses, we find Marxists adding on women and radical feminists adding on class. The question is: how do we develop a coherent and integrated perspective with which to analyse the oppression of women in capitalist society?

This is the question addressed by Pat and Hugh Armstrong and by Michèle Barrett. While these authors agree on many points, they begin from different theoretical positions. The Armstrongs begin by providing an excellent summary and evaluation of the domestic labour debate, which lays the basis for their own analysis in which they 'suggest ways to go forward in developing a political economy that comprehends the fundamental importance of sex divisions at all levels of analysis'. They go on to develop their argument that the subordination of women is inherent in the capitalist mode of production. They say that 'the sexual division of labour is essential to this mode of production, at the highest level of abstraction'. The implication of this argument seems to be that if the inequality of women had not already existed, capitalism would have had to create it. The reason is that capitalism is premised on free wage labour. The reproduction of wage labour must take place in some kind of unit outside of the sphere of production of goods and services. Since women have babies, the separation of home and workplace seems 'to imply a segregation, and denigration, of women'. Indeed, they argue that the separation of home and workplace not only implies the segregation of women; it requires it. Thus 'the existence of a sexual division of labour, although not its form or extent, is crucial to capitalism and therefore to its theorization'. It is significant that they do not distinguish between 'sex' and 'gender', that is, the biologically determined and the socially assigned. Their position is that since these factors are interdependent and since sexual division of labour is the term most often used, no purpose is serviced by distinguishing analytically between them.

Michèle Barrett, on the other hand, uses the term gender and argues that gender divisions are not a necessary element of the capitalist mode of production. For Barrett the question of class is put in terms of the mode of production, while the question of gender is put in terms of the historical development of the social formation. Gender divisions preceded the capitalist mode of production. As capitalism developed, however, it adapted and used this existing division between men and women. Once this had occurred, women's subordination became entrenched in the capitalist system to the point where it became crucial. Nevertheless, gender divisions are an historically constituted integral part of, but not a necessary condition for, the capitalist mode of production.

According to Barrett, to go from the principle that capitalism requires the separation of home and workplace to the position that this separation requires the relegation of women to the home and their exclusion from wage labour is, in fact, precisely to accept the biologistic assumption that this outcome was inevitable. A more historical approach, says Barrett in referring to England, shows that the relegation of women to the home and to low-paid, segregated wage labour was a long and uneven process which involved a struggle between women and the better-organized male craft unionists. The questions of who would be responsible for childcare and whose skills would be recognized as more valuable in the workplace were resolved in the interest of men according to a division of labour and an ideology of gender which pre-dated capitalism and which served to disadvantage women in their struggle. Barrett concludes that women's oppression in capitalist society is characterized by a particular form of family household that has both an ideological and material basis and that has a profound effect on the relationship between women's wage and domestic labour. It is important to point out that Armstrong and Armstrong agree with this conclusion since they argue that the sexual division of labour must be understood at all levels of analysis. The main difference then between the two positions revolves around whether or not the sexual or gendered division of labour is essential at the level of the capitalist mode of production. Let us consider in more detail the distinction that is being drawn.

The capitalist system can be analysed at different levels of its organization. We can analyse it at the most abstract level to determine the structural boundaries of the system and how the economy in its purest form is structured, how it operates, and how it changes. Analysis at this level separates out what is absolutely essential to an understanding of the mechanics of the capitalist system. The focus is on the forces of production and the relations of production. The forces of production are continually developing and societal change occurs as the forces of production and the corresponding relations of production come into contradiction. This key contradiction takes the form of class struggle between those who are the producers and those who benefit from this production. It is through conflict and struggle between these two classes that change comes about. At this level of abstraction the aim is to uncover the underlying economic structures, that is, the logic which governs the operations of a capitalist system. In *Hidden in the Household*, Wally Seccombe makes a strong case for expanding the concept of the capitalist mode of production to include not only the production unit but also the subsistence unit. The subsistence sphere is, however, 'structurally subordinate to the sphere of industrial production where capital presides directly over labour'.[6] With this conception he argues that the household and domestic labour are a necessary part of the capitalist mode of production. However, for an explanation of the particular form of patriarchal family relations which exists in capitalist societies – that is, the prevalence of the nuclear family form, the ownership of household property overwhelmingly by men, the performance of domestic labour overwhelmingly by women – it is necessary to move from 'the sexless and epochal abstraction of the capitalist mode of production' to the 'sexist and historically periodized concrete of the developed capitalist societies'.[7] This points to the fact that the general characteristics defined by the capitalist mode of production become specified by the historical circumstances of particular societies.

This brings us to another level of analysis, that is, to the more concrete and historically specific level of the capitalist social formation. This social formation contains several modes of production but is dominated by the capitalist mode of production with its fundamental labour/capital contradiction. The social formation contains groupings that derive from relations of production (for example, classes) and groupings whose structures are determined by principles other than those of the relations of production (for example, gender). It is within the social formation that struggle takes place. The point of this approach is not to reduce every relationship to economic terms (as at the level of the capitalist mode of production) but rather to disclose the relationship between the economic structure and these other structures (at the more concrete and empirical level of the social formation). An analysis at this level examines how the capitalist mode of production, as it operates in specific societies, determines or redefines particular social, political and ideological forms. At this level the focus is on how the relations of production intersect, combine and conflict with the relations of gender in different classes and in different historical periods within one society, and in different societies. The analysis also raises the question as to how class and gender structures combine, intersect and conflict in social formations dominated by other modes of production.

To use a different example, the reserve army of labour is both a necessary product of the capitalist accumulation process and it is a necessary condition for accumulation to occur. Therefore, a reserve army is essential to the capitalist mode of production. Some group must act as a reserve labour force. It is not, however, essential that this group be composed of women. It is only when we expand the concept of the reserve army and move from the abstract to the more concrete level that we can account for the historical and empirical reality of married women (or different groups of men for that matter) acting as a reserve army in Canada. At different points in history women, despite their childbearing activities, have been brought into capitalist production, and at other points, when they were no longer needed, have been moved out. In recent years, as a result of changes in the economy and in the household, women have been drawn into the labour force on a relatively permanent part-time or full-time basis.[8] To analyse women's position at the level of the social formation in this way is not to relegate women to a secondary position or less important level of analysis. Rather it is a way of using the concepts developed by Marx to explain the operation of the capitalist system, in order to understand specific aspects of women's experience in a capitalist society.

At the same time there are aspects of women's oppression that cannot be understood in terms of these categories, and we should not try to squeeze women's reality into them.[9] We do need to develop new concepts as Angela Miles suggests and we also need to retain the analytic primacy of the mode of production as Armstrong and Armstrong, and Barrett, suggest. The analysis itself, however, should proceed at the level of the historical development of a specific social formation.

At this point it might be asked whether it really matters how or at what level the question is posed, since the reality of the gender division of labour, and of women's oppression as it is experienced, is the same either way. It matters because several theoretical and political implications follow from this distinction. First, since gender divisions preceded capitalism we cannot expect them to disappear necessarily or automatically with the demise of the capitalist mode of production. This has obvious implications for the women's movement. Secondly, this distinction allows us to reject assumptions about the functional necessity of women's work in favour of examining under historically specific conditions the role of female domestic and wage labour and its advantages and disadvantages for capital and/or the family household and/or women.[10] Thirdly, this distinction allows us to focus more clearly on particular issues such as the fact that class struggle and women's struggle do not always coincide and that working-class and middle-class women do not always share the same forms of oppression. The struggle for the male family wage, for example, can both be in the interest of the working-class family household and not in the long term interest of working-class women.[11] Fourthly, it moves us away from the view that women's biology necessarily relegates them to a subordinate position. It is clearly true that women not men bear children, but the responsibility connected to, and the definition of, childrearing are socially not 'naturally' determined. Political issues like the demand for maternity and paternity leave are based on the assumptions that the biological reality of childbearing should be taken into account but that women need not be entirely responsible for childrearing. Fifthly, this distinction keeps us alert to the fact that capitalist penetration of developing countries affects women and the family household quite differently than did capitalist development in Canada. For example, the new international division of labour has created a new female proletariat in the Third World whose cheap labour power is drawn upon while their husbands remain unemployed.[12] And, finally, this distinction directs our focus to an ideology of gender that has been incorporated into the dominant ideology. This in turn raises the issue of the construction of femininity and masculinity, laying the basis for a Marxist-feminist analysis of specifically feminist questions.

More on Marxism and Feminism: A Response to Patricia Connelly

Pat Armstrong and Hugh Armstrong

Building on the work of Michèle Barrett, Patricia Connelly has in *Studies in Political Economy*, no. 12, performed the useful service of clarifying some important differences between her position on women's oppression under capitalism, and our position, as set out in *Studies in Political Economy*, no. 10.[1] While there is much with which we can agree in Connelly's comment, it would in our view also be useful to address some issues of continuing disagreement.

Part of our argument was that free-wage labour is a defining characteristic of capitalism, a characteristic that entails the reproduction of free-wage labourers to a certain extent *outside* the capitalist production process proper. In other words, free-wage labour entails the separation of a public, commodity-production unit from a private, subsistence unit. Given this separation, and given that women, not men, have the babies and can nurse them, mothers are, for a limited time at least, less able than men to participate fully in the labour force. Specifically, under the capitalist mode of production, in which commodities are valued to the point of being fetishized and the work performed to produce non-commodities is devalued, this separation provides a material basis for inequality between the sexes. Because it is the capitalist mode of production, and not biology *per se*, that renders women subordinate, their subordination must be considered when examining capitalism at all levels of abstraction.

For Connelly, by contrast, while women's subordination has become entrenched in the capitalist system to the extent that it has become 'crucial', it has not become a 'necessary condition' for the capitalist mode of production. Rather than being 'essential' to this mode, at the highest level of abstraction, it is the historical result of unequal struggles of women and men in concrete social formations. Following Barrett, she argues that to infer from the separation of production and subsistence units 'the relegation of women to the home and their exclusion from wage labour is, in fact, precisely to accept the biologistic assumption that this outcome was inevitable'.[2] Instead, an ideology of gender that pre-dated capitalism was adapted in concrete historical circumstances by coalitions of the capitalist class and working-class men – especially in male craft unions – to construct a family-household system. This system laid the basis for the relegation of women to the home, for a sex-segregated labour force, and for the mutual reinforcement of these two developments.

We will not stress here our many points of agreement with Connelly and Barrett. Several, such as the observation that the sexual division of labour pre-dated capitalism, and the emphasis on struggle and contradiction in shaping historically the content of sex differences under capitalism, were raised in our initial article.[3] Instead, we will indicate some of the difficulties we have with Barrett's important book and then take up the question posed by Connelly of the theoretical and political implications of our different positions.

One must start with a degree of scepticism regarding an argument that women's subordination should be explained exclusively in terms of historical developments in concrete, capitalist social formations when this subordination is to be found in each and every one of them. In the specific English and American cases examined by Barrett, our scepticism is deepened by her degree of reliance on the exclusivism practised by male craft unions and on the 'protective' legislation promoted by them as a causal factor. As Joanna Brenner and Maria Ramas have recently shown, these unions could not have had such a decisive impact on sex segregation in the English and American capitalist labour forces, given when the legislation was introduced how few men were in these unions, the unions' ambivalent stances on women working for pay, and the inability of the unions to impose their wills on this and on other issues.[4] Barrett offers no explanation of why working-class men enjoyed the success she attributes to them here when they were so clearly unsuccessful elsewhere.

We also have more fundamental, theoretical difficulties with Barrett's analysis. She argues, correctly in our view, against dual systems approaches that posit the independent existence of capitalist and patriarchal structures and that limit Marxist analysis to the former. What is needed is a theory that links the different structures – the different kinds of inequality. Yet in the end, she herself seems to depend on a dual systems approach, as Connelly suggests when she writes that 'for Barrett the question of class is put in terms of the mode of production, while the question of gender is put in terms of the historical development of the social formation'.[5] On the one hand, a sex-blind capitalism; on the other, a seemingly autonomous ideology of gender. But what is the material basis of this ideology? How has it had so profound an impact (or rather, set of impacts) in the several social formations? What are we to make of the distinction between the subordination of women having become so crucial to the capitalist mode of production and its not being essential to it?

The answer provided by Barrett, which we find unsatisfactory, is that the ideology is a precapitalist vestige taken over and shaped as capitalism developed historically in various social formations. Further explanation apparently awaits further historical study. Yet in the meantime we are left wondering why this vestige was shaped so consistently in this way (sex segregation in the labour force and female responsibility for most domestic labour as mutually reinforcing tendencies that promote the subordination of women) and when, if ever, a more general explanation will emerge. Will it only occur when, in positivistic fashion, enough bits of historical evidence have been accumulated? Or is it for Barrett impossible, in principle, to arrive at such a general explanation?

However, while we are wondering there are, as Connelly correctly points out, significant theoretical and political implications attached to the different positions (those of Connelly/Barrett and of ourselves). The first implication discussed by Connelly is that because gender divisions preceded capitalism there is no guarantee that they will automatically disappear with its demise. We agree wholeheartedly, but think our approach offers more than historical precedence on the question. Feminism cannot be collapsed simply into socialism, because with socialism comes the replacement of commodity/market forces with explicitly political forces — with the creation of the conditions for the full flowering of conscious human agency. This, after all, is a large part of socialism's appeal. In such a context, domestic labour will not be devalued by commodity fetishism, but *can* nevertheless be devalued – and women can be subordinated – under socialism unless feminists are vigorous participants in the ongoing struggle to define and achieve the socialist project, and unless socialist women and men are prepared to take their biological differences into account.

Secondly, Connelly warns against yielding to assumptions of functional necessity – assumptions that have often plagued contributions to the domestic labour debate. We think our approach, with its emphasis on a method that is historical and dialectical as well as materialist, and with its focus on struggle and contradiction, avoids such assumptions while also avoiding both the restriction of attention to historically specific conditions – in particular, social formations and theoretically unspecified arguments about what is 'crucial' to capitalism.

Thirdly, she points out that class struggle and women's struggle (as 'class' is now perceived) do not always coincide, and that working-class and middle-class women do not always share the same form of oppression. Our position on class struggle versus women's struggle emphasizes the necessity of stretching the concept of 'class' to cover the subsistence as well as the production units under capitalism. We certainly have no difficulty with the notion of class differences among women, and indeed devoted much of our initial article to an exploration of these differences, especially as they affect human biology.

Fourthly, Connelly argues that her position enables us to move away from assigning to women's biology the responsibility for women's relegation to a subordinate place. It is, however, the capitalist mode of production, with its splitting of commodity production and subsistence units and with its commodity fetishism, that now does the relegating – not biology. Women's biological capacity is a liability, rather than a strength, under the historically specific conditions of capitalism. The severity of the liability is of course a matter of historical developments and struggles in concrete social formations, but it is necessarily and enduringly a liability under capitalism. That is itself a powerful indictment of the inhumanity of capitalism.

Fifthly, for Connelly her position alerts us to the fact that capitalist penetration of the Third World affects women differently than in Canada, with Third World women often being hired while their husbands remain unemployed. But the feminization of certain labour-force jobs is of course not limited to the Third

World. That its explanation is in many instances best found in the examination of particular concrete decisions or struggles does not detract from the position that women are systematically disadvantaged in the capitalist labour market. Indeed, demands for female paid workers in the Third World – as elsewhere – often stem precisely from this disadvantage.

Sixthly, Connelly argues that her position directs our attention to an ideology of gender – incorporated in the dominant ideology – and to the construction of femininity and masculinity. The point, however, is to sort out how this ideology is grounded – to establish its material basis. Only then can an analysis that is both feminist and Marxist be developed. This does not mean that there is a direct correspondence between the economic structure and the dominant ideology of a social formation, but it does mean that there is some sort of link between the two that can in principle be established.

While we would not claim to have presented a definitive feminist-Marxist analysis, our approach does have some implications of its own. First, it allows for, and in fact calls for, the analysis of biological differences between women and men. On the one hand, feminist Marxism is bound to founder if it fails to theorize these differences. On the other hand, the content of these differences is, within limits, historically constituted. Our approach neither ignores them nor treats them as being 'natural' in the sense of being unchangeable.

Secondly, because free-wage labour, and not biological differences (or the sexual division of labour) *per se*, is the defining characteristic of the capitalist mode of production to which we draw attention here, the subordination of women can be eliminated, but only with the elimination of capitalism itself. While our position is in the end optimistic about the possibility of sex equality, it is also revolutionary. While changes, including changes for the better, can and do occur under capitalism, sex equality in our view requires the demise of this mode of production. By contrast, if the explanation of women's subordination is located exclusively at the level of concrete social formations, the implication is ultimately reformist, as it is seen to be possible – however unlikely – to achieve sex equality within such a capitalist social formation.

Thirdly, as Connelly accurately points out, we resist the use of the term 'gender' to distinguish, as she puts it, the socially assigned from the biologically determined. We do so for two main reasons – reasons that are related. In the first place, it is very difficult to distinguish just what is socially assigned from what is biologically determined. To use 'gender' is, at least in some circumstances, to make the misleading suggestion that the distinction is clearly established. Even where sex-specific biological characteristics can be separated from socially assigned ones, these characteristics still have meaning only within a class and historical context and are still influenced by an economic environment. In the second place, to use 'gender' is to imply, inaccurately, that biology itself is outside society and history. A central feature of our argument is that biology is in fact influenced by class society – that it indeed has a history. Biological structures, as well as their evaluation and implications, vary with privilege and over time.

Connelly has made a significant contribution to the project of theorizing sex inequality. The process of refining our analysis of women's subordination under capitalism happens best through public debate of the sort her comment has provoked.

Hegemony and Superstructure: A Feminist Critique of Neo-Marxism

Mary O'Brien

The question for feminists has always been: where do we start? The answer cannot be other than: where we are and with the conditions and problems which history presents to us. Thus neo-Marxism, which marginalizes women but does not obliterate them, may hold heuristic and analytical possibilities which its current androcentrism conceals. For example, it may permit a deeper understanding of the relation of patriarchy and that complex abstraction which we call the state.

The attempt to rescue Marxist understanding of the state from the crude pincers of economism and reductionism has its own intellectual roots in the work of Antonio Gramsci. Gramsci aspired to produce a historical materialist analysis which would revitalize, elaborate and, above all, be tactically useful in the fight against fascism; he also hoped to promote the understanding of the relation of theory to culture, ideology and to political practice. Like all competent dialectical logicians, he had to postulate his problematic in terms of a dialectic of universal and particular. Unlike Hegel, who opposes the universal spirit of Reason to particular historical understandings of rationality, or Marx, who proceeds to the analysis of capitalism from the opposition of generalized commodity production and particular commodity, Gramsci proceeded from a different formulation, one which was historically developed by Marx himself but not adequately explicated.

Gramsci was concerned to analyse the relation of a historically generalized economic substructure and the complex particularity of superstructures. He argued that superstructures, in terms of culture and ideology, have their own dialectical dynamics, and that class antagonisms are mediated in cultural activities, both of social forms and class consciousness. This struggle takes place in a social arena which exists between the economic realm and the apparatus of ruling-class coercion which is but one aspect of the state. Ideology is not a product of naked coercion but of social practice in the realm of everyday life and thought, where consciousness acts on the experiential social context in which the subject is immersed, and where men (*sic*) can only deal with the realities which history presents to them.

This complex theoretical project has two significant dimensions: for Gramsci, the rise of the 'corporate' fascist state had thrown into stark relief the centrality of the state in superstructural and infrastructural formations; the state had developed historically into much more than the executive committee of the ruling class. On the other hand, Gramsci had studied Croce's polemic against materialism, and his positing of historicity as the essence of universal man was perceived by Gramsci to be the culmination of the defects of subjective idealism, an abstract individualism which lay like dead matter in the heart of the reality of community. He did not note that 'universal man' was a male supremicist construct.

For Gramsci, what was important was the creation of a universal class, which meant the abolition of class as such. Gramsci understood class consciousness itself to be dialectically structured – the site of a struggle between 'common sense', or acceptable knowledge, and 'good sense', which has the potential to overthrow common sense and its ideological baggage in the revolutionary struggle to realize true consciousness. Hegemony is the 'motor' of common sense, defining reality and organizing consent to such ruling-class definitions of truth, but in that very process it creates the possibility of counter-hegemony.[1] Hegemony relies on cultural relations. Education is especially vital to elaborate the axioms of practices of 'common sense', yet in doing this it creates the critical 'good sense' which challenges accepted definitions.

There is nothing at all abstract about Gramsci's epistemology. According to him, working-class consciousness is based on economic reality, but this is not a reflexive nor a reductionist relation. It is a *mediated* relation, and the mediator is culture or in Gramsci's terminology, civil society. The significance of the hegemonic and mediative functions of the state becomes clear when the state takes a totalitarian form. Gramsci's understanding of the state is that of class rule working on two superstructural

levels:[2] political society and civil society. These together constitute hegemony, the one protecting the hegemony of the ruling
class 'by the armour of coercion',[3] the other, civil society, representing the needs of individuals and standing between the political level of state and economic structures. For Gramsci, this is
by no means a formal model, nor does he utilize it with particular
consistency, but what he does understand clearly is that the relation between substructure and superstructure must be socially
mediated in the living relations of proletarians and bourgeoisie.

The economic substructure not only produces goods, it 'produces' social relations,[4] but the political drama and 'organic
unity' of these relations is played out in the realm of civil society
where it creates autonomous cultural forms. The state attempts
to control these cultural forms, and does so, when necessary, by
summoning its coercive powers; but it cannot and does not need
to produce detailed blue prints as long as it can prescribe acceptable outlines of common sense and elicit general consent to
these. This has two implications for Gramsci. The first is that the
working class must struggle to define and direct its own cultural
formations. It can, in fact, initiate cultural changes *within civil
society*, 'pre-formations', in Gramsci's terminology, of the eventual destruction of the state and transformation of mode of production. Secondly, Gramsci insists the state *must* wither away if a
universal classless society is to achieve its historic mission of the
negation of class, for the state is no abstraction but the living
totality of class division. Such a doctrine explains why Mussolini
preferred to keep Gramsci locked up, but it hardly made him a
hero in terms of Stalinism either.

This short summary lays no claim to be definitive: there is
much debate about what Gramsci actually understood by 'civil
society', about his actual relation to Marx and Lenin's theoretical
formulation, and whether he really believed that ideological/
cultural relations were not only autonomous but were moments
which took temporal precedence over the transformation of
productive forces in changing a particular 'historical bloc'.[5] Such
questions exercise Gramsci scholars as indeed they should: the
question of whether a new form of state must *enforce* morality
until such time as the masses stop resisting the displaced interpretation of morality is no small matter. It is, in part, an historical
question in terms of whether all states have actually done this,
but is also an ethical concern: is it necessary for new and *revolutionary* states to combine hegemony and force until they achieve

classless consensus? Gramsci claims that, in practice, strong states rule more by hegemony – that is, consensual politics – than by tyranny.

Politics and education become inseparable in Gramsci's work: political action is education. In this broad sense, education is the key to the maintenance of hegemony, but it also leads to the breakdown of hegemony by challenging and, eventually, overthrowing consensus. Where, then, is this activity to be located? Both theoretically and in practice, it is found in that social space and in those social relations which Gramsci calls 'civil society':

> What we can do for the moment, is to fix two major superstructural levels: the one that can be called 'civil society' that is the ensemble of organisms commonly called private, and that of 'political society' or 'the State'. These two levels correspond on the one hand to the function of 'hegemony' which the dominant group exercises throughout society and on the other hand to that of 'direct domination' or command exercised through the State and juridical government.[6]

What is of great interest to feminists, I think, is Gramsci's notion that civil society not only can be but must be transformed in a concrete manner.[7] The concept of 'civil society', so important to Enlightenment thought and to Hegel's notion of its transcendence by the universal state, is not treated systematically by Gramsci. It is for him the realm of *needs* rather than the stern *necessity* for survival which governs economic activity. These needs are deeply felt, and their social expression is shaped by rather than emergent from the economic realm. It is needful but not necessary for the ruling class to perpetuate itself by controlling the state apparatus, just as it is needful but not necessary for the proletariat to prepare itself for the political struggles which will abolish particular man in the creation of universal man and abolish class antagonisms in the abolition of class itself. For such a project, proletarian man, in Gramsci's view, has a need for education: education is therefore a precondition of militant class consciousness and an active promise of the possibility of transforming false consciousness to true consciousness. The notion that patriarchy is or has been needful but not necessary is not part of Gramsci's analysis, but as 'needs' is defined as historical, as opposed to 'necessity' which is biological, the formulation raises some challenging theoretical and practical questions for feminists.

The opposition of particular man and universal man is the second axiom of Gramsci's dialectical logic, an opposition to be mediated only by the revolutionary class activity which will abolish the coercive state in favour of a universalized (that is, classless and stateless) civil society. Gramsci argues strenuously against all notions of 'man-in-general': indeed he scorns all human nature theories. The quest to identify the 'essence of man', so important in the history of political thought, is vehemently rejected: 'man', for Gramsci, is not a concept, nor is he 'natural'. He is a social product, and his subjectivity is grounded in the 'subjectivity of a social group'.[8] However, Gramsci's perception of 'man' at no time denies his masculinity *per se*; Gramsci no doubt thinks it is a non-genderic form, but it is not, for Gramsci has no notion of patriarchal hegemony and the reality of gender conflict.

Non-antagonistic forms of social unity are to emerge from class struggle and the transformation of the production mode. The interesting point is that Gramsci argues that the political strategies which can bring this about involve a preliminary struggle to transform civil society. There is a clear relation between Gramsci's notion of civil and political society and feminist concern with private and public life, and his scheme embodies at least some notion that the personal is political. Indeed, he has been criticized for a tendency to lapse into psychologism. However, apart from the obvious problem of the genderic particularization of 'universal man', Gramsci's notion of civil society is also circumscribed by his fixation on education and his neglect of family relations. He speaks of civil society as local culture centred on school and family but – at least in his translated works – has little to say about family.[9] He is more interested in the birth of organic intellectuals than in the birth of real live babies.

It is not at all clear whether Gramsci envisaged changes in the form and/or content of familial relations. It is one thing to claim that the nuclear form of family is the specific form developed in capitalist society: there is historical evidence for this theory. It is quite another thing to claim that the only content of family which is interesting for Marxists is the economic structure of households and the sexual division of labour, as Marxist-feminists have been wont to affirm. This statement opens the possibility of reforming the economic life of women or even the level and strategy of political involvement for women, but still permits the dismissal of social relations of biological reproduction on the grounds that such an interest can serve only to steer inquiry into the muddy and unproductive waters of biological determinism.[10] The family is functional in so far as it reproduces labour power on an individual and species basis. It also reflects property relations, though less so in terms of corporate power and limited liability than in earlier historical forms of property relations. As understood by most Marxists, the relation of the family to mode of production is at best reflexive and at worst reductionist.[11] The family's role in ideological reproduction – in the socialization of young children, for example – is rarely examined, and its role in the reproduction of the social and ideological relations of male supremacy is thought to be exhausted in the concept of the sexual division of labour. There is thus a dogged evasion of the reality that women are oppressed by men.

The historical definition of 'people' in general as 'universal man' rests on the arbitrary conceptualization of certain *necessities* – such as the continuity of the species as a precondition of history – as mere *needs*. This sort of absurdity is the product of patriarchal hegemony, and it should be theorized as such. The determinant realm in the production of patriarchy is not the mode of production but the 'ahuman' reality of biological reproduction. Patriarchy is a set of social relations, I would argue, grounded in the process of reproduction. All attempts to suggest that 'universal' classless 'man' will share *his* historic triumphs with women are as ideologically absurd as the canons of chivalry. They are absurd because women are not imperfect men with an inferior capacity for abstract thought and concrete action, nor is the oppression of women a sort of cultural by-product which illustrates the versatility of class hegemony. The concept of hegemony strongly points to the problem of ideology and popular consent in capitalist countries, then proceeds to define hegemony in the dialectically posed relations of economy, ideology and culture – the 'mode of production' embracing relations of production, the reproduction of labour power and ideological reproduction. In collapsing the reproduction of labour power, that is, sustenance, into mode of production, the actual reproductive labour of women (what, indeed, women always understand in the first instance by the word 'labour'), which ensures the birth of the individual and the continuity of the species, is negated.[12] In collapsing women's productive labour into labour in general, the actual exploitation of women workers by men workers is negated. In collapsing the particular ideology of male supremacy into the general category of ideological reproduction, the systematic denigration and, indeed, the physical violation of women in the name of that ideology, are negated. The results of this are twofold: in the first place, Marxism has nothing to say about the value of individuals; in the second place, it has nothing to say about gender struggle.

The question of the individual is one which produces a number of kneejerk responses from many Marxists: cries of bourgeois individualism, subjectivism and psychologism rend the air. To be sure, the polemic against liberal individualism, with its greedy sense of 'I'm all right, Jack' and its inability to distinguish between free trade and free people, is one which has to be mounted. Marxist feminists have, on the whole, shared this polemic. We have not yet started to assert the need to pose our materialist problem specifically from our own experience, to ask the forbidden questions and to proclaim that, if the theory does not fit, then the theory is inadequate. For example, we do not ask what, if it is the case that all labour creates value, is the sort of value created by women's reproductive labour? Is it not, in some sense (a sense to be analysed), the value of the individual life poised in dialectical contradiction to the life of the species? Why are we nervous of claiming that feminine experience creates and, in the teeth of patriarchal hegemony, attempts to sustain certain moral values which may not sit comfortably with those whose political imagination chokes in the mouths of cannons? Why do we not give the lie to the claim that birth is merely a biological happening, when our sex has universally created a reproductive culture around this event, consisting of variable, identifiable and persistent sets of social relations among mothers, sisters, midwives, children and (usually rather transitorily) men? Why do we accept the absurd insistence that capitalism has abolished the distinction between private and public life when millions of women are suffering privatization and privation in households? Why should we accept the notion that ideological hegemony is sustained in schools and in political parties when we know quite well that the hand that rocks the cradle is making sure that the swaddling clothes are either pink or blue?

Marxist feminists have no difficulty at all in understanding that social change is a collective endeavour, but we must surely be a little more critical of a collectivity in which the individual members never get born. That women's labour is cheap labour is indisputable and must be changed. That life is cheap is not, I suggest, a careless indifference on the part of a ruling class, but a systematic indifference of a ruling sex to the value produced by women's reproductive labour. Only labour, Marx held, produced value, yet, by denying the capacity of women's reproductive labour power to produce value and failing to analyse and identify that value in social terms, we are left defenceless in the face of idealist claims that the value of a foetus is the same as the cultural value of a human being. There can be no human value without human labour, and no human value which is separate from the social relations which render it material.

All these issues are posed in a still preliminary way. Ironically, the understanding of how hegemony works might well be clarified in an ethnography of Marxist intellectuals. In Gramsci's terms, it may well be that Marxist intellectuals are now traditional because any claim they may have to be 'organic' is destroyed in the vulgar teleology of the unicausality of productive modes on the one hand, and the refusal to come to terms with the social construction of the ideology of male supremacy on the other. This difficulty cannot be cured either by the extension of ethnographies to female sub-groups or by the limitation of Marxist-feminist enquiry to questions of women in the work-force and to domestic labour. What is needed is an historical model which can give an account of male supremacy as an autonomous historical development. The crude superstructural model owes no debt to dialectical logic, and can get along quite well with positivist methodology. The dialectical relations, appearing by definition as class struggle, are found in both levels of structure, but the connection between the two levels is an unsolved problem. Hegemony theory goes some way towards resolution of this problem by Gramsci's positing of 'civil society' as a mediating realm. What is being mediated, however, is a relation which is not dialectical, namely, the realm of economic necessity on the one hand and the need of a ruling class to control by means of violent coercion on the other. Quite apart from the obvious but unaddressed question of why hunger is epistemologically more important than sexuality, this relation is not even dichotomous, far less dialectical. Thus, the conception of civil society is partial, promising in form but very limited in content. The content of civil society cannot be circumscribed by the notions of political party experience as true education, or by faith in organic intellectuals bringing to the masses the knowledge which will make them withdraw consent to ruling-class hegemony. Female reproductive consciousness is an integrative consciousness, linking the generations in a continuity over time and linking people as equal values. Its mediating force is physical labour as the ground of reproductive knowledge. Male reproductive consciousness, on the other hand, is an alienated consciousness. Paternity is essentially ideal: it is based on concept rather than experience, and dependent on a particular mode of reasoning, that of cause and effect. It is thus historical, for modes of reasoning are historical developments, and paternity must be understood as historical discovery. It is a problematic discovery: the discovery of integration in general species being is, at the same time, the discovery of material alienation from species being. Paternity is the discovery of uncertainty, materially grounded in alienation of the male seed. For men, physiology is fate, as I have remarked elsewhere. Paternal praxis arises in the context of efforts to mediate the alienation of the seed. These efforts generally take the forms of collusion with other men, the appropriation of children, and thus of women's reproductive labour, and the building of a hegemonic system to justify these procedures and to engineer consent to their interpretations of gender and knowledge. Historically, these efforts have been successful, and the condition of their success has lain in the involuntary component of women's reproductive labour. The fight for the control of reproductive power has been, on the one hand, a fight to resist the alienation of men from reproductive process and, on the other hand, a struggle to maintain the involuntary nature of reproductive labour, to preserve men's reproductive freedom while cancelling their reproductive alienation. It is precisely because the involuntary component of reproductive labour is now challenged by technology (currently about as sophisticated as the water wheel) that the dialectics of reproduction emerge in a new social form, which challenge patriarchal praxis as a denial of actual female reproductive experience and a wilful transformation of female reproductive consciousness. It is odd indeed that we have still to argue that reproduction is a form of knowledge with profound epistemological significance for women and men, and the fact that the argument must be made is itself a massive triumph for patriarchal hegemonic practice.

There can be no real analysis of hegemony unless it is recognized that cultural forms are subject to the articulation of consent of both a ruling class and a ruling sex. This recognition, in turn, cannot be accomplished on the grounds of economic determinism, however ameliorated or redivided. History has two infrastructures, one concerned with the daily reproduction of individuals (economic activity) and the other concerned with the reproduction of the species (the birth and sustenance of the new generation). Thus, if we are to be successful dialecticians and creative feminologists, we must develop a theoretical model which expresses these relations. Rather crudely, I would suggest that such a model would understand superstructures or, if one prefers, 'civil society', as the level of mediation of the specific forms of contradiction emergent from three sources. The first of these is the economic substructure, in which contradiction emerges concretely as class struggle. The second is the reproductive substructure, in which contradiction emerges concretely as gender struggle. The third is the contradiction between these substructures, the contradiction between individual survival and genetic continuity, or the number of mouths to feed and the resources to feed them. Marxists, blinded by Malthusian antipathies, do not rate this latter question as 'real', for they do not account demography a dialectical science. If they think at all about, for example, the fate of children in the southern Sahara, the clichés of imperialist exploitation serve as adequate explanation. Meanwhile, the children die. The holistic character of dialectical materialism cannot cope, either, with analysis of the social relations of genital mutilation: this is a Third World problem, we are told, and it would be impertinent to comment, far less interfere. Meanwhile, women suffer and die. The responsibility to conserve the natural environment is predicated on a concrete *genetic* relation to the future. Many men share in the social formation of an ethic of conservation, but, again, it is easier to lay the blame for destructiveness on capitalism rather than on men's alienated relation to the natural world.

The implications of a feminist model in terms of hegemony theory go far beyond the formulation of research questions or appropriate ethnographic samples. The question of consent is broadened from the public realm to the private realm: not only why and how a consensual working-class consciousness develops, but why women consent to the ideology and practice of patriarchy. As the latter consensus shows more signs of erosion than the former, it appears to be a promising field for both research and political praxis. As far as education is concerned, the preoccupation with schooling must extend from public institutions to the locus of gender identification and reproductive knowledge in the family. Further, the question of violent coercion cannot be held in abeyance simply because the ruling classes do not find it necessary at a given moment to unsheathe their sabres publicly: violence in the private realm is an ongoing mode of social control which *may* be related to capitalism but *is*, overtly and unquestionably, related to male control of reproduction.

Questions of the social construction of reality must take into account, as Marx noted, such questions which history presents to us. What Marx did not note was that this is done selectively by men in general as well as by bourgeois men in particular. The ruling class and the ruling sex have, at this moment, a joint historical mission, but we cannot understand the current effort to get women back into conventional marriage and unpaid labour simply as emergent from the tribulations of capitalist crisis. We can understand far more clearly how this actually works if we examine, for example, the social production of popular culture. One does not imagine that the state is sending out memos to songwriters to go back to sloppy lyrics about true romance, but they are being written. Why? The state is unlikely to encourage citizens to subvert the system, yet this is certainly happening in America in terms of education in divine creation, abortion and homosexuality. In Britain, of course, class manipulation is generally much clearer, and the major effort at retraditionalizing women which was involved in the Royal Wedding is chiefly remarkable for its capacity to mask the crudity of the objective with the pomp of the execution. These are hegemonic activities which emerge from the reproductive substructure and must be understood as so doing. Only from the standpoint of feminist theory can we analyse how these activities work, and thus proceed to unify theory with knowledge in developing action for social change, a counter-hegemonic thrust which will challenge patriarchal power by translating the contention that 'personal is political' from slogan to strategy, from private to public, from school to family and from theory to practice.

Racism, Ethnicity,
Nationalism

The Social Construction of 'Immigrant Women' in Canada

Roxana Ng

Introduction

Who is an 'immigrant woman'? In the everyday world, when we identify a woman as an 'immigrant woman', we do not only imply that person's legal status, although of course the term presupposes this legal relation. Our common-sense understanding of the term usually conjures up an image of a woman who is visibly different (that is, from a different ethnic or cultural background); who cannot speak English properly; who does not behave appropriately in public situations; and who occupies a certain position in the occupational hierarchy (for example, a cleaning-lady or a sewing-machine operator in a sweat-shop). In other words, the term implies a class relation.[1]

In this paper, I want to proceed from this common-sense connotation of the term, and explicate the processes through which 'immigrant women' come to be constituted as a visible social category in Canadian society. I shall argue that 'immigrant women' are special 'commodities': a special kind of labour, in the labour market. When we call a woman an 'immigrant woman', we are naming, knowingly or unknowingly, the social relations[2] which lead to the commodification of a certain group of people (in this case, women belonging primarily to visible minority groups) in Canada. That is, we are not simply identifying a group of people; more to the point, we are identifying *how* some people are *transformed* in relation to the productive processes of society. This understanding is derived from Braverman's work on changes in the composition of the working class under monopoly capitalism. This is what he says:

The term 'working class', properly understood, never precisely delineated a specified body of people, but was rather an expression for an ongoing process . . . the mark of which is the *transformation* of sectors of the population.[3]

In my work I have identified three moments of how 'immigrant women' are constituted as a group. While I am outlining these moments separately as a backcloth of my discussion, I wish to state that the processes embodied in these moments are intertwined and cannot be isolated easily in the real world. The first of these moments is immigration. Historically, 'immigrant women' are the product of capitalist development, which displaces segments of the population from their indigenous livelihood and draws them to centres of new industrial development where they are more and more tied to an economy based on profit-making: a monetary economy. 'Immigrant women' become a social entity only after the rise of the phenomenon of immigration, which in turn indicates a process whereby different labour supply systems are integrated into the world capitalist economy[4] and where there is an international division of labour.[5]

Secondly, we must take into account the composition of the Canadian labour market, which is stratified by gender and race/ethnicity. The stratified character of the labour market is itself the product of an historical process which has to do with the struggle between capital and labour. In Canada, this process is intimately linked to the history of colonization of North America where immigrant labour was and is used to build up Canada as a nation.[6]

Thirdly, there is a host of institutional processes at work which continually reorganize and reproduce the stratification already existing in the labour market. This includes the work of professional organizations and labour unions which organize groups of workers (and thereby excluding others) to ameliorate the exploitation of capital, intervention by the state to facilitate the accumulation of capital, and various service delivery systems (e.g. education, social and health services) in the state and voluntary sectors. My discussion will focus on a part of this array of institutional processes which serve to constitute 'immigrant women' as a special category of labour.

Specifically, my work deals with the work of a community agency which provided employment counselling and placement services to non-English-speaking women from Chinese, Vietnamese, Italian, and Spanish backgrounds and black women. The agency began as an advocacy group whose goal was to work on behalf of 'immigrant women' in their job search. By examining the work process of the agency in terms of state and labour market relations, my inquiry reveals that the agency's operation underwent certain transformations since its inception so that it came to work on behalf of the state apparatus in organizing and producing 'immigrant women' as a distinctive kind of labour in the labour market.[7] Figure 1 outlines these relations in schematic representations. Further, the constitution of 'immigrant women' as 'commodities' was accomplished through 'a documentary mode of action'.[8]

Diagram 1
Schematic Representation of the Production of Immigrant Women

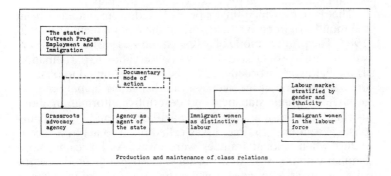

This paper will explicate one component of the work of the employment agency, namely, the counselling and placement process to show how 'immigrant women' came to be constituted through this process. It will become visible in this discussion that gender and race/ethnicity are the threads which are woven into the entire process: they are part of the 'ingredients' in constituting the class locations of 'immigrant women'. Thus, the paper will close with a re-examination of the conceptualization of gender and ethnicity in sociology.

Framework and Data

The analytical procedure used in this paper is one of 'substructing'[9] and has its origin in Marx's method of political economy.[10] In conducting a critique of political economy, Marx began with the categories of political economists; he traced the activities underpinning the origins of the terms and re-embedded them in the social relations out of which they arose. Similarly, in unpacking the term 'immigrant women', I am attempting to explicate some of the social relations which constitute the category 'immigrant women' used to name some members of our society. The practices which constitute this group or category, then, become the basis for understanding the locations of 'immigrant women' and how they are related to other members of society.[11] This approach raises important theoretical and political questions which I will address in the final section of this paper.

The data, on which this paper is based, were obtained from ten months of intensive fieldwork at the employment agency in 1981. The primary mode of investigation was participant observation, with a progressive shift from observation to participation as the fieldwork proceeded. That is, I was permitted to observe the daily routine of the agency in exchange for helping the co-ordinator compile statistical and descriptive information about its clients and its operation for record-keeping and funding purposes. From time to time, I was called upon to act as a receptionist when student trainees were away. As I became more familiar with the work of the agency, I also volunteered to work with clients as a counsellor when the work-load of the agency increased during the summer of my fieldwork. In this way, I gained an encompassing picture of the different work processes involved, from the documentary process which was primarily the responsibility of the co-ordinator to the counselling and placement aspect of the agency's work. My participation as an active member of the agency enabled me to gain an experiential sense of the contradictions involved in working as an advocate in a system where employers' and funding demands exerted constant pressure on one's daily work.

The discussion presented is based on analysis of the field-notes, interviews with workers, selected taped sessions of my interviews with clients (conducted in Chinese), and documents pertaining to the agency which included various forms that the agency filled out as part of its routine operation. In analysing these materials, the object is not to recover the workings of the agency in terms of whether its work is 'typical' of similar community agencies. The enterprise is to situate the agency in its organizational context in order to explicate how it played a determinate part in facilitating labour market processes by examining how it dealt with one segment of the working population, namely women who did not speak English or were from visible minority groups. This approach has been called 'institutional ethnography' by Smith.[12] It places an emphasis on the social relations which are embedded, though not immediately visible, in a local setting (see note 2).

I shall argue that the counselling and placement process through which 'immigrant women' come to be produced as a special group of workers in the labour market is a 'class' process. By 'class' I am not only referring to the locations which they occupy in the occupational hierarchy – the subject of many contemporary Marxist analysts who are concerned to classify and make sense of the gradations of occupations resulting from the increasing fragmentation of the labour process in the twentieth century.[13] I am making use of the original formulation of the concept expounded by Marx and Engels in *The German Ideology*[14] and *The Communist Manifesto*[15] which treats class fundamentally as a *relation.* It refers to the way in which human activities are organized in terms of the productive processes of a particular mode of production; for instance, what we have come to identify as labour market processes in capitalist societies. The strategy here is not to use 'class' as a theoretical concept which needs to be operationalized, but to unfold it as a set of articulated processes which are carried out through organized practical activities fully available for empirical investigation. (See my discussion on Marx's concept of 'social relations', note 2.) I want to preserve the notion of 'class' as a dynamic process whereby people's practices and actions are implicated by virtue of their locations in a determinate organization. This is how Marx describes commodity production.[16] This way we can begin to see how people's work enters them into certain courses of action (as in the case of the employment counsellors studied) which are not necessarily intended by them, the actors, but which nevertheless implicate them in determinate ways. This usage of the concept will become more visible as I proceed.

The Constitution of 'Immigrant Women' through
Job Counselling and Placement

As a general background to the process which I will describe in
due course, it should be mentioned that the agency was funded
through the Outreach Program of the Federal Department of
Employment and Immigration. The objective of the Outreach
Program, according to various departmental documents, was

> To improve, with the help of community-based agencies, the
> employability and employment of individuals who experience
> special difficulties competing in the labour market and who are not
> able to benefit effectively from the services offered by their CEC
> (Canada Employment Centre). The essential purpose of Outreach is
> to complement, and effectively extend, regular services of the Com-
> mission to such groups.

Women, because of their disadvantageous position in the
labour market, were targeted as one of such groups, and the
employment agency was funded under the category 'women'
with special reference to 'immigrant women'. Thus it can be seen
that prior to the provision of services the jurisdictional domain
of the agency's work was already defined, in this instance
through the contract drawn up between the agency and Outreach. Services were provided to people of a certain gender, who
had a certain legal status (that is, immigrant versus citizen), and
who spoke certain languages or who were black. Gender and
ethnicity, however defined, became the most important criteria
for determining who would be eligible for services at the agency.
   A careful analysis of the counselling and placement process
reveals the double character of the agency's work with women. It
is in this process that the class character of the agency comes into
focus. While the intention of the agency was to assist women to
overcome the structural barriers of the labour market and promote their overall status, it was also through employment counselling that 'immigrant women', having the characteristics which
we recognize, came to be constituted as particular 'commodities'. Part of the counselling process involved the counsellor's
discretion and ability to work up the client's work experiences
and skills into 'credentials' which would then be matched with

the requirements of certain job openings. The counsellor selected, out of all the information given to her by the client, the relevant features of the client's social history and worked them up to conform to the kinds of 'skills' and requirements which employers specified in the job orders. While this part of the counselling process was a positive step in helping women with no marketable skills seen to be relevant to a highly advanced and differentiated labour process to secure employment, it was at the same time the way in which 'immigrant women' were organized into certain locations in the Canadian labour market. The counselling process which led to job placement was a way whereby 'immigrant women' were inserted into the class locations which they occupied in Canada. Because of the agency's relation to the state (through Outreach) and the labour market, it played a determinate part in facilitating labour market processes in producing 'immigrant women' as a distinctive kind of labour with certain skills and qualifications by organizing the relation between 'immigrant women' and their potential employers, the buyers of this kind of labour.

What should be noted is that the production of 'immigrant women' as 'commodities' was accomplished through documents. In the counselling process, women's work histories were translated by counsellors into 'skills' and 'abilities' in the agency's records, which were then matched to the types of jobs and requirements requested by employers when they placed job orders with the employment agency. The documentary process mediated the accomplishment of 'immigrant women' as a particular kind of labour in the labour market, and enabled the articulation of clients to available job openings. In turn, the records on clients, notably the Application for Employment (AFE) form, became the basis for calculating the statistical information requested by the funding program, thereby providing for the agency's articulation to the state apparatus.

The Intake Procedure

The intake procedure was the first moment of the screening process which took place at the agency. Whoever was acting as the receptionist at the time[17] ensured that the clients were female and were eligible for services in terms of the mandate of the agency. At the intake, women were asked to fill out an Application for Employment (AFE) form (see Figure 2) in English and were screened in terms of their ethnic backgrounds and linguistic ability. They were then matched to a counsellor according to these criteria. Thus clients who were ethnic Chinese and Vietnamese and who spoke these languages were sent to the Chinese counsellors; the Spanish-speaking clients either from Spain or from Latin American countries ended up with the Spanish counsellor; the black women, whether or not from the Caribbean countries, became the West Indian counsellor's clients, etc. If a client could speak English fluently, then her ethnic origin became less important in this matching process because any of the counsellors would be able to communicate with her.

Diagram 2
Application for Employment

APPLICATION FOR EMPLOYMENT 12.

(1) Date: ______

(2) Type of Job Sought: ______

(3) Name: ______ (family first middle) (4) Tel: ______

(5) Address: ______

(6) Date of Birth: ______ (7) Social Insurance No: ______

(8) Years in Canada: ______ (9) Country of Origin: ______

(10) Marital Status: ______ (11) No. of Children: ______

(12) First Language: ______ (14) English:

	Yes	No	Little
(14a) Speak			
(14b) Read			
(14c) Write			

(13) Immigrant Status: ______

(15) Education Record:

School	grade completed	date completed	course studied	certificate received
(15a) Grade				
(15b) High				
(15c) College				
(15d) Technical				
(15e) Others				

(16) Employment Record (Most recent employer first)

(16a) Company name	(16b) Where	(16c) Position	(16d) Salary	(16e) When

(17) Referral Source: ______

(18) Other Information: ______

(19) Date interviewed	(20) Counsellor	(21) Type of Service-remarks

etc.

(22) Case closed: (22a) when ______

(22b) why ______

Furthermore, as the caseload of the agency increased, women other than the ethnic and linguistic groups which the agency was funded to serve were refused service. Unless they could speak English and a counsellor was willing to undertake the case, they would be referred to other community agencies. The intake thus served as a means to screen out individuals who were seen to be ineligible for the agency's services by virtue of their ethnic origins. Once the AFE form was filled out, a client could proceed to see a counsellor, and the interview process began.

The Interview Process

As a matter of fact, very few clients could fill out the items on the AFE form unproblematically. Even when a client knew English reasonably well, inevitably she would fill in information which was irrelevant to what the counsellor wanted to find out. In the ensuing interview with the client, in addition to finding out the client's marketable skills and the kinds of jobs she wanted, it was also crucial for the counsellor to find out information on the client relevant to the agency's organizational requirements, which included the information necessary for the compilation of the statistics and for a successful placement. The AFE form was used as a way of initiating a dialogue between the counsellor and the client, as well as a way of organizing the interview.

In the interview process, the counsellors invariably referred to the application form to begin the counselling process, and used the form as a basis for eliciting information from the client. Filling in the form organized the interaction between a counsellor and her client. For example, if a client began to discuss things not central to the categories on the form, the counsellor would redirect the conversation or cut the client off altogether, so that the discussion would return to what the counsellor needed to know in order for her to fill in the form properly.

The interview process was central to the agency's work with 'immigrant women' because it was here that the clients of the agency were screened and articulated to jobs available in certain sectors of the labour market. It is in this process, as mentioned earlier, that the class character of the agency's work becomes visible. This includes three major features. First, in the interview, the counsellor selected the relevant features of the clients' work histories and translated them into the kinds of 'skills' and 'experiences' specified by employers, thereby organizing them into available job openings. In the screening process, the counsellor also engaged in a 'classfying practice' by selecting out women with differential skills and inserting them into different locations in the occupational hierarchy. Secondly, in the interview, the counsellor through questioning the client worked up her background as 'skills' and 'experiences' relevant to the job market. In this way the counsellor helped employers to screen potential employees, so that the counsellor herself became an agency of the employers as well as an 'advocate' for her client. The counsellor effectively became a 'gatekeeper'[18] of 'immigrant women's' entry into the labour market. Finally, an aspect of the counsellor's work involved socializing clients into the 'rules' of the Canadian labour market. This included explicit instructions to clients about attributes desired by employers (for example, punctuality, cleanliness, swiftness, and reliability), and implicit transformative work on client's experiences into the terms and categories used by employers (for example, translating a vague statement of the kinds of tasks which a client could do to specific skills and work experience). These features were woven into the entire counselling process, and the transformative work took place most notably during the intitial interview phase when the counsellor attempted to complete the AFE form with a client. In this paper, only this aspect of the counsellor's work will be highlighted.

The interview process, then, covered a range of topics aimed at discovering the marketable skills of the client, the types of jobs for which she was eligible, and what the client was willing to do, given her skills and current labour market conditions. During the interview, information elicited from the client was evaluated according to a set of categories on the AFE form. Usually, the interview session began with questions asked by the counsellor of the client's proficiency in English. Did she understand any English? How much? Had she ever taken an English training (ESL) programme? Where and for how long? (See Item 14 of AFE.) A client's proficiency in English was seen to be crucial in placement, because although the jobs available through the agency were directed primarily at the non-English-speaking segment of the labour force, the ability to understand basic English was an asset in most cases. It opened up more possible areas of employment for the client, as most employers preferred workers who could understand basic instructions, especially when the workers did not have previous work experience in that particular industry or business, and had to go through a period of training.

Educational level (Item 15 of AFE) and previous work experience (Item 16) of a client were two other chief areas to cover in the interview. Since very few of the clients had more than secondary education, and many only had elementary education, discussion about educational background was a cursive part of the interview. Added to this was the fact that levels of education had little relevance to many employers who placed job orders with the agency, so long as the client could understand instructions and do the work.[19]

Work experiences and skills, on the other hand, were a problematic and lengthy part of the interview for both the client and the counsellor. While work experience and its concomitant skills were important in establishing a client's employability, because of the nature of work commonly available to non-English-speaking and working-class black women, which comprised either menial work requiring a host of taken-for-granted skills (for example, domestic skills) or highly repetitive and highly differentiated work, it was usually difficult for them to describe what they did and what the work involved. Many of the clients did not even remember the name of their last employer or the location of their work. A typical answer from a client, when asked about her past employment, would be: 'Somewhere around Main Street' or 'the factory that made plastic things', and the client was unable to describe the commodity which the factory produced. Regarding her work skills, the client was frequently just as vague: 'I did what everyone else did,' or 'I put screws into these round things, you see.' The following example from my field-notes, recorded when I was acting as a counsellor at the agency, illustrates some aspects of this process and how a vague description of tasks was worked up into a specific job category by the counsellor.

> I tried to get her to explain to me what she did in the last place she worked. She said, 'Everything. Just like all the other people.' I told her it didn't tell me what she did and explained to her that she needed to explain her work to me so that I could tell what jobs would be suitable for her.
>
> It was difficult for her to do that. She tried quite hard to explain. They manufactured plastic basins. Like, the basins/sinks were plastic and they came out of a machine. Then she (and other workers) would put screws into the basins. They would wash them first. She also did some general clean-up work, like wiping up the mess and so on.
>
> As I was interrogating her, I realized that what I was doing was to try to categorize what she did so that (1) I could identify what kind of work she was looking for and (2) I could explain to the employers what this client's skills were when I phoned them up. But her description was so vague that after going around the subject several times, I still couldn't figure out what this factory did.[20]

In the case of this client, since I was unable to establish her precise skills based on the interview, I put down 'general factory work' after 'type of job sought' (Item 2) on her AFE. The information entered here was crucial because the type of job sought recorded on the client's record, together with her employment record (Item 16), became the basis for matching her to the job(s) available through the employment agency. (See Item 6 – position opened – and Item 10 – job description/ requirements of the Job Order Record.) Here we see that a description given by the client was translated, by the counsellor, into a category ('general factory work' for the client in question) which could be matched to the description provided by employers. The category of 'type of job sought' was important as it became a way for the counsellor to identify the position suitable for the client later on in the interview, when she had to place the client in a job opening.

Employment Contacts

I want to turn now to another aspect of the agency's work which, though much less visible, was equally central, and this is the agency's relation with employers. In order to arrive at a continual supply of job openings for its clients, employment counsellors had to establish contacts with employers who would place orders with the agency when they needed workers. In the two years since its inception, the agency had established a viable system of 'employer contacts'. While initially contacts were set up through visiting potential employers who were willing to hire immigrant workers and introducing the work of the agency to them, by the time I conducted fieldwork at the agency most of the employer contacts were carried out by telephone and revolved around a fairly stable network of employers. In addition, counsellors daily scanned the classified advertisements sections of the major newspapers to keep on adding employers to the agency's employers file. The process of selection was fairly random. It was to a certain extent shaped by the perceived needs and demands of the clients. For example, most of the agency's clients lived within the city boundaries, especially within the downtown core. Most of them did not have their own transport and therefore would not be able to travel long distances to work; thus it would be impractical to contact employers in the suburbs, for instance.

In terms of the reality of the labour market, non-English-speaking women, particularly those from visible minority groups, tend to concentrate in the bottom rungs of most service and manufacturing sectors in the so-called 'non-skilled' and dead-end positions. They are generally recruited into three kinds of services and industries. First, they are recruited into private service as office cleaners or domestic workers through a network of informal contacts. This kind of employment suits them because they do not have to use English and it offers some flexibility in working hours essential to women with family responsibilities. Secondly, they are employed in manufacturing and retail industries, such as light manufacturing in textile, garment and plastic factories. Thirdly, they are employed in service industries including restaurants, hotels and other food industries. 'Immigrant women' occupy the lowest positions in these types of work. In the garment industry, for example, they are mainly sewing-machine operators with practically no opportunity for upward mobility. In the service sector, they are dishwashers, kitchen helps, chambermaids, and janitors.[21]

According to a survey in Toronto on labour market conditions and training opportunities for non-English-speaking 'immigrant women', the companies which are likely to employ 'immigrant women' are not small companies, but larger institutions, factories and hotels employing a hundred or more people. This is because in a smaller workplace the likelihood of existing employees speaking the same language as the women seeking work is slight, and communication between employer and the new employees may thus be difficult, whereas in a larger place it is easier to accommodate new workers who need help in communicating in English. As well, job opportunities for non-English-speaking women are concentrated in the highly competitive textile and garment industry and in cleaning, laundry, and domestic jobs. Opportunities in the food and manufacturing industries are found to be minimal and generally restricted to the non-unionized places, for example, assembly-line food production and packaging firms.[22] My previous research indicates that small companies and restaurants which consistently hire non-English-speaking immigrants are retail enterprises and restaurants in the so-called 'ethnic' neighbourhoods which service a primarily ethnic clientele.[23] Such industries and businesses usually have poor working conditions and pay low wages, close to minimum wage. Due to the nature of their paid employment (for example, part-time, seasonal or piece work), labour standard legislation is not rigidly enforced in many cases, which further reinforces the poor circumstances under which 'immigrant women' have to work.[24] It can be seen that in order for the employment agency to find work for 'immigrant women', it had entered into those sectors of the labour market which pay low wages and have poor working conditions.

When an employer contacted the agency for workers to fill available job openings, the specifications of the company were recorded on a Job Order Record (JOR) – see Figure 3. In addition to the basic information required by the agency, such as the name, address, and phone number of the employer, types and number of positions opened (Items 6 and 7), etc., there was space on the JOR for the employer to describe the nature and requirements of the position(s) (Item 10 of JOR). The second half of the JOR form was reserved for the counsellor(s) to fill in details regarding the clients referred to this particular employer. Items 6 (position opened) and 10 (job description/requirements) were crucial categories in terms of the counselling process, because this information was used by counsellors to match their clients to available job openings.

Diagram 3
Job Order Record

JOB ORDER RECORD

(1) File no.: _____

(2) Date: _____

(3) Name of employer: _____   (4) Phone no.: _____

(5) Address of employer: _____

(6) Position opened: _____   (7) Number of position opened: _____

(8) Starting salary: _____   (9) Working hours: _____

(10) Job description/requirements: _____

_____

_____

_____

(11)Name of client sent	(12)Date	(13)Counsellor	(14)Remarks

etc.

(15) Date position is filled: _____

Job Placement

While there were several routine procedures which counsellors used to place a client in a job opening, I will focus my discussion on the relation betwen the JOR and AFE of a client, because regardless of the procedure(s) used, the 'match' was conducted using these two sets of forms.

The Job Order Records were filed in a large three-ring binder according to common categories of work received by the agency, such as domestic work, factory work, restaurant work, etc. 'Sewing' became a separate category during the period when I did fieldwork because it was the predominant industry where there was a constant demand for workers by employers. Once the counsellor identified the category of work which the client was seeking (Item 2 of AFE), she consulted the JORs under the appropriate heading in the job order file. She went through the available job openings under this category with the client, and they could decide which of the job(s) would best suit the client.

If a suitable opening was identified, the counsellor would phone up the employer, tell him about the client, and make an appointment for the client to see the employer. Even when an employer regularly made use of the agency to place his orders, very rarely would he hire the client directly over the phone; usually he preferred to look the candidate over himself, or have the candidate go through the firm's application procedure, such as filling out an application form in the personnel department of the company. If the counsellor's telephone conversation with the employer was very positive, she could send the client to see the employer right away, and consider this step a placement. But it is more often the case that the counsellor would ask the client to call her back to inform her of the result of the job interview before closing this client's file.

At this stage of the interview, the counsellor usually attempted to provide the client with more details about the job. In the case of sewing work, for example, she would tell the client the type(s) of machine(s) the client was expected to operate. There might be a discussion on wages and working hours. The counsellor tried to ensure that the client knew as much about the job as possible so that she would not have false expectations. Frequently this phase of the interview process also included instructions to the client regarding bus routes, the appropriate things to say in the interview with the employer, and the way in which the client should present herself. If a client was to start a job, the counsellor often impressed the client with the importance of being punctual. As well, she might act as a messenger for the employer if he had any special instructions for the client, and so forth. What is of interest here is that by placing a client in a job opening with certain characteristics (for example, certain kinds of skills and personal qualities) required by the employer and by providing instructions to the client about the special requirements of a particular employer, the counsellor in effect *produced* a client as a special commodity having these special characteristics. When the client joined the labour force, she in fact *became* an 'immigrant woman' whom we recognize as such in the everyday world.

Thus, the counselling process leading to job placement is one moment in the constitution of 'immigrant women' as a visible social category in Canadian society. The work of employment counsellors did not only dovetail the stratification already existing in the labour market; it actively organized and reproduced such stratification. In the case examined above, we see how gender and race/ethnicity are constitutive features of the organization of 'immigrant women's' class locations in Canada.

Theoretical and Political Implications

This paper has been an attempt to interrogate the phenomenal provenance of the term 'immigrant women', and to locate it in the social relations in which it is embedded. I argued that 'immigrant women' as we understand them are the products of a set of historical and political processes. My examination of the work of a community employment agency captured one moment whereby 'immigrant women' came to be constituted as a social category in the Canadian labour market.

I would like to conclude by discussing the theoretical and political lessons learned from this investigation. While there is a tendency in recent analyses of class relations to investigate class in terms of a set of socio-economic indicators, I suggest that by using Marx's original formulation we can locate class relations empirically in the everyday world. In this formulation, class is not confined to the narrowly defined economic realm. It is a ubiquitous feature of society which penetrates all spheres of social life and is embedded in very ordinary features of everyday life: as people look for jobs and as people go about the daily routine of doing their work. Class relations, then, can be examined as an empirical matter.

In this understanding, ethnicity and gender are not 'variables' to be counterposed against class as competing determinants of social status in society.[25] In a capitalist social formation, they are fundamental to the organization of productive relations; they are integral constituents in the organization of class. I owe much of this insight to the recent development in Marxist-feminist scholarship. In a brilliant article which explores the relationship between women, family, and class, Dorothy Smith makes the following observation:

> In pre-capitalist societies, gender is basic to the 'economic' division of labour and how labour resources are controlled. In other than capitalist forms, we take for granted that gender relations are included. In peasant societies for example, the full cycle of production and subsistence is organized by the household and family and presupposes gender relations. Indeed, we must look to capitalism as a mode of production to find how the notion of the separation of gender relations from economic relations could arise. It is only in capitalism that we find an economic process constituted independently from the daily and generational production of the lives of particular individuals and in *which therefore we can think economy apart from gender.*[26]

I am not arguing that gender and ethnicity are reducible to class. I am suggesting that analyses of gender and ethnic relations cannot be understood by abstracting them from the particular context within which they arise and come to occupy their unique ontological domains. They cannot be understood without the kind of class analysis Marx and Engels expounded. Gender and ethnic relations must be located in a particular social formation. When we take this strategy, we see that ethnicity and gender are constitutive features of productive relations. The fact that we can think of ethnicity and gender as separate social phenomena is itself a product of our kind of society which introduces an artificial separation between economic and social life.

Finally, by adopting this view on class, I imply that social inequalities are not 'frozen' in structural processes over which we have no control. Our own action, though not necessarily intended, can and does contribute to the ongoing production and maintenance of inequality. My analysis of the counselling process of the community agency shows how community advocates can serve to reproduce existing divisions in the class structure. This is another way in which the contradictions generated by capitalist production can divide us from each other and from our common struggles. Thus, it is not simply for theoretical interest that we need to adopt an analysis which can address the contradictions and realities of a continually changing world. We also have a responsibility to other members of society who can really benefit from analyses of their situations which rely on the skills that sociologists learn from their academic training.

Theories of the Family and Family/ Authority Relationships in the Educational Sector in Québec and France, 1850–1960

Nadia Fahmy-Eid and Nicole Laurin-Frenette

The principal Marxist theorists have paid scant attention to the family, and consequently the Marxist theory of the family has hardly progressed beyond the general principles of Engels's formulation.[1] While Marxist research has certainly done a thorough job of analysing the particular forms of the economic processes (of production, circulation and so on) of the capitalist mode of production, the processes which maintain the control and regulation of capitalist society and its reproductive processes remain relatively uncharted. These processes of capitalist production and their associated mechanisms, especially the family and the state, have been the object of numerous studies, but we still have no universal theory of their particular forms and dynamics. Most theories relating to the political and ideological organization of capitalism are based on the study of particular societies or on a particular type of bourgeois society. Consequently, their applications are somewhat limited. We want first to bring out the common elements in the standard discussions regarding the organization of the regulation and reproduction of capitalist societies, and then to show the limits to the application of some of their propositions. A comparison between Québec and other bourgeois societies, especially France, will allow us to illustrate certain special points in the processes of regulation and reproduction in a capitalist society, which cannot be explained by any existing theory. Our study will place special emphasis on questions relating to those structures which are considered most important from the point of view of regulation and reproduction: the state, the church and the family.

It is generally agreed that these structures for the regulation and reproduction of capitalist societies have two main functions.

On one hand, they establish and guarantee various technical, economic and juridical conditions of production, such as the management of land, and the regulation of exchange, etc. On the other, they ensure control of the population. This is a multi-dimensional function, comprising demographic control and the supervision of its geographical movements, as well as education, social services and the police. Most theories assert that the state usually occupies a central place in the network of structures which exercise most of these functions. It is thought that the organization of the technical, economic, and juridical functions of regulation and reproduction rests on a complex articulation between the state and the economic structures of financial, industrial, commercial, labour and other sectors. The organization of control also implies a complex articulation between the state and cultural, religious, academic, medical and other institutions and, in particular, with the family. For structuralists influenced by Althusser, who over the last decade have provided the framework for a substantial reformulation of Marxist theory, the state represents the driving force behind the regulation-repression system of capitalist society. The key mechanisms of this system are termed ideological state apparatuses (ISA), because they 'run' on ideology, as Althusser put it, and because they are more or less completely subjugated to the strategy of the state. Thus, the family, the school, the church, the media and the various institutions of the culture fall into this heterogeneous category of ideological state apparatuses.[2] Yet with regard to the family, neither the nature of its status as an ISA nor the way it fits into the general system of ISA have been explained in Althusserian writings. The same is true for the church, the nature and function of which as an ISA has never been defined or illustrated by the Althusserian school. On the other hand, some recent theoretical tendencies inspired partly by Marxism, and working on the interface between history and sociology, have posited the family as the key element, the organizational pivot of the multi-dimensional control of populations in bourgeois societies.[3]

These theories and research generally propose that the family is at once the target and the agent of the multiple forms of social control. Thus the family would be the favoured object of what have for several years been called the strategies of power. According to these theories, modern forms of the family are determined by the integration of the family structure into networks of regulation and reproduction centered on the bourgeois state. The formation of the modern family in and by the state, had its beginnings around the seventeenth century and it entailed the dissolution or transformation of prior familial forms. Various so-called 'normalizing' interventions affecting the private life of the individual made the gradual achievement of this transformation possible. These 'normalizing' interventions are generated by various institutions framed and co-ordinated by the state – academic institutions, public and private foundations for patronage and social services, medicine, the church and so on. Thus, towards the end of the nineteenth century, the model of the bourgeois family was solidly implanted into society as a whole because, on one hand, it represented the solid guarantee of prosperity and social order, assuring as it did the reproduction of the material and cultural assets of the privileged class; on the other, it allowed the working classes to be immobilized, divided and supervised.

The Diversity of Bourgeois Societies

We agree that the universal result of organization, regulation and reproduction in capitalist society is the integration of the family into the network of power structures, and that this integration makes the family one of the most important of population control mechanisms. However, it seems to us that the social process which historically determines this integration of the family into the network of power structures is not the same in all capitalist societies and, indeed, the modes of integration of the family into power structures in capitalist society present a striking diversity. Current theories of the family derived from Marxism cannot account for this variation. Studies which do account for the transformation of the family into a power mechanism are based on the historical forms this process has taken in certain Western European societies, especially in France.

This research does not take into account the peculiarities that marked the development of the economic, political and ideological organization of capitalism in these societies; peculiarities which thus affected the specific process and mode of integration of the family into the power network of these societies.

First, there is the centralized and bureaucratic form of the bourgeois state which results from its previous form and evolution and which must be related to the development of state and para-state units of officials responsible for normalizing interventions into family life: teachers, social workers, health visitors, doctors, lawyers, scientists and so on. Secondly, there is the absence of a close and permanent alliance between the different parts of the ruling class linked either to the church or to the state and various property bases.

The development of capitalism in other societies does not present these peculiarities where the family, particularly in seventeenth and twentieth-century France, is interwoven with the networks of power through different processes and methods. However it is precisely the case of the French family (and analogous ones) that has been theorized and generalized in recent studies of the history and sociology of the family. In the United States and Canada, the bourgeois state takes a decentralized form, and state or para-state bureaucracy was, until the middle of the twentieth century, poorly developed. In the United States, 'normalizing' interventions into family life took place largely outside of the central state, even if the state did sometimes provide the legal basis for them. Also, local, municipal or state governments are more usually involved, and their activities are only rarely co-ordinated. Among other things, it is notable that the American family is enmeshed in concurrent networks of civic organizations or voluntary associations, which group citizens together on the basis of their age, race, ethnic group, sex, class, profession, religion and so on.[4] These voluntary associations are autonomous and are purely a matter of private initiative, and not supervised by or dependent upon the state. What is more, the contribution of immigration to the reproduction of labour power makes state demographic control unnecessary. Now, we know that elsewhere – in France for example – this kind of control is partly responsible for state investment in the family. In England, the state practises demographic *laissez-faire*, but in a different context from the United States. Historically, it is likely that the politics of the British state have the greatest effect on the material conditions of existence of the family, through laws framing the modes of work of women and children, and through financial assistance in the form of benefit payments.[5]

In several capitalist societies, notably Italy, Spain and Québec, the church plays a privileged role in the development of bourgeois social organization. There the church is integrated in an organic way into the dominant class, an integration which is translated by a stable and efficient division of power between church and state. It might even be thought that it is the weak internal cohesion of the dominant class (that is, of its economic and regional components) that makes the division of power between church and state possible. For the most part, this division removes the family from state control. It is then the church which organizes the family as a mechanism for the regulation and reproduction of capitalist society. The limits of state intervention in the family are fixed by the church, implicitly, as in Québec, or explicitly, as in Italy under the Concordat.[6] In this way, the state must take this ecclesiastical domination of the area of family life into account in the mode, object and frequency of its interventions. Moreover, this investment in the family by the church affects the organization of the family, especially the relationships between its members. A variety of observations point to the hypothesis that the church exercises its influence on the family principally through the mediation of women, in contrast with the state, which uses men as the transmission mechanism.

The church uses a whole range of methods and traditional techniques in its interventions in family life. In societies in which it holds a dominant place in the network of control structures, the church often has partial or exclusive control of population registration, allowing it special insights and the ability to study the various socio-demographic movements of that population, including births, marriages and deaths. Religious groups, associations and confraternities ensure the supervision (and regimentation) of all categories of the population, divided up according to sex, age, profession, etc. The mechanisms of ideological inculcation are put to work in the denominational school structure, by preaching and other modes of diffusion of religious discourse. To this list must be added the various 'personal' means of supervision the church disposes of: confession, family visits and so on. Finally, techniques for the 'normalization' of all kinds of deviants and marginal people, should also be noted, through charitable works for the poor, orphans and others. In the modern period, the church has continued to use these traditional techniques and methods while adapting them to the new living conditions of the population and in particular to those of the urban working class. Thus, the school and hospital systems, and especially the social service system, placed under the control of the clergy and of religious communities, have been expanded on a greater scale and their management has been modernized. Similarly, the system of religious and para-religious organizations which ensures supervision of the population has been diversified and extended to fit these new dimensions of existence, working, for instance, in trade unions and in leisure activities.

As we have already seen, the church's investment in the family in the context of capitalist society, is not unique to Quebec. However, the mode of articulation of the structures of church and state do make a special case of this society, which we think may be even more extreme than the very great influence exercised by the church on the state in Italy, Spain and elsewhere. In fact these two structures have become more or less completely interwoven, not only at the top but on all levels of their respective hierarchies, almost to the point of uniting into a single structure. While this has not excluded the possibility of conflicts between church and state, it has enabled them to exercise together a form of power which may be termed totalitarian. The singular nature of this method of exercising power clearly emerges in the historical comparison between the French and Québecois education systems, presented in the next section.

As far as France is concerned, it should be noted that recent studies may have underestimated the importance and above all the autonomy of the church in the area of the family. The French state has not in fact always succeeded in supervising and managing all modes of church intervention into the family. In this respect it would seem that the church has been able to take advantage of the division in the French bourgeoisie over the problem of religion and its relationship to politics. The historical evidence, which we will analyse later, illustrates certain consequences of this situation, for instance, the education of many bourgeois children in denominational schools and the pre-eminent role of the church in the education of girls. Similarly in the case of the United States, one might be led to disregard the interconnection between the family and the churches. Recent studies indicate that this articulation has taken an original form and that it has brought in its wake hitherto unsuspected cultural consequences. Isolated from political and economic activity at the beginning of the nineteenth century, ministers of the most influential Protestant denominations and bourgeois women formed a stable partnership which procured for them direct or indirect control of a wide area of culture (in its broadest sense) via the production and diffusion of a familialist and religious ideology based on 'feeling'.[7]

The history of these societies calls into question not only theories of the family as an agent of the state, but also the current definition and use of the notion of mode of production. Quite a number of researchers conceive of the mode of production as a formal and ideological model, the application of which allows 'concrete' societies to be analysed and classified. From this point of view a mode of production is a specific combination of processes, classes and particular structures: thus, the combination of serfdom/feudal power/church, or wage labour/liberal state/(laity) bourgeois ideological structure. When a society does not correspond to the model it is treated as an aberration. Thus, feudal societies in which the state takes a non-absolutist form are considered 'advanced' and capitalist societies in which the church carries out important functions are considered 'backward'. According to these rules, a substantial amount of historical reality becomes an exception to the theory, which avoids having to recognize and theorize the variety and complexity of the social organization of a mode of production. The lack of theoretical and empirical interest shown particularly by Marxist studies in analysing the position and function of the Catholic and other churches in capitalist society is one of the most important consequences of this erroneous understanding of the mode of production.

To sum up, our critique of theories and studies relating to the family in bourgeois society is based on the hypothesis that these political and religious structures interact and complement one another in the regulation and control of the social organization of capitalism. In so far as this regulation and this control are exercised in 'private' life, they occur through the mediation of the various practical systems that, on the one hand, form, sustain and reproduce the family and, on the other, depend on it, lean on it and use it. The school and social security systems in particular provide the framework for these modes of intervention. Nonetheless, it is probably the school that provides the principal focus of these complex networks of reciprocal relationships between the family and regulation/control structures, relationships which create and reproduce the distinction between private and public life, and which ensure the functional articulation of these two sectors. A satisfactory illustration of our hypothesis would demand a systematic comparison of different bourgeois societies carried out at a similar stage of their development. This comparison would highlight the respective roles of religious and political structures in the formation and conservation of the form of family organization characteristic of bourgeois societies. We think that in this way one could arrive at an outline for three types of society in which the family is articulated mainly with the church, mainly with the state, or equally with both.

In this article, we have presented a comparison between France and Québec through an examination of the development and mode of functioning of their respective school systems. Up to a point these two societies are exemplary cases in the study of the articulation of family, church and state. In the following section, we will compare the mode of integration of the family with church and state in Québec and in France, starting from a variety of data relating to education and the school system. Then we will touch on the exclusive and universal take-over of the family by the state over the last few decades which will lead us to further remarks and to some new theoretical and historical questions.

The Cases of Québec and France, 1850–1960

The method we will follow and the questions which relate to it will be outlined in a triangular configuration with the family at one corner and, at the other two, state and religious powers.[8] We will be especially concerned with the civil and religious supervision of the child and the family, through the medium of the school. We postulate, first, that as far as power relations (rather than pure apprenticeship) are concerned, the family is as deeply involved as the child. We have also been able to observe that through the rivalry between organisations and the struggles that set different social groups against each other, emerge a discourse and a practice which are largely addressed to families, which are implicitly or explicitly recognized as the principal interlocutors in all questions relating to education.

In comparing the French and Québecois education systems, especially through the second half of the nineteenth century, one is at first particularly struck by the differences between the two systems on many levels, differences which, as we shall see, do not rule out some extremely interesting similarities.

Since its foundation in 1841 and up to the 'Quiet Revolution', the Québec school system provided a social domain in which the effective supervision of child and family by the church was equalled by very few Western societies during the same period.[9] We know how extreme was the degree of denominationalism in secondary schools, colleges and even universities, as well as in primary schools.[10]

For more than a century, Québecois families have realized that as far as the education of their children was concerned, they had to both rely on the church and reckon with it. This was as true for the structure and functioning of the school system as it was for its pedagogic and moral orientation. For its part, the state assumed the role of supplier more than anything else. It provided a source of finance and an administrative agency which were certainly indispensible, but which were always subject to directives emanating from the religious hierarchy. Until the middle of the twentieth century, clerical discourse on the family and education provides a fairly clear reflection of the structure of power relations prevailing at the heart of the educational universe. What is more, this discourse translates the religious and political authorities' view of the role that had devolved upon the familial institution in the framework of these power relations. It then becomes clear that the family is considered the central pivot around which the ensemble of strategies linked to educational politics are worked out. The family is a partner with whom an alliance must be formed, since it is through the family that the trajectories followed by these policies necessarily pass.[11] Now, for more than a century, the dominant ideological discourse has presented the family as the natural ally of the church, against a state which is constantly suspected of wanting to overstep the limits of its competence in the field of education.

In Québec, practice as well as educational discourse have thus maintained a traditional alliance between family and church, thereby contributing to the containment of state power within well defined and above all largely inflexible boundaries.

In France, from the middle of the nineteenth century, power relations in the field of education showed a manifestly different evolution from that of power relations in Québecois society in the same period.[12] We know the extent to which, in contrast with Québec, relations between church and state in France were marked by a confrontation which remained in force for more than half a century, despite the occasional ceasefire.[13] For both church and state the problem was to ensure the effective if not exclusive control of a social domain in which one or the other would constitute the sole valid interlocutor for children and families advancing into its orbit.

The rivalry between church and state expressed itself through different methods, and with different results depending on the educational level. It was in fact the level which determined the particular political strategy to be used, since different social groups were associated with primary, secondary and tertiary levels. The relationship between family, church and state will thus vary both in its form and evolution according to the level of education and the social background of the families involved.

As far as elementary schools are concerned, the church was forced to give up much of its influence in a relatively short period of time.[14] This is why ever since the middle of the nineteenth century the French state has consistently consolidated its hold on what the French educational historian Antoine Prost calls 'l'école du peuple' (elementary public schools). This was of course detrimental to religious power, which up to that point had been the main interlocutor in the field of education, for working-class children and families. The state even acted to the detriment of groups with a history of involvement in education such as the Brothers of the Christian Schools.

Also, unlike their Québecois counterparts, who evolved under the influence of the clergy, lay primary teachers in France were active agents of state power. Especially after 1880, it was on them that a kind of republican and secular missionary spirit devolved.[15] But clearly the call was going out beyond the child to the family. The family in fact is the main recipient of the message transmitted to the child, a message which the child must translate for its parents in his/her own way. Here is the declaration of Ferdinand Buisson, a politician of the Third Republic, and one of the most ardent apostles of secularism.

> You can see that we are hiding nothing, for our ambition is that school should be pleasant, so that it may please the children and so that the children may make it pleasing to others. We are counting on them: into their feeble hands we confide the sacred trust of all our hopes. Little missionary of new ideas, little primary schoolchild . . . as you leave your school, show your parents everything you have learned . . . they will soon understand the importance of the change that has occurred, they will soon understand the worth of such an education, and from whom it comes; and more than once perhaps . . . they will kiss you. In that kiss on your forehead there lies more promise for the Republic than in many an electoral victory.[16]

After 1877 official statistics reveal that at primary level – at least up to the age of twelve – almost 80 per cent of boys compared to only 70 per cent of girls were in a state school.[17] Thus, well before the 'fundamental' laws promulgated in 1880 and 1881 under the Ministry of Jules Ferry, laws aimed at the institution of a free, compulsory and secular system – and before the progressive restrictions which would be directed at religious schools – the French state had succeeded in dominating much of the field of primary education.

In the secondary sector, the state in France made its presence felt differently.[18] Also, the social group concerned consisted largely of children and families from the bourgeoisie or, to some extent, the petit bourgeoisie.[19] It was from a section of these groups – who until then had supplied private secondary schools with their clients – that the initial pressure for more extensive primary schooling, later termed 'upper primary', 'complementary' and, finally, 'secondary' levels, would come, in the middle of the nineteenth century. Nevertheless, the establishment of state power in this domain proved slower and more difficult. The state had to contend with serious competition from the private secondary sector, in which, as we shall see, clerical influence remained omnipresent for a very long time. Still, even at this level, the difficulties experienced by the French state were not nearly as substantial as those of its Québecois counterpart. For in Québec the private and religious 'classical colleges' were pre-eminent in the secondary and college sectors, and the universities also largely escaped interference from the state until the middle of the twentieth century. The French state, on the other hand, acquired a remarkable tool for control in the universities. This was to prove its usefulness particularly under the Third Republic.[20] So in spite of the enormous privileges bestowed by the Falloux Law of 1850 on denominational education – which regained complete freedom of action until 1880 – the universities succeeded, after this interval of thirty years, in reimposing their jurisdiction over the whole of secondary and tertiary education.[21] While it did not completely oust religious influence from this domain, it did permit the state to maintain a presence in a field through which it was able to make contact with a substantial proportion of bourgeois children and families.

Can it be concluded from the above that French and Québecois societies exhibit completely opposite developments in the structure and evolution of relationships between family, church and state in the field of education? Such an opposition often formed the background to controversies current in Québec at the end of the nineteenth century, relating to the secularization of the educational sector in France and the complete expulsion of the church from this domain. Such a perspective, without being totally false, strikes us as somewhat schematic. This opposition should be seen in the context of a Québec receptive to the arguments of French church ideologists, a Québec which felt itself threatened by the contagion of secularization.

In the light of a more attentive reading of recent French historiography, it appears that the position of the church in France at the end of the nineteenth century was not as precarious as many of its defenders here in Canada and overseas have claimed. Until at least the beginning of the twentieth century, the situation of the clergy was not really weakened by the secularizing laws of the 1880s. On the contrary, private secondary education, which was largely secular until the middle of the nineteenth century, came more and more under the aegis of the church after that date. The historian H. Prost even argues

> From 1865 to 1876, on the other hand, it made great progress, and the Third Republic saw an expansion that was all the more remarkable seen in comparison with a general stagnation in secondary education. The draconian measures of 1880 brought only a temporary retreat; in 1898 there were more pupils in Catholic secondary schools than in state schools (*lycées*), not counting the seminaries, some of whose students did not pursue a career in the Church.[22]

Thus, for the year 1898, the official statistics of the Ministry of Education (Conseil Supérieur de l'Instruction Publique) showed that the total number of pupils in Catholic schools had risen to 67,643, with only 52,372 in the *lycées*.[23]

After the suspension of hostilities on the education question brought about by the First World War, which resulted in a holy alliance of clerics and secularizers; and after a period of stability in the inter-war years, the struggle began again in even greater earnest in the early 1940s. This resulted in substantial gains for the church: in 1940 the ban on teaching by those in religious orders, imposed in laws of 1901 and 1904, was lifted. The following year, another law was passed which allowed town councils to fund the independent schools, and gave children attending them access to state scholarships.[24] It was around financial questions that many of the debates over 'independent schools' revolved. Here again, the problem was solved to the great advantage of denominational education, since in 1951 a law was passed which replaced state grants to independent schools (these were withdrawn in 1945) with an allowance given directly to parents of children attending these institutions.[25]

The ruling bourgeoisie in France was clearly divided over the question of education for over a century. The battle over secularization did not take on demarcation lines according to the social class of the participants.[26] However, in the course of this battle to keep clerical influence on education intact, one point is particularly noticeable: the church knew how – or was forced – to integrate the family into its strategies. In the secondary and university sectors, the main concern was to involve bourgeois rather than working-class families, since the former were more affected by educational politics at these two levels.[27] The church in France succeeded both in theory and in practice in identifying its own interests with those of the family, and this without regard for social class.[28] Following the pattern prevalent in Québecois society at the end of the nineteenth century, the church presented itself in French society as the prime defender of paternal authority. This authority was supposed to have been threatened by the pretensions of a state whose inordinate ambitions called into question both the prerogatives of the church and a certain social order connected with the model of the family it was defending. In many rural parts of France until the beginning of the twentieth century, this point of view was translated into an effective alliance between the parish priest and families against the secular schoolteacher.[29] Denouncing the impossible religious neutrality of the teacher, Senator M. Jouin addressed Parliament in these terms, following the secularizing laws of 1881: 'Without wanting to, without the slightest ill will, that unbelieving teacher, by a word, gesture or smile, will breathe heaven knows what icy blasts into the child's soul, paralysing all the efforts of parents and priest.'[30]

It is to the family that church authorities have turned again, towards the beginning of this century, to try to contain state interference in the private school sector. The Parents' Associations for Private Education (PAPE), which were then to emerge, would show their effectiveness in the battles of 1948 to persuade the state to give grants to these – mainly denominational – schools

From the middle of the nineteenth century, the relationship between church and family in French society has been equally close in connection with girls' education, especially in secondary schools.[31] If schools, and the entire education system are driving forces in the elaboration of a precise model of the family, it is clear that the education of girls is a particularly powerful force. State and religious authorities are in complete agreement about that.

After the end of the Second Empire the French state sought to organise and to draw into its field of influence the girls' secondary schools.[32] The famous public secondary classes organized after 1867 by Victor Duruy, who was then Minister for Public Instruction, bear witness to this. After the mitigated success of this type of teaching – the classes did not form a part of a curriculum and did not lead to a certificate – the government of the Third Republic made a second, more coherent and more fruitful attempt, following the adoption in 1880 of a bill framed by Camille Sée, which aimed to create girls' secondary schools (*lycées*) funded by the state. But in this enterprise, as in many others, the state had to reckon with the church, which already had a substantial lead in the field of girls' education. This was to be demonstrated by the extent of the campaign led by church ideologists against state interference in this domain. The state stood accused of trying to trespass on the 'natural' prerogatives of the church, endangering not only its religious and moral authority, but also the stability of a model (Christian) family of which the church was the main guarantor.[33]

If the hostility of the clergy was a decisive factor in the failure of the classes Victor Dury had dreamed of, it proved unable to halt the slow but relentless progress of secondary schools for girls under the Third Republic. Even so, for over half a century these institutions had to deal with serious competiton from convents and private boarding-schools, many of which copied their philosophy and curriculum from the convents.[34] The state took this competition and the moral principles behind it into account when it set aside the idea of mixed schools. The influence of the church was also to be found in the model of the family spread through the secondary curriculum offered to girls. This course of studies was elaborated with consideration to the future role of the girl in the family, hence it was less utilitarian than the curriculum offered to boys; hence also the importance attached to domestic science for many years.[35]

This rather brief analysis, is, undeniably, just a preliminary approach to the enormous field of the relationship between family, church and state in education. It does, however, allow us to uncover some interesting analogies between France and Québec about the role and position of the church at the heart of these relationships. In particular, it leads us to qualify theories relating to the formation of the modern family and to the processes and modes of its integration into networks of state structures. The position underlying these theories, as we have pointed out above, is one that dismisses the power and effectiveness of the church too quickly. Even in France, where the state declared its centralizing and bureaucratic role earlier than in Québec, the influence of the church has shown only a very gradual and partial diminution over a long period.

We believe that socio-historical analyses relating to the family must take this into account and, as a result, must qualify the conclusions they reach concerning relations between the family and the modern state in capitalist society.

Conclusion

Our questions, our hypotheses and our comparative interpretation are concerned only with the stages in the development of bourgeois society at this period in history in Western Europe and in North America. In the second half of the twentieth century, questions about the family in capitalist society raise different problems. In fact, over the last few decades, the almost complete take-over of the family by the state appears to be characteristic of all capitalist and socialist societies, including those like Québec, the United States, Italy, Spain and others, where the state had previously exercised relatively little influence over the family. In these societies, changes in the school and social service systems were a priority.

In Québec, it was towards the end of the 1950s that the organization of Québecois society through the church, based on the family, began to weaken and the state take-over of functions relating to control of the population proceeded. These functions are actually so complex and demand the deployment of such enormous resources that the church could no longer cope. Thus the tasks of registration, regulation and supervision, which had previously been taken on by the church for the most part, were henceforth performed by the state. During the period known as the 'Quiet Revolution', the school system – which was the major prize at stake – as well as the health care and social service systems passed almost exclusively into the hands of the state of Québec. These services were transformed into bureaucratic functions and this transformation precipitated an extraordinary growth in state and para-state structures. In the same way, culture was secularized, and became a state responsibility. Henceforth, the state supervised the Québecois family, and it was towards the state that the family turned to obtain the resources and services it needed. Its 'problems' were to become those of the 'modern' family: contraception, divorce, working women, the crisis of parental authority and so on. The techniques and methods of intervention practised by the State in relation to the family were inspired by the principles governing family politics in most other Western states.

Feminist Reflections on the Fertility of Women in Québec

Marie Lavigne

The new women's history has begun to study the context of women's lives, and there is increasing interest in the history of family life and of fertility. In the case of Québec, this history is at once stereotyped and fertile. The picture is dominated by the 'revenge of the cradle' and by the image of the fertile French Canadian mother. It is claimed that our foremothers differed from other North American women in that they went on having children in order to preserve the race, despite industrialization, urbanization and modernization. And if, perchance, some feminist historian believes that matters might have been rather different or that women's demographic history cannot be reduced to such stereotypes, the demographic data is there to contradict her, as are the conclusions demographers draw from history. Thus, Henripin and Périn assert that 'Perhaps nowhere else in the world has the Catholic ideal of having a large family been observed to greater effect. This ideal was reinforced by vigorous nationalist propaganda in favour of the "revenge of the cradle", and it would be difficult to doubt the success of such ideas.'[1]

The history of our foremothers appears, then, to be the history of women who were dominated by the clergy and the political elites. And yet it is difficult to reconcile that history with the history of the feminists and the working women who, like other women in North America, began to organize and to demand a new status from the late nineteenth century onwards. Why should the history of women in Québec be so similar to that of other North American women when it comes to public life if they were so slow to follow their example in terms of their private lives? It is with this question in mind that I propose to re-examine a number of demographic studies and to attempt to paint a more accurate picture of women's lives.[2] We will begin by retracing the demographic history of the women of Québec over a period of one hundred years, with particular emphasis on women who were of childbearing age during the first half of the century, a period when both the demands put forward by feminists and working women and the pro-family propaganda of the elites were making themselves heard. We will then look into the whys and wherefores of demographic history by tracing those strands in certain studies in population theory which may be of help in trying to understand what was happening in women's lives.

The spectacular decline in the birth rate in Québec in recent decades tends to make us forget that the trend in fact began more than a hundred years ago. Thus, between 1851 and 1951, the overall fertility rate fell by 40.3 per cent.

Jacques Henripin's famous table of fertility rates between 1831 and 1965 shows quite clearly that they fell constantly in Québec (Table 1). If we compare the fertility rate for Québec with that for other provinces, we find that, contrary to popular belief, Québec is far from being the most fertile province. Before 1881, Ontario had a higher birth rate than Québec. It was only in the years 1921–51 that Québec had the highest rate in Canada. Although these high rates suggest at first sight that the women of Québec were exceptionally fertile, they also reveal a radical change. Whereas the fertility rate for Canada as a whole fell by 9 per cent over this period, it declined twice as fast in Québec, where it fell by 22 per cent. It was between 1921 and 1951 that the decline was most pronounced and most irreversible. As a result of the crisis of the 1930s, all provinces recorded a major decline in the fertility rate. But during the so-called 'baby boom' of the 1950s, most provinces returned to the fertility rates of the pre-crisis rates. In Québec, the rate recovered to some extent, but it never reached the levels recorded in other provinces. The crisis appears to have resulted in a definite break in the declining fertility rate of women in Québec. In the light of statistics for overall rates of general fertility, the first half of the century proves to have been a period of rapid and far-reaching change.

Overall fertility rates are a useful index of long-term tendencies, the disadvantage being that they are abstract and shed little light on the changes that take place in women's lives.

Table 1. Overall Rate of General Fertility: Canada and Certain Provinces, 1831–1965 (annual number of births per thousand women aged between 15 and 45)

Year	Canada[a]	Nova Scotia	Québec	Ontario	Manitoba	Saskat-chewan	British Columbia
1831	—	—	271	—	—	—	—
1842	—	—	—	329	—	—	—
1851	203	—	196	212	—	—	—
1861	193	174	187	204	—	—	—
1871	189	174	180	191	—	—	—
1881	160	148	173	149	366	—	202
1891	144	138	163	121	242	—	204
1901	145	132	160	108	209	550	184
1911	144	128	161	112	167	229	149
1921	120	105	155	98	125	135	84
1931	94	98	116	79	81	100	62
1941	87	98	102	73	77	84	73
1951	109	114	117	100	103	110	99
1956	117	121	120	110	109	120	112
1961	112	119	109	108	111	119	104
1965	91	98	88	90	92	100	82

[a] Includes the province of Newfoundland as of 1951.
Source: Jacques Henripin, *Tendances et facteurs de la fécondité au Canada,* Ottawa 1968, p. 21.

Average numbers of children provide more revealing indicators. We can discover how many children women living in the first half of the century had by examining specific cohorts of women who were of childbearing age during that period. In his monograph on the 1961 census, the demographer Jacques Henripin identifies the specific characteristics of groups of women of different ages, all of whom were still alive in 1961. We can therefore discover how many live children were born to women belonging th the birth cohorts of 1887, 1903 and 1913 (approximate dates).[3]

On average, women born around 1887 had 5.5 children; those born around 1903, 4.3; and the 1913 birth cohort only 3.8. Québecoises born in 1913 therefore had 1.7 fewer children than their elders in the 1887 cohort.

These figures refer to all women in Québec, make no distinction between anglophones, francophones and other groups, and represent the average families of our foremothers. Certain demographic studies do separate out the francophone group, which displays different characteristics. As one might expect, the average French-speaking Québecoise had a larger family than women belonging to other ethnic groups. Francophones born in about 1887 had an average of 6.4 children; their daughters, who were born around 1903, had 5.1, and women born ten years later only 4.3. Here we have the basis for French Canadian mothers' reputation for fertility. It should, however, be noted that they probably brought up fewer children than the figures might suggest; the figures refer to live births and take no account of child mortality, which affected francophones more than other groups.[4]

But there are changes here too: in the space of twenty-five years, they were having on average 2.1 fewer children. The change appears even more spectacular if we compare it with the figures for all women in Québec (−1.7) or all women in Canada (−1.2). Table 2 allows us to compare changes in the various groups.

Table 2. Average Number of Live Births per Married Woman: Canada, Québec and French-speaking Women in Québec

Approximate date of birth	Canada	Québec	French Québec
1825	7.8	—	—
1845	6.3	—	—
1867	4.8	6.4	—
1887	4.3	5.5	6.4
1903	3.4	4.4	5.1
1913	3.1	3.8	4.3

Sources: J. Henripin, *Tendances et facteurs*, pp. 339, 52; J. Henripin and Y. Péron, 'La Transition démographique', in *La Population au Québec: études rétrospectives*, p. 41; *Recensement du Canada*, Montréal 1973, 1941, vol. 3, tables 51 and 52.

We can conclude that Québecoises born at the beginning of the century were no longer like their mothers, and that the change resulted primarily from the behaviour of French-speaking Catholic women. Both overall fertility rates and the size of the average family show at least one thing: the 'average' Québecoise was changing. But who was having children? Who had an average family? It is obvious that not every Québecoise born in 1887 had 5.5 children. We have already seen that

French-speaking women had more, and we also know that, on average, women living on farms had more children than women living elsewhere in rural areas or in the towns.[5]

The women born in about 1887 did not all share the same destiny, and the demographic history of women of their generation cannot be discussed solely in terms of fertility or numbers of children. Some of them died without marrying, and others remained single. Some of those who did marry were infertile. Others had few children, whilst some women died in childbirth or before they could have a large family. Some had several children, some were widowed and others went on living with their partners after their children had left home. There are, then, several model life cycles.

The typical life cycle, which we assume to be typical because it is the most probable model, consists of growing up, becoming a mother and then growing old with one's partner once the children have left home. But this has not always been the fate of the majority of women. Only one in five of all American women born in Massachusetts in 1830, for example, experienced this typical life cycle. Women born at the turn of the century were more likely to conform to this pattern, but only 60 per cent of all women born in 1920 went through the same experience.[6] In order to understand the experience of the women of Québec in its entirety, we would have to classify women in terms of different life cycles, and that would imply the study of mortality rates amongst girl children, young people, women of childbearing age and married men, as well as nuptiality and fertility rates.[7]

We will now reconstitute two moments in the life cycles of the 1887, 1903 and 1913 birth cohorts for those groups of women who were still alive in 1961: marriage rate and fertility. While this does not enable us to reconstruct every aspect of the experience of the Québecoises of the generations concerned, it does allow a broad outline to emerge.

The first important point that has to be made is that the history of women born at this time is not simply the history of our grandmothers; it is also the history of those of our great-aunts who either remained unmarried or became nuns. A considerable number of women never married and, proportionally, Québecoises were less attracted to marriage than other Canadian women. Between 14 and 15 per cent of the women belonging to these birth cohorts did not marry.[8] Considerable numbers of them became nuns and lived in 'holy celibacy', but it is still true to say that nuns were in a minority and that most women in this category simply remained single.[9]

The majority of women did marry, but it is far from self-evident that they all led identical lives. Our collective memory does, however, tend to suggest that all our ancestors had large families, mainly because almost half (46.6 per cent) the men and women in Québec whose mothers were born in about 1887 were brought up in families of ten or more children. A large percentage of them therefore retain an image of a mother who was completely preoccupied with bringing up a large family. On the other hand, we might almost say that they are all talking about the same women; only one in five (20.6 per cent) of all married women had ten or more children, and a minority of women therefore produced almost half of all children! If we classify married women in terms of the number of children they had, we find significant variations between them.

Table 3. Birth Cohorts by Number of Live Births: Women Already Married When They Gave Birth, and Still Living in 1961 (%)

	Birth cohort (approximate)[a]		
Number of children	1887	1903	1913
0	12.6	16.1	13.9
1–2	18.4	24.9	29.4
3–5	25.5	26.8	32.0
6–9	22.9	19.2	17.1
10 or more	20.6	13.0	7.6

Note: [a]Women born in about 1887 were over 65 in 1961; women belonging to the 1903 cohort were aged between 55 and 65, and those belonging to the 1913 cohort were aged between 45 and 49 in 1961.
Source: Calculations based upon Henripin, Tendances et facteurs, table 2.8, p. 52.

Table 3 shows that 31 per cent of all married Québecoises born in about 1887 had either no children or only one or two; the same is true of 41 per cent of those born in around 1903, and 43.3 per cent of those born in around 1913. These figures are, however, approximate as they take into account only those women who were still alive in 1961; to produce more accurate statistics we would also have to take into account the mortality rate amongst married women. Even so, the table does give a very different picture of the fate of married women.

For an impressive proportion of Québecoises living in the first half of this century, marriage was not synonymous with a life devoted to bearing and bringing up children; only one in five of all married women born around 1887 had ten or more children. Increasingly, such fertility was becoming the exception, as only 7.6 per cent of women born twenty-five years later had so many children, and only one in four (24.7 per cent) of all married women had more than six children.

A statistical breakdown of women in terms of the number of children they had radically alters the way in which we see their lives and suggests new lines of investigation. We find, first, that by no means all women reproduced. Although all women were capable of procreation, a good number of them were either naturally infertile or controlled their fertility, and only a minority did not control their fertility at all. If we convert the total figures for married and unmarried women into percentage terms, we obtain a picture which suggests even more clearly that there was a degree of specialization (see Table 4).

Table 4. Birth Cohorts of Women by Marital Status and Number of Children

Number of children	Birth Cohort		
	1887	1903	1913
0	10.8	13.7	11.9
1–2	15.8	21.2	25.2
3–5	21.9	22.8	27.4
6–9	19.7	16.3	14.7
10 or more	17.7	11.0	6.5
Unmarried women	14.1	15.0	14.3
Total	100	100	100

Twenty-five per cent of all Québecoises belonging to the cohorts of 1887, 1903 and 1913 never became mothers and did not contribute to the renewal of the population. If we extend this group to include those whose reproductive role was minimal (one or two children),[10] we find that the lives of 40 per cent of all women fail to correspond to the traditional image of the prolific Québecoise. We can, then, put forward the hypothesis that not only did these women have very different historical experiences, but that the biological reproduction of the species was subject to a division of labour and that one quarter of all women took no part in it.

This hypothesis leads us to conclude that we cannot regard 'woman's estate' as being uniform, and that the experiences of the feminists of the early years of this century, the proliferation of religious vocations, the militancy of women workers, the way in which rural women organized around the family, and the apparent contradictions in the elites' discourses on women all have to be seen in the light of this diversity. Those discourses were addressed to different groups of women who experienced woman's estate in different ways. At a rather different level, we also find that the proportion of Québecoises taking no part in reproduction remains constant across the three cohorts under consideration, and that reveals a stable division of reproductive labour. This division was, however, modified by subsequent cohorts: in his monograph on the 1961 census, Jacques Henripin notes both a decline in the proportion of childless women and an increase in the marriage rate.[11]

Whilst the division between reproductive and non-reproductive women persists, there are changes in the distribution of women with children. One in five of all married women belonging to the 1887 cohort had more than ten children; the corresponding figures for the 1913 cohort is only one in thirteen. The total proportion of women with more than six children falls by almost half (from 43.5 to 24.7 per cent) over the same period, whereas the proportion of women with fewer than six children rises (compare Table 3). The explanation is that the proportion of women who did not control their fertility at all fell significantly and that an increasing number of Québecoises were controlling their fertility.

Finally, the changes we have noted in the distribution of married women and of children suggests that we also have to consider the influence of family background on procreation.

As we have seen, 46.6 per cent of all men and women in Québec whose mothers were born around 1887 spent their childhood in a family of more than ten children, and 77 per cent of them came from families of more than six children. We also know that women born in about 1913 were three times less likely to have ten or more children than the women of the 1887 cohort, and almost half as likely to have more than six children. The women of the 1913 cohort were obviously not in literal terms the daughters of those of the 1887 cohort, as the childbearing lives of women born in 1887 stretched from 1903 to 1932. If, however, we do accept the hypothesis that the women born in 1913 were the daughters of women belonging to the 1887 cohort, we can only conclude that they refused to live as their mothers had done.

To say that almost half these women were born into families of more than ten children and that only 6.5 per cent of them were prepared to follow their mothers' example is of course a demographic fiction which could only be verified by reconstructing their families and their life stories. But a comparative study of the behaviour of the cohorts of 1887 and 1913 does suggest that there was a major change in the demographic model. For the majority of women in Québec, the example of a mother with ten or fifteen children was not an example to be followed when they came to have their own families.

In this section, we have tried to use demographic statistics on fertility from the point of view of women's experience. This approach allows us to see more clearly that not all women in Québec shared the same experiences. The experience of women who were of childbearing age during the first half of this century shows that their history is not to be confused with that of mothers. We have also advanced the hypothesis of a division of reproductive labour between women.

The decline in the birth rate has been one of the major upheavals to have occurred in Western societies over the past 150 years. Women are having fewer and fewer children. But although the issue has attracted a lot of attention from historians and demographers, they have rarely shown any interest in its impact on the lives of women. Research into demographic history originated in the United States as a result of concern with overpopulation in the Third World.[12] In Québec, research in this area has to a certain extent been influenced by the political problems posed by the decline in the French-speaking population relative to the English-speaking population. Both the questions asked of the statistics and the methodology used in existing studies therefore make it difficult to use them to reconstruct the lives of women in Québec.

Theoretical explanations as to why fertility has decreased vary. Industrialization, urbanization, the shortage of land in rural areas, ethnic background and access to contraceptive technology have all at various times been invoked as the major factors explaining why fertility rates remain stable or decline. The debate as to which factor is most important has been going on for years.

As a general rule, these theories use global statistics and averages, and take no account of the specific experiences of different groups. Historians and demographers rarely ask why so many women do not marry, why certain groups of women go on having large families in defiance of the new 'small family' model, or why other groups have adopted the dominant model of the restricted family.

The above breakdown of statistics on women in relation to their contribution to reproduction suggests that these changes do not affect all women at the same rate. We therefore have to bear in mind the factors that might have led certain groups of women to go on having large families well into the twentieth century when we discuss studies and hypotheses relating to the history of the family and demographic history. My intention here is not to provide a survey of such studies, but to outline an approach which might help us to get a better picture of women's history.

For a long time, industrialization and urbanization were regarded as factors which modified demographic behaviour. It was thought that industrialization had led to the rise of the nuclear family and to the emergence of the small families with which we are now familiar. Both the new history of the family and demographic history represent a serious challenge to this view.[13] Recent work has shown that the Western family can take a wide variety of forms. Even in the United States, industrialization did not have the levelling effect once attributed to it and, increasingly, it has been found that during the first decades of industrialization, ethnic groups such as French Americans and blacks departed from the model provided by the modern American family.

Tamara K. Hareven's research is of particular relevance to the study of the fertility of French American women living in Manchester, New Hampshire. These women left Québec with their families to work for the Amoskeag Corporation, which was at the turn of the century the world's biggest manufacturer of textiles. French Canadians made up 40 per cent of the work-force.

In Manchester, women, men and children worked side by side in the mills; in other words, a family economy was transplanted into an industrial environment. Because the mills employed children, they helped to increase the family's prosperity rather than constituting a financial burden. It was therefore in their parents' interests to have large families, as their material well-being was at stake. On average, French-speaking families in Manchester therefore had more children than American workers. Rather than adopt the limited fertility model of the 'modern' family when they were transplanted into the industrial world, the Québecois preferred to function as large extended families, as this made it easier for them to adapt to urban and industrial life.[14] Women had lots of children because their economic situation encouraged them to do so. It is also striking to note how the size of families decreased when American legislation on child labour and compulsory school attendance transformed children into little consumers who no longer made any contribution to the survival of their families.[15] Studies of families in Montréal in 1870 appear to confirm Hareven's hypotheses. Bettina Bradbury concludes from her work on Montréal that the type of industrialization adopted in Quebec required only a low level of education and that child labour and the continued existence of large families were essential to it.[16] The work of Hareven and Bradbury suggests therefore that the small family is not necessarily the model best suited to an industrial context.

Many studies in demography spend a lot of time dissecting the differences between urban and rural fertility rates. In general terms, it has often been believed that urbanization was a decisive factor in the falling size of families. Increasingly, studies of nineteenth-century America suggest that this hypothesis has to be modified or even abandoned and that ethnic background, the husband's profession and women's level of education are also decisive factors. Enid Charles's studies, which are based upon the 1941 census, show that, taking Québec as a whole, fertility rates are indeed higher in rural areas than in the towns. Women born in about 1867 had 7.2 children, but those living in towns had only 6. Henripin's statistics, which deal only with French-speaking women born twenty years later, show that whilst urban women were still having six children, rural women living on farms were now having 8.3.[17] A comparison between the two sets of data suggests that environment may be less important than ethnic factors. It is perhaps the case that researchers from Québec are more sceptical about the influence of urbanization than those from other areas; after all, throughout the first half of the twentieth century, the average family in Québec was larger than the North American average, even though most of the population lived in urban areas.

Studies of fertility in certain towns in Québec in 1940 raise certain other problems: the fertility rate for towns like Three Rivers, Hull and Québec was similar to that for the surrounding countryside.[18] The sociologists Falardeau and Lamontagne studied the case of Québec City in detail and concluded their survey by stating that the basic characteristics of families in Québec were rural rather than urban. They explain that phenomenon in terms of a 'French Canadian culture complex' inspired by religion and traditional values relating to family organization.[19]

Philippe Garigue reaches similar conclusions in his sociological studies on the French Canadian family in the 1950s. He argues that the rural–urban distinction is not pertinent in Canada because, he believes, the similarities are greater than the differences, and because the French Canadian family is characterized by its cultural homogeneity.[20] In general, these researchers tend to minimize the impact of industrialization and urbanization and to stress cultural explanations such as religion, conservatism and ethnic factors.

If these researchers had studied the position of the women of Québec in greater depth, they might have reached rather different conclusions. Their work would have had greater interest if they had looked more closely at the economic position of the various members of the families they studied and had related them to the structure of Québec's economy. In, for instance, Falardeau and Lamontagne's study, we find no statistics dealing with women's work outside the home, with homework, moonlighting, or child labour. Could it be that homework, which was very widespread at the time, allowed women to have more children? Could it be that the absence of legislation on compulsory schooling (this was not introduced until 1943) meant that children could work? Could it be that the market for child labour was sufficiently developed for it to be economically profitable for an urban family to have lots of children? Could it be that girls of fifteen and over – an impressive number of whom neither attended school nor made themselves available on the labour market[21] – simply looked after the younger children and therefore allowed their mothers to take in sewing or to go out cleaning? All these questions have to be raised before we can rule out an economic explanation. If the authors had adopted an approach which took into account the labour performed by women and children in the context of a family economy, they might perhaps have reached different conclusions. The model Tamara Hareven discovered amongst French Canadian families working in the textile industry may well have been adopted by working-class families living in Québec during the first decades of this century, when textiles were one of the foundations of the industrial structure.

Historians studying fertility in rural areas are not so quick to discount the influence of economic factors. The decline in fertility rates in the nineteenth century may have resulted from the shortage of land suitable for cultivation, but that question remains open. Chad Gaffield's studies of the rural population of Alfred and Calédonie in Prescott County, Ontario, allow some interesting connections to be made between the economic organization of families and demography, and represent a serious challenge to the view that ethnic factors are the decisive influence on rural demographic behaviour. The French Canadians who settled in these areas of the Ottawa valley did not have many more children than the English-speaking families in the area, and the similarities between the two groups outweigh their differences. It was the family economy model obtaining in this agricultural and forest region, a model in which every man and every woman fulfils a function vital to the survival of the group, which encouraged both French and English-speaking families to have large numbers of children.[22] The demographic characteristics of the village of Laterrière confirm the view that the economics of agriculture and forestry were an inducement to have large families. Until the 1920s, married women in this village in the Lake Saint John area had a child every two years, and their fertility reached *ancien régime* levels at a time when large families were becoming less common by the year in other areas of Québec.[23]

Are we to conclude that these so-called *ancien régime* fertility rates are a reflection of traditional attitudes which meant that women were dominated by an all-powerful clergy and had no knowledge of the contraceptives they needed to control their fertility? Marie Fleury-Giroux's studies of the population of the Gaspé Peninsula in the 1960s shed some interesting light on this question. Rural women had as many children as their eighteenth-century ancestors, but this does not seem to have been because they knew nothing about contraceptive techniques. Certain groups did deliberately control their fertility. Thus, poor and poorly educated families had fewer children than others and limited the size of their families. High-income families, on the other hand, had more children, and Fleury-Giroux notes that 'The adjustment of demographic behaviour to individual economic situations indicates the existence of contraceptive techniques. The behaviour of families therefore appears to be dictated by cultural norms.'[24] Such data suggest that in areas of new colonization or remote areas, women's demographic behaviour was rational and varied according to the available resources. A high income meant that women could have large families, and they were not slow to take advantage of the fact. Poor women, on the other hand, knew how to control their fertility. The rationality we find in groups with large families in the 1960s may also have been characteristic of settler and working-class families at the turn of the century, when having a family which provided a lot of potential workers was obviously a matter of common sense.

There is a common tendency to attribute the decline in the birth rate to the appearance of modern contraceptive devices. By the same criterion, the continued high birth rate in Québec has often been explained in terms of lack of knowledge about contraception. Technology is assumed to have liberated women from their biological destiny. And yet many studies in demography give the lie to this popular belief. We know that birth control was practised in France from the eighteenth century onwards. In North America, birth rates began to fall at the beginning of the nineteenth century, and even in Québec the same trend can be observed from about 1850 onwards. Modern contraceptive devices had not been invented at that time. Women and men alike had to resort to age-old methods such as abstinence, coitus interruptus, abortion, infanticide, abortifacient plants, diaphragms, douches and so on.

The discovery of a way to vulcanize rubber in the nineteenth century made it possible to manufacture better condoms, and this appears to have been technology's major contribution to contraception. On the other hand, the innovation appears to have had little impact in either Canada or the United States before the end of the nineteenth century or the beginning of the twentieth.[25] It was not until the 1920s that the ovulation cycle was understood; until then, periodic abstinence cannot have been effective.[26] Sterilization was performed for eugenic purposes in the 1920s, but it was rarely used for contraceptive purposes, or at least not in the United States. Linda Gordon, who has produced an inventory of both modern and pre-industrial methods of contraception, concludes her survey by saying that until about the 1960s modern medicine had done almost nothing to improve upon methods that had been known for thousands of years.[27]

Quite apart from the fact that modern methods of contraception were slow to be developed, the decline in the birth rate took place against a background of illegality. Article 207 of the nineteenth-century Canadian Criminal Code prohibited not only abortion but also the distribution of information about contraception, and the sale and advertising of contraceptive material. Breach of the law, which was not repealed until 1968, was punishable by two years' imprisonment.

American women were affected by a similar law, the Comstock Law. Despite this, a survey of 1,049 women belonging to the 1901–10 birth cohorts revealed that 70 per cent used contraception. Half of them relied upon condoms, and 45 per cent preferred douches and coitus interruptus; other commonly used methods included the rhythm method and the diaphragm.[28] Such efficient use of contraception (the 1901–10 cohorts had fewer children than any others in American history) invalidates any attempt to explain the falling birth rate in technological terms. Moreover, the fact that most women used illegal methods is an indication both of the state's inability to enforce its norms in this area and of the ability of couples and women to defy those norms.

What was the position of women in Québec? Not only did they have to cope with similar legal restrictions and with the same lack of information about contraception, they, or at least the Catholic majority, belonged to a church which opposed contraception. If we correlate Catholicism with fertility, we find that Catholic Canadians had more children than women belonging to other religions.[29] Are we to conclude, therefore, that they obeyed the church unconditionally and accepted the ideal of having a large family? There are as yet no studies of access to and use of information on contraception in Québec. We therefore have to fall back on hypotheses supported firstly by the demographic facts and secondly by partial and qualitative information.

The fact that the number of children born to French-speaking Catholic birth cohorts fell by 2.1 between 1887 and 1913 speaks for itself. The proportion of married women who did not control their fertility represents no more than 7.6 per cent of all married Québecoises born in 1913; the proportion of families with fewer than six children rises by 18 per cent in twenty-five years. Such changes imply that women did have some knowledge of contraceptive techniques and did use them despite the church.

Québecoises who wanted to control their fertility during the first half of this century must often have had to resort to either traditional methods, to condoms or to periodic abstinence. But who passed on the relevant information? That was the question Henriette Dessaules asked herself on the eve of her wedding. In her journal she records a conversation with a woman friend:

> Jos said to me: 'I hope . . . that you will enjoy your happiness for two or three years before having a baby' . . . 'Don't worry, Jos. It may not seem it, but we are the only two in the family with any sense.' . . . I suppose that Jos is no better informed than I am, but her "*I hope*" would seem to imply that you only have children if you want them. That makes good sense, but what goes on in poor families makes me wonder.[30]

McLaren's research on English-speaking Canada reveals that abortionists and purveyors of contraceptive devices and abortifacient substances advertised their wares in English-language newspapers in Canada and Montréal, using veiled terms to escape the sanctions of the law. Condoms could be obtained from pharmacies and were sold discreetly. Similarly, subscribers to Eaton's catalogue could order 'Every Woman Marvel Whirling Spray', which was specially designed for 'vaginal hygiene'. In order to find out whether these products were also available to francophone women, similar research would have to be carried out on the French-language press.

Surveys or studies carried out during the first half of the century can also provide useful sources of information. Horace Miner's monograph on Saint-Denis, for example, tells us that in the 1930s both the village prostitutes and the young men who had worked in the towns were familiar with contraceptive methods. A spoonful of mustard mixed with gin or beer is reported to have been one well-known abortifacient, but Miner hastens to add that married couples did not use such methods. On the other hand, married couples did not have as many children as one might have expected in the absence of any fertility control; Miner explains this in terms of the high rate of stillbirths resulting from the absence of antenatal care.[32]

The traffic in information was not a one-way flow from town to countryside. Some information may have been brought back by American 'cousins', whose fertility rate was lower than that of those who never left Canada.[33] In Ringuet's *Trente Arpents*, the French American cousin explains why he has only two children in these terms: '*Damn it! Ma femme, et pi moé, on a décidé de mettre les brékes*' (Damn it! We decided to slam the brakes on, first my wife and then me).[34]

Finally, the study of the birth control movement sheds some light on the question of contraception. Unfortunately, the appropriate research has yet to be carried out for Québec, but Diane Dodd's study of the 1936 'Birth Control Trial' does provide some information.[35] The trial involved a woman employed by the Parents' Information Bureau, who was accused of supplying information about contraception to the women of Eastview (now Vanier) in the suburbs of Ottawa. Twenty-one women were called as witnesses; all but one were Francophones. They had all been given a free contraceptive kit by the Parents' Information Bureau containing three condoms and a brochure in French entitled 'Birth Control and Some of the Simplest Methods of Using It'. When questioned by the Crown, all but two or three of the women said that they saw nothing wrong in using contraceptive devices. The Parents' Information Bureau also distributed propaganda in Québec, mainly amongst working-class families in Montréal's Rosemont district.[36] It was probably these actions which prompted Dr Joseph Gauvreau to remark in 1935 that 'An underhand but systematic campaign to encourage sterility and the use of artificial rays to cause sterilization was organized. And then, something unheard of happened: the birth rate in our area began to fall considerably.'[37]

When Dr Gauvreau talks about the use of 'artificial rays to cause sterilization', he is probably referring to a method of radiation treatment which had been in use since 1907 and which resulted in temporary sterility. It would, however, be surprising to find that this method, which was used mainly on tubercular and mentally handicapped women, was in widespread use. His comment is, however, telling in that it reveals that contraceptive information did circulate outside medical circles, despite the church. The counter-propaganda campaign which the church launched in 1944 with its marriage preparation classes for 'engaged couples' may have been an attempt to check or stop this movement.

Religion was certainly an important factor in our foremothers' lives, but it is difficult to assess its impact. The women interviewed by Colette Moreux in the 1960s did not appear particularly influenced by church doctrine despite their outward conformity to religious practices. Some of the oldest women, who had had their children in the first half of the century, had used contraceptives, but that had not prevented from them from going to church.[38] The quantitative and qualitative data supplied suggests that we have to revise our view of the influence of religion on women's decisions as to how many children to have.

If we examine demographic statistics in terms of the experience of women, a very different picture of their history emerges. Several possible life cycles and a plurality of experiences come to light. Women divided the labour of reproduction, and it is clear that the history of the mother with a large family is that of only a minority of the women born at the turn of the century. The prolific minority did, however, have an immense impact on the statistics. They forced up the fertility rate and the size of the average family, and it is the averages provided by this minority that provide the basis for theories as to the fertility of the Québecoise. The use of averages to reduce women's history to the history of 'the average' woman distorts our perception of history, and it is important to correct it by using studies based upon methodologies which allow us to get a better picture of how different groups of women experience historical change.

Current theoretical explanations as to how Québecois society controlled its own reproduction are inadequate. Whereas industrialization and urbanization might have been expected to reduce the size of families, we find that urban working-class families had as many children as rural families. We also find that in some cases, anglophones were as prolific as francophones, which calls into question the correlation between ethnic origins and high birth rates. Finally, the fact that Catholic women, who might have been assumed to have been obedient to a pro-family clergy began to have fewer and fewer children, casts doubt upon the extent of the church's role.   The recent research described here makes a major contribution to answering this question in that it challenges not only existing theories but also their underlying methodology. Most of it deals with small groups, such as the people of Manchester, Alfred, Laterrière and Montréal and it breaks down the wall of anonymity which the use of 'averages' erects around groups of men and women who led similar lives. The approach adopted in this research also situates both women and men in terms of their environment, and takes into consideration all the forms of economic activity in which they were involved. As a result, it reveals what the statistics hide: the work done in the home or on the farm by women, moonlighting and child labour, the way elder daughters, nuns and maiden aunts helped their families, the role of the income brought in by lodgers, etc. In short, it was the family economy which allowed certain restricted groups of women to have an unexpectedly high number of children at a time when they might have been expected to conform to the model of the small North American family. It would appear that it is only by using new methodologies and non-sexist concepts that we can construct more constructive theories as to how societies reproduce themselves.

Nationalism and Feminism in Québec: The 'Yvettes' Phenomenon

Michèle Jean, Jacqueline Lamothe, Marie Lavigne and Jennifer Stoddart

The Yvettes: Or, How a Traditional Political Party Uses Women Once Again

> Come with me and vote No. No to sovereignty, no to economic association, no to sovereignty with association, and no to anything that would separate Québec from the rest of Canada.

A storm of thunderous applause greeted these words, spoken on the evening of 7 April 1980, before an audience of thousands of women demonstrating their solidarity with the federalist option. As early as six weeks before the victory of federalist forces in the referendum on the political future of Québec, the women known as 'the Yvettes' had already carved out their place in history.

Tension between the francophone and anglophone communities of Canada has been a constant feature of Canadian history. But in the 1960s and 1970s a renewed national consciousness on the part of francophones and a growing identification of the province of Québec as a potentially independent nation-state led to a major confrontation on the question of Québec's independence from the rest of Canada. The pro-independence party, the Parti Québecois (literally the Quebec Party; characteristically there is no English equivalent of the name) had been elected by a landslide in 1976. Its support came just as much from those who sympathized with its left-of-centre social programme as from those who identified with its affirmation of French culture and its goal of political independence for the province. The Parti Québecois's election in 1976 was assured by a carefully planned strategy. It promised voters who were hesitant to support it, fearing a sudden break with Canada would have catastrophic economic consequences, that it would commence negotiations to take Québec out of the Canadian Confederation of provinces only if a majority of the province's population mandated it, through a referendum, to take such a step.

The date of the historic referendum was eventually set for May 1980 and as the date approached Canadian and especially Québec political debate rose to a fever pitch. Most anglophones and immigrants, within and outside Québec, were in favour of maintaining the status quo. Francophones within Québec were divided between federalist and separatist options. The Parti Québecois and its supporters were isolated within Canada, while the Official Opposition, the Québec Liberal Party, could count on the support of the Federal Liberal Party holding national power in Ottawa under its leader Prime Minister Pierre Elliot Trudeau. Trudeau's long career as Prime Minister was largely attributed to the widespread perception by Canadian electors that, as an eloquent federalist committed to the concept of the inherent duality – French and English – of Canadian society, he could preserve Canadian unity and fend off the separatist threat.

The referendum campaign in the spring of 1980, the narrow defeat of the 'Yes' (separatist) forces by the 'No' (federalist) vote, and their aftermath were clearly turning points in Canadian political history. But of all the debates that riveted public attention, of all the figures who emerged during the campaign, no phenomenon captured the imagination of the public and the press like the Yvettes.

The phenomenon known as 'the Yvettes', that is, the women who took to the streets of Québec in favour of a 'No' vote, has been interpreted in various ways. Some have wanted to see it as a devastating retort to feminists, whose values were incarnated by the incumbent Parti Québecois Minister, Lise Payette. Others have explained it as the expression of the innate conservative values of women as an apolitical group, values which led these women to reject the innovation of separatism. Yet others have taken the optimistic view that Québec women were waking up to the strategic uses of their political muscle. And finally, there are those who, more pessimistically, have denounced what they saw as the exploitation of women by a political party advocating traditional values.

How can these different interpretations be accounted for? How should we assess the Yvettes? Perhaps the best way is to start with these women themselves. Who were they? How did they manage to gather together in such large numbers? What was their message? And finally, how were these getherings of women viewed by the media and by the general public?

To try to answer all of these questions, we chose to look first at the structure of the organization of the Yvettes, and then to examine their discourse. This gave us information on their origins, their relation to traditional politics and, above all, the values they revealed through the words they used. This, we hoped, would give us an insider's view of the Yvettes. Was there a discrepancy between the phenomenon itself and the ways in which it has been interpreted? In the second part of this article we analyse the reaction of the public and that of intellectuals, particularly as expressed in the press and in the positions that women's groups took up in relation to the Yvettes.

Three things about the Yvettes caught our attention. First, their organization. Was this a spontaneous show of force? What impetus could mobilize so many women in such a short time? Secondly, the political nature of the Yvettes. What exactly was the relationship of the Yvettes to the Québec Liberal Party, the party that managed to dominate the referendum campaign carried out by an alliance of federalist forces? Finally, their image. Were they really as docile and domesticated as their namesake, the little 'Yvette' of the Québec school books? Francophones knew Yvette as the model of femininity – a submissive, helpful young girl whose merits lay in her pliability, her supportiveness of others, and her willingness to accept a never-ending round of domestic chores. French Canadian women, educated by Catholics, had been told to model themselves after Yvette. Was this a sweet revenge on feminists who ridiculed the traditional role of women?

Our conclusions in a few words: first of all, the rallies were cleverly orchestrated by the Québec Liberal Party, which played very skilfully on certain issues which were sensitive for women. Furthermore, the Yvette demonstrations were political rallies like any others and differed only in their exclusively female audiences, and in that only women spoke at them. By pure coincidence, a traditional political party managed to mobilize a section of the electorate whose only common characteristic was its gender. Finally – and we consider this a most important point – it seems difficult to claim that the Yvette movement was fundamentally anti-feminist. The leaders of the Yvettes attacked a political option, using their strategic skills to rally their troops through evocations of women's role as a mother. But it is not possible to infer from this a complete rejection of feminist demands.

In order to reach these perhaps rather surprising conclusions, we have to set out from the beginning, with the very inception of the movement.

Where Did the Yvettes Come From?

Those who hasten to the conclusion that the Yvettes completely rejected feminist values forget too easily the special circumstances surrounding the first 'Yvettes brunch' in Québec. The minister, Lise Payette, made a blunder when, on 9 March 1980, she compared the wife of the leader of the Québec Liberal Party, Madeleine Ryan, to the Yvette of the primary school readers, whose ambition goes no further than doing housework, cooking meals and, above all, being kind, submissive and helpful to others. According to Madame Payette, today's Yvettes were those who, like Madeleine Ryan, were afraid to take Québec out of the Canadian Federation.

At almost the very moment that Lise Payette was describing Madeleine Ryan and the federalist women as Yvettes, a public opinion poll showed for the first time that a small majority of Québecois would vote yes in the referendum. These two events shocked the women's organizers of the Liberal Party into action. Madame Payette's epithet gave them an unhoped for opportunity to take up the challenge of the poll. What better way to capitalize on an opponent's mistake could there be than to adopt the name Yvette of their own free will? The organizers quickly set the massive machinery of the Liberal network into motion. On 30 March 1980 they assembled more than six hundred Yvettes at a 'brunch' in Québec: these women were either members of the Liberal Party or sympathizers with the federal opposition. The extent and speed of the women's response to the call of the party surpassed the most optimistic predictions.

Further meetings were quickly planned throughout Québec, and at least thirty of these took place in every corner of the province during the weeks leading up to the referendum. But the meeting that really aroused public interest was held at the Forum on 7 April 1980. More than fourteen thousand women were present that evening, some from as far afield as Hull and Sherbrooke.

How can the size of this demonstration – the most important political demonstration of the pre-referendum campaign – be explained? The first element in an answer to this question is the efficiency of the Liberal Party organization, which sold tickets only on condition that the buyers came to the Forum, providing coaches for women from distant parts. It must be said here that women are, after a fashion, the pillars of the Québec Liberal Party. At that time they accounted for almost 47 per cent of party members, and they were extremely active, especially at a grass-roots level, where the tiresome but essential work of making contact with the electorate was carried out. Three-quarters of these women were aged thirty-five or over. And over a half of them, according to Liberal Party files, had described themselves primarily as housewives. A second explanation for the Yvettes rally can be found in the latent anxiety of many of these women on the subject of the referendum, an anxiety which the Liberal Party knew very well how to cultivate. One of the principal organizers of the evening said, 'they came because they were thinking of Canada'. They also felt attacked and devalued by Madame Payette's statements. 'We want to prove we are not simpletons,' this same QLP official said to us.

The women who took the floor that night were certainly not mediocrities, and still less were they simpletons. Among the twenty-two women who addressed the crowd were three senators, two Liberal deputies, one minister of the federal cabinet, the Speaker of the House of Commons, women with a distinguished record in community service or in women's organizations, and several successful professional lawyers, administrators and artists. But the organizers took care to disguise the elitism of this gathering by adding a few young students as well as a number of women who described themselves as ordinary citizens. In spite of the fact that only 15 per cent of the Liberal Party are non-French speakers, five English speakers addressed the gathering. What is more, to give the evening a thoroughly multicultural flavour, representatives of Jewish, Black and Italian minorities also spoke in favour of the federal option.

We have chosen here to interpret the speeches given at the forum gathering by analysing the content of the various interventions. Content analysis is an ensemble of techniques for communications analysis which uses systematic and objective procedures to describe the content of messages. The aim is to gain information on conditions of production which may or may not be quantitative.[1] Conditions of production are sociological and cultural variables and they are also variables that relate to the situation of the communication or to the context of the production of the message. It has been applied, for instance, in the comparative analysis of British and German propaganda during the First World War; or in the comparative analysis of news items, for example, the arrival of Krushchev in France as seen by several different Parisian newspapers, or the analysis of messages relayed to the electorate by French electoral candidates.

The types of analysis used for the study of the discourse at the forum are: quantitative; thematic; structural; and an analysis of the structure of the arguments in the discourse.

Here is a brief survey of the results of these different investigations.

Quantitative Analysis
As our corpus, or basic text, was the complete transcription of the speeches made at the Forum by the twenty-two speakers, we have picked out the most frequent words (those occurring more than five times) out of a base of about five thousand, and also the least frequent. The complete absence of certain words seemed equally significant to us.

   a The most Frequent Words
No: 83

Canada/Québec: 21	Yes: 15
Québecois/Canadian: 11	Yvette: 30
Woman: 11	Country: 12
Child: 10	

   b Low Frequency Words
People: 2
Nationalist: 1
Parti Québecois: 1
Position of women: 1

This type of analysis is clearly relatively important. A word only acquires its full meaning in a context. On the other hand, certain meanings can underlie words or phrases which are left unsaid. For example, the idea of morality is never explicitly mentioned, though it is eminently present.

Thematic Analysis

We then classified about five hundred statements from the discourse, regrouping these according to themes imposed by the text and present within it. Three main themes come out.

First, federalism is the best way to safeguard our linguistic and cultural assets. To say yes to separation would be to cut ourselves off from wealth and from all manner of values which were dearly paid for by generations of Canadians before us; for our country is one of the most beautiful, the richest and most civilized in the world. And it is as a land of peace and freedom that it has gained its reputation in the world.

Secondly, those who favour an alternative to federalism are nothing but dream merchants, who shrug away experience, the past, values passed on to us by our ancestors – people who are afraid of the difficulties of life within the federation. And women know how to distinguish fine words from sincerity.

Thirdly, what about women? They show the following attributes:

pride and dignity: they bear witness to their faith in liberty, democracy, the motherland and the language;
solidarity: it is the concerted efforts of thousands of Québec women which have made it possible to safeguard the values of the past, and this effort is being invested today in the cause of federalism;
tenacity and courage: women here draw their strength from the same source as their mothers and grandmothers who were tireless workers as well as stubborn and tenacious when they believed in something;
they are free and independent women, because they are not colonized, dominated or subjugated;
finally, their most characteristic and perhaps most fundamental feature: their moral responsibility.

It is they who, now and in the past, must ensure continuity. On them falls the sacred burden of passing on the values of the race, language and culture. This is a moral obligation which they will not abandon because this role alone ensures their full membership of society.

Structural Analysis

A third way of looking at the discourse is to see it as a structure composed of oppositional elements, articulated along certain axes. Among the main axes found here are values. Two contradictory elements are articulated along this axis, and they are the notions of gain and loss.

Along this same axis there is a linked series of opposites:

wealth/poverty;
safety/violence;
past/possible and uncertain future.

The overriding opposition here is between good and evil.

The speakers, many of whom held positions of political power, presented themselves as active subjects, and the Yvettes as auxiliary helpers in their quest to gain a victory which would ensure the conservation of past gains. To this effect, Madame Thérèse Lavoix-Roux, a Liberal Deputy in the National Assembly, said, 'Dear friends, thank you for coming in such great numbers this evening to lend us your support.'

Lastly, there is a still more obvious opposition, this time situational rather than textual.

In front of fourteen thousand Yvettes, that is, women who had 'reacted', as they said, to the attacks of Lise Payette on housewives, stood twenty-two women, most of them with university degrees, who had acceded to important posts: some of them (seven out of twenty-two) were elected representatives at either federal or provincial level.

It is worth considering that several of the orators had at one time or another proclaimed themselves militant feminists. Their discourse contains no attack on feminism or on feminist demands. Quite the contrary, certain of them went so far as to cite these demands. For example, Minister Monique Bégin speaking on the Commission of Inquiry into the position of women in Canada said, 'everywhere, from north to south and east to west, women were asking for the same things: nurseries for their children, equal opportunities, part-time work, respect for a decision to stay at home, in a word, a greater pride in a simple act of justice'. She affirmed that these demands were among her main concerns as a representative of women in a position of power.

Structure of the Argument

The various interventions constitute so many speeches aiming to convince those listening. By superimposing one on the other we can reconstitute a single discourse, which allows us to reconstruct the argument, the thought processes that were taking place. We therefore conclude this analysis with a schematic reconstruction of the arguments contained in the discourse.

On one hand, we possess a country rich in a variety of resources which were acquired by our worthy ancestors, within the framework of the Canadian federation. On the other, our mothers and grandmothers helped to build this country. The responsibility which falls on us now is to pass this heritage on to our children. Thus, maintaining federal ties becomes the symbol of past, future, and present success. Consequently, we must say no to those who want to cut us off from Canada.

Conclusion

Clearly then the language of the Yvettes is not anti-feminist. But the speeches at the Forum still made an emotional appeal to values traditionally embodied by women. For example, there is much play on the inherent duty of women to transmit not only life, but the whole political and cultural heritage of the status quo, to future generations. How could one give up this heritage without betraying one's duty as a woman?

In a sexist society, in which equal candour for men and women is discouraged, women have learned to survive by mistrusting seducers, people full of empty promises who want only to take advantage of them. This need to say no is recognized as one of the basic elements in male–female relationships. According to the traditional scheme of things, men propose and women are free to refuse. Even rape is justified in this way, on the pretext that this no is not stated clearly enough. Thus, by reminding women of their role of passivity and refusal, one can easily convince them that a real woman, who is no fool and knows how to take care of herself, should quite naturally vote no in the referendum. This is a rejection of a mad seductive adventure which would inevitably lead to failure.

Women's work in traditional spheres is not recognized by society at large but women know the value of the work they do, and they measure the human effort involved in their daily tasks of housework and bringing up a family. When the speakers exhorted them to practise female solidarity, reminding them of their grandmothers, how could they not feel guilty at sweeping away with a single vote what generations of women had struggled to build up?

Finally, it is only very recently that the association of women and morality has been called into question. The women who spoke in the name of the Liberal Party that night at the forum did not hesitate to evoke the evil that would follow from a victory for the separatists. Once again, they drew upon feminine characteristics. How could women associate themselves with this vision of evil?

There is, then, a very subtle shift in the speeches made to the Yvettes. Nowhere is feminism attacked. Nowhere are the new demands of feminists rejected (demands which would still have the effect of transforming the stereotype of the Yvette). But the old feminine characteristics are valued – prudence, moral responsibility, devotion to the future of one's children, good sense, working tirelessly – and are linked with the preservation of the constitutional status quo. In this evocation of the most passive components of collective feminist experience the Liberal Party played on all the most traditional female values in order to render their political option more acceptable.

The 'Yvette' Phenomenon: an Analysis of its Significance

Why was the Yvette movement interpreted as anti-feminist by large sections of the women's movement? How was an ill-chosen phrase from the Québec government's Minister for Women the instigator of the Yvette movement, an unprecedented development in the history of the women of Québec? On the basis of press treatment of the events, that is, from reports, editorials, analyses and readers' letters taken from eleven national and regional newspapers,[2] we shall attempt to bring out certain explanatory features of the phenomenon, and to define its impact on the women's movement, with special regard to the questions it poses for current feminist practice in the political arena.

The Role of the Press

With a few rare exceptions, there is probably no more room today in the traditional press for women's struggles than there was at the beginning of the movement. Often, there is far less: this is rather a time for a frequently violent settling of accounts.[3] In France, explains Liliane Kandel, the press is welcoming its first openly anti-feminist articles with open arms. Its attacks against the 'hysterical' feminists of the 1970s have been replaced by announcements of the death of feminism and the arrival of the post-feminist era.

The Yvette movement aroused a sudden interest on the part of the Québec press in questions of sexist stereotypes, house-wives, and women's relationship to politics. Thus, Minister Payette was continually pestered over her political gaffe. At a press conference, she had to explain what she meant by an 'Yvette' four times. 'Yesterday, the males present at the press conference took up this business again from the most incredible angles . . . as if they wanted to prove yet again that in politics, as in everything else, a woman must not allow herself the slightest mistake.'[4] There were to be numerous attacks on the Minister: almost 10 per cent of readers' letters to the press were in fact personal attacks on Lise Payette. A headline in *The Press* said that at the Forum 'the Québec Party Minister Lise Payette . . . was several times shouted down by the federalist crowd'.[5] Following the example of the editorial writer Lise Bisonette, the newspapers were not content just to pinpoint the Minister's clumsy mistake, but by giving the Yvette phenomenon such excellent coverage they provoked a snowball effect. One example of this is their treatment of two events: the rally at the Forum, attended by fourteen thousand people, made the front page news in all the newspapers, while a celebration in Montréal of the fortieth anniversary of votes for women, organized by the 'Yes' committee which attracted fifteen thousand, made the front page in only one newspaper. Should we see this as the action of a federal press or of a sexist press which is more interested in a woman minister's political misjudgement than in the com-memoration of one of the greatest struggles of the women of Québec?

For their part, the editorial writers all covered the event: such attention for women's political activity was unprecedented. It was also an unprecedented process in the feminist movement:

most in fact put the political involvement of the Yvettes down to 'annoyance and then irritation with the energetic campaigns of the feminists'. Women were even said to be 'outraged on occasion by the way in which the feminist movement endeavours to liberate women while denigrating their present role'.[6]

They were not yet announcing the death of feminism in Québec, but feminism was held responsible for the discontent of women in the home – a clever manoeuvre which avoids the difficult debate on housewives, and who it is that divides women against themselves.

It is common for the press to exploit a political mistake for all it's worth and it always adds interest to campaigns. But it is worth underlining the fact that the first time the press showed a real interest in women in politics, their aims were to hound one woman relentlessly, to highlight a movement stemming from conservative values, and to teach feminists a lesson.

If the Yvette movement was seen by many feminists as a challenge to their practices, and an indication of the growth of right-wing support, it is likely that they were influenced by the treatment of the events by the press: a press which preferred to leap on to the hobbyhorse of anti-feminism, rather than to analyse the question and propose alternative solutions.

Who Is This Yvette Anyway?

From the submissive little girl of our schoolbooks to the thousands of women who adopted the name of Yvette by deciding to vote 'No' in the referendum, there is a considerable change of meaning. Originally, Yvette was an example of the stereotypically passive and devoted little girl who gave Mme Payette the opportunity of announcing publicly that her government was in the process of eliminating sexist stereotyping for schoolbooks.[7] The first shift in meaning came from the Minister herself: she linked the stereotype with fear of change during her famous speech of 9 March. It is difficult, she explained, for a women to take on board political change, to come out of her 'prison of fear'. The association between the Yvette stereotype and supporters of a 'No' vote in the referendum was implicit.

The next shift was the work of Lise Bisonette, the editorial writer who, coming to the defence of Madeleine Ryan, wife of the Québec Liberal Party leader, made great play of her involvement in the community and her role as mother, contrasting this with the career of Lise Payette.[8] From then on, Yvette was synonymous with housewife and, what's more, her curriculum vitae was the opposite of that of a career women.

One of the first reader's comments on the Yvettes shows how the public perceived the concept: in a statement which is full of hatred for Mme Payette, a housewife affirms that she feels dominated by women who work outside of the home (not by men) and by feminists.[9]

The same definition was conveyed by the liberal organizers: they considered that Madame Payette had 'attacked women who have chosen to be Yvettes and hence housewives and mothers, devoting themselves fully and lovingly to the education, care, and needs of their family'.[10] If these Yvettes took the offensive, it was to prove that an Yvette could be politically active and have the courage of her opinions.

Supporters of the 'Yes' option were to try to reclaim or to clarify this title by calling themselves 'Yvettes for a "Yes" Vote'. Feminists would also attempt to remove its partisan flavour by stating that all women are Yvettes. None of this altered the fact that throughout the campaign Yvettes were housewives who chose to vote no in the referendum.

The Yvette Movement: A Takeover Denounced

More than a third of the eighty-five or so letters from daily newspapers that were analysed are centred on the theme of takeover: the Yvette movement is described as a takeover of housewives' discontent, or as a takeover for political ends of womens' aspirations, struggles and demands.

On an organizational level, the statements of Pierre Bibeau, chief organizer of the 'No' committee, would tend to confirm the hypothesis that women were being taken over and used.

> Women are creating the most incredible impetus. They are really turning our campaign in the right direction ... for it to have its greatest momentum in the middle of May, when the 'Yes' camp will be starting to run out of steam.[11]

The 'No' camp, which had made a poor showing at the time of the debate on the referendum question, seemed to be having real problems in organizing its troops. That the Yvettes should have been welcomed so warmly then is quite understandable. They were the driving force that put the whole campaign into gear. Such a co-option by the Québec Liberal Party was not to relegate the militant women for the 'No' option to obscurity. In fact, several women (including Thérèse Casgrain) were to explain that male politicians are in the habit of calling on women when they are having problems, and that women are in the habit of being there when they are needed.

This idea of a co-option was taken up by several editorial writers. While one has the headline ' "No" camp tries to take over Yvettes', another says that 'the frustration of thousands of housewives who are fed up with seeing their role undervalued, is crystallized in a most spectacular way to the advantage of the "No" camp and perhaps the Liberal Party . . .'[12]

On the 'Yes' committee, the Yvette movement was analysed in the same way. Madame Payette as well as the National Vice-President of the Parti Québecois, Louise Harel, saw it as a partisan use of women which would hold back their cause. That was why the 'Yes' camp did not officially reply to the Yvettes on the same ground. It must be stressed here that the efforts of the 'Yes' camp to link women's struggles to the national struggle had met with very little success: the use of Madeleine de Verchères at the beginning of the campaign had aroused little enthusiasm while the use of little Yvette was catastrophic. As it was not really viable to link the two struggles, the minister declared a truce on women's issues until the referendum.

It was even thought that 'No' supporters would put the brakes on the Yvette movement of their own accord, 'for they are beginning to realize how dangerous it is to define oneself in relation to a sexist stereotype . . . the Yvette effect may well backfire'.[13]

If the journalist Lysiane Gagnon is to be believed, there were certain politically experienced women in the Liberal Party who actually did try to slow the movement down. The reticence of a Thérèse Lavoix-Roux, who avoided linking national and women's issues in her speeches, can be easily understood: for a politician committed to the Québec Liberal Party such a linkage would indicate a strategic retreat. How could these political women form the spearhead of a campaign which exploited the social division of women between waged and domestic labour, in a party full of housewives, when they themselves were engaged in the world of work? On the days following the Forum speeches, these politicians were in fact accused of being part-time Yvettes and false Yvettes. It was better for them to keep their distance and let Madeleine Ryan, wife of the party leader, carry the torch. She at least was not a wage-earner and ran no risk of being labelled a 'fake' Yvette!

It does seem, however, that despite the assertion of several newspapers, the Yvette movement did not slow down in the middle of April: on the contrary, committees were formed in every county, and there were Yvette meetings everywhere until the eve of the referendum. The women of the Québec Liberal Party did not succeed in checking a movement that was so useful for the party and the cause.

The Women's Movement and the Referendum

Apart from the Yvette movement, it is interesting to analyse the reactions of the women's movement to the referendum and to derive from this a strategic position on the situation of women in relation to power and political parties. Thinking on the issue of women and power is still at an early stage in the women's movement. Not so long ago, women's groups were content to say that voting was a duty, without suggesting who one should vote for or proposing a political programme. During the 1970s, certain movements, especially the Québec Federation of Women, made a start on the political education of their members, giving them practical preparation for speaking at meetings, through reading, study sessions and publicity leaflets. The referendum marks another stage. The large associations chose neutrality,[14] asking only that women take a stand (for example, the Québec Federation of Women, the Women's Association for Education and Social Action, Christian Women, the Women's League). An abstentionist campaign sprang up among a group of women who had resigned from the Québec Women's Group and among certain others who proposed that women should vote 'Woman', saying that once the battle was over they were always sent back to the kitchen anyway.[15]

For their part, intellectual, progressive feminists called on women to vote yes, equating a 'Yes' vote with a vote for feminism in the wake of the Yvette movement.[16] It became clear then that women were obliged to strike an attitude in relation to the rise of the Yvettes, a phenomenon which urgently raised the problems they had in connecting with the national struggle and, in fact, with any political commitment.

Finally, it can be asked whether this event was positive or negative. Certain evaluations have underlined the fact that this massive mobilization of women marked a stage in the raising of their political consciousness. Others have laid more emphasis on the reactionary aspects and on the co-option of women. But perhaps the question can only be answered in the long term.

Postscript 1986

Five years ago, when we wrote these lines, we were concerned with the political consequences of the 'phenomenon' of the Yvettes. Would the Yvettes turn out to have been a massive mobilization of women, showing the growth of their political consciousness? Or would it be seen instead as an index of the rise of neo-conservatism? Or was it simply another instance of women being used by politicians to serve their own objectives?

If no clear answer can be given to these questions, two statements can be made

First, the Yvettes movement appeared at a time when Reaganism was starting up in the United States and when the media in France were reporting the emergence of 'post-feminism'. In this context it is not surprising that political commentators, and particularly journalists (some of whom were known feminists), should have interpreted the events as part of the 'rise of the right' and thus of the end of feminism.

It was as if we had been expecting the event that would prove that Québec, too, had not escaped this general movement.

Curiously enough, only a few months afterwards the events had been completely forgotten and few significant setbacks could be noted in the files recording women's situation. In fact, in percentage terms, the number of 'Yvettes' (in the sense of full-time housewives) has gone down and the participation of women in the paid labour market has risen and risen. In addition to this, it was not until two years later that the anti-feminist movement called 'Real Women' reached Canada and we notice that even by the beginning of 1986 it has not succeeded in establishing itself in Québec. All of this leads to the conclusion that Québec society probably has a different political culture from the rest of North

America; the 'Quiet Revolution' of the 1960s marked a profound transformation of a society which – linguistically isolated – has had to cling to collective values in order to survive. It is quite possible that such a society would be less likely to espouse the new individualistic values, which often have anti-feminist connotations.

Secondly, it is interesting that the phenomenon of the Yvettes which so coloured the participation of women in politics has had no long-term impact on the number of women candidates. Although Madame Payette withdrew from politics after her ordeal, her principal private secretary went into politics on her own account. In fact, Pauline Marois went on to become a minister and was the first Québec woman to stand for the leadership of a political party in power. In the most recent provincial election in autumn 1985 the Liberal Party – the party of the Yvettes – was re-elected; there were an unprecedented number of women elected as deputies and four are even ministers. It seems that this party had no choice other than to accept the rapidly growing involvement of women in official political power. Nevertheless the Yvettes have certainly left a legacy in the way policy issues about the position of women were treated in the 1985 election campaign. There was almost complete silence. No party dared to take a position and even those candidates who were known to be sympathetic to feminism did not speak up on these issues.

So it has become difficult for women's groups to obtain electoral promises. The politicians are being impartial perhaps, at least they have become more cautious. Maybe they have learned that the women's vote is more complicated than they previously thought and that the diversity of a social movement like the women's movement cannot be contained within the programme of a political party.

The Social Reproduction
of Gender

The Hidden Curriculum of School: Reproducing Gender and Class Hierarchies

Susan Russell

The school is a pivotal social institution mediating between ascriptive factors given at birth, namely social class and gender, and ultimate position in society. It is through schooling, mainstream sociologists posit, that all members of society are offered equal life chances, based on their own ability and achievement. This 'rosy' view (what Mary O'Brien calls 'high-class day-dreaming'[1]) of an egalitarian and just society cannot be taken seriously by feminist and Marxist sociologists, keenly aware of gender and class inequalities in the labour force and the gender hierarchy in the family. For them, the task of a sociology of education is to reveal both the ways in which students in schools are encouraged to consent to these social inequalities, and signs of their resistance to them.

Girls in school, it is revealed through an analysis of the education process, are the focus of pressures to encourage them to accept subordinate positions in both the labour force and the family. They are encouraged to believe that their exclusive role is or ought to be childbearing and childrearing, and that work that they take on in the labour force is secondary to their role in the family. School personnel exert these pressures through job counselling and through undermining the academic ability of girls while focusing on their domestic futures. It is under these pressures that the vast majority of girls sail through school and assume their subordinate roles in the domestic sphere and in the labour force.

It is not that schools 'invent' these social hierarchies. They exist in male-dominated, capitalist society. Students, because of prior pressures from the home and media, enter school with a predisposition to accept these class and gender hierarchies and their place in them. Studies in the sociology of education reveal the ways in which these categories are also accepted in schools and students are encouraged to consent to them and not to consider alternatives. Thus schools contribute to the social reproduction of class and gender inequalities. The signs of resistance on the part of girls to these pressures can also be seen, but these are little, if at all, recognized as valid in schools.

This paper concerns research by Marxist and feminist sociologists of education. It will be divided into three sections, each representing deeper levels of analysis of education: (1) the social organization of schools and how these are established formally to channel students to reproduce class and gender hierarchies; (2) the culture of working-class and middle-class girls, both the elements which they share due to gender and on which they diverge largely because of class differences; (3) phenomenological research in the school, divided into three sections: the advice of guidance personnel, teacher–student interaction in the classroom, and the content of classroom interaction, including 'lessons' in the gender hierarchy and signs of the resistance to them.

Although the second section is not strictly speaking part of the sociology of education, since uncovering the world views and aspirations of students does not necessarily implicate schools, it is included here as an important transition to the subsequent section. What is revealed by this research is that school personnel accept and reinforce the 'motherhood', 'marriage' and 'anti-school' aspects of girls' culture, while ignoring any others.

The primary data presented in this paper were collected in an academically oriented high school in Ottawa, Ontario, and offer insights into the process of schooling.[2] The research was in-depth, employing several modes of data collection: classroom observation in twenty-seven classes in the senior grade; interviews with a random sample of forty senior students, twenty-five of whom were girls, twenty-five teachers of the senior grade, and the five guidance counsellors in the school. Grades achieved by the entire grade 12 class in grades 8 and 11 were also analysed. The initial purpose of the research was to study gender socialization in the school, but this was quickly seen to be impossible without also considering issues of social class. This realization that gender and class are intricately interrelated and must both be explored in analysing students' behaviour and aspirations and school personnel's channelling of students, highlights the importance of using both feminist and Marxist perspectives. The experience of students in school varies enormously by both gender and class, and it is the goal of this chapter to explore some of the ways in which this is true.

Marxist and Feminist Analyses of Schools

Marxist and feminist researchers of education focus their attention on the ways in which schools contribute independently to the perpetuation of male-dominated, capitalist society. Such researchers examine the ways in which schools actively process student behaviour and activity to perpetuate social class and gender divisions.

Social Organization of Schools

The main contribution of schooling, as seen by Marxist sociologists, is to legitimate the existing social hierarchy of jobs and rewards in capitalist society. The work by Bowles and Gintis develops a theory of 'correspondence' between social class, classroom relationships and work in the labour force.[3] They argue that 'ability' tests (IQ tests), used to separate children into 'fast' or 'slow' learners, do not test the children's own potential as students, but, rather, their family backgrounds. Children, streamed by social class, are exposed to different types of education, both in terms of content (academic or vocational), and social relations with teachers and peers in the classroom. These different forms prepare them for different academic futures and, in turn, feed into different types of jobs—working class, bourgeois, or petty bourgeois. A sensitive and personalized account of the Marxist theoretical framework is to be found in *Downtown Kids Aren't Dumb*, a brief presented by Toronto parents concerned with their children's welfare.[4] It shows how ability testing and high school programmes in Canadian schools process working-class children to maintain them in vocational streams which lead into poorly rewarded jobs. On the basis of this evidence, the Marxist argument that schools reproduce the social class division of labour is well established.

Using a similar perspective, some feminist researchers focus on the ways in which schools are formally organized to ensure that girls and boys receive different educational experiences. Gaskell studied girls in Vancouver high school business programmes, showing how they moved directly into the sex-segregated labour force.[5] She demonstrates that there are short-term advantages to both the girls and their employers, but that there are long-term detrimental effects for the girls with limited skill training and jobs without opportunities for advancement.

This type of analysis has prompted some feminist researchers to re-examine the contentious issue of the effects of single-sex versus co-educational schools. In many ways this remains a British and Australian issue. Canadians have tended to follow the American lead into comprehensive and co-educational schools as the ones which, it is argued, offer greater equality (by class, race and sex). Arnot contends that both options should remain open for parents choosing a school for daughters and sons, and urges feminists to continue to study this issue.[6] Shaw argues that although they may provide better facilities for science laboratories, co-educational schools may in fact contribute to greater sex role typing.[7] Even if the move to single-sex schools is perceived as a retrogressive step, perhaps students, especially girls from thirteen to fifteen years whose academic achievement typically falls, might benefit from the segregation. However, as Arnot has pointed out, in a society marked strongly by a sex-segregated labour force, a minimal separation in school would make little difference. Similarly, Canadian data substantiates Wolpe's point that even when girls achieve appropriate credentials in school, they are not likely to obtain positions in the labour force commensurate with their qualifications.[8]

Thus, despite strategic differences, feminist researchers concur that the school system, from sex-typed courses through to its larger organizational structure, reproduces gender, like class, hierarchies.

Student Culture

The work by McRobbie, Llewellyn, Sharp and Willis on the culture of working-class girls and boys, as this is played out in schools, indicates the futility of the functionalist theory of equality of opportunity offered through education, and expands a Marxist structural paradigm. McRobbie finds that working-class girls enter school with a predisposition to marry and have children, and so to ignore other kinds of work which they might also do.[9] The anti-school culture of femininity, and the short-term goal of romance, take priority, in McRobbie's research, for working-class girls. Llewellyn's participant observation study of the culture of girls and girls' friendship groups offers interesting comparative findings to McRobbie's study, while at the same time adding to the underlying finding that school merely provides a setting for the playing out of an anti-school female culture deemed legitimate for young women in a male-dominated school environment.[10] The research by Sharp and her colleagues on the transition of working-class girls from school to work offers added insight into this process which depends on girls' perceiving family and motherhood as their central goals.[11] Similarly, it is found that working-class boys develop an anti-social culture based on a disparagement of academic work, combined with an overvaluation of heavy labour and masculine superiority.[12]

Anyon's recent work on the accommodation and resistance by working-class and upper-middle-class girls to the contradictory expectations of future work and motherhood provides valuable insight into forms of female culture.[13] After exploring both public and private forms of resistance and accommodation to the contradictory expectations of the female sex role, Anyon concludes that overall 'their accommodation and resistance does not seek to remove the structural causes of the contradiction'.[14] Their resistance and accommodation represent creative and individually liberating forms of managing, but ultimately only assist women to survive in a male-dominated milieu where roles which are actually open to them are circumscribed.

The Ottawa study provides support for several of the ideas put forth by Anyon. Of the twenty-five girls interviewed, sixteen were middle- or upper-middle-class from professional or managerial families, while nine were working-class from unskilled or semi-skilled families. For the middle-class group, going to university was an accepted course of action, taken for granted. However, only three of them integrated plans for post-secondary education with a commitment to subsequent careers. For the majority university was seen as a time 'to get my head together' or to fulfil parental dreams. For one it was something to do in case she was 'late' in getting married. As she said, 'When you get to be twenty-five or twenty-six everyone starts looking at you and wondering when you are going to get married.'

For these girls, going to university or art college (a popular choice among the highest status) is mainly a route to motherhood. This, they were quite clear, would put an end to other activities: 'I wouldn't want to work, after I had kids.' 'If I had kids I'd definitely stop working.' 'If I had kids I'd want to stay home and help them.' 'My career would be working with children and having my own kids would be my career.'

Thus these middle-class girls for the most part foresaw a truncated future. Their way of solving the contradictions of being a middle-class woman was a two-stage programme: some further education followed by full-time motherhood. The three who seemed committed to pursuing a career were clearly aware that this might prove problematic. One said she would be expected to do all the housework *and* have a job, while another said, 'Anyone I had an interest in would just have to realise that my career was important to me.'

All but one of the working-class girls were bemused by questions about education after high school. Some mentioned it as an ideal but one quickly dismissed it: 'Sometimes my mother asks me if I'm thinking of going to college, and I say, "I don't know, I think I might get a job first." And she says, "Oh, that's OK." She's pretty reasonable.' Another said, 'I want to do something, but if I don't I won't be upset ... I always wanted to be a housewife.' Another said that she didn't think she could do university work, even though she wanted to be a teacher and had high grades. For the most part they anticipated getting a job at the end of high school. That was what parents wanted: 'They just don't want me to be a slob. They want me to earn a decent living, like being a secretary.' For others the motivation was to be financially independent: 'My boyfriend always said he'd support me, but I don't want that. I can't stand that.' Although university is not in the minds of working-class girls, they share the motherhood ideology with their middle-class sisters: 'If you're going to go on with work and be married at the same time, I don't think you should have children.'

The range of desires and expectations reveals how class differences arise within the structurally prescribed limits of femininity. While middle-class girls may be able to live out both of their typical future plans – full-time motherhood and a cyclical career – this is likely to be at some cost both to their work lives and earning capacities, and to their experience in childcare. Given the levels of female and male working-class wages, it is highly unlikely that the working-class girls will be able to be either financially independent or not to work to help support a household.

This research on the future plans of female high school students adds further support to the critique of functionalist theory and moves beyond organizational analyses where sex and class are all too often rigidly separated. Because functionalism assumes a high degree of consensus on middle-class values of achievement, it cannot see student cultures which develop partly in retaliation to socially imposed gender and class constraints. Given student resistance to what middle-class schooling has to offer in a capitalist, male-dominated society, there is little wonder that the functionalist aspiration that schools provide equal opportunity has failed. Functionalist and critical organizational analyses share a methodological assumption: they separate the formal organizational aspects of the school from the culture of the student population. Phenomenological research which focuses on what happens in schools in a largely informal way shows how the relationship between school personnel and students in the school and classroom contribute to the persistence · of the status quo.

Phenomenological Research on Interaction Between Students and School Personnel

Overall, it becomes evident in this research that at least two processes are operating in the classroom and school to lead students to accept and reproduce society based on class and gender hierarchical divisions. First, it becomes clear that sex and class are recognized by school personnel, usually implicitly, as social categories to consider in guiding students in making 'appropriate' future occupational and educational plans. They do not consider it to be appropriate for individuals to cross the gender division of labour or part ways with their own social class background, despite academic achievement which would allow them to do so. Middle-class girls are encouraged to go to university to achieve some professional or semi-professional skills *before* settling down to childbearing and domesticity, while working-class girls are expected to work, at least part-time, while investing their main attentions in family. Both are actively encouraged to put family first. These decisions are made with little or no consideration of actual school achievement or for individual interests.

The second factor which becomes apparent concerns the implicit devaluation of subordinate (non-middle-class male) cultures. This is most usually expressed by refusing to recognize or deriding resistant or opposing cultures. Girls' interests are particularly subject to derision in the school. In writing about the succesful hegemony of bourgeois culture in the school, Dale states,'what seems to be involved is the prevention of rejection, opposition or alternatives to the status quo through denying the use of the school for such purposes'.[15] Although Dale rejects seeing the school as 'active' in the maintenance of this hegemony, choosing rather to see the status quo as being maintained by the 'normal process' of the relatively autonomous school, it is a matter for research to investigate how much the 'prevention of rejection, opposition or alternatives' is the passive stance of the school, and how much it is actively accomplished. Delamont argues that the school is active in promoting the preservation of the hierarchial gender status quo and in fact is regressive in ignoring social change which has taken place.[16]

Research presented here supports Delamont's view of the school, while at the same time showing how, simply by avoiding issues, the school takes stands supporting existing gender and class hierarchies. The following is broken down into three components: the advice of guidance personnel; teacher–student interaction in the classroom; the content of classroom interaction.

The Advice of Guidance Personnel
The evidence from this research indicates that students are not led to consider future work which would be inconsistent with their social class background or gender, regardless of personal academic achievement. Although survey research has found that scores on mental ability do not correlate very highly with educational aspirations, particularly for working-class students,[17] it is useful to examine how this is accomplished in the school. The statement holds true for girls and boys, but with the added twist that girls, no matter what their social class or academic achievement, are rarely urged to think of work as anything but secondary, with family responsibilities as primary. Thus the surplus labour force of largely unskilled or semi-skilled women who can

be pulled into the labour force as required and pushed out again, back to the family, during times of economic recession, is also reproduced.[18]

The names of the forty students interviewed were given to the guidance counsellors, who were asked what they knew about these students' future plans. The counsellors knew nineteen of the students well enough to discuss their plans and, in a few cases, students were discussed by more than one counsellor. The counsellors assumed that none of the students aspired to break with their social class backgrounds. They were unaware of the one working-class girl who did aspire to go to university and study science. Instead, two counsellors claimed that this student was planning to be a legal secretary; and both thought that this was a good choice. On the other hand, the student herself stressed several times in her interview that she did not want to be a secretary. She realized that the counsellors knew of this 'plan' because her mother had spoken with them about it. This was the only student interviewed who was consciously trying to overcome both social background and stereotyped gender roles, and she obviously received no support from counsellors.

In some cases, counsellors discussed students whose academic achievement was inconsistent with what might be anticipated for their future work – that is, where it was 'too high' for a working-class job, or 'too low' for a middle-class or professional job. The working-class girl with the highest achievement of all forty in the sample had wanted to be a doctor but now planned to become a hospital technician. Her lowered goal met with approval from a counsellor: 'She's always been an A student . . . She is someone who is independent and doesn't have any financial backing behind her, so it's a case of economic necessity that she takes on a job.'

Another counsellor positively accepted a high achieving working-class boy's decision to go directly into the army:

As a counsellor I'm not going to say to someone who is unfamiliar, let us say, with the university career situation, perhaps not monetarily too well off, they have no aspirations in that line for that sort of thing, it's no use *my* saying, 'You should go to university.'. . . My idea of guidance is to present to the student what opportunities there are for them to take what suits them, what they feel comfortable with. And a lot of that comfort and advice and discussion goes on in the family.

These examples of working-class experience show that not only do most students seem predisposed to train for jobs that will maintain their social class background, but also that there is little positive encouragement and sometimes active discouragement from the school to alter these patterns.

Upper-middle-class students also seemed likely to maintain their class position, regardless of low academic achievement. Of the two boys in this situation, one intended to go to an American college and eventually to enter the marine business owned by his uncle. Doing this, he would probably be able to maintain his social class position. The second would also go to college, much as he preferred not to. In the meantime one had football, the other a jazz group to deflect attention from poor achievement. In both cases, family resources and direction, not advice from school, were instrumental in assuring their futures. In fact, the counsellors chose not to offer any comment or information on these two students, thereby showing the school's passivity in allowing the reproduction of class relations.

One upper-middle-class girl, who was managing the academic programme with great difficulty, wished to move into the technical stream of another high school. Her parents forbade such a move and thus forestalled her chance of acquiring a skilled manual job. The guidance counsellors were unaware of her desire to go to the technical school and merely viewed her as a problem student.

Gender was a category used more explicitly than class in advising students, particularly girls. Several middle-class girls also had aspirations for working-class jobs. However, this was not seen as problematic, as long as the jobs were in the female segregated segment of the labour force. In four of five interviews, counsellors explicitly stated that girls had to realize that being future wives and mothers was of primary importance to their future plans. As one said: 'I have certain feelings about home, etc. . . . Can a surrogate or substitute mother . . . replace the mother? There's no way. The bond is simply not there.' Another felt that a woman could do neither properly if she tried to have both a family and a job. A third said, 'I think that the girl who is interested in marriage and children . . . might look for a career that she can leave for a few years and then go back to . . . where the knowledge of the job takes second place to the personality of the job.' He then proceeded to list several jobs in the predominantly woman's branch of the labour force: social worker, teacher, saleswoman, secretary.

Overall, maintaining social class background was seen as appropriate by the counsellors. For the most part this implied also maintaining the sexual division of labour, but in several cases gender took precedence over social class. This meant that some of the sixteen girls from the middle class were heading for working-class jobs which were conspicuously open to women and would be compatible with their jobs as mothers, since they could be dropped and perhaps resumed. It would be incumbent upon these girls to maintain their social class position through marriage.[19]

An important way in which counsellors sidestep issues of class, is by 'converting social hierarchies into academic hierarchies':[20] upper middle class translates perniciously into 'bright', working class into 'dull'. According to Keddie, teachers talk about the 'dull' students in the lower stream (mostly working-class students) and the 'bright' students in the higher stream (mostly middle-class students).[21] It is through doing this that school personnel are able to maintain the myth of being 'class-blind'. Thus the words themselves may be neatly avoided, and a great step may be made in the social reproduction of class.

Student class origins affect the interpretation of falling grades by school personnel. Low achieving middle-class children were labelled by guidance counsellors as 'bright' but not well enough motivated. One middle-class girl whose grades had declined was 'probably very bright. Her father's in the diplomatic corps.' Another was 'extremely bright, as are her brothers . . . but there's no effort there whatever'. On the other hand, working-class students whose grades declined were not seen as presenting problems. They were achieving according to what was expected of them. A girl from a divided family was a 'very, very average student'. A working-class boy whose grades dropped was a 'solid sixty per center. . . . It may be that there isn't the drive, the motivation in the family.'

Social class and gender played closely connected roles in the advice of the high school counsellors. A content analysis of comments made about students indicated that counsellors knew as much about student family background as they did about academic achievement. Thus, school personnel actively contributed to homeostasis in the class and sex divisions of labour.

Teacher–student Interaction

The observation of classroom activity confirmed previous findings that boys dominate in the classroom and that teachers contribute to this male dominance by focusing greater attention on the boys.[22] Furthermore, teachers' interviews clearly revealed that they evaluated female and male academic abilities differently. Together, these teacher practices devalued girls and rendered them invisible in the classroom.

In the observation sessions in twenty-seven grade 12 classes (eleven English literature, twelve mathematics, two chemistry, two world religion), girls were found to dominate verbal interaction with the teacher in only 7 per cent of the classes, while boys dominated in 63 per cent. There were only minor discrepancies by sex in the remainder. On the one hand, in the English and mathematics classes it was found that teachers directed between one and a half and five times as many questions to boys as to girls. On the other, in two exceptional classes (the woman teacher in the chemistry class and the man teacher in the numerically female-dominated world religion class), teachers directed equal numbers of questions to girls and boys. In all class periods boys independently asked more questions and made more comments than girls. Thus it was clear that both teachers and students were responsible for the dominance of boys in the classroom. Why teachers directed more attention to boys in their classes is illustrated by their comments on the behaviour of girls and boys in class. Although the typically non-disruptive behaviour of girls and their relative silence is often a relief to teachers, this does not lead teachers to appreciate them as students.[23] Girls do not fit the 'ideal client' image which Becker found was the student who responded to and appeared to learn as a result of the teacher's efforts.[24] Several comments made by the women in their interviews revealed that they preferred boys as students; the men indicated that they thought boys were brighter. Teachers responded to girls' quietness in class and their decline in achievement over the years in school in ways which turned quietness into invisibility. Ultimately teachers' attitudes fostered girls' further rejection of the school.

Eight of the ten women in the school who taught academic courses at the grade 12 level confirmed that they preferred the classroom behaviour of boys. As one said: 'The boys are very pointed in their questions. They want very specific information.

The girls have a tendency to be vague, whereas the boys will be very specific. And I appreciate that, because then I can help more.'

Boys were also seen as more fun than girls, as evident from this statement from another teacher, which opens with a clearly stated preference for male students: 'The fellows I prefer to teach, more than the girls, because they don't get as uptight about little things. Like I find in my grade 10s they don't hold grudges and they're fun, while the girls are taking themselves far more seriously.'

The issue of holding grudges and the duplicity of the girls was taken up by two other teachers. One talked with great admiration about how easy the boys made it for her, a petite young woman, to discipline them: 'You know I even scold some of them, those tall guys. But the next day it's "Good morning, miss" and "Good-bye, miss" and that's it.' Girls, she said, were less forgiving. Another said; 'I think in general that the boys are a bit more forthright. You're not as inclined to see somebody and say "now I wonder what he's thinking" as "I wonder what she's thinking". You feel that the boys are pretty much more open about things.'

The women teachers spent much more time during the interview discussing the behaviour of the boys than that of the girls. One spoke extensively about the boys, comparing the dedicated student with the 'he-men' whom she 'tamed' in her classes. When prompted to discuss the girls, she said briefly; 'Girls haven't caused me any trouble in years and years. They tend to talk a bit much, but it's never been any problem for me for years to stop the girls.'

Boys were the subject of other 'plugs' from the women, but the girls never were. A chemistry teacher noted that boys liked to put on airs about doing well, even though they did not work. 'But mind you,' she said, 'whenever you look at their homework it's done, and you only assigned three questions but they've got twenty-three done.'

The sexual dynamic is a clear underpinning to the attraction between women teachers and the young adult males in their classes. It is only half perceived and unspoken, but it clearly led to admiration and respect. The mirror attraction, on the other hand, which must have existed (and had led to one marriage in the recent history of the school), did not generate a parallel respect of men teachers for female students. On the contrary,

twelve of the fifteen men clearly denigrated the academic abilities of the girls. They were more aware than the women that the
early high achievement of girls declined in the later years of high
school. They called the girls in the junior grades 'over-achievers';
they did not see them as 'under-achievers' in later years. Rather,
girls' decline in achievement over the years was felt to be due to
the fact that in the upper grades 'ability starts to take over'.
Another, who said that most over-achievers were girls, defined
the term: 'By an over-achiever I mean somebody who's getting
marks above and beyond their innate ability level. Which can be
done very easily at the 9 and 10 level by doing two hours of
homework a night.' Implicit in this statement is a judgement that
achievement is more a sign of ability in the upper grades, since it
is impossible to exceed ability at this level. The same teacher
remarked that, as he looked back, more boys stood out in his
mind as 'really bright students'.

The 'over-achievement' of girls in the lower grades is, according to several teachers, a result of their docility and conscien-
tiousness. Girls gave the 'party line', as one teacher said, and as a
result were more successful than boys. They noted that girls
passed through puberty and 'settled down' before boys, and so
they were initially able to do better. It took boys a bit longer to
settle down and achieve according to their ability. One teacher
said that girls did well in the early grades because at that stage
they were still keen to learn things 'by rote', and that 'they could
cope with this'.

Girls did continue to excel in senior English classes. The male
English teachers recognized this but attempted to explain away
the success. Girls did well because 'their work habits were so
good' and 'they read more'. One painted a scenario of a girl
spending the evening babysitting, since she had to wait for an
invitation out, and this would provide a lot of quiet time to read.
One noted that the pattern of girls excelling in English ended at
the university level.

Two corollaries followed from the over-achievement thesis.
First, girls who declined in achievement and were doing relatively poorly by the end of high school were seen as achieving
according to their ability. Boys, on the other hand, who did *not*
do well by the end of high school were under-achieving. The
teacher of the 'slow' senior mathematics class said: 'Girls are
there pretty well because they should be there. I don't find too
many under-achievers amongst the females. You're going to get

the boys in there who are capable of doing well but don't do well. They have *decided* not to achieve the way they should,' (my emphasis). Thus for boys there was seen to be an aspect of low achievement not strictly related to ability; but this possibility was not suggested for girls.

As a second corollary, girls who did manage to achieve high grades in the upper years were seen not as clever, but as plodders. In other words, they merely continued in the pattern of over-achievement. As a teacher of chemistry said about the girls in his class: 'they tend to be very good workers. Maybe not the brightest, maybe not the cleverest, but they have plugged and done all their work to get there ... Some of the boys have got there completely on their cleverness. But the girls who are there tend to be the ones who have worked.' Although it is not a disparaging comment to say that the girls worked hard, it was unnecessary to say that they were not really bright. The message was clear that these male teachers felt that the low achievement of the girls but not the high achievement was related to ability.

Thus there is an important, although largely hidden way, in which teachers in school undervalue the female students and encourage their withdrawal from the educational field. Certainly the emphasis in the wider society on marriage and children is a source of their limited future aspirations, but the undervaluation of their behaviour and achievement in school is an important contribution to this outcome. It is probable that teachers themselves are also influenced by what they 'know' about the future expectations of girls. It is not a finding particular to this research that teachers perceive boys as the better students.[25] However, this merely serves to add support to the thesis that this is one way in which girls are rendered invisible in the school, and are undervalued as students.

These assessments of the unequal relation of achievement to ability in boys and girls echoes those made about class and achievement. In both cases the dominant group – male and middle-class students – were assumed to be capable but unmotivated, whereas the subordinate group – female and working-class students – were judged to be simply intellectually unable. The conversion of pre-existing social hierarchies of class and gender external to the school into achievement hierarchies in and by the school serves to reproduce them in the educational system and for the whole society.

The Content of Classroom Interaction

Ideology of male-superior, female-subordinate arises frequently in classroom conversation and discussion, and is accepted uncritically as natural. Previous research has shown that the acceptance of a gendered status quo has profound implications for girls' classroom experience and ability to learn. Spender cites the example of a male history teacher who encountered problems in getting girls to participate in a class discussion on war. When one girl did speak, she was ridiculed by boys in the class. Since most topics covered in classes do traditionally have a male orientation and since girls are discouraged from speaking to these topics, they withdraw and learn silence and passivity – a lesson well learned, judging from the classroom observation sessions.

One example from classroom observations in the Ottawa study shows how patriarchal culture is reproduced. In the world religions class, the teacher asked who in the Christian religion might be a good role model. When no one answered, he suggested St Paul, but then added that Paul would not be a good model for a woman, because he did not like women. Then he went on to note that few religious leaders had liked women. He also stated that women had been created from a rib from Adam's side, to help and please him. At this stage I heard a girl in the class whispering that women and men had the same number of ribs. The misogyny inherent in the great religions of the world is an important topic, but it was never critically discussed or presented as in any way problematic. Instead misogyny was presented as 'objective' classroom knowledge.

In another class, an English teacher criticized a play written by a student because in it the daughter did not cry or show enough emotion in pleading for the family car. A mathematics teacher merely smiled and nodded when a girl in his class said she wouldn't have to learn how to complete an income tax form because her 'husband' would do it.

In each of these classroom episodes, the status quo is accepted as normal and natural. In the first, gender stereotypes are actively offered as legitimated knowledge; in the second, they are used to judge student work; while, in the third, the student is silently rewarded for conforming to gender stereotypes. None of them led to any critical discussions. Nor did any of the teachers challenge gender typing. Consequently, gender hierarchies are removed from the purview of education and given a status as fact of life.

In contrast is the example provided by a discussion in an English literature class which was remarkable because of the overwhelming participation of the girls. The content of this discussion is worth exploring. In this class, the teacher raised questions for discussion on Hardy's novel *Tess of the d'Urbervilles.* Did Tess know she was being seduced (it is often difficult to tell in Victorian novels!)? Did she love her baby as she said, or was she secretly relieved when the baby died? The girls participated fully in this class, not because the teacher altered his usual pattern of calling more often on the boys, but because the girls were eager to discuss these questions and independently raised issues elaborating on them. In fact, the teacher was overwhelmed by the flood of discussion he had started and actually appeared withdrawn and even embarrassed by it.

The fact that the teacher and the boys withdrew from the discussion suggests that the cultures of the girls and boys are kept very separate in the school. Male culture dominates in the school, as elsewhere, and the alternate culture, the feminine voice, is silenced, either by being ignored or undervalued when it does surface. The discussion about Tess obviously did strike a very responsive note among the girls. Since they are not even encouraged to discuss the issues which are of immediate concern to them, they learn to be silent generally in class, and the process of learning, of pursuing important questions, is stunted. Teachers encourage passivity on the part of girls and then criticize them for being silent and not participating in class. By conforming to female standards of passivity in patriarchal culture, the intellectual growth of girls is undermined and teachers judge them as being less capable students.

The class discussion which I heard on *Tess* was in all probability rare, given that most topics covered in classes are from a masculine orientation. If the girls had been encouraged and respected for their participation in that discussion, they would feel more free to pursue their own orientation to issues in others.

Conclusion

A great deal occurs within the school and classroom to encourage students to accept the sex and class divisions of labour, at both a societal and personal level. In part, alternatives are seen as unacceptable, in part the status quo is assumed to be just and appropriate.

As a result the school is characterized by these two related patterns which contribute to the social reproduction of society marked by economic and sex inequality. One way of accomplishing this is by ignoring that inequalities do in fact exist in male-dominated, capitalist society. The dominant culture is accepted as the only reality. The experience of students whose background or sex indicates that they are living another face of this reality is not recognized in the school. Consequently, students from subordinate cultures tend to reject schooling and all it represents.

A related way in which the school contributes to the hegemony of the dominant culture is by accepting that students' choices concerning their educational 'and occupational futures be consistent with the sex-segregated labour force and their social class background. Very often students who have not rejected schooling (usually because of parental pressure, or because they are very bright and curious) are encouraged because of their own financial limitations, or because of their future 'plans' to become wives, mothers and low-status workers; in other words, to make sex- and class-appropriate future choices. In these cases, actual academic achievement is placed second to factors of sex and class.

Thus these two components of schooling interact to contribute to the persistence of the dominant culture: at one level, subordinate cultures are undervalued and most students make their own choices to reject schooling; at another, students are not encouraged to make 'inappropriate' choices, given their sex and social class. They are, on the other hand, lauded for making 'appropriate' choices. In this way, schools do in fact contribute to the inequalities inherent in male dominated, capitalist society.

The enthusiasm that the girls showed in their discussion of *Tess* indicates that schools might be forced to change if girls generally assert themselves and do not rest with whispering, 'Women and men have the same number of ribs.' However, the subordinate position of women in society is clearly reflected and promoted in schools as they exist now.

Conceptions of Skill and the Work of Women: Some Historical and Political Issues

Jane Gaskell

Assumptions about what constitutes 'skilled' and 'unskilled' work have been fundamental to the division of labour in the workplace, to ideological divisions within the working class and to academic and policy discussion about the labour force. The terms have been important in the ways workers and employers describe and understand differences among workers. They have been adopted by academics and policy makers seeking to understand labour markets and the nature of work. Their use is based on the common understanding that skilled workers have more to offer their employers, and thus rightfully enjoy higher esteem, and a better bargaining position in relation to management and others workers. Recently the terms have taken on added importance in Canada, as the state has argued that a shortage of 'skilled' workers constitutes a major problem for the economy even in a time of general unemployment.[1] This definition of the problem suggests a reallocation of resources towards attracting and training skilled workers, while the unskilled are left to fend for themselves.

Women are rarely considered to be skilled workers. One can find constant references to women's lack of skills in the research literature. Studies of the socialization and education of girls are often premised on the assumption that we need to understand the ways in which girls become deskilled – learning the attitudes (passivity, fear of success) and intellectual styles (docility, dependence) which fit them for less skilled areas of work.[2] Studies in the human capital tradition explore how women's lower earnings at work are explained by their lack of 'human capital' that is, relevant work skills. In this tradition, Polachek characterizes female occupations as 'requiring lesser amounts of training' and 'menial'.[3]

Even theorists who are explicitly feminist and/or Marxist characterize women's jobs as demanding less skill. Women 'are still overwhelmingly slotted into specific industries and occupations characterized by low pay, low skill requirements, low productivity and low prospects for advancement'.[4] 'Women are paid less even for the same job. They usually get less skilled jobs. They are given proportionally less responsibility in the hierarchy, and they are the last hired and first fired.'[5] Wolpe describes women 'clustering at the lowest levels of the occupational hierarchy, in terms of both pay and skills'.[6]

A more careful analysis of the jobs women do reveals that these claims are entirely too facile. We usually take schooling as an important index of 'skill' but women in the labour force are more educated on the average than men in the labour force. Picot, Gaskell and Boyd have shown that on indices of occupational status, women do not appear disadvantaged in relation to men.[7] Englund shows that jobs in which women predominate require as much formal schooling and as much 'cognitive complexity' as the jobs in which men predominate. Indeed, she concludes, based on the official government ratings in the *American Dictionary of Occupations,* that 'females actually have an advantageous occupational skill distribution on balance'. This analysis is immensely valuable in showing that the problem for women is not in their skills, but in the way these skills are rewarded. With the same education and skills as a man a woman gets paid less. Occupations which employ a large number of women pay less for the same skills than occupations which employ a large number of men.[8] But the argument about skill can be taken in another direction, to explore how the assumption that women are unskilled has come to be so widely shared. Most discussions proceed as if skill were an easily identified and quantified characteristic of a job, like pay and prospects for advancement. But skill is a socially constructed category and we need to inquire about how it is constructed. What counts as a 'skill' and why? The ability to manage social interaction, the ability to put up with routine tasks, the ability to analyse problems or the possession of a particular kind of credential? Different things may count in different circumstances. Different people will count different things. In this paper it will be argued that managing skill definitions is a political process, one that organized workers engage in continually. Women have been at a disadvantage in this process of managing skill definitions because they have not been represented by strong collective organizations. As a result, the notion of skilled work is used in a way that devalues the work women do. Understanding how this happens will provide women with more awareness of how to combat continuing attempts to downplay the skill involved in their work. This paper will begin to look at these processes as they have influenced working-class jobs. Others have explored how professional groups have engaged in similar political struggles, acting to monopolize access to, mystify and charge high prices for, the skills they have.[9] Women professionals have had less political power than their male counterparts, and the consequences for women can be explored. They include, arguably, the classification of women's professional work as only 'semi-professional' (nursing, teaching, librarianship), the under-representation of women in the male professions, and the take-over of some areas of women's work, notably midwifery, by more 'skilled' professionals.

Rethinking Skills

Some recent work has begun to challenge the taken for granted nature of skill labels. Braverman especially urged a rethinking of the way we accept official designations of what is skilled or unskilled work. He points out that, according to census categories, work today is considerably more skilled than work a century ago because more people work with machines. But the reality behind the census classifications is considerably more complex. For instance, although the census classified drivers of motorized vehicles as skilled and drivers of horsedrawn vehicles unskilled, Braverman comments,

> Today, it would be more proper to regard those who are able to drive vehicles as unskilled in that respect at least, while those who can care for, harness and manage a team of horses are certainly the possessors of a marked and uncommon ability. There is certainly little reason to suppose that the ability to drive a motor vehicle is more demanding, requires longer training or habituation time, and thus represents a higher or intrinsically more rewarding skill.[10]

But having pointed out that the government classification system does not accurately describe skill levels, Braverman reverts to his own definition of skill as one that is accurate. He sees skills as 'traditionally bound up with craft mastery', and, as he indicated above, tied to training time and the 'commonness' of skills. He assumes this definition is shared with his readers and validated by common sense. He does not want to pursue issues in the sociology of knowledge, being uneasy with definitions of skill that depend on 'relativistic or contemporary notions', especially as he sees 'skilled' coming to mean 'able to perform repetitive tasks with manual dexterity', a usage which is produced by changes in the organization of work and which he deplores. But his own concern with changing the wrongheaded notions of skill suggests the importance of inquiry into the processes involved in producing skill labels. Some feminist work has also begun to question the connection between skill labels and the actual content of work. Margaret Mead has written:

> One aspect of this social evaluation of different types of labour is the differentiated prestige of men's activities and women's activities. Whatever men do – even if it is dressing dolls for religious ceremonies – is more prestigious than what women do and is treated as a higher achievement.

More recently, Phillips and Taylor have argued:

> The classification of women's jobs as unskilled and men's jobs as skilled or semi-skilled frequently bears little relation to the actual amount of training or ability required for them. Skill definitions are saturated with sexual bias. The work of women is often deemed inferior simply because it is women who do it. Women workers carry into the workplace their status as subordinate individuals and this status comes to define the work they do.[11]

In this passage Phillips and Taylor see gender-distorting skill classification, much in the way that Braverman sees skill labels being distorted by capitalism. For Phillips and Taylor, the amount of training and 'ability' required are legitimate bases for differentiating among skill levels. But what might be called, in social psychology, a 'halo' effect acts to increase the status of men's work, because men do it. While this process surely occurs, Phillips and Taylor do not go far enough in exploring how the social construction of skill categories works against women. Ability itself is a socially defined concept. Which abilities count? It depends on who is using what criteria, which returns us to the original problem that employers do not value women's abilities. Training time is also not a clear indicator of the difficulty of learning to do a job. How are we to determine the amount of training 'necessary' to an 'adequate' performance of a job? Rather, the length and form that training will take is decided through political and economic struggle. So what Phillips and Taylor take as potentially objective valuations of skill levels are themselves socially produced.

Barrett places her discussion of skill squarely in the context of political struggles between men and women under capitalism:

> Women have frequently failed to establish recognition of the skills required by their work, and have consequently been in a weak bargaining position in a divided and internally competitive work force . . . we need to know precisely how and why some groups of workers succeed in establishing definitions of their work as skilled.

By asking about the political processes responsible for skill labelling, she is pointing to the questions I will pursue here. She goes on to suggest that training requirements may be part, not of 'real' skill requirements, but of the way skill categories are constructed. 'Training and recruitment may be highly controlled and skill rendered inaccessible for the purposes of retaining the differentials and privilege of the labour aristocracy.'[12]

Education and the Creation of Skill

It has been shown above that even those who point to the ideological content of skill ratings (Braverman, Phillips and Taylor) tend to rely on time spent in training as a legitimate way to differentiate between skilled and unskilled work. This is not the only criterion, but it is an important one. Time is a useful measure for administrators or social scientists trying to come up with ratings, as it can be turned into a number and used to compare things that are actually quite unlike. Time becomes a mode of exchange of value, like money, and its creates the same problem of 'fetishizing the commodity', in Marx's terms, losing sight of what it actually represents and how it is produced. Thus time in training is turned into skill ratings, reifying skill into a unidimensional 'thing'. This is the assumption built into the *Canadian Classification and Dictionary of Occupations (CCDO)*, which is the state's attempt to systematically 'classify and define occupational activity in the world of work'.[13] The skill level of a job in the CCDO is expressed partly in terms of general educational development (GED) and specific vocational preparation (SVP). GED measures the levels of numeracy, literacy, comprehension and reading skills necesssary for performing a job. While this is not identical with the number of years of schooling required, it is 'assumed to result from participation in the educational system'. The SVP, which is highly correlated with the GED rating, is based on the 'time necessary for acquiring specific skills'. This is estimated from time in 'vocational training, apprenticeship, in-plant and on-the-job training, as well as from experience in other occupations'. Taking training time as a sign of skill assumes that the length of training depends on the difficulty, complexity and breadth of understanding necessary for performing the work. There is a long tradition in the sociology of education that treats skill in just this way, as something accumulated through years of formal education. This view of skill has been used to explain why more educated workers are preferred by employers, paid more and enjoy lower unemployment rates. It underlies human capital theory, and the analysis of schooling as a 'fair' mechanism for allocating jobs in the society.[14] But many recent strands of the sociology of education have raised questions about this common scenario. Educational attainment may act as a 'signal' or a 'screen', without imparting any necessary skills. Some have argued that the skills learned at school have very little importance on the job.[15] The time training takes can vary for the same job and changes when the actual skills involved in the work do not. The training of teachers is an example. It has been suggested that what is learned in school is not any technical skill, but social orientation that employers prefer because they produce a quiescent workforce. As Collins summarizes his critique:

> The great majority of all jobs can be learned through practice by any literate person. The number of esoteric specialities 'requiring' unusually extensive training or skills is relatively small. The 'system' does not 'need' or 'demand' a certain kind of performance; it 'needs' what it gets, because 'it' is nothing more than a slip shod way of talking about the way things happen to be at the time. How hard people work, and with what dexterity and cleverness, depends on

how much other people can require them to do, and on how much they can dominate other people.[16]

In other words, the correspondence between schooling and work need not be very strong, and certainly does not need to be based on 'skill'. While there undoubtedly are instances where training does develop necessary skills, this must not be assumed to be the case.

Secondly, the notion that education serves the employer in some straightforward way has been increasingly questioned. It is more useful to see educational institutions and the state in general as a site of class struggle than as a mechanical reflection of what employers want.[17] Employers will have more resources, power and access to decision-making than most other groups, but education does have some independence and other groups are able to exert some influence. This has produced innumerable struggles over what will be in the curriculum, when and how it will be taught, and what will be left in the hands of parents or employers or unions. The form that specific skill training and vocational education will take has been one of the major areas of this struggle, within the public school system as well as in the workplace and in state-run training programmes.

To summarize, although length of training is taken as a sign of the skill level of a job, there is no necessary relation between the time spent in school and level of difficulty of the work. Many political factors influence the length and kind of training. Research has often shown little relationship between the skills workers use at work and what they learned in school. Schooling and forms of training can, however, have a material impact on the operation of labour markets by influencing the supply of workers and the way that qualified workers are recognized—both legally through licensing and more informally in personnel practices. For this reason there has been considerable contention over what forms training will take, and what kinds of skills are recognized and regulated. The usefulness of this framework can be illustrated by looking briefly at the way craft unions have struggled over kinds of training to maintain definitions of their work as skilled. This paper will then consider clerical workers to see how they have been unable to win similar battles, and how the organization of training there contributes to the work's 'unskilled' character. This is a very preliminary overview, but will suggest a new set of questions about skill, and work, and education, which need to be addressed by further research.

The 'Skilled' Trades

In most employment documents and sociological texts, as well as among most workers, a 'skilled' labourer is equivalent to an artisan, a craftsperson who performs a licensed trade. The sign of a skilled labourer rather than a semi-skilled or unskilled one is the existence of an apprenticeship which leads to licensing. Which trades are apprenticed, and exactly what an apprenticeship involves, varies from country to country,[18] but in North America apprenticeships are reserved for relatively few trades and involve a period of three to six years of on-the-job training while the trainee is employed at less than a full journeyman's wage.[19] This form of training is rarely applied to the work women do. There are only a few trades where women are represented – hairdressing and cooking being the main ones. A 1978 study showed 3 per cent of the participants in apprenticeship programmes in Canada were female. Mitchell found that 7.5 per cent of all participants in apprenticeship and pre-apprenticeship programmes in British Columbia were women.[20] Briggs has pointed out that:

> of the multitude of potentially apprenticable jobs and occupations ... those that have been recognized and approved for formal apprenticeship had with only one or two outstanding exceptions happened to fall in the traditionally male occupational category.[21]

How does this 'happen'? The previous section of this paper argues that we can look for the reasons in the history of political struggles over apprenticeship, rather than simply in characteristics of the work performed. Briggs herself argues that job descriptions show few skill differences between apprentices and much non-apprenticed and female work, even when official skill ratings systematically underrate the skills involved in women's work. Apprenticeships have their origin in the practices of the medieval guilds or 'mysteries' as they were sometimes called. The name 'mystery' emphasizes the special and complex nature of craft knowledge, and the long process of apprenticeship that was necessary to learn it adequately. Apprenticeships have always been subject to political struggle between labour and capital. Apprenticeships were made a universal and compulsory form of job training in Britain in 1563 through an act of parliament.

It shall not be lawful to any person . . . to exercise any craft now used within the realm of England or Wales, except he shall have been brought up therein seven years at the least as an apprentice.[22]

In fact, these regulations seem to have been mostly applied to men and male work although a few women's trades (for example millinery) were well organized. Women's work in the home meant that most women learned the arts of textile manufacture, sewing, food processing, cleaning and, to a certain extent, trading.[23] This made it difficult to monopolize the skills, to create 'mysteries'. Women also worked in trades that were carried on as family industries with the male as head and journeyman, so that they picked up the necessary skills without being formally apprenticed.[24]

It is unlikely that even in male trades, the apprenticeship law was applied very strictly, except where the power of the crafts was great enough to ensure it. However, the law acted as a symbol of the legitimate claims of the craft unions to control entry and training into work. The repeal of the act in 1814 followed a prolonged struggle between organized skilled labour and manufacturing employers seeking a free labour force.[25]

The discussion at the time sounds remarkably similar to contemporary discussions of training requirements.[26] At a time when new technologies were altering jobs in the workplace and employers feared that the working classes represented a growing and serious threat, apprenticeship regulations came under attack. Much evidence was produced to show that far from teaching complex skills apprenticeships were a way of exploiting young labourers at low wages and creating artificial shortages of workers. Adam Smith maintained that any trade, even a skilled one like watch-making, could be learned in a matter of weeks. The craft unions fought the repeal of the law and attempted in many job-specific actions to enforce its provisions. Learning took place on the shop floor through the precept and example of older workers, and the artisans considered the knowledge involved their property, not to be taken from them by the state or the employer. Apprenticeships served to limit the supply of labour, to stop wages being undercut by non-union members, and to enhance the status and skill of the journeyman. During the nineteenth century some trades were still able to consolidate their position enough to limit, regulate and enforce apprenticeships. There is a continuing record of work stoppages and other forms of job action over apprenticeship provisions into the twentieth century.[27] They represent a continuing attempt by workers whose skills were still officially recognized to retain their power in the labour market in the face of continued reorganization of production that threatened to displace them.

> Only where working people were able to establish powerful trade societies, as in the case of male mule-spinners and the engineers, could a lengthy apprenticeship be enforced.[28]

Men were better organized than women to resist attacks on apprenticeships. In their struggles to maintain their skilled status, their power, and their wages, the craft unions excluded women workers from training and from union memberhsip. This was done not simply because of prejudice, but because women could be paid lower wages and used to undermine the union's position.[29]

Women were then used by employers as strikebreakers. The fact that untrained women were used by employers to replace male workers suggests that the skill necessary for work could still be picked up more casually than through a formal apprenticeship. The apprenticeship served to control the supply of labour and to mystify the skills involved as much as it served to teach skills. The enforcement of apprenticeship regulations and the exclusion of women became tactics to preserve the skilled status of jobs under attack. The consequence was that women were pushed into areas of employment that did not demand an apprenticeship.

There has been much debate in the literature on apprenticeship as to whether it imparts necessary skills to workers or whether it is simply, as Lee puts it, 'a period of ritual servitude designed to reinforce exclusive unionism'.[30] From James Howell (1877) and the Webbs to more recent critics,[31] commentators have argued that apprenticeships do not in fact teach much that is necessary for doing the job. Others[32] argue that this is at least overgeneralized, and that important skills are picked up through apprenticeships and are used on the job.

Whatever its training functions, it is clear that where apprenticeships exist they are an important institution in the labour market, regulating entry into some jobs. The important point is that the training has remained in a form that controls entry by demanding that trainees be hired by an employer who is willing to sponsor and subsidize their training on the assumption that the worker will be an ongoing part of the organization of production. That this form of training has been preserved, and has not been turned into either specific skill training modules on the job, or generalized technical training in the high school or community college, is due to continuing union pressure, an ability to import trained workers from abroad, and employers' willingness to undertake training for some men who, they assume, will stay on the job. However, it is clear that the number of apprenticeships is still declining.[33]

Clement's study of hard rock mining in Canada describes a contemporary Canadian example of the continuing struggle over apprenticeship.[34] As technology has changed in mining, management has reorganized work in a way that de-skills it. Management has also replaced traditional training with a company controlled modular training programme that teaches the particular processes necessary to operate particular machines, but provides no overall understanding of the mining process or the variety of technological processes involved. The union has responded by trying to introduce the 'miner-as-a-trade' programme, which would certify mining apprentices and require a three-year period of apprenticeship with eight weeks a year in school in addition to the time spent working in specific areas. This is an attempt by the union to counteract the de-skilling strategy of management. The union has had limited success persuading the government and management to recognize the programme, although in Manitoba the New Democratic Party government did so and the mining company was forced to participate.

At present, the Canadian government is officially concerned about a shortage of 'skills', especially the availability of people in licensed trades.[35] This is signalling new attention to processes of training in the trades, a new training act, and a new assault on apprenticeships. Ways of increasing the supply of labour and circumventing training requirements increase when there is a labour shortage. We can expect new initiatives in the area of training for craft work. Some of the signs of this can already be seen. New research on generic skills in the trades has been funded by the Canadian Department of Employment and Immigration in an attempt to examine the transferability of skills among occupations.[36] This is undertaken with the explicit purpose of reorganizing training, and developing a comprehensive curriculum based in the high schools and the community colleges. Pre-apprenticeships are being introduced in the high schools in specific trades. A common core programme for pre-apprenticeships in all trades is being introduced into British Columbia community colleges. Employers complain about having to pay for training, and demand more government subsidies, while they criticize the traditional apprenticeship system as inefficient and failing to produce enough skilled workers.[37]

The result is that the use of the apprenticeship as a way of controlling the supply of labour is continuing to slip away from the unions. A more open system based in the public schools and community colleges is developing. The unions' control of the content of training is also undermined. While unions have direct input into what courses will be offered in apprenticeship training, their control is weakened in the public school system.

It is not clear what the result of these changes will be for women. The traditional structure of apprenticeship did not result in much access to the trades for women. The demise of the apprenticeship system and the emphasis on general skills taught in educational institutions may open recruitment more widely and permit more women to at least compete for training places and employment. Women are more likely to be able to move into new areas of employment when these areas are expanding. On the other hand, some have argued that special initiatives for women, affirmative action programmes, and the holding of a certain quota of training 'seats' for women – all of which have been tried recently in the trades – will disappear as training is reorganized. If women do gain more access to the trades as training becomes more widely available, shorter and therefore less valued, it will continue the tradition of women moving into new areas of work as they get designated as 'unskilled'. This is a process we can see by looking at clerical work.

Clerical Work

The training for clerical work contrasts clearly with the training for licensed trades. Clerical work is quintessentially 'women's work'. In any bureaucracy, clerical workers are at the bottom. Their work is considered unskilled and routine and is paid accordingly. Career ladders for clerical workers are short, and end within clerical or secretarial work, not allowing a move into managerial or technical areas, which are considered skilled, and paid considerably more.

Clerical work in the nineteenth century, and earlier, was a male field, a skilled and small one. Clerical jobs were primarily managerial, allowing promotion into partnerships.[38] The training was similar to an apprenticeship.

> Master craftsmen, such as bookkeepers or chief clerks, maintained control over the process in its totality, and apprentices or journeyman craftsmen – ordinary clerks, copying clerks, and office boys – learned their crafts in office apprenticeships, and in the ordinary course of events advanced through the levels by promotion.[39]

Around the turn of the century the typewriter was introduced and what Braverman calls the 'factory office' began to appear. Clerical work expanded rapidly, and women entered the new jobs, which became increasingly cut off from promotion opportunities and seen as 'unskilled'. In Canada, clerical work more than doubled from 2 per cent of the workforce in 1891 to 5 per cent in 1901, and in 1911 almost doubled again to 9 per cent. The percentage of women doing clerical work rose from 14 per cent in 1891, to 22 per cent in 1901 and 33 per cent in 1911.[40]

> Mechanization afforded considerable socioeconomic status and craft-like work to a select group of female clerks. Early stenographers closely approximated the ideal of craft work, as evident in the range of their skills and their greater mastery and control over the work process.[41]

To begin with, stenographers were able to translate this into high wages. However, employers were able to reorganize work so that skills were fragmented and typing pools were created. Private business schools opened. Clerical training became part of the high school curriculum. The skills of the stenographer flooded the market, and the work lost its 'skilled' status rapidly. Wages and promotion opportunities declined.

The striking thing about the training for office work today is that it is widely available in many settings, most importantly in the public high schools. Commercial courses in the high school have a unique status in relationship to the labour market. They are seen as job training much more directly than any other part of the high school curriculum. They specifically include typing, shorthand and office machines: technical skills with little traditional academic content. They include social skills in courses like office practice and work experience, as well as academic skills in English and communications courses. Course descriptions make no bones about their vocational goals – 'as many types of written language projects as are relevant to office work will be included', 'should be capable of handling books in a small business firm', 'qualifies a student for a high-standard secretarial position',[42] and teachers are explicit in their concern for job-related social skills – being feminine, dressing well and handling an interview.[43]

Taking these courses is important in securing a secretarial job. Typing and shorthand particularly are skills which cannot be picked up in a matter of weeks on the job, which can be learned at school, and which are likely to be tested during a job interview. As clerical work employed 47 per cent of females with a high school education in 1971, these courses take on an enormous importance for girls who are not planning to continue post-secondary education, and they are seen as an occupational safety net even for girls who do plan to go to college. The courses have relatively low status in the school; good students are encouraged to stay in the more academic courses. Hall and Carlton (1977) have suggested that clerical work is the only type of job obtained by a significant number of high school graduates that demands significant technical skills.[44] They arrive at this conclusion by asking employers whether their employees have the skills necessary for their work. Only the employers of clerical workers want their employees to know more.

Why then is training for clerical work incorporated into the high school curriculum when training for other types of work is added on after high school, on the job or in post-secondary education? The forms of training which we now take for granted were historically constructed. The incorporation of vocational education courses into the public high school was subject to negotiation between employers, labour, and educators.[45] Progressive educational reformers argued that the academic curriculum was elitist, and needed to be adapted to the needs of working-class children. They argued that vocational courses would provide skills to make pupils more productive and well paid workers, and would mesh schooling with the economy to make it a more socially efficient institution.

Employers saw vocational education as a means of breaking workers' control over skills training. Bowles and Gintis quote the National Association of Manufacturers, 'It is plain to see that trade schools properly protected from the domination and withering blight of organized labor are the one and only remedy for the present intolerable conditions.'[46] Rogers and Tyack describe business' response as a 'noisy, ambitious campaign to insert training for jobs into schools'.[47]

Labour was split on the wisdom of more vocational schooling in the public domain, wanting to use it to increase the skills of workers and their access to advancement, but fearing management motives. While the Trades and Labour Congress declared itself in complete sympathy with the recommendations of the Canadian Royal Commission on Technical Education in 1913, working-class testimony in 1891 opposed more technical education in schools on the grounds that it would lead to a congested labour market and teach skills imperfectly.[48]

While the introduction of industrial education, home economics and business education into the public schools did occur in the early twentieth century, this 'victory' obscures the fact that there were differences in the forms of training that were introduced, and in their relation to getting a job. As we have seen, some apprenticeships continued outside the school, and school-based industrial training was not producing students qualified for skilled industrial jobs. Only in business education did the training for craft-like skills come to be lodged in public schooling.

Studies of the specifics of business education are much less numerous than studies that inquire more broadly into what is called vocational education, so conjecture about the differences exists in something of a vacuum. Weiss (1978) suggests that business education courses were brought into the school in an attempt to increase enrolments, especially of boys who were attending the flourishing private business schools. This explanation seems to correctly reflect the public discussion in schools at the time, and it has been offered for other forms of vocational courses, but it leaves various factors, especially related to the developing organization of work, unanswered. As Poss[49] and Rogers and Tyack point out, schools in the late nineteenth century were already serving to train students for jobs in business.

> Youths who gambled on clerkships as the entry point could gain a
> good deal of specific vocational training from the schools, at least as

far as penmanship and ciphering. By the end of the century and in
still greater numbers, young, urban, native born women could capitalize on the same instruction to work their way through schools into
the expanding secretarial and commercial positions opened to
women.[50]

This existence and organization of the private business
schools was itself noteworthy, when we compare it with, for
example, the organization of training for mechanics. The training
was provided off the job, was not subsidized by employers and
was open to anyone willing to pay the fee. Why did the training
develop in this form outside the public school, a form which
allowed it to be incorporated into the school relatively easily?

The organization of clerical workers appears to be a critical
variable. They were not unionized and were not able to collectively organize to control access to the job at a time when the
need for labour was rapidly expanding. Moreover, as clerical
work became increasingly feminized, employers were reluctant
to invest in on-the-job training, seeing women as temporary
workers, with short working lives, in whom investment would be
wasted. Thus the resistance of workers was less and the push for
subsidized training by employers was greater. As a result, clerical training was available for public school educators to take
over, while real training for the male crafts eluded their grasp.

Clerical training is still not confined to the high school,
important as its existence there is, but is widely available to anyone who wants to take a night course, a short day programme at a
private secretarial college, or a variety of courses at the community college level. The training is short and intensive.
Entrance involves no negotiations with a union or an employer,
and few prerequisites, although a high school diploma may be
required.

What results then is a large pool of labour, so identified with
women that the assumption that all women can type becomes
prevalent. Clerical skills become part of every women's skills,
along with the ability to manage her personal appearance, support the men around her and handle interpersonal relations. The
training does not appear scarce, long and arduous but easy,
taken for granted (as long as you are female) and thus no skill at
all.

The process shows signs of continuing with the introduction
of computer technology into the office. It is reducing the number

of clerical jobs and further truncating the career ladders available to clerical workers. Although new jobs involving work with computers are opening up, these are not being filled by women who were clerical workers, but by men with 'more' and certainly different skills.[51]

The reasons for this are complex. Employers prefer to hire workers who already have the skills they need, instead of mounting the training at their own expense. This is particularly true if the workers are women. Employers then hire directly from the public schools, and streaming within the schools becomes critical for understanding why women do not have access to new technical and managerial jobs in offices. The curriculum guides for British Columbia's high schools illustrate how processes of streaming in the public schools are taking place. 'Data processing' is being introduced into the commercial curriculum. In it, students learn to operate electronic equipment. The objectives of the courses are set out explicitly. For example, students will learn to 'process data with a) edge notched cards, b) embossed plates, c) carbon paper'. They will 'prepare source documents for input' using a variety of techniques and they will learn to 'use a variety of input media and devices'.[52] They are learning to feed the machine, which must involve some understanding of how the machine works, but their knowledge is officially minimal.

In the mathematics department, however, 'computer science' is offered. The name as well as the course description tell the difference. In this course, students learn to write programmes using various computer languages, and discuss how the computer will affect society. They get defined as potential technical experts. The commercial teachers I have talked to see no reason for their students to take this course, as it does not provide skills an office worker will use.

Processes of gender differentiation are displayed in the placement of these courses. We know that girls drop out of mathematics much more quickly than boys, and grade eleven is the beginning of this process of differentiation. More boys than girls then will take the computer mathematics courses. We also know that girls tend to take the office courses preparing clerical workers. More girls will take the 'data processing' course. Instead of mounting courses that introduce all students equally to computers, courses are being implemented in a way that ensures differential access to knowledge for boys and girls.

The clerical worker is not being given training that allows her to understand the machines she works with, that would allow her to be a 'skilled' worker or enter further training. Her training is defined in such a way that it is distinct from management training or computer training. It is not just the lower end of a continuum. It is a different 'programme'. One cannot graduate from one to the other. Entering the commercial programme rather than the academic programme acts as a barrier to taking the courses necessary to be recognized as a manager or a computer technician. Students who take business courses do not have the prerequisites they need to get into university training in business administration or computer science. Furthermore, the necessary training for advancement is not offered on the job, as employers prefer employees who have higher educational credentials, even when much of the training occurs on the job. The training process operates to give men without office experience the recognized attributes for advancement, while women's skills are downplayed.

Conclusions and Implications

The time and form that training for a job takes are created through a process of political struggle between workers and capital. This paper has argued that some male workers have been able to retain relatively lengthy apprenticeships with restricted access while women in clerical work are trained in programmes that are short and widely available. While one might argue that neither job is actually very difficult to learn, or that both are quite difficult, there is little basis for arguing that one is significantly more difficult to acquire than the other. The differences arise in the power of organized male workers, their ability to monopolize access to their skills and the unwillingness of employers to invest in training women.

These two examples have shown how training programmes can help to create 'skilled' workers through limiting access to jobs and institutionalizing and mystifying the 'skills' involved. Women's unskilled status is produced at least in part by training that is widely accessible and formally short. Differences in what one needs to know to do the job are less important than differences in the ways this knowledge is transmitted and made available in the labour market. The way it is transmitted to new workers can vary and this process is a process of managing the image of skill as much as it is learning to do a job. To manage it successfully, you need power, and male craft unions have had more power than secretaries. Neither seems to be doing very well at the moment however. It is professional groups that have been most successful in this enterprise, and the traditional male professions have been the most successful of all in both uniting access and mystifying their skills.

This analysis suggests that 'skill' should not be seen as an independent variable, a fixed attribute of a job or a worker which will explain higher wages or unemployment, as it is in human capital theory or neo-classical economics. The 'skilled' label instead stands for a political process in which some workers have more economic power than others. It is this power that allows them both to make the 'skilled' label stick, and to demand higher wages, limit entry into the job and increase the stability of their employment. Skill will only be exchanged for wages if it represents resources that the workers have to get their way – that is if they are not easily replaceable, and if they are able to organize job action when it is necessary to preserve their position.

Women should not assume that when the state moves to increase the length of training, it will necessarily benefit women by increasing the employer's perception of their skill and the difficulty of access. Changes may occur because the existence of a surplus of workers makes it possible for employers to demand more for the same wages. For example, clerical workers with university degrees may be preferred by some employers, but job descriptions and wage rates remain the same. Even when it constitutes an attempt by an occupational group to upgrade the image of the work and limit access, the effect may be small. Childcare workers for example, are increasingly required to fulfil training and licensing requirements and this is supported by childcare workers who want to have their skills recognized, but their power to demand better wages is limited by the structure of financing for childcare.

This analysis suggests that we should not accept the notion that the only way to become a skilled worker is to do the jobs men do, the way men do them. Organizing to demand recognition of the skills involved in women's labour is critical, using strategies like equal pay for work of equal value. Even with more programmes designed to move women into what have been male areas of work, we can assume the workplace will remain largely segregated for a long time. One of the ways to increase the wages and improve working conditions for women is to demand recognition for the skills and jobs we have.

Subjectivity, Sexuality, Motherhood

The Collusion with Patriarchy: A Psychoanalytic Account

Roberta Hamilton

The most important insight that feminist theory and practice has given to traditional Marxist theory is the insistence that the reproduction of the species, the institutions within which this occurs, and the entire network of relationships which result from it *must* be analysed if the nature of society is to be understood and transformed. Within Marxist-feminist theory, this has led to the analysis of the role played by the family in perpetuating both the social relations of capitalism and patriarchy.

While it is recognized, in the words of Christopher Lasch, that 'the development of capitalism and the rise of the state reverberate in the individual's inner being', understanding the mediations for this interchange has proven an elusive task.[1] It is not just Marxists who have faltered in the attempt to understand why and how individuals collude with social and personal structures which exploit and oppress them, or for that matter why they resist, as miraculously they do, so often. It was Dennis Wrong who pointed out in his seminal article 'The Oversocialized Conception of Man in Modern Sociology', that sociologists have tended to generate a view of man sufficiently 'disembodied and non-materialistic to satisfy Bishop Berkeley, as well as being desexualized enough to please Mrs Grundy'. As a result, he argues, there has been a marked failure to keep in mind the long-time sociological and philosophical question: 'How is it that man becomes tractable to social discipline?' He called for a sociological reassessment of the nature of man which would incorporate the findings of Freud and psychoanalysis. And he did not have in mind the kind of truncated version of psychoanalysis that Talcott Parsons produced, extracting the concept of the super-ego from the rest of the theory to explain that men internalize the values of their society. Rather, Wrong insisted that full weight be given to Freud's understanding of the human psyche as a complex, conflict-ridden arena in which there is a lifelong attempt to reconcile the desires of the material body with social possibilities.[2]

While mainstream sociology has, with few exceptions, resisted Wrong's challenge, tending, as Edward Boldt pointed out, to return to symbolic interactionism and George Herbert Mead for an understanding of human motivation,[3] the particular intersection of questions posed by Marxist-feminists are now leading to some tentative explorations of psychoanalytic theory.[4] What conjuncture of interests has brought this about? As Eli Zaretsky has put it:

> Marxists have rightly pointed out that society must organize the production of food, clothing and shelter, but they have forgotten that it must equally organize the sexual and instinctual life of its members and the process of human reproduction.[5]

This lacuna was, of course, particularly important to feminists whose primary concern with the hierarchical relationship between men and women, even in their intimate day-to-day encounters, led them to the appreciation expressed in the slogan, 'the personal is political'.

The analysis that resulted from the Marxist-feminist encounter led to the breakdown of the mystification that there were two autonomous arenas for human activity: the public world of work and social relations of production and the private world of the family and personal relations.[6] Engels's understanding of the family as historically shaped by the particular mode of production has been extended to show the role of the family in capitalist society as both producer and reproducer of 'appropriate' kinds of labour power for capitalist enterprise and, also, as a unit of consumption for the products of that enterprise. The sexual division of labour, both in the family and in the work world, has been analysed and used to help account for the perpetuation both of social relations of production and of patriarchy.[7]

This work has, however, tended to rely upon superficial assumptions about human motivations. The collusion of men and women with the social structure has been variously accounted for by political and economic coercion, behavioural conformity and individual intention. It is not surprising that this inadequacy has been more acutely felt in Marxist-feminist theory than in other theoretical perspectives. Our interest in that inter-section between social and economic structure and the behaviour of individuals has forced us to be peculiarly sensitive to individual resistance to change. We have had to wonder in new and bitter ways about the cliché, 'she is her own worst enemy'. Kate Millett's application of the expression 'interior colonization' to women is an effective description but also raises questions about how and why. Since our interest is not simply to understand the world but to change it, our theories are flawed if they do not include viable formulations about the nature of human beings. Just as we need to understand the social structure in order to participate actively in its transformation, so we need to understand how the psychosexual structure of men and women will lead them to conform to, or to resist, the social order that they encounter. At the same time, the consequences of the transformations of social systems without the transformations of underlying psychosexual structure are becoming apparent. This, together with the longevity of capitalism and the tenacity of patriarchy, can lead us to cynical answers to the old questions, 'Can men and women in fact live by bread alone, and under what circumstances will they demand more that that?'

It has not been easy for feminists to turn to psychoanalysis. Freud's personal chauvinism was often reflected in his writings about women and has been an easy foil for feminist anger.[8]. This anger resonated with that of most Marxists who believe that their theory is irreconcilable with Freud. Yet, as Paul Robinson argues, a serious controversy about the nature of Freud's theories has long existed among the left:

> The question can be formulated in both political and sexual terms. Did Freud's theoretical achievement imply a revolutionary or a reactionary attitude towards the human situation? Was Freud truly the apologist of sexual and political repression, drawing a picture of inevitable unhappiness, unfreedom, and aggression, or did his new science contain within it the promise of gratification, liberty and peace?[9]

In the last ten years or so, sparked by Juliet Mitchell's *Psycho-analysis and Feminism*, Marxist-feminists have begun to draw out the radical implications of Freud's theory as part of their attempt to show that patriarchy is not a universal but an histori-cally specific phenomenon. It is my own view that what we can have minimally from psychoanalytic theory are serious answers to questions about how and why women and men come to *collude* with the system of male dominance and female subordination and thereby participate in its perpetuation. It cannot explain *why* men are dominant and women subordinate. For that we must look elsewhere: to the implications of the unequal role men and women play in the perpetuation of the species and to the ramifications of the development of private property and social relations of production.[10] Here, I will argue that we internalize and legitimate this hierarchy in the course of the early development of our ego; that it becomes enmeshed in what we feel about our bodies, our behaviour and our actions, in our fantasies and dreams and in our self-concepts.

In particular, in this article I want to outline the specific kind of contribution that I believe psychoanalytic theory can make.

1. It can account for, as Freud put it, how men and women are made in social terms and for how they are so *tenaciously* made.[11]
2. It can account for the social reproduction of primarily heterosexual human beings out of bisexual human infants.
3. It can account for the social devaluation of what is perceived as femininity (with its more extreme manifestations in mysogyny) and the overvaluation of what is perceived as masculinity.

The social reproduction of heterosexual men and women who place unequal value upon masculinity and femininity implies its corollary: that a whole range of needs, feelings, attitudes, desires and behaviours have had to be repressed in the process.[12] In other words, we have individuals who, in the course of their development, come to collude both with patriarchal and social structures. I would, of course, not argue that economic, political and social coercion do not play a crucial role in ensuring this conformity. I maintain, however, that the system does not, nor could not, rely simply on coercion to ensure that individuals perform the thousands of small and large acts which sustain it from day to day.

To start, 'we must remember that in the beginning is the body'.[13] Radical feminists have had no difficulty with this departure. Their concern has been with the social consequences of the biological differences between the sexes, differences which have made possible the reproduction of the species.[14] The question arising from biological differences that has been posed most fruitfully within psychoanalysis is at what point, and in what ways, do these biological differences register themselves in the psychic development of the human child? Before discussing this further, it is necessary to look briefly at Freud's theory of ego development. Our interest is in that phase in the development of the ego (if indeed at all) that it becomes a *gendered* ego.[15] While Marxists have had difficulty accepting the concept of repression, feminists have reacted negatively to the argument for penis envy. Both these aspects of Freud's theory have been the focus of new research, clarification, systematization and reformulation.

The first concern is the link which Freud drew between repression and civilization. On the surface at least, he advanced an image of the nature of man which is antithetical to Marx's formulation. For Marx, man's alienation from himself, from his fellows and from nature, is not an inevitable aspect of humanness but is historically specific, located in his alienation from the productive process and from the products of that process.[16] In an attempt to reconcile Marx's theory with Freud's concept of repression, Herbert Marcuse and, more recently, Gad Horowitz have undertaken the task of analytically separating basic repression from what they call 'surplus repression'.[17]

What is basic repression and why is it fundamental to the Freudian account? Under its rubric come many different processes. As Horowitz says, repression includes, for example, the physiological renunciation of certain infantile pleasures as the libido shifts to different areas of the body and sublimation, the process whereby some neutralization and redirection of libido occurs (painting instead of smearing).[18] Repression also explains the resolving of the oedipus complexes in which incestuous love objects are renounced and the subsequent identification with parental figures occurs. This neutralization, sublimation and substitution of desires occurs in the unconscious which operates according to its own laws and does not recognize realities of time, space or 'logic'.

The nature of the human child makes repression intrinsic to human development. On the one hand, she arrives on this earth dependent and helpless, unable to satisfy her bodily drives without the active intervention of caretakers. On the other hand, unlike the young in the rest of the animal kingdom, she possesses no automatic script for the playing out of those drives.[19] What we have, therefore, is a small being alive with potential, but inevitable contradictions. She is not a *tabula rasa*, awaiting the imprint of her society. But, on the other hand, her dependence, helplessness and the very diffuseness of her drives means that she is unable to seek their gratification except in so far as they are being channelled, fashioned, controlled, redirected and mediated by others. This process does not result only from the social pressures being exerted by the primary caretakers who engage in a 'training' process. It is also very much a *physiological* process, in which the ego and the concept of the ego are developing in response to the body's sexual maturation. That is, the libido (the sexual instincts) successively organizes around four erotogenic zones, the mouth, anus, phallus and genitals. Each stage does not simply replace the next but, in a dialectical fashion, the content of former stages persists in similar and altered forms within the new.[20] Although with each successive stage, there is some repression of the wishes of earlier stages (it is unlikely even in the millennium that most adults would spend a lot of time sucking their thumbs), Marcuse and Horowitz argue that, in our society, there is *more* repression at each stage than is called for by the requirements of ego development or civilization (maybe thumbs would be better than cigarettes).

Repression is, then, our guarantee of humanness; in Marcuse's words, it is that which enables the child 'to transform the blind necessity of the fulfilment of want into desired gratification.'[21] But Freud believed that the amount of renunciation necessary for civilization had become so intolerable that he could characterize man in society as discontented, even though man apart from society was a logical and practical absurdity. Marcuse saw as his task the rescuing of the idea of repression but without its devastating implications for man which Freud foresaw. His solution was to separate repression into 'basic' and 'surplus' components. This was an analytic distinction only; for, in experience, they were intertwined. Basic repression, necessary for civilization, is intrinsic to ego development and is not itself especially burdensome. Surplus repression, which he posited as by far the greater component, refers to renunciation in order that man accept patriarchal domination and toil. Robinson refers to Marcuse's argument as follows:

> He was able to correlate the repression of pregenital sexuality with the economic needs of the capitalist order – the requirement that libido be concentrated in the genitals in order that the rest of the body might be transformed into an instrument of labour.[22]

Working with Marcuse's concepts, Horowitz's contribution was to separate out what constitutes basic repression and what surplus repression. He has provided an analysis which explains the internalization of patriarchy and which has important implications for feminism. Horowitz's argument is that the main component of surplus repression involves the renunciation of all non-reproductive sexuality and therefore, primarily, of bisexuality. In a society informed by scarcity, either actual or controlled, the libido will be free to pursue bodily pleasure in so far as it serves the perpetuation of the species; that is, heterosexual, genital sexuality. All other libidinal desires will be renounced and that energy will ultimately be redirected towards toil. This renunciation, first in the service of meeting human survival needs, but finally (and most evidently in capitalist society) in the service of the ruling class involves individual collusion with patriarchy.

Central to Horowitz's critique is an analysis of the oedipus complex and it is at this point that his analysis intersects with the concept of penis envy which, as I pointed out earlier, has been a particular 'problem' for feminists. Freud posited the essential bisexuality of the human child.[23] As the child proceeds through the first three stages of ego development (oral, anal and phallic) she remains psychically bisexual. The biological differences between male and female do not yet register themselves psychically; for, the function of the dominant organ is experienced and represented in the same way in the two sexes.[24] It is, then, a psychically bisexual child which arrives at the oedipal stage. Furthermore, for each sex, there is not *one* oedipus complex but two: the active and the passive. The resolution of these two oedipal dramas will determine the biological maturation of the child and its subsequent entry into 'human' society through the incorporation of the parents' social standards. When we consider the oedipus complex we can start with the assurance that for almost all children everywhere their first love object has been a female primary caretaker or caretakers.[25] In our society, because of the nuclear family structure (which has taken its shape from, and in the course of, the development of capitalist social relations of production), it is likely to be one woman, the mother, who will carry out her mothering task in virtual isolation from all other adults. While a Marxist-feminist analysis has revealed the consequences of this for the hierarchical sex division of labour, the incorporation of a psychoanalytic account of ego development can demonstrate the manner in which children are prepared during their early psychosexual development for collusion with that structure. In other words, the renunciation of the oedipal complexes will also reflect the *particular* nature of the socializing society – in our case, a patriarchal, heterosexual, sexually monogamous one, based on a sexual division of labour that the infant will have experienced profoundly through her primary caretaker, in all likelihood the female parent.

Under these circumstances, both sexes will emerge from the stage of pre-oedipal attachment and identification with the mother towards the inevitable mother-infant separation and the taking up of the mother as a love object. The father, because he distracts maternal attention from the child, is experienced as a rival. The male child fears that his father will do to him what he would like to do to his father; namely, castrate him. In such a struggle, the child acknowledges his powerlessness, represses his oedipal love for his mother, and compensates himself for his loss through identification with his father. This internalization of the father's standards forces part of the child's ego to split off into the observing and judging function which Freud called the superego. This is the renunciation of the male child's active oedipus complex; 'active' because active libidinal aims are called up in the desire to possess the mother. For the male child, however, the active *aims* are not forfeited, since he will one day have what his father now has. The vehicle for the incorporation of society's standards is, therefore, castration anxiety. But it is precisely this experience of castration anxiety which, Horowitz argues, is felt much more intensely than it has to be because of the child's perception of the undoubted value of the penis, and what it represents in patriarchal society.[26]

The overvaluation (hyper-cathexis) of the penis in patriarchal society will also help determine the fate of the boy's passive oedipal complex. The male child will also take his father as love object and see his mother as rival. When he realizes, however, that to desire his father means, in a patriarchal, heterosexual world, that he cannot have a penis, his desire for his father will arouse all the intense castration anxiety that was involved in his active oedipus complex. The 'normal' way to deal with this will be for him to repress not only his incestuous desire for his father in particular, but his homosexual desires in general and, therefore, his passive libidinal aims (including his desire to be penetrated), for when roused they will summon up the anxiety surrounding castration.[27] What he represses, then, are his passive aims which he equates with femininity since only females do not have a penis. These desires will be projected on to the female, who, as the possessor of those anxiety-creating desires, will be threatening.[28] She will have to be mastered or controlled and since this is an uncertain business, even in patriarchy – hostility and contempt for women will also be summoned to aid in controlling his castration anxiety.

The male repudiation of femininity, which Ruth Brunswick described as 'what we have come to consider the normal male contempt for women', is an intrinsic feature of male psychosexual structure in patriarchal society.[29] Wollheim puts it this way: 'What women have suffered from over the centuries is man's inability to tolerate the feminine side of his nature.'[30] This, then, as I understand it, would be, in skeletal form, the psychoanalytic case for male collusion with patriarchy.

Let us turn now to female children. Like the little boy, the little girl will emerge from pre-oedipal attachment to her mother to the taking of her mother as her first love object. In Freud's early formulations, the girl child passed directly from pre-oedipal attachment to her mother to the oedipal relationship with her father. He was, however, forced to reconsider:

> We knew, of course, that there had been a preliminary stage of attachment to the mother, but we did not know that it could be so rich in content and so long-lasting, and could leave behind so many opportunities for fixations and dispositions. During this time the girl's father is only a troublesome rival: in some cases the attachment to her mother lasts beyond the fourth year of life. Almost everything that we find later in her relation to her father was already present in this earlier attachment and has been transferred subsequently onto her father.[31]

More concisely put by Brunswick, 'the pre-oedipal sexuality of the girl becomes her active oedipus complex with the mother as its object'.[32] The taking of the mother as love object will, however, be resolved in different ways by the male and female child. The little girl does experience her father as rival for her mother's attention, but this problem is soon eclipsed by a new dilemma. As she enters the genital phase she becomes aware of the significance of the fact that she does not have a penis and that a penis is what you need in a heterosexual world in order to possess your mother. The resulting penis envy then has two sources: the wish of the bisexual child to possess the organs of the other sex (penis envy, uterus envy, breast envy);[33] and the desire to do the things that having those organs permits one to do. Lampl-De Groot puts it this way:

> The acceptance of castration anxiety has for her [the girl] the same consequences as for the boy. Not only does her narcissism suffer a blow on account of her physical inferiority (the boy finds himself and his penis unbearably puny compared to his father; the girl finds her clitoris unimpressive compared to the larger and handier penis), but [secondly] she is forced to renounce the fulfilment of her first love longings. (Just as the boy had to renounce his mother to avoid castration anxiety, the girl has to renounce her because, lacking a penis, she cannot possess her.)[34]

Horowitz argues, however, that penis envy becomes *intense* penis envy, just as castration anxiety becomes *intense* castration anxiety for the male, because the phallocentric civilization, the patriarchal, heterosexual world announces to the girl child that she cannot possess her mother, or indeed any other women, *because* she has no penis. She will be forced to repress not only her desire for her mother but also her homosexuality, in her case, her active libidinal aims. Intense penis envy is for her then, just as castration anxiety is for the male, a repudiation of 'femininity'. But in her case, it is a repudiation of precisely what patriarchal civilization insists that she be – feminine – that is, passive and submissive. In this resolution of her active oedipal complex, she gives up her active libidinal aims.

I have not yet dealt with the passive oedipal complex in which the girl takes her father as love object and experiences her mother as rival. By the time she turns to her father as love object, the girl child cannot be threatened by castration since, in the course of resolving her active oedipus complex, she has already accepted her 'castration' and, more importantly, its implications.[35] As a result, she does not have the same motivation to renounce her father as love object. Equally interesting, however, is why she takes him as a love object *at all* in a society in which he is not her primary caretaker. Is it only, as Freud suggested, in defensive flight from her active oedipal complex? 'The girl is driven out of her attachment to her mother through the influence of her envy for the penis and she enters the oedipus situation (with her father) as though into a haven of refuge.'[36] Or is it, as

Nancy Chodorow posits, a question of seduction by her father?[37] In other words, she responds to *his* treatment of her as a little girl. Or is it, rather, a result of her 'essential' bisexuality? While I would not deny the role of the first two processes, particularly in patriarchal society, I agree with Horowitz that the acquisition of heterosexual genital aims by women (the acquisition of which is the species guarantee of survival; rape surely not being a viable alternative) cannot be an entirely learned behaviour (as Chodorow seems to posit) and is rather *one* of the outcomes of the normal psychosexual development of a bisexual child.[38] Horowitz's aim is to show that the presence of these heterosexual genital aims is not incompatible with the retention both of pre-genital sexuality and homosexuality. The male child need not give up his homosexuality and his passive aims and the girl child need not give up her homosexuality and her active aims, *except* in surplus repressive civilization.[39]

The argument that both men and women repudiate femininity in the course of their early psychosexual development provides, I believe, a plausible explanation of the collusion of men and women with patriarchy. As Wollheim argues, 'psychoanalysis can at best explain why men and for that matter women have colluded', have conspired with the organization of society to secure male dominance and female subordination.[40] Part of this explanation demonstrates how both sexes come to repudiate their 'female' side, though only one sex is expected to live it.

Horowitz states categorically, 'revolutionary movements which do not revolutionize the psychosexual structure formed by surplus repression must fail, for this psychosexual structure is both product and source of domination'.[41] But if we are now trying to understand a world through such concepts as 'basic' and 'surplus' repression, are we in a realm that is not so much antithetical to Marxist theory, as foreign to it? And if that is the case, how can we view the relationship between the dismantling of patriarchy and the overthrow of capitalism? At this point, I can only indicate where one important point of convergence would seem to lie. I would suggest that the concepts of objectification and alienation in Marx have some affinity with the concepts of basic and surplus repression in Marcuse and Horowitz.

Psychoanalytic theory informs us that the young child's passage into human society involves an initial erotic dependence upon its primary caretakers, followed by the renunciation of that dependence and the internalization of the adults' socializing standards. This involves processes which Horowitz describes as basic repression. Intrinsic to this process is the child's separation from her primary caretakers and, more especially, her growing realization that she is separate from the people and objects around her. In the course of ego development she moves from identification with the mother – 'briefly one may state that every successful act of identification with the mother makes the mother less necessary to the child'[42] – to objectification, the separation of the self from the other, the capacity to reflect upon oneself, that is to take oneself as object and to take the other as love object. This occurs in the very process in which she interacts with others and achieves growing mastery over her environment. Compare Marx who, we must remember, did not, like some of his disciples, ever believe that consciousness started at the factory door:

> In creating a world of objects by his practical activity, in his work upon organic nature, man proves himself a conscious species being, i.e. as a being that treats the species as its own essential being, or that treats itself as a species being . . . Through and because of this production, nature appears as his work and his reality. The object of labor, is therefore, the objectification of man's species life: for he duplicates himself not only, as in consciousness, intellectually, but also actively, in reality, and therefore *he contemplates himself* [emphasis added] in a world that he has created.[43]

This activity in and upon the world commences with birth. We participate in the creation of our world even as we undergo its primary initiation rights. And this capacity for objectification is made possible through basic repression without which we could never experience separateness, without which we would never come to treat ourselves as the 'actual living species'. In our society, the human capacity of objectification turns against itself:

> In tearing away from man the object of his production, therefore, estranged labor tears from him his *species life* [emphasis added], his real objectivity as a member of the species and transforms his advantage over animals into the disadvantage that his inorganic body, nature, is taken away from him.[44]

In the very process of producing objects which will be controlled by others and used by others to enhance their life, man is alienated from his labour, the objects of his labour, himself and his fellows. His preparation for this has been lifelong, and his willingness is both the result and the cause of surplus repression, a surplus repression that has been fashioned by scarcity, real and controlled. For, in the course of renouncing many forms of bodily gratification, we renounce many pleasures to be found in our own company and in the company of others. This is true not just in directly sexual pleasures but in all the derivatives of sexuality including general sociability, affection and in the activities arising from non-surplus repressive sublimation. We not only come to reflect upon ourselves, but also to experience a painful separation from self and from others.

Marx's concept of alienation includes estrangement from self, other people and nature. Its transcendence involves the reclamation of work and the productive process as the species activity of man. A psychoanalytic account informs us that our understanding of what constitutes 'work' must include *all* the activities in which we engage as we produce and reproduce our social world.[45] Its reclamation, therefore, must include the re-eroticization of the body, the retention of pregenital sexuality and the re-fusion of passive and active libidinal aims. Such a perspective brings the struggles for sexual liberation away from the sidelines and into the centre of the struggle against capitalism and patriarchy.

Embracing Motherhood:
New Feminist Theory

Heather Jon Maroney

Women give birth to children whom they then mother. Given the level of contemporary medical achievement, the former is an apparently inescapable biological fact, but nevertheless, from the moment of childbirth (and often before) women's role as mothers is historically malleable.[1] This complex of birthing and social action is not only the basis of a unique social relationship between the individual woman and her child/ren but of a social institution, motherhood. Because of the way it mediates between the biology of procreation and historical institutionalization, motherhood provides a prime site for exploring and constructing boundaries between nature and culture. Historically, the division in Western thought has been dichotomous and drawn in such a way as to exclude women from the social and historical.

What to make of this apparently pre-social reality and its political and cultural institutionalization has always been a central question in the history of feminist theory and ideology. It also occupies a particularly vexed place in understanding the origins and basis of women's oppression. Much of the suffrage movement staked its claim on what was, after all, a demand that the domestic importance and private skills of women as mothers be officially recognized and given full reign in the public domain.[2] On the other hand, an ideological vanguard of the contemporary women's movement, confronting the possibilities of new contraceptive technology, rejected patriarchal prescriptions for compulsory motherhood to lead a struggle against both the socialization patterns and economic constraints that serve to restrict women's lives to ahistorical maternity. Despite differences in their global ideologies, both Betty

Friedan and Juliet Mitchell found the family to be the lynchpin in an ideology which offered feminine fulfilment within the confines of the home and apart from a world of self-creative and paid work.[3] Extending the male option of splitting public and reproductive life, Germaine Greer thought maternity possible – and even enjoyable – if it included an Italian hill farm where she could go to visit her child, carefully cared for by maternal peasants, once a month or so.[4] The most radically anti-maternalist position, that women's liberation requires extra-uterine reproduction, was argued by Shulamith Firestone in line with a generally biologistic analysis of the sources of male – female power differentials in patriarchal society.[5]

More recently however, and linked to a larger concern with biological and social reproduction, a quite different thematization has begun to emerge, one that reflects the evaluation of motherhood as an essentially positive activity and insists on its disalienating recuperation by and, in the first instance, for women themselves. A first step in this reconstruction has been untangling the social, historical, biological and psychological dimensions of maternity. Beyond formulating a critique of contemporary family, medical and state practices, the more radical proponents of this perspective have seen in sexual asymmetries with respect to birth and childcare a material key for understanding not only masculine and feminine character differences but also constituent features of dominant Western cultural developments, including the coded relation between 'man' and 'nature' and the modality of formal knowledge systems. Understanding motherhood then is crucial for understanding the specificity of human self-constitution and has wide-ranging implications for theory whether feminist, political, psychological or philosophical. The critical appropriation of maternity also implies a transformation in human practice of truly redemptive proportions.

In this paper, I trace the way in which the new thematization of motherhood has emerged and has become manifest in three different areas of feminist discourse and then, against the background of some of the more global claims about the necessity of placing biological reproduction and social and psychological mothering at the centre of theory, consider some of the profound issues they raise for feminist and other dimensions of emancipatory theory.

The Emergence of a Feminist Problematic of Motherhood

In one sense, history not feminism has problematized motherhood. The relatively rapid development of medical technologies, collectively if somewhat inaccurately known as 'the pill', dissolved the biological given which inextricably linked sexuality and reproduction for women. As a result of these developments, pregnancy and birth became a choice for women who to this extent were placed in a position of equality with men. What has made facing this decision awesome for individuals and impossible to absorb into the smooth operation of the child-centred nuclear family complex is that it arose in the context of a political, social, and demographic conjuncture which had already seen the patriarchal institutional model of motherhood come slowly to its full fruition and abort of its own contradictions.

Exclusive childcare by women, isolated in independent households, is an historically exceptional family form. The object of care, the child and its location, the 'non-producing' household, were fused over the flame of a naturalistic argument into a specialized role for women.[6] As mothers, women were defined as the moral guardians of Western civilization with immediate responsibility for children's character development and ultimate responsibility for the moral texture of public life. With its origins in a rising European bourgeoisie, this family form owes its mass realization to the wealth generated by capitalist production and the requirement to shape a schooled and self-regulating labour force out of neonatal plasticity. The ideology of mother–child coupling pervaded the working classes at any rate only from the 1920s to the 1960s. However, even as the post-Second World War boom, a reduction in fertility, and the development of housing and household technology combined to permit women to play out an intensified and extended 'motherhood-per-child', its limitations began to become clear.[7] The cult of domesticity and the cult of the child proved too thin and too demanding to sustain its mystified feminine acolytes who were struck with 'the disease that has no name' symptomatized in depression, over-medication, and loss of self.[8] These costs were noted by a de-radicalized Freudianism but glossed as the problem *of* women.[9] At the same time, with changes in the structure of the labour market and attempts to maintain family-household incomes in the face of inflation, its material base began to be eroded as women with school age and then pre-school children were recruited wholesale into retail, clerical and public sector employment.[10]

In the 1960s, a growing women's movement defined the contradictory non-choice – housewives' syndrome or the double day – as a problem *for* women and attempted to intervene in the ideological and structural organization of marriage and family as central institutions organizing gender and generational relations. One of its central tactics was the contestative denial of sexist ideology, one of its central preoccupations reclaiming free sexual activity for women. Whatever patriarchy had said, 'Women are . . .', feminists fought against. 'Biology is destiny' was its cry; ours that biology could and more importantly *should* be transcended. Of course this abstract negation of patriarchal ideology was, in the first instance, reactive, a battle fought on the opponent's ground within given categories. In rejecting the hegemonic patriarchal construction of feminity whole hog, women were also led to deny the importance of motherhood as such and to devalue any specialized skills or values associated with this admittedly limited sphere of feminine practice. New conditions, not least the changes in the institutional framework and activity of mothering sketched above, have encouraged a positive revalorization of maternity that is at once radical and feminist. It has been the simultaneous coming into play of demographic, biographical and political changes that has permitted this kind of reformulation.

During the 1970s, some potentially significant demographic patterns of delayed and reduced fertility became visible. Certainly, for at least a socially and ideologically important cohort of 'middle-class' post-war boom babies now between twenty and thirty-nine, well into the 'normal' range of fertility, a number of factors – the increase in post-secondary schooling for women, some increase in the age at first marriage, the ideological impact of the women's and ecology movements and economic constraints – have contributed to an initial postponement of and a likely reduction in childbearing.[11] The early indications of these changes have already been culturally significant; for example, a rapid increase in first births among American women over thirty received the cultural cachet of a *Time* cover story.[12] Altogether, these changes have brought the encouragement of population replacement to the attention of the state as well as cultural interpreters.

The psychological ramifications of ageing of this population cohort are complex: they involve not merely ageing, nor just a change in status and life style for those who have actually given birth, but also a major impact at the level of the unconscious on all women. Those of us who were and have remained daughters (by age and family relationship) are becoming mothers (again by age and even if only vicariously). If as Nancy Friday suggests from her 'daughter's' perspective, sexuality is 'a powerful force in the fight to separate from [the mother] and grow up' and our first jobs provide the opportunity 'to prove to ourselves that we are agents in our own lives', then marriage provides a formal structure to repeat parental models and childbirth 'speeds up' 'the unconscious drive to become the mothers we dislike'.[13] If we have acquired through work, economic independence and feminism a certain measure of the autonomy we sought as individuals and as a movement, then encapsulated conflictual relations with our mothers no longer need dominate practically or psychologically in any simple sense. This situational autonomy also makes possible greater empathy in reconsidering and re-evaluating the mother–daughter relationship.

The release of powerful psychological processes of fantasy, displacement, regression and desublimation which invert and blur mother–daughter differentiation need not be triggered by a real decision to give birth, a real pregnancy, a real child. Being with the children of our friends, reading the articles on childbirth, late, voluntarily unpartnered or lesbian motherhood can be enough.[14] We begin to regard our mothers, our – real, fantasied, potential – daughters and ourselves from a new position fulcrumed on three generations. Signe Hammer describes this perspectival shift as a maturational imperative:

> Not all women become mothers, but all, obviously are daughters, and daughters become mothers. Even daughters who never become mothers must confront the issues of motherhood, because the possibility and even the probability of motherhood remains.[15]

Finally, the political and ideological maturation of the women's movement demands more rigorous and comprehensive theories of motherhood and family. In a situation where women's cultural, economic and political gains have been met with inertia, resistance and, in the extreme, right-wing opposition gilded in the glories of motherhood and apple pie, the

further development of feminist theory of family and motherhood is both politically important and constrained. It must be
both offensive and defensive. Susan Harding argues that the
conflicts between feminists and their opponents are rooted in
the adoption of conflicting 'family strategies' that are either
egalitarian (emphasizing the individual and a breakdown of
roles) or hierarchical (stressing 'the symbolic authority of the
father' and 'protecting and celebrating the role of the family in
defining a woman's life and identity').[16] Exploiting the contradictions in a contested ideological terrain, the mass media tell
large numbers of women who attempt to develop social strategies to juggle work, childcare, conflicts with men, and personal
life and psychological strategies to resolve conflicts over sexuality, femininity, competition, accomplishment and children that
this whirlpool which saps energy is the result of feminism.
Indeed, the easy public acceptance of some aspects of the new
motherhood discussion as witnessed by the *Time* cover story still
rests on assumptions of the propriety and endurance of gender
divisions of labour.

Here the women's movement walks a tightrope strung
between offensive and defensive poles: it must assert feminist
theory in our own terms, validating 'what women do' (and have
done historically) in mothering at the same time as it contests
patriarchal glorification of the role at the expense of the occu-
pant. It must also offer insightful support to those women and
men caught in the toils of institutional transition who place a high
value on having and caring for children as well as on their own
individuality and gender equality – those who 'believe in' day-
care, maternity and paternity leave, equal pay and reproductive freedom but do not yet identify themselves as feminists –
if it is to gain their political allegiance and active support for
both liberated family structures and the larger feminist programme.

In developing the theoretical underpinnings of the new problematic, feminism has woven together lesbian-feminism, psychoanalysis, and as yet untheorized female experience. The first of
these, radical lesbian ideology, adopted matriarchy as an idyllic
and strategically useful myth.[17] Since this focus is congruent with
a more sociological interest on the part of Marxist feminism in
pre-class social formations, it provides a rare point of agreement
between these competing politico-theoretical tendencies, which
has allowed it to be more easily popularized. Its adoption by a

radical feminist current also served to undercut the anti-maternalism of Firestone's version of radical feminism. The second, psychoanalytic theory, shares an object with feminist theory – the role of the mother–child–father triangle in producing sexual difference. The form of investigation which grounds both these theories was also congruent; that is, uncovering socially illicit but sociologically normal experience in the interests of therapeutic catharsis.[18]

The third strand has been, however, perhaps the most provocative especially linguistically. Using motherhood as a metaphor/m, melding anaylsis and poetics, outside the rule of phallocentric linear logic, it has striven to delve down and back through body, sexuality and time to create new rationality capable of uniting nurturing and strategy, past and future, the conscious and unconscious:

> Somehow the questions raised here did not take on a problem-solving or strategy-laden dimension but rather concerned mothers, mothering, motherhood. As we found them inside of us. No feminist theory of motherhood? Well, we will start to invent one. We start with our hands on our pulses.[19]

Much of this writing has been formally experimental, in Hélène Cixous's term, 'woman writing woman'[20] and so more easily ignored than assimilated by traditional disciplines with their fundamentally sexist foundations and territorial jealousies. While no systematic integration has been made of these theoretical foundations increasingly the themes overlap in feminist discourse.

Obviously, given the uneven development and ideological differences of the women's movement as a whole, the refocusing has been uneven. But as well as tracing a general movement in feminist theory, a change of orientation appears in the work of individual writers. Robin Morgan is a case in point. In 1969, mother is 'emptiness', the person who won't let you wear a bra, the abstraction who 'spent her days with kids and housework'. Her characterization is perhaps surprising only when we recall that Morgan, already a mother, who defended her right to raise a boy against separatist attacks, helped to organize collective childcare and faced conflicting demands of work, mothering and politics. Like that of the movement as a whole, her attitude to motherhood changed by confronting first lesbian, matriarchal theory and then the ecology movement – Mother Nature indeed. Ultimately she rejected 'the notorious correct line which . . . conceived of turning real babies into real soap' so that 'throwing out the baby with the bath appeared to the correct liners as both sensible and sanitary'. In her artistic endeavours, she began to play a maternal theme, lamented Mary Wollstonecroft's death in childbirth and celebrated her love for her son. She was moreover quite aware of this transformation:

> They said we were 'anti-motherhood' – and in the growing pains of certain periods some of us were . . . Patriarchy commanded the women to be mothers (the thesis), we had to rebel with our own polarity and declare motherhood a reactionary cabal (the antithesis). Today a new synthesis has emerged; the concept of mother-right the affirmation of childbearing and/or rearing when it is a woman's choice.[21]

Motherhood: A Patriarchal Institution

Conceptualizing motherhood as an institution has had three main effects. First, it was removed from the biological and invariant and placed in the social and historical. Secondly, on the basis of historical and anthropological comparisons, a categorization has been developed of two distinct orders of motherhood – matriarchal and patriarchal – which echoes in psychoanalytic and metatheoretical discourses. Thirdly, it has helped to clarify programmatic demands for the women's movement. For it uncovers an apparent paradox: as patriarchal ideology has relegated mothering to women, women have lost control and authority in childbirth and childraising.

In her influential book, Adrienne Rich denies that the 'patriarchal institution' is a necesary part of the human condition:

> Motherhood . . . has a history, it has an ideology, it is more fundamental than tribalism or nationalism. My individual private pains as a mother, the individual and seemingly private pains of the mothers around me and before me, whatever our class or colour, the regulation of women's reproductive power by men in every totalitarian system and every socialist revolution, the legal and technical control by men of contraception, fertility, abortion, obstetrics and extrauterine experiments – are all essential to the patriarchal system, as is the negative or suspect status of women who are not mothers.[22]

Here she specifies themes central to feminist investigation: prescriptive ideologies of motherhood, the medicalization of childbirth and the experience of women as mothers.

Breaking with academic convention, many feminist scholars contend that female-dominated mother-centred social formations existed historically. Obviously they recognize that their reconstructions of matriarchal societies through an interpretative synthesis of evolutionary biology, archaeology, myth, law and comparative anthropology are necessarily speculative, but perhaps no more than received views. In any case, the images of 'matriarchal' and 'patriarchal' motherhood presented in the literature are in sharp contrast.

Rereading the evidence of archaeology and evolutionary biology 'to visualize how the hominid line could have arisen', Nancy Tanner and Adrienne Zihlman propose a theory of early hominid evolution centred on and dynamized by the exigencies of the mother–child relationship.[23] As a result of complex interactions that followed the early development of bipedalism and neonatal dependence, infants needed to be carried, supervised, fed and protected. In response, mothers, as the most consistent food-gatherers, developed material and social techniques to make their tasks more efficient: storage containers, carrying slings, digging sticks and regular patterns of food sharing. As primary socializers, they also taught these patterns to both daughters and sons who replicated them in turn with siblings and in wider social groups. With increasing evolutionary complexity the intimacy of the mother–infant relationship and the necessity of communicating complex technical and environmental information facilitated language development. Given a flexible kin-based family structure most likely to be congruent with gathering as a mode of subsistence and the implications of loss of oestrus, these evolutionary tendencies were reinforced through kin and sexual selection. Males who shared with, carried, protected and played with their siblings helped them to survive. In addition, 'mothers chose to copulate most frequently with these comparatively sociable, less disruptive sharing males – with males more like themselves'.[24] Zihlman later concludes that the success of the human species was made possible only through a reproductive strategy that combined independence and innovation for females with the co-operation of males and females in caring for their young through both sharing food and nurturing.[25]

The Mother-Goddess appears as a compelling image of female power and creativity, especially in radical and lesbian feminist writing. Merlin Stone's interpretation of the significance of Mellart's excavation of the late neolithic site at Çatal Hüyük is representative:

> The definition and worship of the female divinity in so many parts of the ancient world were variations on a theme, slightly differing versions of the same basic theological beliefs. . . . It is difficult to grasp the immensity and significance of the extreme reverence paid to the Goddess. . . . But it is vital to do just that to fully comprehend the longevity as well as the widespread power and influence this religion once held.[26]

Representations of female figures, pregnant or in childbirth, with plants or weaving provide archaeological evidence of the association of females with social power, technological innovation and birth that Zihlman and Tanner saw as central to human evolutionary progress. In a scholarly article, Anne Barstow warns against extrapolating social conclusions from archaeological remains but concurs that a civilization whose religious and social life centred on female fertility and accomplishment flourished at Çatal Hüyük.[27]

The defeat of women and the imposition of newly elaborated forms of power may have come about in two ways. Stone suggests that women were deprived of the direction of religion, public welfare and commercial activity as a result of military defeat by northern invaders who imposed patrilineal clan systems. Their patriarchal religious superstructures triumphed with increasingly repressive and misogynist practices towards female sexuality.[28] In an examination of pristine state formation at Sumer, Ruby Rohrlich identifies a different dynamic of internal subordination by militarily organized males. Although 'matriarchy seems to have left more than a trace in early Sumerian city states' where women once owned land and were trained in professional religious occupations, warfare and military organization undermined their status and, incidentally that of some males. 'What seems to have happened is that as class society became increasingly competitive over the acquisition of commodities . . . warfare became endemic and eventually led to the centralization of political power in the hands of a male ruling class.'[29]

Our concern in evaluating this problematic is not the 'scientificity' of these reconstructions, for in one sense their accuracy is beside the point, but identifying the associational clusters connected with patriarchal and matriarchal motherhood. Matriarchal society and motherhood are thought to be co-operative, natural, sex positive and permissive, peaceful and able to integrate males on a basis of equal exchange. In contrast, patriarchy is hierarchical, ultimately technologically rational, sexually repressive and violent for women, associated with militarism and the state and based on the oppressive exploitation of female productive and reproductive powers. Evidence of these configurations continue to be found in periods where the historical record is more detailed and comprehensive.

In these periods, when motherhood is appropriated by male theoretical authority, these correlations become conscious social norms. This theft did not of course include the work of childcare, which was left as before to women, but it did include control; thus the female activity of childcare was subordinated to male expertise operating within a reified, mechanized and sexist paradigm. While medieval theology had considered maternity as an aspect of the problem of Christology, feminist theorists suggest it was only in the early phases of capitalist development that political and medical theory deemed the issue worthy of theoretical attention.[30] Within a post-Renaissance patriarchal optic motherhood was construed as at once biological and transcendental – an instinct and so less than fully human yet infused with a redemptive morality of sacrifice and altruism as a counter to the competitive behaviour of political-economic man. These theories consistently sought legitimation in the welfare and social utility of the child, not the mother's happiness or autonomy; they posited a tension between mother and child, which was to be resolved in favour of the child.

Although couched in a rhetoric of natural necessity, these developments in nineteenth-century patriarchal theory in fact broke the 'naturalness' of the mother–child connection in order to permit the intervention of progressive 'scientific' childraising practices.[31] The break between the natural and social and the consequent expansion of the realm in which the social takes precedence over the natural was disguised not just by language but by the prescriptions for intensive and exclusive mothering elaborated in these theories. Alarmed, on one hand, by high rates of infant mortality revealed by early population surveys and on the other, enraptured by Rousseauian views of childhood educability, medical and social theorists expanded the role of the good mother from one who suckled her child to one who was all to her child – teacher, companion and devoted nurse. If comparisons of mothers to hens and plants were sometimes dehumanizing, nevertheless, this role offered certain rewards:

> Motherhood became a gratifying role because it was now a repository of the society's idealism. . . . The mother was frequently compared to a saint, and it was believed that the only good mother was a 'saintly' woman. The natural patron saint of the mother was the Virgin Mary, whose whole life bespoke her devotion to her child.[32]

For the woman limited by middle-class social horizons and newly excluded from work in family-based production, the new role as the central axis of the family also offered improved personal status and power over her children.[33] But sainthood precluded sexuality and power in the family meant isolation, however glorified, from social life outside it.

Barbara Ehrenreich and Deidre English trace the growing ascendency of similar patriarchal prescriptions in North America. For them, the transition is a response to the industrial revolution's disruption of an 'Old Order' where women's centrality to household-based production modified formal patriarchal power. A shift to centralized production posed 'the question of how women would survive and what would become of them in the modern world'.[34] Two answers were offered. The first, a radical ideology of sexual assimilation and rationalism extended middle-class liberal ideals of individual freedom and equality to women. The second, a romantic reaction that, linked to a strategy to contain class conflict, became dominant after the Civil War, promoted a sentimentalized vision of women as half outside the world of men which was derived also from liberal social philosophy.[35] In pragmatic America medical and technical 'experts', not political philosophers, were the advance men for scientific domesticity and exclusive maternal childraising:

> The idea that the child was the key to the future . . . had a definite political message. . . . By concentrating on the child – rather than on, say, political agitation, union organizing, or other hasty alternatives – the just society would be achieved painlessly, but slowly.[36]

This solution was weakened by the internal contradiction between triumphant romantic ideology and the needs of industrial society. 'In the sexually segregated society built by industrial capitalism . . . there is, in the end, no way for women to raise men,' that is, according to proper patriarchal principles.[37] Thus, the connection between exclusive childcare by women and its domination by male experts articulated in France was reinforced by North American social developments.[38] Although the scientific fashion in childcare changed in response to changing infrastructural needs, its various perceived failures were all blamed on mothers who were alternately castigated as too sentimental and overprotective or as too ruthless, the power-hungry mom.[39] Overall, the modern patriarchal construction of parenting was, like its enlightened romantic predecessor, based on difference and inequality and the domination of private relations by public requirements for order in a sex and class stratified society.

In contemporary motherhood, the contradictions which have emerged from competing patriarchal, feminist and ecologist ideologies on the one hand and structural transformations which have bisexualized the labour market without similarly affecting childcare on the other have created a recurrent dilemma for women: 'I hate motherhood, but I love my kids.'[40] An enormous literature, ranging from practical self-help books, through the wryly recuperated accuracy of Lynn Phillips's cartoons to a professional literature seeks to explain this tension and develop a programme for ideological and institutional reform. In so far as this work seeks to reclaim women's experience, define women as individuals and expand the area of legitimate female activity, it operates within a feminist paradigm. In the main, it views conflicts in mothering – between emotional nurturance and the work it entails or paid work in the labour force and unpaid childcare, for example – as rooted in social changes that it analyses at best only scantily.[41] These tensions are compounded for women in paid employment who are most often the primary or 'psychological parent' responsible not only for the material functioning of the household but also 'for the whereabouts and the feelings of each child'.[42] Other problems, like the contradiction between adult, particularly sexual, identity and ideologies of motherhood are described if not analysed.[43] Unlike patriarchal prescriptions, however, it seeks to resolve them equitably to the benefit of both mother and child.

Despite the severity of the problems uncovered by listening to women, the popular and scholarly literatures generally remain reformist. For the most part they continue to accept the inevitability of motherhood-in-the-family and offer apparently moderate solutions suggesting, for example, that women engage in a developmental process of identity synthesis because 'the models of femininity . . . presented . . . do not fit [women's] current adult lives' which in fact seek to resolve these structural and historical contradictions at the psychological level.[44] The most consistent 'feminist' influence is found in the treatment of the 'working mother'. Paid work, while still occasionally justified by an appeal to financial need, is increasingly construed as good in itself. The failure to analyse structural determinants fully and to explore possibilities for institutional reorganization leaves this literature vulnerable to suggesting new 'permissive' norms which may turn out to be new performance criteria for women.[45] These will not alter an experience of motherhood which is at best ambivalent, at worst masochistic: 'Motherhood simply confirms what we knew before — that pleasure and pain are rarely far apart.'[46]

If some historians and sociologists bewail the effects of exclusive mothering, others decry the loss of female control over the ideological, mystical and practical dimensions of childbirth. Several studies trace the rise of obstetrics and gynaecology as male-dominated professions, which they contend 'desexed' and denaturalized childbirth. In this process, women healers were forced from their last niche as midwives in the name of paridigmatically scientific and mechanical norms, as a result of interprofessional rivalry, in the interest of private profit and in an attempt to tame female creativity.[47] The specialization and professional self-defence of 'male midwives' began with the invention of obstetrical forceps – 'hands of iron' – by the Chamberlen family in the late sixteenth century and their subsequent generalization after 1773. Although male midwifery based its claim on cleanliness and superior knowledge, its practices were often medically irrational and, indeed, dangerous. The supine position, which inhibits control in contractions, was introduced in order to afford Louis XIV a better view of his mistresses giving birth and later adopted for the convenience of the physicians. Under male control, birth was all too often a precarious experience in part as the result of technical innovations like destructive obstetrics and in part from the systemic blood poisoning called 'puerperal' fever caught when surgeons imported germs from cadavers to the birthing room.

Contemporary medical management of childbirth continues to claim scientific rationality as a cover for practices that from the point of view of women are irrational and costly. Shiela Kitzinger contends that pre-labour prep – shaving, enemas obstetrical masks and gowns, the exclusion of the husband and episiotomy – are mainly of ritual significance. They serve to purify the woman, exclude her from her normal community, return her to a pre-pubertal and dependent state and, above all, confirm the obstetrician's control over birth. 'The previously mysterious power of childbirth has been analysed and he bends it to a masculine purpose and according to a masculine design.'[48] Based on her findings in a psychoanalytically influenced study, Dana Breen argues that the redesign of the birth process undermines a woman's confidence in herself and in her ability to care for her infant:

> When a woman can only have a child by her body being provoked into it, by substances being continually pumped into it and more substances injected to dull the pain which has been thus increased, finally giving in to having the baby pulled out by forceps because she is paralysed from the waist down, she feels she hasn't given birth to her baby.[49]

Stripped of this gift and separated from her child who is appropriated by the hospital staff, she loses all sense of the essential goodness of her body. In addition to psychological costs, the technological transformation of birth increases the risk of medical complications in many cases.[50]

The alternatives proposed to the over-medicalization of birth reveal the degree to which critical problematics are biological, social or, indeed, feminist. 'Natural childbirth', and calls for the revival of lay or professional midwifery fit several strategies from reinforcing the hierarchical or nuclear family, to widening the family-community or the repossession of female power.[51] Despite the biological essentialism and the assumption of the exclusivity or dominance of mother–infant care that it imports, bonding or immediate skin to skin contact between the mother and child is promoted enthusiastically as a way of overcoming the alienation of hospitalized delivery.[52] A certain faith in the wider importance of unmediated biological influences is accorded more general significance as well. Although she does not elaborate her position theoretically, Rich thinks that birth can be a source of knowledge and discovery of 'our physical and psychic resources, one experience of liberating ourselves from fear, passivity and bodily self-alienation'.[53] At the extreme Alice Rossi's call for 'A biosocial perspective on parenting' rejects cultural and historical explanations of the persistence of gender divisions of labour along with egalitarian family values and childcare arrangements in favour of a theory of biologically determined, sexually differentiated learning capacities, particularly with regard to childcare and a return to not merely female, but mother-care for children.[54]

Despite its limitations, this literature substantiates the claims made in campaigns for day care, midwifery and the reorganization of the relationship between paid labour and childcare among other issues. Addressing these concerns is one step in advancing feminist strategy so that in responding to the everyday issues of sexual and maternal politics in the 1980s, it can bridge the ideological gap between politicized feminists and the women who are their constituency and transmit its larger transformative vision.

Minoan-Mycenaean revivification

A feminist psychoanalytic archaeology has set out to uncover the pre-oedipal mother–daughter relationship and to consider its significance for contemporary gender arrangements. Freud thought that femininity was fundamentally shaped in this region, 'so grey with age and shadowy and almost impossible to revivify', which was inaccessible to men.[55] The effect of this work is first, to move the analysis from historical, social relations to their representation in the unconscious and, once there, to displace the creation of heterosexual femininity from the anatomical difference between the sexes, the father and the faeces–penis–baby connection of classical Freudian analysis, on to the mother and her relations with infants of either sex. Because they weigh cultural and biological realities differently, Nancy Chodorow and Dorothy Dinnerstein, the main initiators of this project, arrive at somewhat different conclusions. But their common view that asymmetries in parenting serve to reproduce gender differences, substructure mysogyny, and connect masculinity with productivism has been highly influential.

Rejecting all biological or libidinal determinations, Chodorow adopts object relations theory to relativize and historicize distortions in Freud's own work.[56] She argues that gender asymmetries in parenting shape differentiated female and male capacities and desires to mother. Because they are of the same gender and because of taboos against sexualizing the mother–son relationship, women tend to experience their daughters more intimately, more ambivalently and as less separate than their sons. The experience of maternal identification and ambivalence sends girls through pre-oedipal and oedipal development preoccupied with 'those very relational issues that go into mothering – feelings of primary identification, lack of separateness or differentiation, ego and body-ego boundary issues under the sway of the reality principle'.[57] In the oedipal resolution, female personality structure embeds relational capacities and a sense of self-in-relationship necessary to fulfil the psychological role of mothering and the desire for a triangular relational configuration which encompasses both the masculine object and patriarchal power of the father and the merging identification with the mother. Since the boy is unlikely to have been intimately 'fathered' by a man his adult character structure is less shaped to be able to 'mother' or, indeed, to want to.[58] He is also less able to provide a return to the mother in coitus that women offer men.[59] Adult women then feel a double sense of incompleteness in dyadic relationships with men that they seek to mend by replicating the mother–infant–father triangle, this time in the position of mother.

Influenced both by Melanie Klein's more biologically oriented theory of the inevitable infantile discovery of loss, powerlessness and rage and Norman O. Brown's historical pessimism, Dinnerstein's picture is altogether more bleak.[60] The infant's dependence is more frightening, its rage greater and adult heterosexual alienation starker. For Dinnerstein, the exclusive power that mothers have over biologically dependent infants of both sexes leaves a residue at the level of the unconscious of the infant's ambivalent attraction to women: a desire for their nurturing and a fear of their will. Thus, the source of mysogyny is identified with matriphobia arising from a dialectic of absolute power/powerlessness:

> Power of this kind, concentrated in one sex and exerted at the outset over both, is far too potent and dangerous a force to be allowed free

sway in adult life. To contain it, to keep it under control and harness it to chosen purposes, is a vital need, a vital task, for every mother-raised human.[61]

Chodorow agrees that a wellspring of mysogyny lies in the contradictions of power and sensuality in gender arrangements that leave mothering exclusively to women but disagrees about its source. For Chodorow, the absence of fathers from child-raising allows masculinity to be glamorized. Seeking autonomy, the girl turns to her father to open up the relationship with her mother.[62] Boys, forced to seek masculinity through a positional identification with its cultural symbols rather than a personal identification with a nurturing father, find continuing identification with the mother threatening yet attractive.[63] Their quandary is resolved by the creation of psychological and cultural mechanisms to cope with their fears without giving up women altogether.

> The structure of parenting creates ideological and psychological modes which reproduce orientations to and structures of male dominance in individual men, and builds an assertion of male superiority into the definition of masculinity itself.[64]

Both see bisexualizing parenting as a way to overcome mysogyny, mutual heterosexual erotic dissatisfactions and issues of autonomy endemic to 'mother-raised' children, although neither offers a strategy for the restructuring of the psychic structures of 'non-nurturant' males. In addition, such a reorganization of parenting would go some way to overcoming the ambivalence among mother-raised *women* that, as Jane Flax has persuasively argued, constrains the political development of feminism.[65]

More theoretically intriguing, however, are the implications of the gender differentiated unconscious in shaping a relation to production and nature. Here, Dinnerstein makes explicit a thesis that is merely implicit in Chodorow that gender differences in values and consciousness are not superficial but go so deep as to be of epistemological and anthropological significance. Chodorow's perception is limited to adaptation; female personality structure is adapted to the diffuse multi-phasic demands of childcare, male personality to class differentiated relations to economic participation. Dinnerstein argues that matriphobic mysogyny substructures a destructive relation with nature that cannot be explained by mere economic rationality. It is to this difference in consciousness that feminist metatheory turns.

Motherhood and Metatheory

The most provocative of all the initiatives at recentring feminist theory on the maternal are the metatheoretical revisions of O'Brien, Daly and Dinnerstein all of which are predicated upon a conviction that patriarchal theory has ignored and suppressed the importance of motherhood. They carry the themes of matriarchal motherhood, the historicization of mothering and gender differences in consciousness to a more general, indeed universal, level. For all three, the denigration of motherhood in political theory is symptomatic of a global deformation of consciousness which substructures a potentially catastrophic opposition between culture and nature which at its limit threatens life on this planet.

At the centre of O'Brien's analysis is a claim that 'genderically differentiated processes of human reproduction itself' give rise to gender differences in consciousness and the theoretical and political projects they invoke.[66] Her brilliant relocation of Marx's production-centred alienation problematic in the fatalities and constraints of sexual reproduction should make it impossible to think of alienation in simple workerist terms any more. Distinguished from Rossi's biologism, she sees sexual differences in reproduction as material, mediated by consciousness and labour, further conditioned by historical development in productive and reproductive relations.[67] For both men and women, reproduction contains a moment of alienation to be overcome, but the modalities differ. After the discovery of the male role in reproduction, 'negation [for men] rests squarely on the alienation of the male seed in the copulative act' with the result that male reproductive consciousness and the rationality to which it gives rise is fraught with dualism, separation and opposition from the race, from its continuity and from nature.[68] Overcoming this alienation and separation have been male projects which can be traced in the attempts of political theory to create artifical forms of community and continuity and, in the face of uncertain paternity, to organize social systems designed to appropriate the child and to ensure control over female sexuality and reproductive powers in marriage and the family. The structures of patriarchy and male potency which accomplish this task have then a particular relation to nature, both rest on the capacity to transcend natural realities, whether benign or malign, with man-made realities.

In contrast with paternity, O'Brien sees maternity not as an abstract idea but a material relation. Although women also face a moment of alienation in birth it is mediated by their own voluntary and involuntary labours. 'Women, unlike men, do not have to take further action to overcome their alienation from the race, for their labour assures their integration' and structures a consciousness informed by suffering and labour that unites the actual with potential and confirms the integrations of women with the generationally renewed species in both nature and history.[69] These synthetic dimensions of consciousness are, like the child, values created by labour in birth. Unlike men who are doomed by biology to a destiny of attempts to mediate reproductive alienation, women have lived their alienation in the private sphere of family and household.

These differentiated relations and consciousnesses have, however, been undermined by the development (from within the male sphere of alienated technology) of new contraceptive techniques incompatible with proprietary right to women and children. Because of their new ability to control reproduction by separating the 'moment of copulation' from the 'moment of conception' women are now placed in a situation of equality with men, thrust into a world of freedom. Women must begin to evolve their second nature and develop a feminist philosophy of freedom in the particularly difficult and urgent historical conditions inherited as a result of masculine hostility to nature; that is, a world 'choked with technological sewage, a wasteland strewn with the garbage of the brotherhood's machines of war and electronic chatter'.[70] For O'Brien, the growth of feminism as a revolutionary historical force permits and requires a theoretical elaboration of its synthetic consciousness in an integrated social science which comprehends birth not metaphorically but as a critique of power.[71] The women's movement must proceed from individual consciousness-raising to the political expression of transformed universal feminine consciousness, which demystifies the opposition of alienation and integration, the particular and the universal in the real world. In effect, she offers one version of the new form of rationality that Cixous sought and that feminist strategizing requires. Her project, although dependent upon women's practice is open to men who can be reintegrated into the genderal harmony of people and nature by co-operative decisions between reproducing adults.

For Dinnerstein, too, masculine subjectivity is bound up with the entrepreneurial control over nature and exclusive female mothering with its insane elaboration. Weaving together de Beauvoir's notion that women mediate men and unconscious uncontrollable nature and Brown's pessimistic reading of Western culture as obsessed with fear of the body, she argues that women appear as a Dirty Goddess, representing but repressing nature.[72] It is not simply the burden of childcare but also a greater sense of compunction for the mother, which grows out of a more intense identification with her on the part of girls that has served 'to keep women outside the nature-assaulting parts of history – less avid than men as hunters and killers, as penetrators of Mother Nature's secrets, plunderers of her treasure, outwitters of her constraints'.[73] Although the male project appears to be freely chosen and equally valued for its technical results by both genders, it reveals a hollow core. Uncontrolled, the drive for transcendence that both sexes can assign to males because their power is less contaminated with the sediment of infantile angst threatens to produce a world that is totally denatured and fit only for machines.[74]

Reflecting her training as a Catholic theologian, Mary Daly's problematic centres on a critique of religion and its underlying mythologies, a critique that subsumes Christianity under a notion of patriarchy as itself, 'the prevailing religion of the entire planet'.[75] Although her interpretation and solutions change radically in the course of her work from *Beyond God the Father* to *Gyn/Ecology: The Metaethics of Radical Feminism*, their common core is a perception that male-dominated theologies have attempted to excise Goddess religions and their devotees and to substitute 'the honour of the father' to take over her maternal powers.[76] Thus, Apollo, Dionysis and Athena who respectively control, madden and betray women and later Christ are moments in the evolution of legitimating patriarchal myths of 'Monogender Male Motherhood'.[77] In this process women are, like Mary, raped and emptied or, like Joan of Arc, a real Dianic heretic defeated by an alliance of French and English patriarchs whose common masculinist interests are stronger than those dividing their warring states.[78] The site of this struggle for control is typically medical knowledge acquired fom childbirth and handed down through Goddess cults. Today the struggle is with role enforcing practices of gynaecology and psychiatry.[79]

As her analytic position evolved, Daly's solutions changed. In her early work, she urged a transvaluation of 'phallic morality' to give women existential courage to face ontological nothingness. Male–female/paternal–maternal differences were to be overcome through 'a qualitative leap into psychic androgyny' which would integrate the repressed figure of the Goddess into new symbols of transcendence and provide the religious basis for an emancipatory politics that avoided the 'idolatry of single issue limited goals'.[80] Later, however, she rejected God as a pseudototality contaminated with necrophiliac patriarchy and androgyny as an abominable semantic suppression of totally woman-identified concepts.[81] Instead of mundane political action, she offers Hags and Crones, Spinners and Searchers — a metapatriarchal journey into self-discovery and collective ecstasy.[82] In both cases, the building of female solidarity requires rejecting mother–daughter relations as at least ambivalent and at worst destructive, for 'mothers in our culture are cajoled into killing off the self-actualization of their daughters' who learn, in turn, to hate them.[83] Her first metaphor for female solidarity is a cosmic convent where the realization of the mother–daughter relationship entails its destruction: 'mother and daughter look with pride into each other's faces and know that they have both been victims and are now sisters and comrades'.[84] Later she offers the vision of a celebratory coven united by Daughter-Right, since daughterhood is the universal social condition of women and the disalienated condition of mothers.[85] Either way, the dissolution of mother–daughter ties and the exclusion of men represents the positive sublation of motherhood, but at the cost of maternity.

In *Gyn/Ecology,* Daly's analysis of the effects of the biological division of labour in reproduction is extended from religion to science. Unable to incubate their own connections with immortality through pregnancy and birth and preoccupied with the reproduction of their own male selves, men envy, not just the womb but women's creative energy in all its forms. Their envy gives rise to an identification with the foetus for, like the foetus, they draw on female energy to fuel projects of pseudocreative technology. Because Apollonian science feeds parasitically on women, loves only those victimized into a state of living death and ultimately deals deathly pollution to the heavens and the earth, it results in necrophilia:

Since the passion of necrophilia is for the destruction of life and since their attraction is to all that is dead, dying and purely mechanical, the fathers' fetishism with 'fetuses' (reproductions/replicas of themselves) with which they passionately identify, are fatal to the planet. Nuclear reactors and the poisons they produce, stockpiles of atomic bombs, ozone destroying aerosol spray propellants, oil tankers 'designed' to self-destruct in the ocean.[86]

Even without the final solution of war, technology fosters the mechanization of life, a living death.

There is no doubt that these totalizing visions have extended the power and range of feminist theory, but as metatheoretical elaborations of the motherhood problematic they each in different ways suffer from a onesidedness at variance with the global complexity they aim to embrace. Thus, despite her groundbreaking rethinking of alienation theory, O'Brien's reassessment of classical political philosophy lacks historical concreteness (for all its appeal to history) particularly in its failure to specify the mechanisms which permit the patriarchal appropriation of motherhood to continue. In her work the move from the experience of reproductive biology to consciousness, whether formalized or spontaneous, is not mediated by a psychoanalytically understood unconscious. On the one hand, this analytic strategy avoids the necessity of imputing particular psychic motivational structures to political theorists whose texts can then be read for crucial absences (of reproduction) and demarcations (of nature/culture) which reveal political and ideological commitments. On the other hand, it cannot elucidate the ways asymmetries in reproduction and childcare generate fears of empowered women which divide women not just from men but from one another.

The same ahistorical historicism flaws Dinnerstein's work, but in contrast there a disregard for the historical constitution of motherhood and production relations leads to an overinflation of psychical power, its confusion with social power and a reinforcement of the matriphobia she wants to contest. Despite their different emphases on the relative importance of biologically based power and social powerlessness, both Chodorow and Dinnerstein can be read as reinforcing the mother-bashing of conventional psychology. Because it does not encompass actual biological reproduction and in fact rejects any male participation, Daly's theological transcendence of motherhood remains congruent with Firestone's earlier radical feminist rejection of the mother. Furthermore, her assertion of instant recognition among women has been only partially substantiated by the actual political dynamics of feminist struggle. Prescriptively neutral with respect to other dimensions of political action, her retreat to a coven cannot stop ecological disaster. Concerned as they are with the dynamics of heterosexual reproduction, neither O'Brien nor Dinnerstein articulates the implications of lesbian sexual choice that Daly values. It seems, then, that both a focus on maternity and a concern with the practical organization of human reproduction are necessary if the full theoretical implications of the transformation implied by critically revalorized motherhood are to be fully and successfully drawn.

Conclusion

There is some irony in the fact that feminist theory is renewing itself by embracing motherhood. After all, did not nineteenth-century feminism hold a similar perspective? And was this not a mark of its co-optation and containment? The thesis that there is a redemptive moment in feminine psychology which is connected with birth and nature is disturbing to the contemporary feminist emphasis on the similarity of women and men. Yet, as an authentic extension of radical-feminist critique the new motherhood problematic's assertion of the superiority of feminine modes of action and interaction holds a certain appeal. Rethinking motherhood begins a process in which feminist not androcentric theory defines what is good mothering and good in mothering.

While there are some obvious similarities in the maternal feminism of the first wave and the new motherhood problematic of the second there are also crucial differences that are more telling; they may theorize the same object but they do so with different values and strategies. In general, limited by a lack of effective contraceptive technology and a commitment to an anti-sexual moral propriety, nineteenth-century feminists did not challenge contemporary hegemonic claims that gender differences and labour divivions were biologically determined facts of life. Instead, they made the ideology of difference their own. Women's moral, cultural and practical skills and values were meant to *extend* the boundaries of differentiated spheres, not break them down; men were not to put nappies on babies, although women were to read Latin. The social conditions in which earlier feminist political ideologies arose also inflected their approach to maternity, particularly in relation to the women/nature dialectic, and the tendency to identify these terms. While there were certainly problems arising from the relation of an industrial society to nature and from the dislocations of workers in the course of its development, these were, except for prolonged high rates of infant mortality, usually seen as local and specific.

The ideological character and historical situation of second wave feminism mitigates against an automatic equation of its new focus on motherhood with conservatism. Its commitment to a radical extension of egalitarian principle is supported by a sophisticated understanding of the oppressiveness of imposed gender divisions. Moreover, its radical transformative project is to create a feminized world. Although there is now beginning to be some pressure to return women to the family, the liberatory character of the new motherhood theory is reinforced both by the historical and anthropological discourses examined above and by some aspects of practical life. Adopting the first wave metaphor of spheres, we can say that the second wave of the women's movement wants not merely to *overflow* boundaries but to *abolish them altogether* by extending the feminine sphere until it becomes coterminous with the human totality. In this optic, the liberation and integration of men lies in their reintegration into such a transformed world, not least as full participants in the reproductive practices of childcare and birth, no longer as experts nor just as 'fathers'. Second wave motherhood theory goes beyond that of the nineteenth century not just to the extent that it envisions men as, among other things, also nurturers – mothers, if you like – but also in so far as it defines their assimilation as necessary for human and planetary survival.

In narrower terms, a number of practical and political questions about the organization of birth and the social reproduction of human beings are posed. The critique of medicalized birth points to a need for the appropriation of knowledge and technology of the birth process by women and those with whom they wish to share it from its thrall in the hands of medical specialists. Existing contrasting outcomes of population policy in capitalist and self-identified socialist states also raise a democratic question of what social structures are necessary to empower individuals freely to make decisions about their reproductive lives and how to ensure a balance between population and resources.

Perhaps the most interesting contribution of the new motherhood problematic is its critical re-examination of the culture/nature distinction in relation to the prospects for a liberated technology and its location of this intersecting problematic at the point of birth. Here it shares the malestream philosophical perception of the unity of women and nature but interprets this as an evolutionary strength rather than a less-than-human weakness. It argues that birth, nature and female power and creativity are indeed linked and moreover that they each and all conflict with the outcomes of the male reproductive condition: exploitation, mechanistic rationalization and death. This strategic juncture has evidently become of immense political significance in a biosphere threatened with the exhaustion of resources, pollution and nuclear war, and in a situation where microtechnology is about to reduce drastically and globally the demand for productive labour. In these conditions, simply increasing production will neither end the gender division of labour nor ensure distributive justice on a world scale. The anti-Malthusianism of early Marxism and the technological faith of the Soviets to which it gave rise absolutely need revision. The analysis offered by the new theories of motherhood underlines an intimate connection among women's liberation, global social emancipation and biospheric renewal. Whether elaborated in philosophical or psychoanalytic modes, these arguments, although they have visionary moments, are more than sentimental and must be examined by other currents of emancipatory philosophy.

Feminism and Revolution

Mary O'Brien

The fastest way to evade and trivialize the question of the revolutionary potential of feminism is to play the definitional game: 'It all depends on what you mean by feminism' – or, for that matter, by 'revolution'. Having then subscribed implicitly to the notion that meaning inheres in words rather than in happenings, it is a relatively easy task to go on to define the terms in such a way that almost any proposition can be 'proved', including the contentions that feminism is 'really' *not* revolutionary or that there is 'in fact' no such thing as feminism. However, the crass things which can be done with definitional games do not get us off the hook of having to try to say clearly what we mean. For example, it can be argued that feminism is revolutionary because feminism attacks the integrity of the family, that the family is traditionally and actually an irreplaceable foundation brick in the structure of all known societies, and that the removal of this particular brick would bring the whole edifice tumbling down, and thus entail a revolution in social structure. As a matter of fact, what I am going to argue is not all that different from this. What is very different is the way in which I want to argue it. The importance of the family is a gospel of reactionary groups, yet the family and the private realm increasingly engage the attention of active feminists as the social organizations which must be examined in a critical way, and which can only be examined in a critical way from a standpoint within the social realities of feminist experience.

Such a project must go beyond the recovery of women's history and the description of contemporary situations, yet the past and present of feminism constitute the framework of theory and practice. Feminism is revolutionary because it is historical, but also because this is a history of struggle. The perception of history as a process with a revolutionary dynamic was grasped with great clarity and creative intensity by Marx, yet Marx's analysis of history as class struggle does not elucidate the dynamics of the reproductive realm with anything like the clarity which he brings to the understanding of the dynamics of the productive realm. Starting from the history of the lived lives and relations of real people, Marx found in these relations the reality of division by socio-economic class growing out of the historical divisions of labour. Class struggle is revolutionary because it is historical, and history is revolutionary because it is the history of class struggle. This is not just one of these tedious verbal trick circles: actual class struggle and revolutionary activity break through the merely abstract enclosures of circles. Yet there is nothing in this view of history which says that *feminism* is revolutionary, or that the social relations of reproduction generate their own contradictions. Indeed, if it could be demonstrated theoretically that generic struggle is an integral part of class struggle, then there would be no problem for Marxist feminists. This approach may have been Marx's own, and was certainly that of Engels, and still appeals strongly to large sections of the Left, particularly of the vanguard type. However, 'pure' theory is not enough for Marxists, and the available evidence from both simple and complex societies falls far short of demonstrating that gender relations can be subsumed in class relations. In practical terms, it would be nice if it could be shown that only the bourgeoisie beat their wives, or that existing socialist societies have been able to make really substantial inroads on the ideology and practice of male supremacy. The truth is that *male supremacist praxis is transhistorical*, and increasing numbers of women are sceptical of the notion that the inevitable motion of class dialectic will ultimately liberate them.

This does not mean that feminists should abandon class struggle, nor regretfully dismiss Marx as a great guy but a hopeless patriarch. What it does mean is that the ways in which productive and reproductive social formations relate to each other must be opened up to a more rigorous and refined critique. Marx once said, in speaking of his own development of historical materialism, that the route he took was through a critique of Hegel, but it was a critique which necessarily had to be made from *inside* Hegel's systematic philosophy of history. I believe that the critique of male supremacy which can uncover the revolutionary structure of women's history and create a living feminist praxis must be conducted from within Marxism. Some Marxists find the implications of this disturbing, for it is, in a necessary way, 'revisionist', yet women must reject the comforts of an orthodoxy which does not reflect the actual conditions of their lives. Female experience affirms that class oppression and sex oppression are related in many ways, but they are not the same. Class oppression and exploitation are the realities within which wage labourers come to reject the false definition of human freedom which bourgeois ideology and practice attempts to lay on them. Women's consciousness and women's oppression is this class experience, but it is also more than this, for in all male-dominated societies the oppression and exploitation of women by men crosses class barriers.

Feminism is the history of resistance to male exploitation, and is therefore not a history which can be understood fully in terms of the theory of class struggle. The fact that class struggle and genderic struggle are related has meant that, in the more cataclysmic historical moments of class struggle, women have been there, more so than we can know if we read only men's accounts of these events. There is, however, a different struggle and a real struggle which is the true history of feminism. To be sure, this struggle has not produced the dramatic social upheavals which class struggle has precipitated. This fact has lent fuel to the smug notion that women are not, in fact, oppressed by men, but are oppressed by Nature, their own dear mother. But the 'invisibility' of women's real resistance to oppression cannot be ascribed, particularly by historical materialism, to the ideological strength of male supremacy, or to biological determinism. It must be understood in terms of visible social structure. If the visible social structure of male oppression is not class struggle, it is incumbent upon feminists to say what it is. I submit that the structure in question is the structure in which the social relations of reproduction have developed historically, and that this is the structure by which private life and the personal have been separated from public life and the political. The opposition of public and private is to the social relations of reproduction what the opposition of economic classes is to the social relations of production.

The significance of the events which this formulation attempts to grasp has not, of course, gone unnoticed. It is the basis of Marx's and Engels's view of the need to socialize domestic labour, thus breaking down the privatization and devaluation of women's work. Much recent discussion on the Left has zeroed in on this question of domestic labour, but there appears to linger in domestic labour and its products the same sort of elusiveness which Marx found in the bourgeois version of a commodity. A commodity, Marx noted, seems a straightforward and even trivial thing, yet 'analysis shows that it is, in reality, a very queer thing, abounding in metaphysical subtleties and theological niceties' (*Capital*, Part I, 1, i. 3.14). Domestic labour and its products have proven to be resistant to analysis in terms of value or of productive and non-productive labour. There is no dispute that domestic labour constitutes a useful bonus to capitalism: there is a certain reluctance to include in the discussion the fact that it also constitutes a very real value to its immediate appropriators, men of all economic classes. Further, there is no analysis at all of the actual process of reproductive labour as the material ground of both species continuity and the separation of public and private life.

Contemporary feminism started off with an uncritical acceptance of the low value of reproductive labour assigned to it by 'malestream' thought. In terms of theory, this position, which was the early position of de Beauvoir, perhaps reached its apotheosis and its negation in the popular work of Shulamith Firestone. With impeccable logic, Firestone argued that as the historical oppression of women was grounded in female reproductive function, the emancipation of women depended upon our escape from our biological destiny. This theory is unsound, for its premise that women's oppression stands in causal relationship with biological function cannot be demonstrated empirically. It is also incapable of providing a rallying point for a widely based women's praxis, for many women resist the notion that their maternal experience has no value. But the inadequacies of early feminist theory have not prevented the growth of the movement, not out of theory but out of change in the material conditions of women's lives. The conditions of early theory were the conditions of male reproductive experience, which has not been subjected to radical change. Female reproductive consciousness is radically transformed by the development of contraceptive technology, a transformation which has not yet been subjected to sustained theoretical critique from a materialist perspective. The truth is that contraceptive technology is qualitatively different from all other technologies in that it makes its major impact on the social relations of reproduction, and that it does this in a radical way which has nothing to do with the attractive marketability of 'the pill', the joys of liberated sexuality, nor even the serious and sombre political considerations involved in the dizzy dreams of controlled genocide which no doubt colour bourgeois visions of absolute power. Contraceptive technology is a world historical event because it actually transforms the process of reproduction. Just as the development of capitalism not only changed productive relations but exposed to the light of day the inner workings of the true substructure of these relations, so the transformations wrought in reproductive relations by recent changes in contraceptive technology expose the material grounds of genderic oppression and open them up to a heretofore impossible critical analysis. This sort of enterprise is one which Marx could no more have undertaken than could Malthus, for the fact that the substructure of reproductive relations is the *process of reproduction itself* was simply not visible at a time in history in which that process appears to be mired eternally in the realm of determinism, contingency and brute biology. This is now no longer the case. The process of reproduction is not simply the route from ovulation to birth, but the total sociobiological process from copulation through birth to the nurture and care of dependent children. Reproduction in this sense has always been a unity of thinking and doing, and the fact that the woman engaged in the strenuous process of reproductive labour cannot help what she is doing does not mean that she does not *know* what she is doing and what she has still to do. Women's place in the reproduction of the species involves her body and her mind. So does men's. It is precisely here that the dialectics of reproduction differ from the dialectics of production. Both produce particular forms of consciousness, but the forms of productive consciousness are related to the standpoint of class. The forms of reproductive consciousness are related to gender. Men and women are joined together by class consciousness, but they are separated by reproductive consciousness.

We must note, further, that although reproductive consciousness is differentiated by gender, it is not therefore an individual, atomized, purely subjective consciousness. Women do not need to bear children to partake in female reproductive consciousness, for such consciousness is a socially and culturally transmitted collective consciousness. Women have a particular form of reproductive consciousness, not because they are mothers, but because they are women. Likewise, it is not necessary to *be* a father to partake of patriarchal consciousness: indeed male reproductive consciousness has managed to develop patriarchal forms in the teeth of the radical uncertainty of paternity.

There are several aspects of the reproductive process which can be released by dialectical analysis from the straitjackets of conventional wisdom. Take, for example, the proposition that women have a 'special relationship' with nature, which, in its extreme form, says that women are *identified* with nature. The fact that this view is a hardy staple of malestream thought, and has been used historically to draw conclusions which are hardly in women's best interests, should not obscure the fact that it has a significant element of truth. What is wrong with the hand-me-down view is that it suggests that women are *immediately* related to nature when in actual fact women's relationship with nature is *mediated*, and the mode of mediation is reproductive labour. The separation of all people from the natural world is mediated in the process of productive labour, but the relation of women to the biological world of species continuity is mediated by reproductive labour. This is not, of course, the case with men: the process of reproduction entails a *separation* of men from nature in the necessary alienation of the male seed in copulation. Furthermore, this alienation is more than alienation from the natural world, for it also involves a real separation from genetic time. Male experience of time is the experience of species discontinuity, a discontinuity which is, in the female experience, mediated in the reproduction of successive generations.

The profound significance for materialist dialectical science of the fact that man's reproductive consciousness is an alienated consciousness has not been examined with sufficient thoroughness. In Marx's perception of human consciousness, consciousness resists alienation in terms of both thinking and doing. Have men, then, resisted their experienced alienation from biological continuity? The historical record shows quite clearly that they have, in both ideological and practical ways. The most common and most profound mode of resistance which they have employed is the familiar one of appropriation. Men have erected a huge social edifice to facilitate and justify that appropriation of women's children which we call patriarchy. The sealing off of the private realm, the institutions of marriage and the establishment of a 'right' to the children of a particular woman are the social acts of a class of appropriators, striving to resist alienation and to make real the idea of a paternity. Not the least of the contradictions of reproductive consciousness lies in the fact that paternity is essentially an idea while maternity is experienced fact.

Paternal rights of appropriation without labour are shared by men of all classes; they are actual social relations, and are a significant building block in the ancient notion of a brotherhood of man. How can all men be brothers when they are so experientially remote from one another in diverse and significant ways? Yet this notion of brotherhood is a historically pervasive one which cannot be understood as some kind of simple humanistic opiate or a noble lie cynically generated by a historical succession of ruling classes. It has a material ground in the dialectics of reproductive process, in which men are, by virtue of the alienation of their seed, forced into co-operative efforts to resist this universal male mode of alienation. The brotherhood notion is an essential and materially grounded plank in the ideological platform of male supremacy, which, like reproductive consciousness, transcends class.

The question of the ordering of strategic priorities between the related but opposing needs of class and generic struggle is not one that can be worked out neatly in theory and imposed on political practice. Its resolution must be lived, including the fundamental question of whether the necessary transformation of the social relations of reproduction must be a violent one. The working out is not exclusively a women's problem but a human problem, however women are the progressive social force in the struggle. Men can and do join in, though they must recognize that their participation carries with it the same kind of uncomfortable ambivalence as that experienced by the bourgeois intellectual who opts to join the proletariat in their historic mission.

Karl Marx, in one of his more celebrated pronouncements, once suggested that in the humane diversity of a classless society, men could be fishermen in the morning, farmers in the afternoon and critical critics in the evening. I wonder how many women have, as I did when I first heard the passage, wondered who was minding the kids. This question is no longer a suppressed disloyalty to the hegemony of the class struggle. It is an upfront problematic in the struggle to abolish generic inequality, now that the material base has been transformed by the fact that motherhood is now a choice as fatherhood has always been.

The bringing to light of the dialectics of reproduction is reflected in the recent history of the women's movement. Proclaimed dead, it lives and flourishes. Proclaimed frivolous, it invades ever more deeply the citadels of male intellectual dominance. Proclaimed dependent and derivative, it continues to emancipate itself from the mindcuffs of malestream thought and the petty potency of private realm imperialism. Accused of shrillness, it nurtures beneath its disagreements a joy in the discovery of sisterhood so profound that it is expressed in silence. Attacked from the right as life destructive, it joyfully celebrates life's femaleness. Assailed from the left as a bourgeois deviation, it maintains a thoughtful and activist probe into the deeper realities of the relation of generic struggle and class struggle. In doing these things, feminism moves erratically but irresistibly towards the feminist praxis which understands its past, lives its present for itself, and prepares to make its future.

Note

For a fuller exposition of these ideas, see Mary O'Brien *The Politics of Reproduction*, London 1981.

Select Bibliography
(Canadian Sources)

Acton, Janice *et al.*, eds., *Women at Work: Ontario 1850–1920*, Toronto 1974.

Andersen, Margret, *Mother Was Not a Person*, Montréal 1972.

Armstrong, Pat, *Labour Pains: Women's Work in Crisis*, Toronto 1984.

Armstrong, Pat and Armstrong, Hugh, *The Double Ghetto: Canadian Women and Their Segregated Work*, Toronto 1978.

Armstrong, Pat and Armstrong, Hugh, *A Working Majority: What Women Must Do for Pay*, Ottawa 1983.

Bacchi, Carol Lee, *Liberation Deferred? The Ideas of the English Canadian Suffragists, 1877–1918*, Toronto 1982.

Backhouse, Constance, 'Involuntary Motherhood: Abortion, Birth Control and the Law in 19th Century Canada', *Windsor Yearbook of Access to Justice*, no. 3, 1983.

Backhouse, Constance and Cohen, Leah, *The Secret Oppression of Working Women*, Toronto 1978.

Bashevkin, Sylvia B., *Toeing the Lines: Women and Party Politics in English Canada*, Toronto 1985.

Benston, Margaret, 'The Political Economy of Women's Liberation', *Monthly Review*, vol. 21, no 4 (September 1969).

Benston, Margaret, 'For Women, the Chips are Down', in Jan Zimmerman, ed., *The Technological Woman: Interfacing With Tomorrow*, New York 1983.

Bradbury, Bettina, 'The Family Economy and Work in an Industrializing City: Montreal in the 1870s', *Canadian Historical Association Papers*, 1979.

Bradbury, Bettina, 'Women and Wage Labour in a Period of Transition: Montreal, 1861–1881', *Histoire sociale/Social History*, no. 17, May 1984.

Briskin, Linda and Yanz, Lynda, *Union Sisters. Women in the Labour Movement*, Toronto 1983.

Brown, Jennifer S. H., *Strangers in Blood: Fur Trade Company Families in Indian Country*, Vancouver 1980.

Burstyn, Varda, 'Economy, Sexuality, Politics: Engels and the Sexual Division of Labor', *Socialist Studies/Etudes Socialistes: A Canadian Annual*, 1983.

Burstyn, Varda, 'Masculine Dominance and the State', in *The Socialist Register 1983*, London 1983.

Burstyn, Varda, ed., *Women Against Censorship*, Vancouver 1985.

Canadian Women's Educational Press, *Women Unite!*, 1972.

Clark, Lorenne and Lewis, Debra, *Rape: The Price of Coercive Sexuality*, Toronto 1977.

Clark, Lorenne and Lange, Lynda, eds., *The Sexism of Social and Political Theory: Women and Reproduction from Plato to Nietzsche*, Toronto 1979.

Cohen, Yolande, ed., *Femmes et politique*, Montreal 1981.

Le Collectif Clio, *L'Histoire des femmes au Québec depuis quatre siècles*, Montréal 1982.

Connelly, Patricia, *Last Hired, First Fired: Women and the Canadian Work Force*, Toronto 1978.

Dubinsky, Karen, 'Lament for a "Patriarchy Lost"? – Anti-feminism, Anti-abortion and REAL Women in Canada', Ottawa 1985.

Eichler, Margrit, 'And the Work Never Ends: Feminist Contributions', *Canadian Review of Sociology and Anthropology*, vol. 22, no. 5 (December 1985).

Eichler, Margrit, *The Double Standard: A Feminist Critique of Feminist Social Science*, London 1980.

Fahmy-Eid, Nadia and Dumont, Micheline, eds., *Maîtresses de maison, maîtresses d'école: Femmes, famille et éduction dans l'histoire du Québec*, Montréal 1983.

Fitzgerald, Maureen, Guberman C. and Wolfe, M., eds., *Still Ain't Satisfied: Canadian Feminism Today*, Toronto 1982.

Fox, Bonnie, ed., *Hidden in the Household: Women's Domestic Labour Under Capitalism*, Toronto 1980.

Fox, Bonnie J. and Fox, John, 'Women in the Labour Market 1931–81: Exclusion and Competition', *Canadian Review of Sociology and Anthropology*, vol. 23, no. 1 (1986).

Gorham, Deborah, 'Birth and History', *Histoire sociale/Social History*, vol. 18 (1984).

Horowitz, Gad, *Basic and Surplus Repression in Psychoanalytic Theory: Freud, Reich and Marcuse*, Toronto 1977.

Jamieson, Kathleen, 'Multiple Jeopardy: The Evolution of a Native Woman's Movement', *Atlantis*, vol. 4, no. 2 (1979).

Kealey, Linda, ed., *A Not Unreasonable Claim: Women and Reform in Canada 1880s–1920s*, Toronto 1979.

Kealey, Linda, 'Canadian Socialism and the Woman Question, 1900–1914', *Labour/Le Travail*, no. 13 (Spring 1984).

Laurin-Frenette, Nicole, 'The Women's Movement, Anarchism and the State', *Our Generation*, vol. 15, no. 2 (1982).

Lavigne, Marie, and Pinard, Yolande, eds., *Travailleuses et féministes: Aspects historiques*, Montréal 1983.

Lowe, Graham S., 'Women, Work and the Office: The Feminization of Clerical Occupations in Canada, 1901–1931', *Canadian Journal of Sociology*, vol. 5, no. 4 (Fall 1980).

Luxton, Meg, *More than a Labour of Love: Three Generations of Women's Work in the Home*, Toronto 1980.

Luxton, Meg, 'Taking on the Double Day: Housewives as a Reserve Army of Labour', *Atlantis*, vol. 7, no. 1 (Fall 1981).

Luxton Meg and Heather Jon Maroney, *Women's Jobs, Women's Struggles: Feminism and Political Economy*, Toronto 1986.

Marchak, Patricia, 'Canadian Political Economy', *Canadian Review of Anthropology and Sociology*, vol. 25, no. 5 (December 1985).

Maroney, Heather Jon, 'Feminism at work', *New Left Review*, no. 141 (September–October 1983).

MacDonald, Martha, 'Economics and Feminism: The Dismal Science', *Studies in Political Economy*, no. 15 (1984).

McLaren, Angus, 'What Has This to Do with Working-Class Women?: Birth Control and the Canadian Left, 1900–1939', *Histoire sociale/Social History*, vol. 14, no. 28 (November 1981).

Meissner, Martin, Humphreys, Elizabeth W., Meis, Scott M. and Scheu, William J., 'No Exit for Wives: Sexual Division of Labour and the Culmination of Household Demands', *Canadian Review of Sociology and Anthropology*, vol. 12, no. 4, part 1 (November 1975).

Mitchinson, Wendy, 'Gynecological Operations on Insane Women: London, Ontario, 1895–1901', *Journal of Social History*, vol. 15, no. 3 (Spring 1982).

Mitchinson, Wendy, 'A Medical Debate in Nineteenth-Century English Canada: Ovariotomies', *Histoire sociale/Social History*, no. 17 (May 1984).

Montreal Health Press, *A book about birth control.*

Montreal Health Press, *A book about sexual assault.*

Montreal Health Press, *A book about sexually transmitted diseases.* Montréal (PO Box 1000, Station La Cité, Montréal, Canada H2W 2NI).

Morris, Cerise, '"Determination and Thoroughness": The Movement for a Royal Commission on the Status of Women in Canada', *Atlantis*, vol. 5, no. 2 (Spring 1980).

Morton, Peggy, 'Women's Work Is Never Done', in *Women Unite*, Toronto 1972.

Parr, Joy, ed., *Childhood and Family in Canadian History*, Toronto 1982.

Parr, Joy, *Labouring Children: British Immigrant Apprentices to Canada, 1869–1924*, Montréal 1980.

Payette, Lise, *Le Pouvoir? Connais Pas*, Montréal 1982.

Phillips, Paul and Phillips, Erin, *Women and Work: Inequality in the Labour Market*, Toronto 1983.

Pierson, Ruth, *They're Still Women After All: The Second World War and Canadian Womanhood*, Toronto 1986.

Prentice, Alison and Trofimenkoff, Susan Mann, eds., *The Neglected Majority: Essays in Canadian Women's History*, Toronto 1977.

Prentice, Alison and Trofimenkoff, Susan Mann, eds., *The Neglected Majority: Essays in Canadian Women's History*, Volume 2, Toronto 1985.

Seccombe, Wally, 'The Housewife and Her Labour Under Capitalism', *New Left Review*, no. 83 (January–February 1974).

Seccombe, Wally, 'Domestic Labour – A Reply to Critics', *New Left Review*, no. 94 (November–December 1975).

Seccombe, Wally, 'Marxism and Demography', *New Left Review*, no. 137 (January–February 1983).

Smith, Dorothy E., 'Women's Perspective as a Radical Critique of Sociology', *Sociological Inquiry*, vol. 44, no. 1 (1974).

Smith, Dorothy E., 'A Peculiar Eclipsing: Women's Exclusion from Male Culture', *Women's Studies International Quarterly*, vol. 1 (1978).

Smith, Dorothy E., 'A Sociology for Women', in Sherman, J. A. and Beck, E. T., eds., *The Prism of Sex: Essays in the Sociology of Knowledge*, Madison 1979.

Smith, Dorothy E. and David, S., ed., *Women Look at Psychiatry*, Vancouver 1975.

Smith, Dorothy E., 'Women, Class and Family', *The Socialist Register 1983*, London 1983.

Stephenson, Marylee, ed., *Women in Canada*, Don Mills 1977.

Stoddart, Jennifer, 'Quebec's Legal Elite Looks at Women's Rights: The Dorion Commission 1929–1931', in Flaherty, D. H., ed., *Essays in the History of Canadian Law*, Volume 1, Toronto 1981.

Strong-Boag, Veronica, 'The Girl of the New Day: Canadian Working Women in the 1920s', *Labour/Le Travailleur*, vol. 4, no. 4 (1979).

Strong-Boag, Veronica, 'Working Women and the State: The Case of Canada, 1889–1945', *Atlantis*, vol. 6, no. 2 (Spring 1981).

Strong-Boag, Veronica and Fellman, Anita Clair, *Rethinking Canada: The Promise of Women's History*, Toronto 1986.

Trofimenkoff, Susan Mann, 'Nationalism, Feminism and Canadian Intellectual History', *Canadian Literature*, no. 83 (Winter 1979).

Trofimenkoff, Susan Mann, *The Dream of Nation: A Social and Intellectual History of Quebec*, Toronto 1983.

Valverde, Mariana, *Sex, Power and Pleasure*, Toronto 1985.

Van Kirk, Sylvia, *'Many Tender Ties': Women in Fur Trade Society in Western Canada, 1700–1850*, Winnipeg 1980.

Vickers, Jill McCalla, ed., *Taking Sex into Account*, Ottawa 1984.

Bibliographies

Light, Beth and Strong-Boag, Veronica, *True Daughters of the North. Canadian Women's History: An Annotated Bibliography,* Toronto 1980.

Prentice, Alison and Trofimenkoff, Susan Mann, eds., *The Neglected Majority,* Volume 2, Toronto 1985, pp. 174–87.

Drache, Daniel and Clement, Wallace, eds., *The New Practical Guide to Canadian Political Economy,* Toronto 1985.

Journals

Atlantis: A Woman's Studies Journal/Journal d'études sur la femmes, Halifax: Mount St Vincent University.

Canadian Journal of Women and the Law.

Canadian Woman Studies/les cahiers de la femme, Toronto: York University.

Histoire sociale/Social History, Ottawa: University of Ottawa Press.

Labour/Le Travail.

Resources for Feminist Research/Documentation sur la Recherche Feministe, Toronto: Ontario Institute for Studies in Edcuation.

Studies in Political Economy: A Socialist Review.

Special Issues

Alternate Routes: A Critical Review, Special issue: 'Feminism', vol. 6, Ottawa: Department of Sociology and Anthropology, Carleton University 1983.

Sociologie et sociétés, 'Women in Sociology', 13 October 1981; 'Femme, Travail, Syndicalism', 6 October 1974.

Canadian Journal of Political and Social Theory, Issue title: 'Feminism Now', vol. 9, nos. 1–2 (1985).

Notes on Contributors

Hugh Armstrong, Department of Sociology, Vanier College, Montreal.

Pat Armstrong, Department of Sociology, Vanier College, Montreal.

Patricia Connelly, Department of Sociology, St Mary's University, Halifax, Nova Scotia.

Bruce Curtis, Department of Sociology and Anthropology, Wilfrid Laurier University, Waterloo, Ontario.

Bonnie Fox, Department of Sociology, University of Toronto.

Nadia Fahmy-Eid, Département d'Histoire, Université de Québec à Montréal.

Jane Gaskell, Department of Social and Educational Studies, University of British Columbia.

Michèle Jean, Ministère de la Main-d'Oeuvre et Sécurité de Révénue, Montréal.

Jacqueline Lamothe, Département de Linguistique, Université de Québec à Montréal.

Nicole Laurin-Frenette, Département de Sociologie, Université de Montréal.

Marie Lavigne, Ministère des Affaires Culturelles, Hull, Québec.

Meg Luxton, Department of Social Science, Atkinson College, York University, Toronto.

Martha MacDonald, Department of Economics, St Mary's University, Halifax, Nova Scotia.

Suzanne Mackenzie, Department of Geography, Carleton University, Ottawa.

Angela Miles, Department of Sociology and Anthropology, St Francis Xavier University, Antigonish, Nova Scotia.

Roxana Ng, Faculty of Education, Queen's University, Kingston, Ontario.

Mary O'Brien, Department of Sociology in Education, Ontario Institute for Studies in Education (OISE), Toronto.

Ruth Roach Pierson, Department of History, Ontario Institute for Studies in Education (OISE), Toronto.

Susan Russell, Department of Sociology and Anthropology, Concordia University, Montreal.
Jennifer Stoddart, Canadian Human Rights Commission, Ottawa.
Wally Seccombe, Department of Sociology in Education, Ontario Institute for Studies in Education (OISE), Toronto.

Notes on the Editors

Michèle Barrett teaches sociology at the City University, London, England, and is a member of the *Feminist Review* collective. She is author of *Women's Oppression Today* (1980) and, with Mary McIntosh, of *The Anti-social Family* (1982).

Roberta Hamilton is at Queen's University, Kingston, Ontario, where she teaches sociology and history and is co-ordinator of women's studies. She is author of *The Liberation of Women* (1978).

Notes

Introduction

1. See the recent companion volumes *Labour and Love: Women's Experience of Home and Family, 1850–1940*, Jane Lewis, ed., and *Unequal Opportunities: Women's Employment in England, 1800–1918*, Angela V. John, ed., London 1986.
2. The essays published here have almost all been published only in Canada and are difficult to obtain in Britain. We have excluded from the book a number of directly relevant and useful papers that have already been published in Britain on the grounds that such duplication is undesirable. Two authors in particular, Dorothy Smith and Varda Burstyn, have papers in the 1983 issue of *Socialist Register* which have been excluded for this reason. Both of them, however, have made long-standing contributions to feminist debate in Canada, and reference to their work is made elsewhere in this volume.
3. Hubert Guindon, 'The Modernization of Québec and the Legitimacy of the Canadian State', in D. Glenday, A. Turowetz and H. Guindon, eds., *Modernization and the Canadian State*, Toronto 1977.
4. Le Collectif Clio, *L'Histoire des femmes au Québec depuis quatre siècles*, Montreal 1982, pp. 481–7, forthcoming in English from the Women's Press in Toronto.
5. *Unequal Union* is the title of Stanley Ryerson's book on the formation of the Canadian state, Toronto 1968.
6. Denys Delâge, *Le Pays Renversé: Amérindiens et européens en Amérique du nord-est 1600–64*, Montréal 1985, p. 48.
7. *Report of the Royal Commission on the Status of Women*, Ottawa 1970. Kathleen Jamieson, 'Multiple Jeopardy: The Evolution of a Native Women's Movement', *Atlantis*, vol. 4, no. 2, part 2 (Spring 1979). Marjorie Mitchell, 'The Indian Act: Social and Cultural Consequences for Native Indian Women on a British Columbia Reserve', *Atlantis*, vol. 4, no. 2, part 2 (Spring 1979).
8. David Boisvert, and Keith Turnball, 'Who are the "Métis"?', *Studies in Political Economy*, no. 18 (Fall 1985).
9. Warren Magnusson, *et al.*, eds., *The New Reality*, Vancouver 1984. See in particular Stella Lord's 'Women's Rights: An Impediment to Recovery'.
10. Sylvia B. Bashevkin, *Toeing the Lines: Women and Party Politics in English Canada*, Toronto 1985.

11. Roberta Hamilton, 'Sexual Politics', *The Canadian Forum*, February 1980.

12. Audrey Doerr, 'Women's Rights in Canada: Social and Economic Realities', *Atlantis*, vol. 9, no. 2 (Spring 1984), pp. 35–47.

13. Cerise Morris, 'Determination and Thoroughness: The Movement for a Royal Commission on the Status of Women in Canada', *Atlantis*, vol. 5, no. 2 (Spring 1980).

14. For its effect on the Native Women's Movement, see Jamieson, 'Multiple Jeopardy'.

15. See, for example, comments in Margret Andersen, ed., *Mother Was Not a Person*, Montreal 1972.

16. *The Radical Future of Liberal Feminism*, Boston 1981.

17. Cerise Morris, 'Pressuring the Canadian State for Women's Rights: The Role of the National Action Committee on the Status of Women', *Alternate Routes*, no. 6 (1983).

18. Penney Kome, *The Taking of Twenty Eight: Women Challenge the Constitution*, Toronto 1983.

19. Varda Burstyn, *Women against Censorship*, Toronto 1985. See also the critical review of this by Susan Cole in *Canadian Journal of Women and the Law*, vol. 1, no. 1 (1985).

20. The publications are listed in the bibliography. The collective's pre-history is recorded by its founders Donna Cherniak and Allan Feingold, 'Birth Control Handbook', *Women Unite!*, Toronto 1972.

21. This anthology reprinted Peggy Morton's important article 'Women's Work Is Never Done'.

22. Linda Briskin, and Linda Yanz, *Union Sisters: Women in the Labour Movement*, Toronto 1983; Fitzgerald, Maureen C. Guberman and M. Wolfe, eds., *Still Ain't Satisfied*, Toronto 1982.

23. Jacques Dofny, 'The PQ Government: Year One', in Nicole Arnaud and Jacques Dofny, eds., *Nationalism and the National Question*, Montreal 1977.

24. Kari Levitt, *Silent Surrender: The Multi-national Corporation in Canada*, Toronto 1970. Harold J. Innis is generally regarded as the progenitor of political economy in Canada. See *Journal of Canadian Studies*, 1977, special edition on Harold Innis. For an overview of 'Canadian Political Economy', see Patricia Marchak's article in *Canadian Review of Sociology and Anthropology*, vol. 22, no. 5 (December 1985).

25. Daniel Drache and Wallace Clement, eds., *The New Practical Guide to Canadian Political Economy*, Toronto 1985, p. ix.

26. Their work is referenced in the bibliography.

27. 'The Housewife and Her Labour under Capitalism', *New Left Review*, no. 83.

28. See 'More Than Just a Memory: Women and the 1984–5 NUM Strike' in which Sheila Rowbotham interviews Jean McCrindle, *Feminist Review*, no. 23 (1986).

29. *Last Hired, First Fired: Women and the Canadian Work Force*, Toronto 1978.

30. See Annette Kuhn and Ann-Marie Wolpe, eds. *Feminism and Materialism*, London 1978; and Women's Studies Group, Centre for Contemporary Cultural Studies, ed., *Women Take Issue*, London 1978.

31. 'Class Struggle and the Persistence of the Working-Class Family' *Cambridge Journal of Economics*, vol. 1, no. 3 (1977).

32. See Michèle Barrett and Mary McIntosh, 'The "Family Wage": Some Problems for Socialists and Feminists', *Capital and Class*, no. 11 (1980); Colin Creighton, 'The Family and Capitalism in Marxist Theory', in Martin Shaw, ed., *Marxist Sociology Revisited*, London 1985; Hilary Land, 'The Family Wage', *Feminist Review*, no. 6 (1980).

33. Angela Coyle, 'Going Private: The Implications of Privatization for Women's Work', *Feminist Review*, no. 21 (1985); Teresa Perkins, 'A New Form of Employment: A Case Study of Women's Part-time Work in Coventry', in Mary Evans and Clare Ungerson, eds., *Sexual Divisions: Patterns and Processes*, London 1983; Sheila Allen and Carol Wolkowitz, 'The Control of Women's Labour: The Case of Homeworking', *Feminist Review*, no. 23, (1986).

34. *A Working Majority*, Ottawa: Canadian Advisory Council on the Status of Women, 1983.

35. For the most recent bibliography of the debate, see Creighton, 'The Family and Capitalism in Marxist Theory', p. 208.

36. See Margaret Coulson, Branka Magaš and Hilary Wainwright, 'Women and the Class Struggle', *New Left Review*, no. 89 (1975).

37. 'Wiping the Floor with Theory – a Survey of Writings on Housework', *Feminist Review*, no. 6 (1980).

38. *Women's Oppression Today: Problems in Marxist Feminist Analysis*, London 1980.

39. Johanna Brenner and Maria Ramas, 'Rethinking Women's Oppression', *New Left Review*, no. 144 (1984); Michèle Barrett, 'Women's Oppression: A Reply', *New Left Review*, no. 146 (1984); Jane Lewis, 'The Debate on Sex and Class', *New Left Review*, no. 149 (1985).

40. London 1981, p. 43.

41. Winnipeg 1980.

42. Toronto 1982.

43. *The Vertical Mosaic: An Analysis of Social Class and Power*, Toronto 1965.

44. See her article, 'Bourassa and the "Women Question"' in Susan Mann Trofimenkoff and Alison Prentice, eds., *The Neglected Majority*, Toronto 1977, and her book, *The Dream of Nation*, Toronto 1983, chapter 12.

45. Marie Lavigne, Yolande Pinard and Jennifer Stoddart, 'The Federation Nationale Saint-Jean-Baptiste and the Women's Movement in Quebec', in Linda Kealey, ed., *A Not Unreasonable Claim: Women and Reform in Canada, 1880–1920s*, Toronto 1979.

46. Marta Danylewycz, 'Changing Relationships: Nuns and Feminists in Montreal, 1890–1925', in Alison Prentice and Susan Mann Trofimenkoff, eds., *The Neglected Majority*, volume 2, Toronto 1985. Marta's tragic and violent death in March 1985 created shock, sadness and anger among feminist historians in Québec and throughout the country. See *Resources for Feminist Research*, vol. 14, no. 2 (July 1985), for tributes to her work.

47. Even in the late seventeenth century in New France, such policies apparently had no effect. Le Collectif Clio, 'L'Histoire', p. 49.

48. Quoted in Hamilton, 'Sexual Politics'.

49. Montréal, Editions Québec/Amérique, 1982, p. 117.

50. Kenneth McRoberts and Dale Posgate, *Québec: Social Change and Political Crises*, Toronto: McClelland and Stewart, 1980.

51. For an elaborated discussion of the ways in which political ideologies can be articulated in varying combinations, see the illuminating discussions of

populism in Ernesto Laclau, *Politics and Ideology in Marxist Theory*, London 1977.

52. See Payette *Le Pouvoir?* *Connais Pas!*, and Roberta Hamilton, 'Politics in Québec: Pronatalism, Nationalism and Feminism', in Hugh Armstrong, ed., *Women and the State*, forthcoming.

53. 'Sex and Skill: Notes Towards a Feminist Economics', *Feminist Review*, no. 6 (1980).

54. Harmondsworth, Middlesex 1975.

55. See Jane Gallop, *Feminism and Psychoanalysis: The Daughter's Seduction*, London 1982; Juliet Mitchell and Jacqueline Rose, eds., *Feminine Sexuality: Jacques Lacan and the Ecole Freudienne*, London 1982.

56. See Michael Rustin's apologia for Kleinianism, 'A Socialist Reconsideration of Kleinian Psychoanalysis', *New Left Review*, no. 131 (1982), and Michèle Barrett and Mary McIntosh, 'Narcissism and the Family', *New Left Review*, no. 135 (1982), pp. 47–8.

57. Joanna Ryan has pointed to the explicit anti-feminism of the specific appropriation of psychoanalysis currently gaining ground in Britain through the publishing house of Free Associations. In a critical review of one of their central early works, Barry Richard's collection entitled *Capitalism and Infancy* (1984), she shows the connections between the revival of Kleinianism and the 'object relations' theory and the celebration by these same authors of the anti-feminist writer Christopher Lasch. Margaret and Michael Rustin, for instance, speak of lesbianism as 'powered by despair and pessimism' (about the possibility of better relations between women and men). Ryan regards this as a 'backlash' against feminism; certainly it represents heterosexism, if not homophobia (Joanna Ryan, 'Mind Over Matter', *New Socialist*, no. 32 (1985) p. 44.)

58. See Hester Eisenstein, *Contemporary Feminist Thought*, London 1984; Lynne Segal, *Is the Future Female?*, forthcoming.

59. For a critique of 'dualism' see Veronica Beechey, 'On Patriarchy', *Feminist Review*, no. 3 (1979).

60. 'Women, Class and Family', in Ralph Miliband and John Saville, eds., *The Socialist Register 1983*, London 1983, p. 2; for a major new study of the 'gender-saturated' quality of social class, see Leonore Davidoff and Catherine Hall, *Family Fortunes: Men and Women of the English Middle Class, 1780–1850*, London 1987.

61. Joan Kelly, 'The Doubled Vision of Feminist Theory', *Feminist Studies*, vol. 5, no. 1 (1979).

Two Hands for the Clock: Changing Patterns in the Gendered Division of Labour in the Home

This paper reports the results of research carried out in Flin Flon, Manitoba, in 1981. All the quotes cited in the paper without references are from interviews conducted as part of that research.

The article is a revised version of a paper presented at the Canadian Sociology and Anthropology Association meeting in Ottawa in 1982. For critical comments I am grateful to Margaret Benston, Pat Connelly, Heather Jon Maroney, Pat Marchak, Ester Reiter, Harriet Rosenberg and Wally Seccombe.

1. Heidi Hartmann, 'The Family as the Locus of Gender, Class and Political Struggle: The Example of Housework', *Signs*, vol. 6, no. 3 (Spring 1981), pp. 377–86.

2. Rayna Rapp, 'Family and Class in Contemporary America: Notes Towards an Understanding of Ideology', *Science and Society*, no. 42 (Fall 1978), pp. 278–301; Michèle Barrett, *Women's Oppression Today*, London 1980; Michèle Barrett and Mary McIntosh, *The Anti-Social Family*, London 1983.

3. For example, see Deirdre Gallager, 'Getting Organized in the CLC', and Debbie Field, 'Rosie the Riveter Meets the Sexual Division of Labour', in Maureen Fitzgerald, Connie Guberman and Margie Woolf, eds., *Still Ain't Satisfied: Canadian Feminism Today*, Toronto 1982.

4. Canadian Institute of Public Opinion, *The Gallup Report*, Toronto 1981, pp. 1–2.

5. Meg Luxton, *More than a Labour of Love: Three Generations of Women's Work in the Home*, Toronto 1980.

6. The problem here, however, lies in trying to determine what consititues economic need. All of these women (twenty-four) maintained that they were working outside the home for economic reasons, because their families needed the money. In all likelihood, this is true. However, it may be that these women, like most employed housewives who have been studied, also have non-economic reasons for accepting paid employment. Economic necessity is a more socially legitimated reason and some of these women may be dealing with the contradictory feeling they have towards their family obligations and their pleasure in employment by convincing themselves and others that they are only working because they 'have to'.

7. There were no obvious sociological factors that might explain the differences in opinion and behaviour. While a large-scale survey might reveal correlations between these different strategies and such factors as political or religious affiliation, ethnicity, and husbands' attitudes, at least among this group of women, and given the available data, no such patterns emerged. It is also important to point out that while these three approaches are typical, they are not the only available options. Some women have fully egalitarian relations with the men they live with; others live alone or with other women.

A creative strategy was developed by one couple (not included in the study). The man worked a forty-hour week in the mines; the woman was a housewife. They determined mutually what work she was responsible for during a forty-hour week. She did childcare while he was at work, as well as heavy cleaning and certain other chores. The rest of the domestic labour – childcare, cooking, cleaning, laundry, shopping – they divided equally between them. As a result, each worked a forty-hour week at their own work and shared all remaining labour.

8. It seems to me that the involvement of men in the actual birth of their children is of enormous significance – something which has not yet been appreciated, or studied.

9. Pat Mainardi, 'The Politics of Housework', in Robin Morgan, ed., *Sisterhood Is Powerful*, New York 1970, pp. 449–51.

10. Nellie McClung, *In Times Like These*, first published 1915, Toronto 1972; Michael Young and Peter Willmott, *The Symmetrical Family*, London 1973.

11. Hartmann, 'Family as the Locus', p. 379.

12. In Québec the unions of CEGEP teachers have won paternity leave. This has made it possible for some men to take equal responsibility for infant care.

13. Susan Harding, 'Family Reform Movements: Recent Feminism and Its Opposition', *Feminist Studies* vol. 7, no. 1 (Spring 1981), pp. 57–75.

Women's Work: Domestic and Wage Labour in a Nova Scotia Community

We would like to thank the people in the community we studied, particularly, of course, the women we interviewed as well as other key informants on the development of the fishing industry. We would also like thank Shirley Buckler for her excellent typing effort and Saint Mary's University for providing some funding for this research.

1. W. Seccombe, 'Domestic Labour and the Working-Class Household', in B. Fox, ed., *Hidden in the Household: Women's Domestic Labour Under Capitalism,* Toronto 1980; M. Barrett, *Women's Oppression Today: Problems in Marxist Feminist Analysis,* London 1980; M. Barrett and M. McIntosh, 'The "Family Wage": Some Problems for Socialists and Feminists', *Capital and Class,* no. 11 (1980), pp. 51–72; J. Humphries, 'The Working Class Family, Women's Liberation, and Class Struggle: The Case of Nineteenth Century British History', *The Review of Radical Political Economics,* vol. 9, no. 3 (1975), p. 25ff.; J. Humphries, 'Class Struggle and the Persistence of the Working Class Family', *Cambridge Journal of Economics* vol. 1, no. 3 (1977), pp. 241–58; B. Fox, 'Women's Double Work Day: Twentieth Century Changes in the Reproduction of Daily Life', in *Hidden in the Household;* P. Connelly, 'Women's Work and the Family Wage in Canada', in A. Hoiberg, ed., *Women and the World of Work,* New York 1982, pp. 223–37; M. MacDonald, 'Women in the Workforce: Meeting the Changing Needs of Capitalism', Institute of Public Affairs, Halifax 1979; P. Armstrong and H. Armstrong, *The Double Ghetto,* Toronto 1978; D. Smith, 'Women, Class and Family' (paper presented at the Social Sciences and Humanities Research Council of Canada's Workshop on Women and the Canadian Labour Force, University of British Columbia, 1980).

2. V. Beechey, 'Some notes on Female Wage Labour in the Capitalist Mode of Production', *Capital and Class,* no. 3 (1977); M. Simeral, 'Women and the Reserve Army of Labour', *Insurgent Sociologist,* no. 8 (1978); P. Connelly, *Last Hired, First Fired: Women in the Canadian Workforce,* Toronto, 1978; Fox, *Hidden in the Household.*

3. Connelly, *Last Hired, First Fired.*

4. On women and class, see M. Luxton, 'Taking on the Double Day: House-wives as a Reserve Army of Labour', *Atlantis,* vol. 7, no. 1 (1981); Smith, 'Women, Class and Family', Fox, *Hidden in the Household.*

5. L. Johnson, 'Independent Commodity Production: Mode of Production of Capitalist Class Formation?', *Studies in Political Economy,* no. 6 (1981), pp. 93–112. Johnson points out that the degree to which they produced for their own consumption or for exchange depended upon local conditions. Both, however, were necessary for survival.

6. S. Ostry and M. Zaidi, *Labour Economics in Canada,* 3rd edn, Toronto 1979.

7. Fox, *Hidden in the Household;* T. Copp, *The Anatomy of Poverty: The Condition of the Working Class in Montreal, 1897–1929,* Toronto 1974.

8. National Council of Women of Canada, *Women of Canada: Their Life and Work* (distributed at the Paris International Exhibition, 1900; reprinted Ottawa 1975).

9. Ostry and Zaidi, *Labour Economics;* Fox, *Hidden in the Household.*

10. L. Johnson, 'The Political Economy of Ontario Women in the Nine-teenth Century', in *Women at Work: Ontario, 1850–1930,* Acton, Goldsmith and Shepard, eds., Toronto 1974.

11. G. Leslie, 'Domestic Service in Canada, 1880-1920', in *Women at Work*.

12. F. Denton, *The Growth of Manpower in Canada*, Ottawa 1970.

13. Canada, Dominion Bureau of Statistics, *Reserve of Labour Among Canadian Women*, Ottawa 1942.

14. R. Pierson, 'Women's Emancipation and the Recruitment of Women into the Labour Force in World War II', S. Mann Trofimenkoff and A. Prentice, eds., in *The Neglected Majority: Essays in Canadian Women's History*, Toronto 1977.

15. V. Strong Boag, 'The Girl of the New Day: Canadian Working Women in the 1920s', *Labour/Le Travailleur*, vol. 4, no. 4 (1979), pp. 131–64.

16. S. Ostry, *The Occupational Composition of the Canadian Labour Force*, Ottawa 1967.

17. L. Johnson, *Poverty in Wealth: The Capitalist Labour Market and Income Distribution in Canada*, Toronto 1974.

18. S. Amin, 'Accumulation and Development: A Theoretical Model', *Review of African Political Economy*, no. 1 (1974).

19. For reviews of the international literature on dependency, see H. Veltmeyer, 'A Central Issue in Dependency Theory', *Canadian Review of Sociology and Anthropology*, vol. 17, no. 3 (1980), pp. 198–213; C. Leys, 'Underdevelopment and Dependency: Critical Notes', *Journal of Contemporary Asia*, vol. 7, no. 1 (1977). For analyses of Canada's dependent development, see K. Levitt, *Silent Surrender: The Multinational Corporation in Canada*, Toronto, 1970; G. Teeple, ed., *Capitalism and the National Question in Canada*, Toronto 1972; W. Clement, 'The Canadian Bourgeoisie–Merely Comprador?', in J. Saul and C. Heron, eds., *Imperialism, Nationalism and Canada*, Toronto 1977. For a critical review of this Canadian literature, see L. Panitch, 'Dependency and Class in Canadian Political Economy', *Studies in Political Economy*, no. 6 (1981), pp. 7–34.

20. For a review of the controversies in the international literature on the mechanisms of underdevelopment see Veltmeyer, 'A Central Issue in Dependency Theory'. For a summary of the debates on the nature of regional underdevelopment in the Atlantic Provinces, see G. Barrett, 'Perspectives on Dependancy and Underdevelopment in the Atlantic Region', *Canadian Review of Sociology and Anthropology*, vol. 17, no. 3 (1980), pp. 273–87.

21. Barrett, 'Perspectives on Dependency'.

22. H. Veltmeyer, 'The Underdevelopment of Atlantic Canada', *Review of Radical Political Economics*, Special Issue on Regional Development (1978), pp. 198–213.

23. See Veltmeyer, 'A Central Issue in Dependency Theory'; J. Sacouman, 'Semi-Proletarianization and Rural Underdevelopment in the Maritimes', *Canadian Review of Sociology and Anthropology*, vol. 17, no. 3 (1980), pp. 232–45; Johnson, 'Independent Commodity Production'; E. Laclau, 'Feudalism and Capitalism in Latin America', *New Left Review*, no. 67 (1971), pp. 24–6.

24. J. McMahon, 'The New Forest in Nova Scotia', *Round One*, no. 6 (1975).

25. G. Barrett, 'Underdevelopment and Social Movements in the Nova Scotia Fishing Industry to 1938', in R. Brym and J. Sacouman, eds., *Underdevelopment and Social Movements in Atlantic Canada*, Toronto 1979.

26. Laclau, 'Feudalism and Capitalism'.

27. Leys, 'Underdevelopment and Dependency'.

28. Veltmeyer, 'Underdevelopment of Atlantic Canada'.

29. Ibid.

30. Sacouman, 'Semi-Proleterianization'.

31. Veltmeyer, 'Underdevelopment of Atlantic Canada'.

32. Sacouman, 'Semi-Proletarianization'.

33. R. Williams, 'Inshore Fishermen, Unionization and the Struggle Against Undervelopment Today', in Bryan and Sacouman, *Underdevelopment.*

34. For a fuller discussion of this concept, see Sacouman, 'Semi-Proletarianization', and Williams, 'Inshore Fishermen'.

35. Williams, 'Inshore Fishermen'.

36. Another aspect of 'cheap labour' is that fishermen produce *more* as prices drop relative to costs, just to stay even. Wage labour does the opposite. There are examples of companies reverting from wage arrangements with primary producers back to price-for-product arrangements in order to take advantage of this.

37. Sacouman, 'Semi-Proletarianization'.

38. This plant was first visited by MacDonald in 1978 as part of a study for the Marginal Work World Project at the Institute of Public Affairs, Dalhousie University. This was a five-year programme of research funded by the Canada Council, the Department of Health and Welfare and Dalhousie University. Separate interviews were conducted for this paper; however, the earlier research provided background on the industry and the community.

39. J. Sacouman, 'Underdevelopment and the Structural Origins of Antigonish Movement Cooperatives in Eastern Nova Scotia', in Brym and Sacouman, *Underdevelopment.*

40. According to Barrett, in 'Underdevelopment and Social Movements', this was the first wave of centralization and capitalization of the fishing industry, and of the distorted transformation of independent commodity production.

41. See Sacouman, in 'Underdevelopment', for an analysis of the Antigonish Movement and its relationship to underdevelopment.

42. These were multi-purpose boats, doing longlining in fall and winter, seigning in the spring, and swordfish in the summer. These were relatively large boats compared to the typical inshore boat in Nova Scotia. This tradition of bigger boats reflects the fact that there were no good inshore grounds close to Big Harbour; the boats had to be capable of going further out.

43. This pattern has continued and in fact intensified. The cost of buying a new licence and boat is prohibitive and people in the community agree that the inshore fishery is being decimated by attrition. Those who stayed, however, did well.

44. Boat owners average $30,000, whereas crew make $10,000–$30,000 and average $15,000. In this community, this is considered a minimum 'family wage' for an adequate standard of living.

45. It is not clear that the introduction of the ferry was a complete coincidence since the member of the legislature who introduced the bill for the ferry was also the manager of the plant during the period when they were experiencing this labour supply problem. When we speak of Pleasant Bay, we are referring to several small communities side by side on 'the other side of the river'.

46. There is great variance by community. The recent rationalization of the industry has meant better incomes for the fewer bigger-boat fishermen, as in Big Harbour, but the smaller-boat fishermen who remain (and communities dependent on them) have become even more marginalized. Big Harbour tradi-

tionally had larger boats and thus prospered when that became the size necessary to make a good living in the new industry conditions.

47. Here we are pointing to the fact that while individual women do make choices or decisions about entering the labour force, these choices are defined and limited by the economic context within which they are made.

Women's Responses to Economic Restructuring: Changing Gender, Changing Space

1. Both quotes are from homeworkers interviewed as part of a larger project on homework, funded by the Social Science and Humanities Research Council of Canada. Interviews were carried out in the interior of British Columbia and Eastern Ontario in spring of 1985. All the women interviewed in this study were self-employed homeworkers and this is the group to which I am referring when I use the term homeworker.

2. The feminist work includes, for example: Pat Armstrong, *Labour Pains: Women's Work in Crisis*, Toronto 1984; Priscilla Connolly, 'The politics of the informal sector: A Critique', in Nanneke Redclift and Enzo Mingione, eds., *Beyond Employment: Household, Gender and Subsistence*, London 1985, pp. 55–91; Wendy Faulkner and Erik Arnold, eds., *Smothered by Invention: Technology in Women's Lives*, London 1985; Redclift, Nanneke 'The Contested Domain: Gender, Accumulation and the Labour Process', in Redclift and Mingione, pp. 92–125; Hilda Scott, *Working Your Way to the Bottom: The Feminization of Poverty*, London 1984.

Some discussions of the relation between feminist analysis and geography as a whole are: Sophie Bowlby, Jo Foord and Suzanne Mackenzie, 'Feminism and Geography', *Area*, vol. 13, no. 4 (1981), pp. 711–16; Janice Monk and Susan Hanson, 'On Not Excluding Half the Human in Human Geography', *The Professional Geographer*, vol. 34, no. 1 (1982), pp. 11–23; Suzanne Mackenzie, 'Catching Up with Ourselves: Ideas on Developing Gender-sensitive Theory in the Environmental Disciplines', *Women and Environment*, vol. 6, no. 3 (1984), pp. 16–18; Suzanne Mackenzie and Damaris Rose, 'On the Necessity for Feminist Scholarship in Human Geography', *The Professional Geographer*, vol. 34, no. 2 (1982), pp. 220–23; Linda McDowell, 'Some Gloomy Thoughts from Britain', *Women and Environments*, vol. 7, no. 2 (1985), pp. 10–11.

3. Not all feminists would agree with this statement, nor with the subsequent analysis of 'human' which flows from it. Certainly radical feminists, who have been more concerned with 'human nature' and with biological and psychological questions than have socialist feminists, see the project of feminism as more concerned with 'women's liberation', and the nature of human, especially of 'man', as more immutable. See, for example, Angela Miles, 'Feminist Radicalism in the 1980s', *Canadian Journal of Political and Social Theory*, vol. 9, nos. 1–2 (1985), pp. 16–39.

4. This conceptualization of people and environment is related to developments in historical materialist and humanist concepts of human-environmental relations which have developed within or have influenced geography. There are parallels with Bertell Ollman's work on the creation of nature and human nature through environmental appropriation in work: Bertell Ollman, *Alienation: Marx's Conception of Man in Capitalist Society*, Cambridge, 2nd ed., 1976, Anthony Giddens' ebullient discussion of space and time in Anthony Giddens',

Central Problems in Social Theory: Action, Structure and Contradiction in Social Analysis, London 1979, and Anthony Giddens, *A Contemporary Critique of Historical Materialism: Volume 1, Power, Property and the State,* London 1981. In geographical work, this concept is connected to work by Ted Relph, *Rational Landscapes and Humanist Geography,* London 1981 and David Ley and Marwyn Samuels, 'Introduction: Contexts of Modern Humanism in Geography' in Ley and Samuels, *Humanistic Geography: Prospects and Problems,* London 1978 in their concern for intentionality and created meaning in environmental relations, a theme which is also central, although from a different perspective, in Andrew Sayer's 'Epistemology and Conceptions of People and Nature in Geography, *Geoforum,* vol. 10, no. 1 (1979) pp. 19–43.

5. For a fuller discussion of restrictions and alternatives see Dolores Hayden, *The Grand Domestic Revolution: A History of Feminist Designs for American Homes, Neighbourhoods and Cities,* Cambridge, Massachusetts 1982; Matrix, *Making Space: Women and the Man-made Environment,* London 1984. Also see the collection of fiction, Carol Kessler, *Daring to Dream: Utopian Stories by United States Women: 1836–1919,* Boston 1984.

6. Activities of production and reproduction to on in both the wage work sphere and the domestic community sphere. The household and community are sites providing means of reproduction and structuring the process of reproduction. Wage workplaces are also sites of reproduction as well as production.

7. A more detailed discussion of this period is found in Suzanne Mackenzie, *Women and the Reproduction of Labour Power in the Industrial City: A Case Study,* Urban and Regional Studies Working Paper 23, University of Sussex, Brighton 1980.

Some sources utilized in the discussion of pre-industrial and early industrial cities are: Canadian Women's Educational Press Collective, *Women at Work, Ontario, 1850–1930,* Toronto 1974; Michael Cross, ed., *The Workingman in the Nineteenth Century,* Toronto 1974; Peter Goheen, *Victorian Toronto, 1850–1900: Pattern and Process of Growth,* Chicago 1970; National Council of Women of Canada, *Women of Canada: Their Life and Work,* Ottawa 1900.

8. Such organization includes the establishment of Women's Institutes and Co-operative Guilds to improve education and consumer services, groups which pressured for better housing, for family allowances, for nursery schools and extended welfare services. For a discussion of this process in Britain, see Suzanne Mackenzie and Damaris Rose, 'Industrial Change, the Domestic Economy and Home Life', in James Anderson, Simon Duncan and Ray Hudson, eds., *Redundant Spaces in Cities and Regions? Studies in Industrial Decline and Social Change,* London 1983.

9. For discussion of this period see: Pat Armstrong *Labour Pains: Women's Work in Crisis,* ch.3.

10. These conflicts have been documented in work on women and environments. For a review of the geographic literature, emphasizing the empirical work, see Wilbur Zelinsky, Janice Monk and Susan Hanson, 'Women and Geography: A Review and Prospectus', *Progress in Human Geography,* vol. 6, no. 3 (1982), pp. 317–66.

Interdisciplinary collections on women and environment include Suzanne Keller, ed., *Building for Woman,* Lexington, Mass. 1981; Catharine Stimpson, Elsa Dixler, Martha Nelson and Kathryn Yatrakis, eds., *Women and the American City,* Chicago 1981; Gerda Wekerle, Rebecca Peterson and David Morley, eds., *New Space for Women,* Boulder, Colorado 1980.

11. It is difficult to establish the number of people working at home for pay with any precision. According to estimates, between 1980 and 1984, the self-employed category in Canada, which would include the homeworkers interviewed in this study, increased at a faster rate that did the numbers in paid work as a whole. Rates of growth were especially high for women. For example, between 1980 and 1982, numbers of paid workers of both sexes decreased by 4.7 per cent, numbers of self-employed increased by 6.2 per cent and numbers of self-employed women increased by 11.3 per cent. Between 1982 and 1984, numbers of paid workers increased by 5.9 per cent, self-employment by 9.5 per cent, self-employment by women by 20.5 per cent. Jean-Marc Levesque, 'Self-employment in Canada: A Closer Examination', *The Labour Force*, February 1985, pp. 91–105.

In the United States, the Small Business Administration estimated that in 1984 more than 2 million American women were running businesses from their homes. Sharon Johnson, 'When Home Becomes Your Corporate Headquarters', *Working Woman*, October 1984, pp. 75–7.

12. Johnson, 1984; see also Wendy Dennis, 'Mothers who turn Entrepreneur', *Châtelaine*, (September 1984), pp. 52 and 102–6; Phyllis Gillis, 'Enterprising Mothers', *Parents*, (September 1983), pp. 47–54.

13. Homework was in fact a common strategy for Canadian women in the period of transition to monopoly capitalism, both in the form of 'self-employment' and as part of a putting-out system. See, for example, Bettina Bradbury, 'The Family Economy and Work in an Industrializing City: Montreal in the 1870s', *Canadian Historical Association Historical Papers,* 1979; Michael Katz, *The People of Hamilton, Canada West: Family and Class in a Mid-nineteenth-century City,* Cambridge; Mass. 1975.

14. For child care-givers, training ranged from seminars and drop-in centres co-ordinated by family day care agencies with the assistance of statutory bodies or by the Board of Education and Recreation Commissions, through formal adult extension courses in first aid, recreational training and creative education to certificates in early childhood education. For craftworkers, training ranged from seminars given by local artists and crafts councils to university or art school extension courses or degrees in fine arts. Many craftworkers had also travelled and attended numerous shows and conferences.

15. Most frequently mentioned networks for care-givers included drop-in centres for home care-givers or local playgroups and regional or national child-care groups, as well as the *ad hoc* local groups. For craftworkers, most frequently mentioned groups included local craft councils or arts councils, Women's Institutes and *ad hoc* local groups.

16. The majority of homeworkers had carried out some renovation, the amount varying positively with the time they had been doing homework and with their satisfaction with the job. Such renovation varied from redesignating and adding small equipment or minor furniture to the addition or 'finishing' of new rooms or major yard work.

17. For example, home care-givers discussed their neighbourhoods in terms of their capacity to provide safe, accessible play space and public transport or settings for outings. They also assessed the neighbourhood in terms of the number of local families requiring childcare and in terms of the ages of local children, thus measuring the actual and potential market demand for their services. Craftworkers assessed communities in terms of potential markets as well as in terms of available local outlets for their products.

18. Not only have they become to some extent, union issues (see Maureen Fitzgerald, Connie Guberman and Margie Wolfe, eds., *Still Ain't Satisfied: Canadian Feminism Today*, Toronto 1982), but in some cases, childcare is located in the workplace (Martha Friendly and Laura Johnson, *Perspectives on Work-related Day Care*, Child in the City Report 11, Centre for Urban and Community Studies, University of Toronto 1981).

19. In 1983, of children receiving some form of non-family care, home caregivers in Canada were providing care for 84 per cent of children aged two to six and 95 per cent of children under two (Canada, National Health and Welfare, National Day Care Information Centre, *Status of Day Care in Canada, 1983*, Ottawa 1984).

20. See references in note 13, also discussion in Nanneke Redclift and Enzo Mingione, eds., *Beyond Employment: Household, Gender and Subsistence*; also Christine Oppong, 'Women's Roles and Conjugal Family Systems in Ghana', in Eugen Lupri, ed., *The Changing Position of Women in Family and Society: A Cross National Comparison*, Leiden 1983, pp. 331–43; Anna Steyn and J. Uys, 'The Changing Position of Black Women in South Africa', in Lupri, pp. 344–70.

21. Raymond Williams, *Politics and Letters*, London 1971, pp. 150–51.

22. For a fuller discussion of some of these arguments, see Sheila Rowbotham, Lynne Segal and Hilary Wainwright, *Beyond the Fragments: Feminism and the Making of Socialism*, London 1979; also Sheila Rowbotham, 'Women's Liberation and the New Politics', in Michelene Wandor, ed., *The Body Politic: Women's Liberation in Britain, 1969–1972*, London 1972, pp. 3–20.

Women's Emancipation and the Recruitment of Women into the War Effort

1. Barry Broadfoot, *Six War Years 1939–1945: Memories of Canadians at Home and Abroad*, Toronto 1974, p. 353. Work is beginning to be done on the relation of women's wartime employment to the long-term trends in women's participation in the labour force. See Hugh and Pat Armstrong. 'The Segregated Participation of Women in the Canadian Labour Force, 1941–1971', *Canadian Review of Sociology and Anthropology*, vol. 12, no. 4, part 1 (November 1975), pp. 370–84; Paul Phillips, 'Women in the Manitoba Labour Market: A Study of the Changing Economic Role (or "plus ça change, plus le même")', paper given at the Western Canadian Studies Conference, University of Calgary, 27–8 February 1976; and, for the First World War, Ceta Ramkhalawansingh, 'Women during the Great War', in *Women at Work: Ontario 1850–1930*, Toronto 1975, pp. 261–307

2. Betty Friedan, *The Feminine Mystique*, New York 1963. For the impact of *The Feminine Mystique* on Canadian society, see the report of the *Royal Commission on the Status of Women in Canada*, Ottawa 1970, p. 2.

3. Chapter on 'Employment of Women and Day Care of Children' (completed sometime before 24 August 1950), Part 1, pp. 5–6, in the 'History of the Wartime Activities of the Department of Labour', Public Archives of Canada [PAC], RG 35, Series 7, vol 20, file 10. Hereafter cited as 'Wartime History of Employment of Women' or 'Wartime History of Day Care of Children'.

4. 'The Development of the National Selective Service (Civilian) Organization in World War II to 31 December 1945', n.d., p. 7, PAC, RG 35, Series 7, vol. 19, file 2; 'History of the National Employment Service 1939–1945', n.d., p. 5, PAC, RG 35, Series 7, vol. 19, file 3.

5. 'Wartime History of Employment of Women', p. 6.

6. PAC, RG 27, Vol. 605, file 6–24–1, vol. 1.

7. 'Wartime History of Employment of Women', p. 15. Emphasis mine.

8. Government Notice, 8 September 1942, Registration of Women, Order, Department of Labour/National Selective Service, PAC, RG 27, Vol. 605, file 6–24–1, vol. 1. By Order-in-Council PC 1955 (13 March 1942), every employer subject to the Unemployment Insurance Act (7 August 1940) was required to register all persons in his employ on forms provided by the Unemployment Insurance Commission. 'History of the National Employment Service 1939–1945', p. 6.

9. 'Wartime History of Employment of Women', p. 16.

10. 'Listing of Women Starts 14 September, Says Mrs Eaton', *The Globe and Mail*, 21 August 1942, p. 12; 'Mrs Rex Eaton Announces Registration of Canadian Women', PAC, RG 27, Vol. 605, file 6–24–1, vol. 1.

11. Ibid.

12. A. Chapman, 'Female Labour Supply Situation', December 15, 1942, PAC, RG 27, Vol. 605, file 6–24–1, vol. 1.

13. Ibid.

14. General Report on National Selective Service – Employment of Women, 1 November 1943, PAC, RG 27, Vol. 605, file 6–24–1, vol. 2.

15. Chapman, 'Female Labour Supply Situation', 15 December 1942.

16. General Report on NSS – Employment of Women, 1 November 1943.

17. 'Wartime History of Employment of Women', p. 8.

18. General Report on NSS – Employment of Women, 1 November 1943.

19. A. Chapman's phraseology.

20. Letter of 18 May 1943, from Mary Eadie, Supervisor, Women's Division, Employment and Selective Service Office, Toronto, to Mrs Norman C. Stephens, President, Local Council of Women, Toronto, PAC, RG 27, Vol. 605, file 6–24–1, vol. 1.

21. General Report on NSS – Employment of Women, 1 November 1943.

22. 'Wartime History of Employment of Women', p. 20.

23. Memorandum of 7 May 1943, from Mary Eadie, Supervisor, Women's Division, Toronto, to Mr B. G. Sullivan, Ontario NSS Regional Superintendent, PAC RG 27, Vol. 605, file 6–24–1, vol. 1.

24. 'Wartime History of Employment of Women', p. 20.

25. Report on Recruitment of Part-time Workers – Toronto, by Mrs Rex Eaton to the NSS Advisory Board, 28 July 1943, PAC, RG 27, Vol. 605, file 6–24–1, vol. 1.

26. Letter of 22 May 1943, from Mary Eadie to Mrs Rex Eaton, PAC, RG 27, Vol. 605, file 6–24–1, vol. 2.

27. The National Council of Women of Canada is a federation of women's organizations, organized nationally, provincially, and locally. For its early history, see Veronica Strong-Boag, *The Parliament of Women: The National Council of Women in Canada, 1893–1929*, Ottawa 1976.

28. Letter of 8 September 1943, from Mrs Rex Eaton to Mrs H. L. Stewart of the Local Council of Women, Halifax, PAC, RG 27, Vol. 605, file 6–24–1, vol. 2.

29. Report on Recruitment of Part-time Workers – Toronto, by Mrs Rex Eaton to the NSS Advisory Board, 28 July 1943.

30. 'Wartime History of Employment of Women', p. 22.

31. Report on Recruitment of Part-time Workers – Toronto, by Mrs Rex Eaton to the NSS Advisory Board, 28 July 1943.

32. NSS Circular No. 270–71, 18 August 1943, Employment of Women – Campaign for Part-time Women Workers, PAC, RG 27, Vol. 605, file 6–24–1, vol. 2.

33. Draft letter of 31 August 1943, signed by Mr A. MacNamara and Mrs Rex Eaton to be sent to Local Councils of Women, PAC, RG 27, Vol. 605, file 6–24–1, vol. 2.

34. 'Appeal to Women to Take Part-time jobs in Essential Civilian Work', radio address, 20 September 1943, Public Archives of Nova Scotia, RG 35–102, Elective Municipal Government Records, Series 2, Section B. Vol. 16, no. 178, Correspondence of the Mayor of Halifax with the Women's Voluntary Services, 1943–5.

35. 'Wartime History of Employment of Women', p. 23.

36. Ibid., pp. 20–21.

37. Draft letter of 31 August 1943, signed by Mr A. MacNamara and Mrs Rex Eaton, to be sent to Local Councils of Women.

38. 'Wartime History of Employment of Women', p. 24.

39. Mrs Rex Eaton's Report to the NSS Advisory Board on Recruitment of Women for Work in War Industries, 28 July 1943, PAC, RG 27, Vol. 605, file 6–24–1, vol. 1.

40. Letter of 16 August 1943, from B. G. Sullivan, Ontario Regional Superintendent, to Mrs Rex Eaton, PAC, RG 27, Vol. 605, file 6–24–1, vol. 2.

41. Minutes of 26 July 1943, Toronto, meeting of NSS with local Employers about the Campaign for War Plants, PAC, RG 27, Vol. 605, file 6–24–1, vol. 2.

42. Letter of 1 September 1943, from Mrs Rex Eaton, to Mr A. Mac-Namara, with copy to Humphrey Mitchell, PAC, RG 27, Vol. 605, file 6–24–1, vol. 2.

43. Memorandum of 22 September 1943, from Mrs Rex Eaton, to Mr A. MacNamara, PAC, RG 27, Vol. 605, file 6–24–1, vol. 2.

44. Letter of 13 October 1943, from Mrs Eaton to Mme Florence F. Martel, NSS, Montreal, PAC, RG 27, Vol. 605, file 6–24–1, vol. 2

45. 'Wartime History of Employment of Women', p. 23.

46. Minutes of Employers' Committee Meeting held on 2 November 1943, in Mr Leonard Prefontaine's office, re Recruiting Campaign for Women War Workers, PAC, RG 27, Vol. 1508, file 40–5–1.

47. Letter of 2 December 1943, from V. C. Phelan, Director of Information, Information Division, Department of Labour, to Mr MacNamara, PAC, RG 27, Vol. 615, file 17–5–11, vol. 1.

48. 'Wartime History of Employment of Women', p. 25.

49. Memorandum of 8 May 1944, from Mrs Rex Eaton, to Mr A. Mac-Namara, PAC, RG 27, Vol. 605, file 6–24–1, vol. 3.

50. 'Wartime History of Employment of Women', p. 25.

51. Letter of 8 August 1944, from Gordon Anderson, Public Relations Officer, Department of Labour, to Mr Arthur MacNamara, Deputy Minister, Department of Labour, PAC, RG 27, Vol. 615, file 17-5-11, vol. 1.

52. 'Wartime History of Employment of Women', p. 26.

53. Ibid.

54. Memorandum of 25 July 1944, from Mrs Kate Lyons, Supervisor of Women's Work, Edmonton, to Mrs Rex Eaton, PAC, RG 27, Vol. 605, file 6–24–1, vol. 3.

55. NSS Report on 'Wartime Employment of Women in Canadian Agriculture', 17 August 1944, PAC, RG 27, Vol. 985, file 7.

56. Ibid.

57. Although the war did see a rise in the collective provision of domestic services, such as communal kitchens and commercial laundries, their main purpose was to ease the burden on women working outside the home in essential industries, who still had primary responsibility for their families' domestic chores.

58. *Labour Gazette*, vol. 42 (1942).

59. Issued by Public Information, for National Salvage Office, Ottawa, under authority of Hon. J. G. Gardiner, Minister of National War Services, PAC, APC C-87541.

60. PAC, Department of National War Services, RG 44, Vol. 34, file 'Appointment of a Director'; Department of National War Services, 'Wartime History of the Women's Voluntary Services Division', PAC, RG 35, Series 7, Vol. 18.

61. Alice Sorby, 'A Volunteer Bureau Emerges', *Junior League Magazine*, October 1940, pp. 51–2.

62. PAC, RG 44, Vol. 6, file 'Canadian Women's Voluntary Services (Ontario Division)', Vol. 34, file 'WVS – Reorganization'.

63. Thelma LeCocq, 'Lady in Control', *Maclean's*, 1 August 1942, pp. 7, 29–30, RG 44, Vol. 3, file 'Fats Salvage Advisory Committee'.

64. Marjorie Wispear, 'Canadian Women Take to the Block Plan', *National Home Monthly*, July 1943, pp. 45–6.

65. 'Christmas "Warsages" by WVS', *Saturday Night*, 16 December 1944, p. 31.

66. PAC, RG 44, Vol. 34, file 'National Week'.

67. PAC, RG 44, Vol. 33, Women's Voluntary Services General, vol. 11.

68. BC Provincial Archives, Add. MSS. 174, vol. 1, Women's Institute, Burton, BC, Minute Books, 1912–50, Meeting of 28 September 1942.

69. 'Report on War Services, FWIC, 1943–45', presented June 1945 by Convenor for War Services for the FWIC, Mrs E. E. Morton, Vegreville, Alberta PAC, RG 44, vol. 45, file 'Women's Institute – Alberta'; 'Mrs E. E. Morton of Vegreville to Give War Services Report', *Edmonton Journal*, 2 June 1945.

70. Women's Voluntary Services, Regina Centre, 'Report of Voluntary Services in Regina, 1941–46', Provincial Archives of Saskatchewan. See also Joyce Hibbert, ed., *The War Brides*, Toronto 1978.

71. Lillian D. Millar, 'Price Control Depends Largely on the Women', *Saturday Night*, 10 October 1942, p. 20; Lillian D. Millar, 'Has this Structure of a Million Women Post-War Potentialities?', *Saturday Night*, 8 July 1944, pp. 22–3.

72. For an excellent account of its composition and functioning, see Gail Cuthbert Brandt, '"Pigeon-Holed and Forgotten": The Work of the Sub-committee on the Post-War Problems of Women, 1943', *Histoire sociale/Social History*, vol. 15, no. 29 (May 1982), pp. 239–59.

73. PAC, MG 28, I 25, Vol. 83, letter of 23 April 1943, from Jessie I. A. Archer, Corresponding Secretary, Local Council of Women of Toronto, to Miss Beatrice Barber, Honorary Corresponding Secretary, National Council of Women.

74. PAC, MG 28, I 25, Vol. 85, letter of 14 March 1944, to Humphrey

Mitchell, Minister of Labour, from Miss Beatrice Barber, Honorary Corresponding Secretary, National Council of Women; letter of 24 March 1944, to Miss Beatrice Barber, Honorary Corresponding Secretary, National Council of Women, from H. R. L. Henry, Private Secretary, Office of the Prime Minister.

75. Clement W. Cook, 'Problems of the Wartime Advertising Campaign', *Canadian Business* (March 1944), pp. 56–7, 170, 172.

76. *Maclean's*, 15 November 1942, p. 50.

77. Poster C 94056, PAC, Picture Archives Branch.

78. *Maclean's*, 1 April 1943, p. 44.

79. *National Home Monthly*, August 1943, p. 34.

80. *Maclean's*, 15 May 1942, p. 48.

81. Poster C 93633, PAC, Picture Archives Branch.

82. *Maclean's*, 1 July 1942, p. 28.

83. General Report of NSS – Employment of Women, 1 November 1943.

84. 'Wartime History of Employment of Women', p. 8.

85. 'Comments re Wartime Programme', p. 5, Preface to 'Wartime History of Employment of Women'.

86. NSS Report on 'Wartime Employment of Women in Canadian Agriculture', 17 April 1944.

87. Draft letter of 31 August 1943, signed by Mr A. MacNamara and Mrs Rex Eaton, to be sent to Local Councils of Women.

88. NSS Circular No. 270–1, 18 August 1943, Employment of Women – Campaign for Part-time Women Workers.

89. December 1943 Design for Full-page Newspaper Ad. to Recruit Women for War Industry, PAC, RG 27, Vol. 615, file 17–5–11, vol. 1.

90. Memorandum of 9 May 1944, from Mrs Rex Eaton, to Mr A. MacNamara, with Suggested Draft Circular re Tightening of NSS Regulations for Women, PAC, RG 27, Vol. 605, file 6–24–1, vol. 3.

91. Moffats 'Help Wanted' Campaign Breaking 20 July 1944, PAC, RG 27, Vol. 615, file 17–5–11, vol. 1.

92. Memorandum of 5 March 1943, from Renée Morin, NSS Montreal, to Mrs Rex Eaton, PAC, RG 27, Vol. 605, file 6–24–1, vol. 1.

93. Letter of 8 April 1943, from B. G. Sullivan, Ontario Regional Superintendent, NSS, to Mrs Rex Eaton, PAC, RG 27, Vol. 605, file 6–24–1, vol. 1. Unfortunately, Sullivan's report of the questionnaire results does not give the number of women questioned.

94. Memorandum of 11 May 1943, from Percy A. Robert, Montreal, to Mrs Eaton and Mr Goulet, PAC, RG 27, Vol. 605, file 6–24–1, vol. 1.

95. Memorandum of 30 April 1943, from Dr F. H. Sexton, Director of Technical Education, Department of Education, Technical Education Branch, Province of Nova Scotia, PAC, RG 27, Vol. 605, file 6–24–1, vol. 1.

96. December 1943 Design for Full-Page Newspaper Ad. to Recruit Women for War Industry.

97. PAC, RG 27, Vol. 615, file 17–5–11, vol. 1.

98. 'The Income Tax Change Applying to Married Employees in 1947', n.d., PAC, RG 27, Vol. 66, file 6–24–11.

99. Letter of 7 November 1946, from A. MacNamara, Deputy Minister of Labour, to Mr Fraser Elliott, Deputy Minister of National Revenue, PAC, RG 27, Vol. 606, file 6–24–11.

100. 'Income Tax Change Benefits Employed Married Women/Aims to Keep Wives from Quitting Posts', *The Globe and Mail*, 16 July 1942, p. 1.

101. Explanation received from the Minister of Finance, J. L. Ilsley, by Douglas Hallam, Secretary of the Primary Textiles Institute, Toronto, and conveyed in his letter of 4 November 1946, to Humphrey Mitchell, Minister of Labour, and in his letter of 13 November 1946, to A. MacNamara, Deputy Minister of Labour, PAC, RG 27, Vol. 606, file 6–24–11.

102. Full-page advertisement 'To the Man and Wife Who Are Both Working', *London Free Press*, 26 December 1946, promoted through the Employer Relations Division of the Unemployment Insurance Commission Office, London, Ontario, and sponsored by the London Chamber of Commerce, PAC, RG 27, Vol. 606, file 6–24–11.

103. Minutes of the 24 January 1947, Meeting of the Vernon Local Employment Committee, a copy of which was sent to officials in the Departments of Labour and National Revenue, PAC, RG 27, Vol. 606 file 6–24–11.

104. J. R. Moodie Company, Hamilton. Information conveyed in memorandum of 17 April 1947, from Margaret McIrvine, Acting Regional Employment Adviser, UIC, Toronto, to B. G. Sullivan, Ontario Regional Superintendent, PAC, RG 27, Vol. 606, file 6–24–11.

105. Memorandum of 31 December 1946, from George G. Greene, Private Secretary, Department of Labour, to A. MacNamara, Deputy Minister of Labour, PAC, RG 27, Vol. 606, file 6–24–11.

106. Memorandum of 30 January 1947, from W. L. Forrester, Manager, Local Employment Office, Prince George, B.C., to William Horrobin, Pacific Regional Employment Officer, PAC, RG 27, Vol. 606, file 6–24–11.

107. School Board of Charlotte County, New Brunswick. Information communicated in a telegram of 7 November 1946, from A. N. McLean, Saint John, New Brunswick, to A. MacNamara, Deputy Minister of Labour, PAC, RG 27, Vol. 606, file 6–24–11.

108. T. Eaton Company Ltd., Toronto, reported that 453 married women had left their employ since 1 January 1947. Information in a letter of 26 April 1947, from G. W. Ritchie, Chairman, Ontario Regional Advisory Board (Department of Labour), to A. MacNamara, Deputy Minister of Labour, PAC, RG 27, Vol. 606, file 6–24–11.

109. Letter of 12 February 1947, from A. MacNamara, to F. Smelts, Chairman, Pacific Regional Advisory Board, Department of Labour, PAC, RG 27, Vol. 606, file 6–24–11.

110. Letter of 13 November 1946, to A. MacNamara, from Douglas Hallam, Secretary, Primary Textiles Institute, Toronto, PAC, RG 27, Vol. 606, file 6–24–11.

111. 'The Income Tax Change Applying to Married Employees in 1947', n.d., PAC, RG 27, Vol. 606, file 6–24–11.

112. Ten Points Enumerated in the Prime Minister's Speech of 24 March 1942, with a View to Bringing Women into Industry, PAC, RG 27, Vol. 605, file 6–24–1, vol. 1.

113. According to the 1931 census, there were 128,132 married women, including those divorced or widowed, who were gainfully occupied. Less than half that number were married women living with their husbands. In 1941, the single women who were working outside their own homes numbered about 688,000, and the others, 166,000. Letters of 23 September 1943, from the Chief, Legislation Branch, Department of Labour, Ottawa, to Miss Marion Royce, Secretary for Young Adult Membership, World's Young Women's

Christian Association, Washington, DC, PAC, RG 27, Vol. 610, file 6–52–2, vol. 2.

114. Memorandum of 13 June 1942, from Mrs Rex Eaton, to Mr George Greene, Private Secretary to the Minister of Labour, Ottawa, PAC, RG 27, Vol. 609, file 6–52–1, vol. 1

115. Report on Day Care of Children, 1 July 1943, PAC, RG 27, Vol. 609, file 6–52–1, vol. 1

116. Mrs Eaton's memorandum of 13 June 1942, to Mr George Greene.

117. 'Need for Day Nurseries', editorial, *The Globe and Mail*, 16 July 1942, p. 6.

118. Mrs Eaton's memorandum of 13 June 1942, to Mr George Greene.

119. Letter of 30 April 1942, from E. M. Little, Director of NSS, to G. S. Tattle, Deputy Minister, Department of Public Welfare, Ontario, PAC, RG 27, Vol. 611, file 6–52–1, vol. 1.

120. Letter of 14 May 1942, from Fraudena Eaton, to E. M. Little, Director of NSS, PAC, RG 27, Vol. 609, file 6–52–1, vol. 1.

121. Letter of 28 April 1942, from George F. Davidson, Executive Director, Canadian Welfare Council, to Mr E. M. Little, Director, NSS, PAC, RG 27, Vol. 609, file 6–52–1, vol. 1.

122. Memorandum of 30 April 1942, to E. M. Little, Director of NSS, and R. F. Thompson, Supervisor of Training, Training Branch, Department of Labour, subject: conference with Dr W. E. Blatz, Director of the Institute of Child Study of the University of Toronto, PAC, RG 27, Vol. 609, file 6–52–1, vol. 1.

123. Report on 'Day Care of Children', 1 July 1943, no authorship specified, PAC, RG 27, Vol. 609, file 6–52–1, vol. 1.

124. Letter of 17 March 1943, from Miss Margaret Grier, Assistant Director NSS, to H. F. Caloren, Assistant Director of Administrative Services, Department of Labour, PAC, RG 27, vol. 609, file 6–52–1, vol. 1.

125. Memorandum of 10 November 1943, from Mrs Rex Eaton, to Mr V. C. Phelan, Director of Information, Information Division, Department of Labour, PAC, RG 27, Vol. 609, file 6–52–1, vol. 1.

126. Letter of 27 April 1944, from Mrs E. C. (Marjorie) Pardee, Representative of NSS on the Albertan Provincial Advisory Committee on Day Nurseries, to Mrs Rex Eaton, PAC, RG 27, Vol. 611, file 6–52–9.

127. PAC, RG 27, Vol. 611, file 6–52–9.

128. Mothers were charged fees under the agreement. For day nursery care, mothers in Ontario paid 35 cents per day for the first child, 15 cents for additional children; in Québec, 35 cents per day for the first child, 20 cents for additional children. Where both parents were working, the fee was 50 cents per child. For day-care of school children, mothers in Ontario were charged 25 cents per day for the first child, 10 cents for additional children. No school projects were established in Québec. Memorandum of 27 May 1943, from Mrs Rex Eaton, to Mr George Greene, Private Secretary to the Minister of Labour, PAC, RG 27, Vol. 609, file 6–52–1, vol. 1.

129. Memorandum of 8 February 1943, from Mrs Rex Eaton, to Mr A. MacNamara, PAC, RG 27, Vol. 609, file 6–52–1, vol. 1.

130. Letter of 17 March 1943, from Miss Margaret Grier, to H. F. Caloren, Assistant Director of Administrative Services, Department of Labour, PAC, RG 27, Vol. 609, file 6–52–1, vol. 1.

131. 'Wartime History of Day Care of Children', p. 3, PAC, RG 35, series 7,

vol. 20, file 10; Memorandum of 8 February 1943, from Mrs Rex Eaton, to Mr A. MacNamara, PAC, RG 27, Vol. 609, file 6–52–1, vol. 1.

132. Memorandum of 16 June 1943, from Mrs Eaton, to Mr Eric Strangroom, in response to request for information on day nurseries for the Minister of Labour, PAC, RG 27, Vol. 609, file 6–52–1, vol. 1; NSS Circular No. 291, 15 October 1943, on Women Workers – Day Care of Children, PAC, RG 27, Vol. 610, file 6–52–2, vol. 2.

133. Memorandum of 4 March 1943, from Mrs Rex Eaton, to Mr A. Mac-Namara, PAC, RG 27, Vol. 610, file 6–52–2, vol. 2.

134. July 1943 Monthly Summary of Dominion-Provincial Wartime Day Nurseries, Ontario, PAC, RG 27, Vol. 611, file 6–52–6–1, vol. 1.

135. September 1943 Monthly Summary of Dominion-Provincial Wartime Day Nurseries, Ontario, PAC, RG 27, Vol. 611, file 6–52–6–1, vol. 1.

136. Mary Weeks, 'Nursery Schools in Canada Have Come to Stay', *Saturday Night*, 26 February 1944, p. 4; Marjorie Winspear, 'The New Fashioned Woman: Angels in Nurseries', *National Home Monthly*, February 1943, pp. 44–6; Frances Thompson, 'On the Kitchen Front: Nursery Nutrition', *National Home Monthly*, February 1943, pp. 36–8; Anne Fromer, 'Caring for Children of War-Working Mothers', *Saturday Night*, 24 October 1942, pp. 22–3.

137. Memorandum of 10 November 1944, from Mrs Rex Eaton, to Mr V. C. Phelan, PAC, RG 27, Vol. 609, file 6–52–1, vol. 1.

138. Survey of the Dominion-Provincial Wartime Day Nursery Programme in Ontario, submitted on 29 October 1945, to Mr B. Beaumont, Director of Child Welfare, Department of Public Welfare, Ontario, by Miss Dorothy A. Millichamp, Organizing Secretary, Wartime Day Nurseries, Department of Public Welfare, Ontario, PAC, RG 27, Vol. 611, file 6–52–6–1, vol. 3.

139. Report of the Québec Ministry of Health on the Dominion-Provincial Wartime Day Nurseries, 15 November 1946, PAC, RG 27, Vol. 611, file 6–52–5–2, vol. 2.

140. Memorandum of 7 July 1945, from Margaret Grier, to Miss Norris, PAC, RG 27, Vol. 609, file 6–52–1, vol. 2.

141. Letter of 30 April 1942, from E. M. Little, Director of NSS, to G. S. Tattle, Deputy Minister, Department of Public Welfare, Ontario, PAC, RG 27, Vol. 611, file 6–52–6–1, vol. 1.

142. Memorandum of 22 May 1942, on Proposals for Day Nurseries for Mothers Working in War Industry, for file in Deputy Minister's Office, Department of Labour, PAC, RG 27, Vol. 609, file 6–52–1, vol. 1.

143. Memorandum of 13 June 1942, from Mrs Rex Eaton, to Mr E. M. Little, Director, NSS, PAC, RG 27, Vol. 609, file 6–52–1, vol. 1.

144. 'Wartime History of Day Care of Children', Appendix, Part 2.

145. NSS Circular No. 291, October 15 1943, on Women Workers – Day Care of Children.

146. Report on 'Day Care of Children', 1 July 1943.

147. PAC, RG 27, Vol. 610, file 6–52–2, vol. 1.

148. Minutes of the 10 June 1943, Conference on the Day Care of Children, Confederation Building, Ottawa, PAC, RG 27, Vol. 609, file 6–52–1, vol. 1.

149. Memorandum of 19 May 1943, from Mrs Eaton, to Mr A. Mac-Namara, PAC, RG 27, Vol. 610, file 6–52–2, vol. 1, and RG 27, vol. 1508, file 40–5–6.

150. 'An Inequitable Division', editorial, *The Globe and Mail*, 28 October 1943, p. 6.

151. Memorandum of 1 December 1943, from Mrs Rex Eaton, to Mr A. MacNamara, PAC, RG 27, Vol. 610, file 6–52–2, vol. 3.

152. Ibid.

153. Memorandum of 22 November 1943, from Mrs Rex Eaton, to Mr A. MacNamara, PAC, RG 27, Vol. 1508, file 40–5–6.

154. Memorandum of 1 December 1943, from Mrs Rex Eaton, to Mr A. MacNamara.

155. Order-in-Council PC 2503, 6 April 1944, PAC, RG 27, Vol. 610, file 6–52–2, vol. 4; Order-in-Council PC 3733, 18 May 1944, PAC, RG 27, Vol. 610, file 6–52–2, vol. 5.

156. PAC, RG 27, Vol. 609, file 6–52–1, vol. 2.

157. Memorandum of 30 August 1945, from W. S. Boyd, National Registration, Department of Labour, Ottawa, to Mrs Rex Eaton, PAC, RG 27, Vol. 609, file 6–52–1, vol. 2.

158. PAC, RG 27, Vol. 609, file 6–52–1, vol. 2.

159. Ibid.

160. Letter of 20 September 1945, from Miss Gwyneth Howell, Assistant Executive Director, Montreal Council of Social Agencies, to Miss Margaret Grier, PAC, RG 27, Vol. 611, file 6–52–5–2, vol. 2.

161. Letter of 3 October 1945, from Renée Morin, NSS Welfare Officer, to Miss M. Grier, PAC, RG 27, Vol. 611, file 6–52–1, vol. 2.

162. PAC, RG 27, Vol. 609, file 6–52–1, vol. 2.

163. Letter of 3 October 1945, from Renée Morin, NSS Welfare Officer, Montreal, to Miss M. Grier, PAC, RG 27, Vol. 611, file 6–52–5–2, vol. 2.

164. Memorandum of 11 September 1945, from Mrs Rex Eaton, to Mr Arthur MacNamara, PAC, RG 27, Vol. 609, file 6–52–1, vol. 2.

165. Letter of 22 October 1945, from B. W. Heise, Deputy Minister, Department of Public Welfare, Ontario, to Mrs Rex Eaton; letter of 29 October 1945, from A. MacNamara, to Mr B. W. Heise, PAC, RG 27, Vol. 609, file 6–52–1, vol. 2.

166. Memorandum of 8 November 1945, from Mrs Rex Eaton, to Mr Arthur MacNamara, PAC, RG 27, Vol. 609, file 6–52–1, vol. 2.

167. Ibid.

168. Memorandum of 9 November 1945, from A. MacNamara, to Mrs Rex Eaton, PAC, RG 27, Vol. 609, file 6–52–1, vol. 2.

169. Letter of 22 November 1945, from A. MacNamara, to Mr B. W. Heise, Deputy Minister, Department of Public Welfare, Ontario, PAC, RG 27, Vol. 609, file 6–52–1, vol. 2.

170. Ibid.

171. Letter of 17 December 1945, from Mary Eadie, Supervisor, Women's Division, Unemployment Insurance Commission, Toronto, to Miss Margaret Grier, Assistant Associate Director, NSS, Ottawa, PAC, RG 27, Vol. 611, file 6–52–6–1, vol. 3.

172. Memorandum of 15 February 1946, from Margaret Grier, to Mr. Arthur MacNamara, PAC, RG 27, Vol. 609, file 6–52–1, vol. 2.

173. Letter of 18 February 1946, from Fraudena Eaton, Vancouver, to Mr. A. MacNamara, Deputy Minister of Labour, Ottawa, PAC, RG 27, Vol. 609, file 6–52–1, vol. 2.

174. Emphasis mine. Letter of 26 February 1946, from Humphrey Mitchell, Minister of Labour, Ottawa, to W. A. Goodfellow, Minister of Public Welfare, Province of Ontario, PAC, RG 27, Vol. 609, file 6–52–1, vol. 2.

175. Letter of 7 March 1946, from W. A. Goodfellow, Minister of Public Welfare, Ontario, to Humphrey Mitchell, Minister of Labour, Ottawa, PAC, RG 27, Vol. 609, file 6–52–1, vol. 2.

176. Letter of 2 April 1946, from Humphrey Mitchell, to W. A. Goodfellow, PAC, RG 27, Vol. 609, file 6–52–1, vol. 2.

177. Bill No. 124, An Act respecting Day Nurseries, 1946, PAC, RG 27, Vol. 609, file 6–52–1, vol. 2.

178. Letter of 17 May 1946, from W. A. Goodfellow, Minister of Public Welfare, Ontario, to Humphrey Mitchell, Minister of Labour, Ottawa, PAC, RG 27, Vol. 611, file 6–52–6–1, vol. 3.

179. Letter of 17 May 1946, from Mrs G. D. (Beatrice H.) Kirkpatrick, Chairman, Board of Directors, United Welfare Chest, A Federation of Greater Toronto's Social Services, Welfare Council Department, to Humphrey Mitchell, PAC, RG 27, Vol. 611, file 6–52–6–1, vol. 3.

180. Letter of 29 May 1946, from Mrs G. D. (Beatrice H.) Kirkpatrick, Chairman, Board of Directors, Welfare Council Department, United Welfare Chest, A Federation of Greater Toronto's Social Services, to Humphrey Mitchell, PAC, RG 27, Vol. 611, file 6–52–6–1, vol. 3.

181. Letter of 21 May 1946, from Humphrey Mitchell, Minister of Labour, Ottawa, to Brooke Claxton, Minister of National Health and Welfare, Ottawa, PAC, RG 27, Vol. 611, file 6–52–6–1, vol. 3.

182. Letter of 7 June 1946, from Brooke Claxton, to Humphrey Mitchell, PAC, RG 27, Vol. 11, file 6–52–6–1, vol. 3.

183. Letter of 12 June 1946, from Humphrey Mitchell, to W. A. Goodfellow, Minister of Public Welfare, Ontario, PAC, RG 27, Vol. 611, file 6–52–6–1, vol. 3.

184. Memorandum of 28 November 1946, from J. C. McK., to Mr. Mac-Namara, PAC, RG 27, Vol. 611, file 6–52–6–1, vol. 4. For information on post-war centres, see Patricia Vanderbelt Schulz, 'Day Care in Canada, 1850–1962', in Kathleen Gallagher Ross, ed., *Good Day Care: Fighting for It, Getting It, Keeping It*, (Toronto 1978), pp. 137–58.

185. Report on 'Day Care of Children', 1 July 1943, PAC, RG 27, Vol. 609, file 6–52–1, vol. 1.

186. Ibid.

187. Letter of 4 April 1946, from Mrs Rex Eaton, Associate Director, to Miss R. M. Grier, Assistant Associate Director, National Employment Service, Ottawa, PAC, RG 27, Vol. 609, file 6–52–1, vol. 2.

188. Marie T. Wadden, 'Newspaper Response to Female War Employment: *The Globe and Mail* and *Le Devoir* May–October 1942' (history honours dissertation, Memorial University of Newfoundland, May 1976).

189. 'Wartime History of Employment of Women', pp. 80–81. In February 1944, Mrs Eaton estimated the number of women in the labour force at approximately 600,000 in 1939, rising to 1,200,000 by early 1944. Letter of 2 February 1944, from Mrs Rex Eaton, Associate Director NSS, to Mrs J. E. M. Bruce, Convenor, Trades and Professions Committee, Local Council of Women, Victoria, BC, PAC, RG 27, Vol. 605, file 6–24–1, vol. 3.

Working at Home

1. Bonnie Fox, ed., *Hidden in the Household: Women's Domestic Labour Under Capitalism*, Toronto 1980; Meg Luxton, *More than a Labour of Love:*

Three Generations of Women's Work in the Home, Toronto 1980.

2. *Women Unite!*, Women's Press, ed., Toronto 1972.

3. Peggy Morton, 'Women's Work Is Never Done', in *Women Unite!*

4. Meg Luxton notes that the term 'domestic labour' appears to have been first applied to women's work in the home in an article by Wally Seccombe, 'The Housewife and Her Labour under Capitalism', *New Left Review*, no. 83 (1974), pp. 3–24.

5. According to Eva Kaluzynska over fifty articles have been published in this debate in the socialist and feminist press alone in the past decade. For a partial list see her article, 'Wiping the Floor with Theory – a Survey of Writings on Housework', *in Feminist Review*, no. 6 (1980), pp. 27–54.

6. Ibid. p. 27.

7. Alice Clark, *Working Life of Women in the Seventeenth Century*, London 1919, p. 118.

8. Karl Marx, *Capital*, Volume 1, Chicago 1906, p. 190–91.

9. The debate on the transition from feudalism to capitalism was sparked by Maurice Dobb's *Studies in the Development of Capitalism*, New York: New World Paperbacks, 1947. The responses have been republished in Paul Sweezy, ed., *The Transition from Feudalism to Capitalism*, London 1976. An interesting account of a different sort is C. H. George's 'The Making of the English Bourgeoisie 1500–1750', *Science and Society*, 1971, pp. 385–414. Discussion comparing women's work in feudalism, pre-industrial capitalism and industrial capitalism can be found in Alice Clark; Roberta Hamilton, *The Liberation of Women*, London 1978; Ann Oakley, *Women's Work: The Housewife Past and Present*, New York 1974; and Eli Zaretsky, *Capitalism, the Family and Personal Life*, Santa Cruz 1973. See also the recently published article by Chris Middleton, 'Peasants, Patriarchy and the Feudal Mode of Production in England', parts 1 and 2, *Sociological Review*, vol. 29, no. 1 (1981), pp. 105–54, for a graphic illustration of the complexity and variation over space and time of feudal society and the place of women within it. Seccombe's dismissal of Laslett in a footnote without citing the sources he uses to do so is another example of his rather cavalier approach to historical materials.

10. My phrasing here is, of course, a direct steal from E. P. Thompson, 'The Peculiarities of the English', in John Saville and Ralph Miliband, *The Socialist Register, 1965*, London 1965.

11. Clark; Bettina Bradbury, 'The Family Economy and Work in an Industrializing City; Montreal in the 1870's', in *Historical Papers*, 1979, pp. 71–96. Suzanne Cross, 'The Neglected Majority: The Changing Role of Women in 19th Century Montreal', in Alison Prentice and Susan Mann Trofimenkoff, eds., *The Neglected Majority*, Toronto 1977, pp. 66–86; Ruth Pierson's 'Women's Emancipation and the Recruitment of Women into the Labour Force in World War II', in *The Neglected Majority*, pp. 125–45 and Ceta Ramkhalawansingh's 'Women during the Great War', in Janice Acton *et al.*, *Women at work 1850–1930*, Toronto 1974, pp. 261–308, are useful studies showing the attempts by the Canadian government to draw women into the labour force during the wars and usher them out again after.

Fox also fails to draw upon either of the two major Canadian studies that deal with her question. Patricia Connelly's *Last Hired, First Fired*, Toronto 1978, is barely mentioned while Pat and Hugh Armstrong's *The Double Ghetto*, Toronto 1978, is ignored.

12. This constitutes a very basic argument within contemporary Marxism. See E. P. Thompson, *The Poverty of Theory*, London 1978, and Perry Anderson, *Arguments within English Marxism*, London 1980.

13. Curtis does not consider the recent historical interpretations on either side of this question. Although it is very recent some of it was available in time for citation by Seccombe (p. 98, fn. 60). See Michèle Barrett and Mary McIntosh, 'The Family Wage: Some Problems for Socialists and Feminists', *Capital and Class*, Summer 1980, pp. 51–2; Hilary Land, 'The Family Wage', *Feminist Review*, no. 6 (1980), pp. 55–78. Jane Humphries's most recent contribution to the interpretation espoused by Curtis is 'Protective Legislation, the Capitalist State, and Working-Class Men: The Case of the 1842 Mines Regulation Act', *Feminist Review*, no. 7 (Spring 1981), pp. 1–34.

14. Armstrong.

15. See, for example, Ann Oakley, *The Sociology of Housework*, Bath 1974; Hannah Gavron, *The Captive Wife*, London 1966.

16. Laura Oren, 'The Welfare of Women in Labouring Families: England 1860–1950', in M. Hartman and L. W. Banner, eds., *Clio's Consciousness Raised: New Perspectives on the History of Women*, New York 1974.

17. For different perspectives on these relationships see, for example, Nancy Chodorow, *The Reproduction of Mothering*, California 1978; Dorothy Dinnerstein, *The Mermaid and the Minotaur*, New York 1977; Gad Horowitz, *Repression: Basic and Surplus Repression in Psychoanalytic Theory: Freud, Reich and Marcuse*, Toronto 1977; Gayle Rubin, 'The Traffic in Women' in Rayna Reiter, ed., *Toward an Anthropology of Women*, New York 1975.

18. Ibid.

19. See Zillah Eisenstein's *The Radical Future of Liberal Feminism*, New York 1981, for a good discussion of this potential.

Reply to Bruce Curtis

John McMullan helped me to develop and clarify my ideas. I am grateful to him and to Pat Armstrong and Susan Russell for their critical reading of an earlier draft and their many helpful suggestions.

1. Lise Vogel, *Science and Society* (Spring 1982), pp. 94–7.

2. Raymond Williams, *Keywords*, London 1976, p. 267.

3. Karl Marx, *The Poverty of Philosophy*, New York, p. 109.

4. Marx to J. B. Schweitzer, ibid., p. 197.

5. Williams, p. 99.

6. Karl Marx, 'Critique of the Hegelian Dialectic and Philosophy as a Whole', *The Economic and Philosophic Manuscripts of 1844*, New York 1964, p. 172.

7. Raymond Williams, *Culture*, London 1981, p. 35.

8. E. P. Thompson, 'The Peculiarities of the English', *The Poverty of Theory and Other Essays*, London 1978, p. 296.

9. Jane Humphries, 'The Working-Class Family, Women's Liberation and Class Struggle', *The Review of Radical Political Economists*, vol. 9, no. 3 (Autumn 1977), pp. 25–41.

10. Sheila Lewenhak, *Women and Trade Unions: An Outline History of Women in the British Trade Union Movement*, London, Ernest Benn, 1977; Sheila Rowbotham, *Women, Resistance and Revolution*, Penguin Books, 1974;

Dorothy Thompson, 'Women and Nineteenth-Century Radical Politics: A Lost Dimension', in *The Rights and Wrongs of Women*, Anne Oakley and Juliet Mitchell, eds., Harmondsworth, Middlesex, Penguin Books, 1976, pp. 112–38; Sally Alexander, 'Women's Work in Nineteenth-century London; A Study of the Years 1820–50', ibid., pp. 59–111.

11. E. P. Thompson, 'the Poverty of Theory', in Thompson, p. 124.

Economism and Feminism: A Comment on the Domestic Labour Debate

1. See Mariarosa Dalla Costa, *The Power of Women and the Subversion of the Community*, Bristol 1972; Selma James, *Women, the Unions and Work*.

2. For an introduction to this theory in English see Guido Baldi, 'Thesis on Mass Worker and Social Capital', *Radical America*, vol. 6, no. 3 (1973), pp. 3–21.

3. See Selma James, 'Sex, Race and Working Class Power', *Race Today* (January 1974), pp. 12–15.

4. For examples of this literature see Sheila Rowbotham, 'The Carrot, the Stick and the Movement', Caroline Freeman, 'When is a Wage Not a Wage?' and Joan Landes, 'Wages for Housework: Political and Theoretical Considerations', all anthologized in Ellen Malos, ed., *The Politics of Housework*, London 1980. See also Linda Briskin, 'Toward Socialist Feminism? The Women's Movement: Where Is It Going?', *Our Generation*, vol. 10, no. 3 (1974), pp. 23–34.

5. Wally Seccombe's article, 'The Housewife and Her Labour Under Capitalism', *New Left Review*, no. 83 (1974), is an important example of this approach. Other examples are 'The Housewife and Her Labour Under Capitalism – A Critique', by Margaret Carlson, Branka Magas and Hilary Wainwright; 'Women's Domestic Labour' by Jean Gardiner, Susan Himmelweit and Maureen Mackintosh (also anthologized in *The Politics of Housework*).

6. See Ian Gough, 'Marx's Theory of Productive and Unproductive Labour', *New Left Review*, no. 76 (1972).

7. Bonnie Fox, ed., *Hidden in the Household: Women's Domestic Labour Under Capitalism*, Toronto 1980.

8. Wally Seccombe, 'Domestic Labour and the Working Class Household', in *Hidden in the Household*, p. 31.

9. Ibid., p. 33.

10. Ibid., p. 27.

11. Bonnie Fox, 'Introduction', in *Hidden in the Household*, p. 15

12. Ibid., p. 21.

13. Bruce Curtis, 'Capital, the State and the Origins of the Working Class Household', in *Hidden in the Household*, p. 121.

14. Linda Briskin, 'Domestic Labour: A Methodological Discussion', in *Hidden in the Household*, p. 136.

15. Emily Blumenfeld and Susan Mann, 'Domestic Labour and the Reproduction of Labour Power: Towards an Analysis of Women, the Family, and Class', in *Hidden in the Household*, p. 267.

16. Curtis, 'Capital', p. 109.

17. Briskin, 'Domestic Labour', p. 137.

18. Bonnie Fox, 'Women's Double Work Day: Twentieth-century Changes in the Reproduction of Daily Life', in *Hidden in the Household*.

19. Seccombe, 'Domestic Labour', p. 83.

20. Ibid., p. 84.

21. Bruce Curtis's article is the only one in this volume to focus theoretically on the question of women's oppression. In doing so it falls outside the limits of the domestic labour debate strictly defined. It is not by chance that his is also the only article to engage the wages for housework perspective directly.

22. Fox, 'Introduction', pp. 13, 14–15.

23. Seccombe, 'The Expanded Reproduction Cycle of Labour Power in Twentieth-century Capitalism', in *Hidden in the Household*, p. 217.

24. Briskin, 'Domestic Labour', p. 169.

25. Curtis, 'Capital', p. 130.

26. Blumenfeld and Mann, 'Domestic Labour', p. 293.

27. Briskin, 'Domestic Labour', p. 143.

28. Seccombe, 'Expanded Reproduction', p. 228.

29. Fox, 'Women's Double Work Day', p. 190.

30. Blumenfeld and Mann, 'Domestic Labour', p. 273.

31. Seccombe, 'Expanded Reproduction', p. 228.

32. Ibid., p. 239.

33. Ibid., p. 222.

34. For an examination of differential material conditions for men and women in marriage, see Laura Oren, 'The Welfare of Women in Labouring Families: England, 1860–1950', in *Feminist Studies*, vol. 1, nos. 3–4 (1973), pp. 107-25.

35. Bonnie Fox, 'Introduction', pp. 11–12. Similar assertions include: 'The argument concerning the enduring nature of patriarchy from precapitalist to fully capitalist societies often obscures, however, the revolution which has occurred *in the way* in which patriarchal domination is sustained within the household of the working class' (Seccombe, 'Domestic Labour', p. 81); 'Once the historical nature of the family is established, the theory of a continuous system of patriarchy, identified with the family is called into question,' (Briskin, 'Domestic Labour', p. 147).

36. For references to the socialist-feminist literature of this project and a feminist examination and critique of the progress made so far, see Iris Young, 'Socialist Feminism and the Limitations of Dual Systems Theory', *Socialist Review*, nos. 50–51 (1980), pp. 169–88.

37. Curtis, 'Capital', 121.

38. Blumenfeld and Mann, 'Domestic Labour', pp. 268, 269.

39. Briskin, 'Domestic Labour', p. 153.

40. Seccombe, 'Expanded Reproduction', p. 273.

41. Blumenfeld and Mann, 'Domestic Labour', p. 273.

42. Seccombe, 'Domestic Labour', p. 86.

43. Briskin, 'Domestic Labour', p. 146.

44. Curtis, 'Capital', pp. 121,126.

45. Briskin, 'Domestic Labour', p. 138.

46. This article is reprinted in Anne Koedt, ed., *Radical Feminism*, New York 1973.

Never Done: The Struggle to Understand Domestic Labour and Women's Oppression

I would like to thank Karen Anderson and Penni Stewart for helping me think through some of this material. Also, I thank John Fox for reading the draft of this essay and for providing constant support.

1. Perhaps the hesitancy comes from the brevity of the period (three weeks) in which this essay had to be written.

2. Thus, 'discourse theory' is currently popular.

3. One of the disturbing things abour Roberta Hamilton's review of *Hidden in the Household,* which involved its juxtaposition with Luxton's empirical study, is its implicit (but strong) anti-theory stance. The point is that Luxton would not have looked for, or seen, what she did without the theoretical understanding of domestic labour provided by the debate: for example, assuming that the household reproduced labour power led her to look for the way in which the 'long arm of the job' extends into the home. The tone of Hamilton's review was also disturbing: it did not promote dialogue around issues of women's oppression.

4. This argument, best stated by McDonough and Harrison in *Feminism and Materialism* (Annette Kuhn and Ann Marie Wolpe, eds., London 1978) about the relationship of 'patriarchy' and capitalism, does not imply that capitalism is the source of male dominance. The argument also does not reduce to one that says that gender oppression is different for different social classes, as Barrett claims it does. She omits a consideration of social structure.

5. Luxton's book is a very fine elaboration of these processes (for example, the nature of the man's job shaping his needs and thus the work of his spouse, the effect on housework of commodified means of subsistence). My article in *Hidden in the Household* draws out implications of the fact that the means of household production are commodities, to explain why married women are in the wage labour force.

6. Benston, Morton, Harrison and Seccombe (to an extent) make functionalist arguments. (See John Harrison, 'The Political Economy of Housework', *Bulletin of CSE,* Winter 1973.

7. In contrast, answering the question whether women constitute a class probably requires theoretical abstraction. We have not pursued that question far enough yet.

8. See p. 184.

9. Michele Barrett, *Women's Oppression Today,* London 1980; Johanna Brenner and Maria Ramas, 'Rethinking Women's Oppression', *New Left Review,* no. 44 (March/April), pp. 33–72; Michèle Barrett, 'Women's Oppression: A Reply', *New Left Review,* no. 146 (July/August 1984). Barrett's idealism is clearest and starkest in her reply to Brenner and Ramas. While denying an idealist tendency, she argues that 'the degree of determination of the social by the biological is a social or – more precisely – a political *choice'.* She is decidedly anti-structural as well in her insistence that men take 'responsibility' for nineteenth-century exclusionary union practices. To emphasize individuals' sexist behaviours in the context of a labour market where low-paid female workers represented competition and an ideological climate with rigid notions of gender roles (which Barrett herself emphasizes) involves poor sociology (or social analysis) and needless moralism.

I emphasize Barrett's idealist tendencies although it is also the case that she is often careful to argue simply that ideology must be considered, in an analysis of gender inequality, as it is grounded in material reality *and* in addition to social structure.

10. To illustrate this point, assume we were to prove that biological differences were the current source of the division of labour and gender inequality

(although this clearly is not the case). In some future society, in which babies developed in test tubes, women might still be oppressed and subordinate to men – although they might not bear or rear children. In that society of the future, biology would not be the basis and perpetrator of women's oppression. Understanding that biology originally was the source of women's subordination would not help much in the struggle for an end to gender inequality.

11. See, for example, Philippe Ariès, *Centuries of Childhood,* New York 1962, and Nancy Cott, *The Bonds of Womanhood,* New Haven 1977.

12. She cites the fact that children raised in institutions bear gendered identities. Aside from the fact that such studies have been notoriously poor in quality, it is also true that men are rarely the dominant caregivers in institutions. (See Nancy Chodorow's discussion of the significance of the fact that women mother for people's psyches and their gender identities.) Barrett, pp. 97, 251, 206. See Michel Foucault's, *The History of Sexuality,* New York 1980.

13. Jean-Louis Flandrin, *Families in Former Times,* Cambridge 1979.

14. See Eleanor Leacock, *Myths of Male Dominance,* New York 1981; Karen Anderson's article in Luxton and Maroney *Women's Jobs, Women's Struggles,* Toronto, forthcoming; and Kay M. Martin and Barbara Voorhies, *Female of the Species,* New York 1975.

15. Maccoby, E.E. and C. Jacklin, *The Psychology of Sex Differences,* Stanford 1974.

16. Jessica Benjamin, 'Master and Slave: The Fantasy of Erotic Domination', in Ann Snitow, C. Stansell and S. Thompson, eds. *Powers of Desire,* New York 1983, pp. 280–300. See also Alice Miller's provocative explanation of the ways in which traditional childrearing practices can create violent adult personalities. (*For Your Own Good,* 1983). Her analysis can easily be made sociological by underscoring the importance of the privatization and isolation of motherwork (see Rosenberg's article in Luxton and Maroney for a fine discussion of this), which leads to the tendencies of childrearing that she is discussing. Carol Gilligan, *In a Different Voice,* Cambridge, Mass., 1982.

17. Rosalind Coward, in her final chapter of *Patriarchal Precedents,* London 1983, seems to be arguing the importance of this point.

Reflections on the Domestic Labour Debate and Prospects for Marxist-feminist Synthesis

1. The 'domestic labour debate', as it came to be known on the left, was a wide-ranging discussion among Marxists and socialist feminists which endeavoured to situate women's work in the home in specific relation to wage work and to the dynamics of capital accumulation more generally. Its main focus was on working-class households in developed capitalist formations in the contemporary period. The debate was initiated in the late 1960s in the early stages of the contemporary rise of the women's movement (in Canada, interestingly, by Maggie Benston and Peggy Morton). See the appendix for a bibliography of contributors.

2. Lise Vogel, *Marxism and the Oppression of Women,* London 1983, p. 23.

3. Wally Seccombe, 'Patriarchy Stabilized: The Construction of the Male Breadwinner Wage Norm in Nineteenth-century Britain', *Social History,* vol. 11, no. 1 (1986).

4. Louis Althusser and Etienne Balibar, *Reading Capital,* London 1970.

5. Louis Althusser, *Lenin and Philosophy and Other Essays*, New York 1971, pp. 141–8.

6. 'The Housewife and Her Labour Under Capitalism', *New Left Review*, no. 83 (1974), p. 4. The entire edifice of value analysis was subsequently thrown into question by the neo-Ricardian challenge, inspired by Sraffa's *The Production of Commodities by Means of Commodities* (see Ian Steedman's *Marx after Sraffa*, London 1977). Significantly, the vexed question of value equilibration within the reproduction cycle of labour power (which does not go away merely because one discards the labour theory of value) failed to become a prominent issue in the value controversy.

7. 'The Reproduction of Labour Power: A Comparative Study', PhD dissertation, University of Toronto, 1982.

8. John Harrison, 'The Political Economy of Housework', *Bulletin of the Conference of Socialist Economists*, 1973, pp. 35–52.

9. Ivy Pinchbeck, *Women Workers and the Industrial Revolution, 1750–1850*, first published 1930, London 1981, pp. 1–2.

10. For a preliminary account of this reversal, see W. Seccombe, 'Patriarchy Stabilized: The Construction of the Male Breadwinner Wage Norm in Nineteenth-century Britain', *Social History*, vol. 11, no. 1 (1986).

11. Kathryn Walker, and Margaret Woods, *Time Use: A Measure of Household Production of Family Goods and Services*, Washington, DC 1976.

Alexander Szalia, ed., *The Use of Time: Daily Activities of Urban and Suburban Population in Twelve Countries*, The Hague 1972.

12. Ruth Cowan, *More Work for Mother*, New York 1983.

13. Sarah F. Berk, *The Gender Factory: The Apportionment of Work in American Households*, New York 1985; J. G. Condran, Bode and Rashomon, 'Working Wives and Family Division of Labour: Middletown, 1980', *Journal of Marriage and the Family*, no. 44 (1982) pp. 421–6; Joan Vanek, 'Time Spent on Housework', *Scientific American*, no. 231 (1974) pp. 116–20; M. Geeken and W. R. Gove, *At Home and the Work: The Family's Allocation of Labour*, Beverly Hills, Calif. 1983; Meg Luxton, 'Two Hands for the Clock: Changing Patterns in the Gendered Division of Labour in the Home', *Studies in Political Economy*, no. 12 (1983), pp. 27–44.; M. Meissner, E. M. Humphreys, S. M. Meis and W. J. Scheu, 'No Exit for Wives: Sexual Division of Labour and the Cumulation of Household Demands', *Canadian Review of Sociology and Anthropology*, vol. 12, no. 4 (1977), pp. 424–39.

14. Kathryn Walker and Margaret Woods, *Time Use: A Measure of Household Production of Family Goods and Services*, Washington, DC 1976; Alexander Szalia, ed., *The Use of Time: Daily Activities of Urban and Suburban Population in Twelve Countries*, The Hague 1972.

15. Meg Luxton, June Corman, David Livingstone and Wally Seccombe, *Steelworker Families: Workplace, Household and Community in Hamilton, Ontario* (in progress).

16. Meg Luxton, 'Two Hands for the Clock: Changing Patterns in the Gendered Division of Labour in the Home', *Studies in Political Economy*, no. 12 (1983), pp. 27–44.

17. As my mate persistently reminds me, doing a defined chore and taking responsibility for household planning are two different things. Like most men I know whose domestic practice has improved somewhat under feminist pressure, I find the latter much harder to accomplish than the former.

18. Gary Becker, *A Treatise on the Family*, Cambridge, Mass. 1981.

19. *Capital*, Volume 1, Moscow 1954, pp. 168–9.

20. Mark Killingsworth, *Labour Supply*, London 1983, p. 38.

21. Jacob Mincer, 'Labour Force Participation of Married Women: A Study of Labour Supply', in National Bureau of Economic Research, *Aspects of Labour Economics*, Princeton 1962; Gary Becker, *A Treatise on the Family*, Cambridge, Mass. 1981.

22. Reuben Gronau, 'Leisure, Home Production, and Work: The Theory of the Allocation of Time Revisited, *Journal of Political Economy*, vol. 85, no. 4 (1977), pp. 1099–1124; R. A. Pollack and M. L. Wachter, 'The Relevance of the Household Production Function and Its Implications for the Allocation of Time', *Journal of Political Economy*, no. 83 (1975), pp. 255–77; T. J. Wales and A. D. Woodland, 'Estimation of the Allocation of Time for Work, Leisure and Housework', *Econometrica*, vol. 45, no. 1 (1977), pp. 115–32; Richard Berk, and Sarah F. Berk, *Labour and Leisure at Home: Content and Organization of the Household Day*, Beverly Hills, Calif. 1979.

23. Nancy Folbre, 'Exploitation Comes Home', *Cambridge Journal of Economics*, no. 6 (1982), pp. 317–29.

24. Marilyn Manser and Murray Brown, 'Marriage and Household Decision-making: A Bargaining Analysis', *International Economic Review*, no. 21 (1980), pp. 31–44.

25. The best available summary, comparing twelve Western countries, is Patricia Roos, *Gender and Work: A Comparative Analysis of Industrial Societies*, Albany, New York 1985.

26. See the very useful discussion in Michèle Barrett's *Women's Oppression Today*, London 1980, chapter 5.

27. Michael Piore, 'The Dual Labour Market: Theory and Implications', in David M. Gordon, ed., *Problems in Political Economy: An Urban Perspective*, Lexington, Mass. 1971, pp. 90–4.

28. William Dickens and Kevin Lang, 'A Test of Dual Labor Market Theory', *American Economic Review*, vol. 75, no. 4 (1985), pp. 792–805.

29. Mark Killingsworth, *Labour Supply*, London 1983, pp. 185, 205.

30. Shelley Coverman, 'Explaining Husband's Participation in Domestic Labour', *Sociological Quarterly*, vol. 26, no. 1 (1985), pp. 81–97.

Appendix

The following is a list of English language contributions to the domestic labour debate. To make the compilation manageable, I have defined the debate narrowly; even so inadvertent omissions will surely be found. No offence is intended.

Olivia Adamson, Carol Brown, Judith Harrison and Judy Price, 'Women's Oppression under Capitalism', *Revoultionary Communist*, no. 5 (1976), pp. 2–48.

Anonymous, *On the Political Economy of Women*, London n.d. (a collection of articles by British Marxist feminists).

Pat Armstrong and Hugh Armstrong, 'Political Economy and the Household', *Studies in Political Economy*, no. 17 (1985).

Margaret Benston, 'The Political Economy of Women's Liberation', *Monthly Review*, no. 21 (September 1969), pp. 13–27.

Melanie Beresford, 'The Domestic Mode of Production Revisited', *Refractory Girl*, no. 6 (1974), pp. 44–8.

Lucy Bland, Rachel Harrison, Frank Mort and Christine Weedon, 'Relations of Reproduction: Approaches through Anthropology', *Women Take Issue*, 1978.

Teresa Brennan, 'Women and Work' *Journal of Australian Political Economy*, October 1977, pp. 34–52.

Renate Bridenthal, 'The Dialectics of Production and Reproduction in History', *Radical America*, no. 10 (1976), pp. 3–14.

Mia Campioni, Elizabeth Jacka, Paul Patton, Pat Skenridge, Margo Moore and David Wells, 'Opening the Floodgates: Domestic Labour and Capitalist Production', *Refractory Girl*, no. 7 (1974), pp. 10–14.

Margaret Coulson, Branka Magas and Hilary Wainwright, 'The Housewife and Her Labour Under Capitalism – A Critique', *New Left Review*, no. 89 (1975), pp. 59–71.

Christine Delphy, *Close to Home: A Materialist Analysis of Women's Oppression*, 1st edn. 1978, Amhert, Mass. chapter 5.

Mariarosa Dalla Costa, *Women and the Subversion of the Community*, Bristol 1972.

Hodee Edwards, 'Housework and Exploitation – a Marxist Analysis', *No More Fun and Games*, no. 5 (July 1971), pp. 92–100.

Terry Fee, 'Domestic Labour: An Analysis of Housework and Its Relation to the Productive Forces', *Review of Radical Political Economics*, 8 (1976), pp. 1–9.

Nancy Folbre, 'Exploitation Comes Home', *Cambridge Journal of Economics*, no. 6 (1982), pp. 317–29.

Jean Gardiner, 'The Political Economy of Domestic Labour in Capitalist Society', in Diana Barker and Sheila Allen, eds., *Dependence and Exploitation in Work and Marriage*, London 1976, pp. 109–21.

Jean Gardiner, 'Women's Domestic Labour', *New Left Review*, no. 89 (1975), pp. 47–59.

Jean Gardiner, Susan Himmelweit and Maureen Mackintosh, 'Women's Domestic Labour', *Bulletin of the Conference of Socialist Economists*, no. 4 (1975), pp. 1–11.

Ira Gerstein, 'Domestic Work and Capitalism', *Radical America*, no. 7 (1973), pp. 101-31.

Ian Gough and John Harrison, 'Unproductive Labour and Housework Again', *Bulletin of the Conference of Socialist Economists*, no. 4 (1975).

John Harrison, 'The Political Economy of Housework', *Bulletin of the Conference of Socialist Economists*, no. 2 (1973), pp. 35–52.

Susan Himmelweit and Simon Mohun, 'Domestic Labour and Capital', *Cambridge Journal of Economics*, no. 1 (1977), pp. 15–31.

Heidi Hartman, 'Capitalism and Women's Work in the Home', PhD dissertation, Yale University 1975.

Joan Landes, 'Wages for Housework: Subsidizing Capitalism?', *Quest*, no. 2 (1975), pp. 17–31.

Joan Landes, 'Women, Labour and Family Life: A Theoretical Perspective', *Science and Society*, no. 41 (1977–8), pp. 386–409.

Michael Lebowitz, 'The Political Economy of Housework: A Comment', *Bulletin of the Conference of Socialist Economists*, no. 5 (1976).

Ellen Malos, 'Housework and the Politics of Women's Liberation', *Socialist*

Review, no. 8 (January–February 1976), pp. 41–73.

Bonnie Fox, ed., *Hidden in the Household: Women's Domestic Labour Under Capitalism*, Toronto 1980.

Maxine Molyneux, 'Beyond the Domestic Labour Debate', *New Left Review*, no. 116 (1979), pp. 3–28.

Peggy Morton, 'A Woman's Work Is Never Done', in *Women Unite!*, Toronto 1972.

Mary Rowntree and John Rowntree, 'More on the Political Economy of Women's Liberation', *Monthly Review*, no. 21 (1970), pp. 26–32.

Wally Seccombe, 'The Housewife and Her Labour Under Capitalism', *New Left Review*, no. 83 (1974), pp. 3–24.

Wally Seccombe, 'Domestic Labour – Reply to Critics', *New Left Review*, no. 94 (1975), pp. 85–96.

Paul Smith, 'Domestic Labour and Marx's Theory of Value', in A. Kuhn and A. M. Wolpe, eds., *Towards a Materialist Feminism*, London 1978.

Lise Vogel, 'The Earthly Family', *Radical America*, no. 7 (1973), pp. 9–50.

Batya Weinbaum and Amy Bridges, 'The Other Side of the Paycheck: Monopoly Capital and the Structure of Consumption', *Monthly Review*, no. 28 (1976), pp. 88–103.

Beyond Sexless Class and Classless Sex

As Roberta Hamilton would say, like all publications this is only a draft gone public. Many people have provided critical comments on earlier drafts, and while a few may still recognize the current paper, and while fewer still may want to be linked with it, we would like to thank Jacques Chevalier, Patricia Connelly, Roberta Hamilton, Jared Keil, Angela Miles, George Mitchell, Mary O'Brien, Shirley Pettifer, Wally Seccombe, Dorothy Smith, Pam Smith, Erica Van Meurs and Bonnie Ward in particular.

1. Heidi Hartmann, 'The Unhappy Marriage of Marxism and Feminism: Towards a More Progressive Union', in Lydia Sargent, ed., *Women and Revolution*, Boston 1981, p. 2.

2. C. Wright Mills, *The Marxists*, New York 1962, p. 98.

3. Juliet Mitchell, 'Marxism and Women's Revolution', *Social Praxis*, vol. 1, no. 1 (1972), p. 24.

4. Wally Seccombe, 'Domestic Labour and the Working-Class Household', in Bonnie Fox, ed., *Hidden in the Household: Women's Domestic Labour Under Capitalism*, Toronto 1980, p. 27.

5. Shulamith Firestone, *The Dialectic of Sex*, New York, 1970, pp. 4, 5, 9.

6. Charnie Guettel, *Marxism and Feminism*, Toronto 1974, pp. 2, 36.

7. Margaret Benston, 'The Political Economy of Women's Liberation', reprinted in Leslie Tanner, ed., *Voices from Women's Liberation*, New York 1971, p. 285.

8. M. Patricia Connelly, *Last Hired, First Fired*, Toronto 1978, pp. 6, 33.

9. Peggy Morton, 'Women's Work Is Never Done', reprinted in *Women Unite!*, Toronto 1972.

10. Wally Seccombe, 'The Housewife and Her Labour under Capitalism', *New Left Review*, no. 83 (1974), and Jean Gardiner, 'Women's Domestic Labour', *New Left Review*, no. 89 (1975).

11. Margaret Coulson, Branka Magaš and Hilary Wainwright, 'The House-wife and Her Labour under Capitalism – A Critique', *New Left Review*, no. 89 (1975).

12. Paul Smith, 'Domestic Labour and Marx's Theory of Value', in Annette Kuhn and Anne Marie Wolpe, eds., *Feminism and Materialism*, London 1978.

13. Seccombe, 'Domestic Labour', p. 9.

14. Coulson, Magas and Wainwright, p. 49.

15. Jean Gardiner, 'Political Economy of Domestic Labour in Capitalist Society', in Diana Leonard Barker and Sheila Allen, eds., *Dependence and Exploitation in Work and Marriage*, London 1976.

16. Maxine Molyneux, 'Beyond the Domestic Labour Debate', *New Left Review*, no. 116 (1979), p. 9.

17. Wally Seccombe, 'Domestic Labour – A Reply to Critics', *New Left Review*, no. 94 (1975), p. 89.

18. Ibid., p. 92.

19. Wally Seccombe, 'The Expanded Reproduction Cycle of Labour Power in Twentieth-century Capitalism', in *Hidden in the Household*.

20. Patricia Connelly, 'Women's Work and Family Wage in Canada', in Anne Hoiberg, ed., *Women and the World of Work*, New York 1982, pp. 223–38.

21. Seccombe, 'Expanded Reproduction Cycle'.

22. Christine Delphy, 'L'ennemi principal', reprinted in Partisans, ed., *Libération des femmes année zéro*, Paris 1972.

23. See Roberta Hamilton, *The Liberation of Women*, London 1978, Bonnie Fox, 'Women's Double Work Day: Twentieth-century Changes in the Repro-duction of Daily Life', in *Hidden in the Household*, and Dorothy Smith, 'Women, the Family and Corporate Capitalism', in Marylee Stephenson, ed., *Women in Canada*, Toronto 1973, for Canadian theorists who have discussed class differences amongst women.

24. Jean Gardiner, 'Women in the Labour Process and Class Structure', in Alan Hunt, ed., *Class and Class Structure*, London 1977, p. 158.

25. Christine Delphy, 'Women in Stratification Studies', in Helen Roberts, ed., *Doing Feminist Research*, London 1981, p. 115.

26. Gayle Rubin, 'The Traffic in Women: Notes on the Political Economy of Sex', in Rayna R. Reiter, *Toward an Anthropology of Women*, New York 1975, p. 165.

27. Richard W. Wertz and Dorothy C. Wertz, *Lying In: A History of Child-birth in America*, New York 1979, p. ix.

28. Louise A. Tilly and Joan W. Scott, *Women, Work and Family*, New York 1978, p. 27.

29. Wertz and Wertz, *Lying In*, p. 3.

30. Margaret Llewelyn Davies, *Maternity: Letters from Working Women*, first published 1915; Tiptree, Essex 1978, p. 6.

31. Neil Sutherland, *Children in English-Canadian Society*, Toronto 1976, pp. 62–3.

32. Janice Delaney, Mary Jane Lupton and Emily Toth, *The Curse*, New York 1977, pp. 42–3.

33. Joyce Leeson and Judith Gray, *Women and Medicine*, London 1978, p. 93.

34. Quoted in Sheila Rowbotham, *A New World for Women: Stella Browne – Socialist Feminist*, London 1977, pp. 62, 63.

35. Linda Gordon, 'The Struggle for Reproductive Freedom: Three Stages of Feminism', in Zillah Eisenstein, ed., *Capitalist Patriarchy and the Case for Feminist Socialism*, New York, 1979, p. 108.

36. For accounts of the historical development of regulations related to abortion, see Angus McLaren, 'Women's Work and the Regulation of Family Size: The Question of Abortion in the Nineteenth Century', *History Workshop*, no. 4 (1977); and Angus McLaren, 'Birth Control and Abortion in Canada, 1870–1920', *Canadian Historical Review*, vol. 59, no. 3 (1978), pp. 319–40.

37. Wertz and Wertz, *Lying In*.

38. *Women, Work and Family*, p. 100.

39. 'Women's Work', p. 76.

40. Sutherland, *Children*, p. 56.

41. Canada, Statistics Canada, *Canada Year Book 1975*, Ottawa 1975, p. 153.

42. Leroy O. Stone and Claude Marceau, *Canadian Population Trends and Public Policy Through the 1980's*, Montréal 1977, p. 37.

43. Adrienne Rich, *Of Woman Born*, London 1977.

44. Barbara Ehrenreich and Deirdre English, *Complaints and Disorders*, Old Westbury, New York 1973, p. 72.

45. Quoted by McLaren, 'Birth Control', p. 320.

46. 'Reproductive Freedom', p. xiii.

47. 'Women's Work', p. 79.

48. McLaren, 'Birth Control', p. 320.

49. Suzann Buckley 'Ladies or Midwives? Efforts to Reduce Infant and Maternal Mortality', in Linda Kealey, ed., *A Not Unreasonable Claim*, Toronto 1979, p. 140.

50. Ehrenreich and English, p. 16.

51. Wertz and Wertz, *Lying In*.

52. Rainer Baehre, 'Victorian Psychiatry and Canadian Motherhood', *Canadian Women's Studies*, vol. 2, no. 1 (1980), p. 45.

53. Davies, *Maternity*, p. 3.

54. For an outstanding example of the type of historical investigation we have in mind, see Patricia Connelly and Martha MacDonald, 'Women's Work: Domestic and Wage Labour in a Nova Scotia Community', in this volume.

On Marxism and Feminism

1. Angela Miles, 'Economism and Feminism; *Hidden in the Household*: A Comment on the Domestic Labour Debate', *Studies in Political Economy*, no. 11 (Summer 1983), reprinted in this volume.

2. Pat Armstrong and Hugh Armstrong, 'Beyond Sexless Class and Classless Sex: Towards Feminist Marxism', *Studies in Political Economy*, no. 10 (Winter 1983), reprinted in this volume.

3. Michèle Barrett, *Women's Oppression Today: Problems in Marxist Feminist Analysis*, London 1980.

4. For an excellent discussion of the different uses of the concept of patriarchy, see Barrett.

5. Z. Eisenstein, ed., *Capitalist Patriarchy and the Case for Socialist Feminism*, New York 1979; A. Kuhn and A. Wolpe, eds., *Feminism and Materialism*, London 1978; L. Sargent, ed., *The Unhappy Marriage of Marxism*

and Feminism, London, 1981. R. Hamilton, 'Working at Home', *Atlantis*, vol. 7 no. 1 (1981); B. Curtis, 'Rejecting Working at Home', *Atlantis*, vol. 8, no. 1 (1982); R. Hamilton, 'Reply to Curtis', *Atlantis*, vol. 8, no. 1 (1982). These three articles are reprinted in this volume.

6. Wally Seccombe, 'Domestic Labour and the Working-Class Household', in Bonnie Fox, ed., *Hidden in the Household: Women's Domestic Labour Under Capitalism*, Toronto 1980, p. 37.

7. Ibid., p. 59.

8. M. P. Connelly, *Last Hired, First Fired: Women in the Canadian Workforce*, Toronto, 1978; Bonnie Fox, 'Women's Double Work Day: Twentieth-century Changes in the Reproduction of Daily Life', in *Hidden in the Household*.

9. Hamilton, 'Working at Home'.

10. For a discussion of this point, see M. P. Connelly, 'Women's Work, The Family Household and the Canadian Economy', paper delivered at the Canadian Sociology and Anthropology Association Meetings, Learned Societies, Vancouver, 1983.

11. M. Barrett and M. McIntosh, 'The "Family Wage": Some Problems for Socialists and Feminists', *Capital and Class*, no. 11 (1980); J. Humphries, 'The Working-Class Family, Women's Liberation and Class Struggle: The Case of Nineteenth-century British History', *Review of Radical Political Economics*, vol. 9, no. 3 (1981).

12. H. Safa, 'Runaway Shops and Female Employment: The Search for Cheap Labor', *Signs*, vol. 7, no. 2 (1981).

More on Marxism and Feminism

1. Michèle Barrett, *Women's Oppression Today*, London 1980; Patricia Connelly, 'On Marxism and Feminism', *Studies in Political Economy*, no. 12 (Autumn 1983, reprinted in this volume); Pat Armstrong and Hugh Armstrong, 'Beyond Sexless Class and Classless Sex: Towards Feminist Marxism', *Studies in Political Economy*, no. 10 (Winter 1983, reprinted in this volume).

2. Connelly, 'On Marxism and Feminism', p. 241.

3. See, for example, Armstrong and Armstrong, 'Beyond Sexless Class', p. 208.

4. Joanna Brenner and Maria Ramas, 'Rethinking Women's Oppression', *New Left Review*, no. 144 (March–April 1984), especially pp. 40–7.

5. Connelly, 'On Marxism and Feminism', p. 241.

Hegemony and Superstructure: A Feminist Critique of Neo-Marxism

1. *Selections from the Prison Notebooks of Antonio Gramsci*, Quintin Hoare and Geoffrey Nowell Smith, eds., London 1971 (hereafter *PN*); Antonio Gramsci, *Letters from Prison*, Lynne Lawner, ed, London 1975; Antonio Gramsci, *The Modern Prince and Other Writings*, Louis Marks, trans., New York 1975.

2. Hoare and Nowell Smith note (*PN*, p. 5, fn.) that the Italian word *ceto* which they translate as 'strata', does not mean quite that. Gramsci for political reasons avoids the use of the word 'class'. 'Levels' also suggest a hierarchical

relation, where Gramsci clearly means to delineate a dialectical relation. Both political relations of the former to the ruling class is much more direct – although, of course, instrumentally individual proletarians do become soldiers and policemen/women.

3. *PN*, p. 263.

4. See, for example, Norberto Bobbio, 'Gramsci and the Conception of Civil Society', and Jacques Texier, 'Gramsci, Theoretician of the Superstructures', in Chantal Mouffe, ed., *Gramsci and Marxist Theory* (London, Boston, Henley 1979). For discussion of 'historical bloc' and sex also see Waller L. Adamson, *Hegemony and Revolution* (Berkely, Los Angeles, London 1980), pp. 176–9.

5. See discussion by Leonard Paggi, 'Gramsci's General Theory of Marxism', in *Gramsci and Marxist Theory*, pp. 122–3.

6. *PN*, p. 12.

7. In 'the enigmatic mosaic that Gramsci laboriously assembled in prison, the words "State", "Civil Society", "Political Society", "domination" or "direction" all undergo a constant slippage'. Perry Anderson. 'The Antinomies of Antonio Gramsci', *New Left Review*, no. 100 (November 1976–January 1977).

8. Gramsci, *11 Materiali Storico e la filoso fia di Benedetto Croce*, p. 191. Quoted by Paggi in *Gramsci and Marxist Theory*, p. 123.

9. Gramsci's notion of schooling is traditional, centring on the primary need for literacy and a concern with discipline. Harold Enthwhistle appears to believe that Gramsci's quite conservative notions of curriculum undermine the radical integrity of the 'new' sociology of education. See Harold Enthwhistle, *Antonio Gramsci: Conservative Schooling and Radical Politics* (London, Boston, Henley 1979). It should be added that, in his personal life, Gramsci's concern for the welfare and education of his family is dignified and humane, as his moving *Letters from Prison* attest. He had two sons, no daughters.

10. Michele Barrett, *Women's Oppression Today: Problems in Marxist Feminist Analysis*, London 1980, pp. 12–13.

11. Ibid., p. 12.

12. Mary O'Brien, *The Politics of Reproduction* (London, Boston, Henley 1981), chapter 1.

The Social Construction of 'Immigrant Women' in Canada

This paper was first presented at the Canadian Sociology and Anthropology Association annual meeting in May 1985. The data are taken from my PhD dissertation entitled, *Immigrant Women and the State: A Study in the Social Organization of Knowledge*, Ontario Institute for Studies in Education, 1984. I wish to thank my friends, too many to name, in the immigrant and academic communities for comments on earlier versions of the paper.

1. I am aware of the fact that the term 'immigrant women' has gained popularity in Canada in recent years, expecially since the International Women's Year and as a result of agitation by middle-class women immigrants. It is not uncommon for middle-class women who were or are immigrants, and who work with working-class immigrant women, including myself, to call themselves, 'immigrant women' from time to time, for political and ideological reasons. However, we should not confuse this kind of self-labelling with the common-sense implication of the term.

2. The term 'social relation' is used in a Marxian sense in this paper, and is different from the standard sociological usage which divides social realities into social, political and economic relationships.

In his investigation of commodity production, Marx uses this term to identify a series of co-ordinated processes of a capitalist mode of production which is located temporally and spatially in the everyday world and is carried out by individual's activities. Yet the sum total of these processes is more than the activities of individuals and has this strange objective character which transcends each individual act. To use Marx's original example, a commodity is an objective ordinary feature of capitalist society. But a commodity becomes a commodity only through productive activities (which are carried out by workers in a factory) and activities of exchange in the market (which are in turn accomplished by merchants, capitalists, consumers, etc.). Each one of these acts does not produce an object as a commodity. An object becomes a commodity at the end of the productive and exchange activities: it becomes a commodity at the point when it is exchanged for money (*Capital*, vol. 1). Thus, when we identify an object as a commodity, we in effect presuppose that it is the result of the social relations of production and exchange in a capitalist society. Furthermore, every time we purchase an object (a commodity) we enter into the relations of production and exchange without necessarily intending to do so. The individual act of shopping, in a capitalist mode of production, is not *merely* an individual act; it presupposes and is connected to larger processes of the society. This is the understanding that the present inquiry makes use of. See I. I. Rubin, *Essays on Marx's Theory of Value*, Montréal 1973; D. Smith, 'On Sociological Description: A Method from Marx, *Human Studies*, no. 4 (1981), pp. 313–37.

3. Harry Braverman, *Labor and Monopoly Capital: The Degradation of Work in the Twentieth Century*, New York and London 1974, p. 24.

4. S. Sassen-Koob, 'Toward a Conceptualization of Immigrant Labour', *Social Problem*, vol. 29, no. 1, pp. 65–85.

5. F. Frobel, J. Heinrichs, O. Kreye, *The New International Division of Labour*, Cambridge 1980.

6. Canada as a nation is built on immigrant labour. The classic study is Pentland's work on the organization of labour up to 1860 (Pentland 1981). A review of the history of Canada shows case after case of the use of immigrant labour: Scandinavian and Ukrainian labour was brought in to open up frontier, the Chinese to build the railway, etc. Indeed, immigration is *the* process through which the stratification of the Canadian labour market is produced in the first place, and how it is maintained in the second place; ethnicity is thus an integral part of the composition of the labour market. By the same token, in order to protect themselves from exploitation by employers, men have organized themselves against capital by exluding women, children, and ethnic minorities, thereby contributing to the creation and maintenance of the gender and ethnically segregated character of the labour market. See H. Potrebenko, *No Street of Gold, A Social History of Ukrainians in Alberta*, Vancouver 1977; D. Avery, *'Dangerous Foreigners': European Immigrant Workers and Labour Radicalism in Canada, 1896–1932*, Toronto 1979; G. S. Basran, 'Canadian Immigration Policy and Theories of Racism', in P. Li and S. Bolaria, eds., *Racial Minorities in Multicultural Canada*, Toronto 1933; H. Hartmann, 'Capitalism, Patriarchy, and Job Segregation by Sex', in M. Blaxall and B. Reagan, eds., *Women and the Workplace: The Implications of Occupational Segregation*, Chicago 1976; M. L. Campbell, 'Sexism in British Columbia Trade Unions, 1900–1920', in C. Kess

and B. Latham, eds., *In Her Own Right: Selected Essays on Women in BC History*, Victoria 1980; C. Cockburn, *Brothers: Male Dominance and Technological Change*, London 1983.

7. R. Ng, *Immigrant Women and the State: A Case Study in the Social Organization of Knowledge*, PhD dissertation, Department of Sociology, Ontario Institute for Studies in Education, Toronto. R. Ng, 'Sex, Ethnicity, or Class? Some Methodological Considerations', *Studies in Sexual Politics*, no. 1, pp. 14–45.

8. D. Smith, 'The Social Construction of Documentary Reality', *Sociological Inquiry*, vol. 44, no. 4, pp. 257–68.

9. D. Smith, 'On Sociological Description: A Method from Marx', *Human Studies*, no. 4, pp. 313–37.

10. K. Marx, *Grundrisse: Foundations of the Critique of Political Economy*, New York, 1973.

11. A detailed discussion of Marx's critique has been offered by Jackson, *Describing News: Toward an Alternative Account*, MA thesis, Department of Sociology and Anthropology, University of British Columbia, Vancouver, 1977.

12. D. Smith, 'Instituting Ethnography: A Feminist Method', *Resources for Feminist Research*, vol. 15, no. 1, forthcoming, Economy of Gender Relations, Ontario Institute for Studies in Education, Toronto.

13. G. Carchedi, *On the Economic Identification of Social Class*, London 1977; N. Poulantzas, *Classes in Contemporary Capitalism*, London 1978; E. D. Wright, 'Class Boundaries in Advanced Capitalist Societies', *New Left Review*, no. 98, pp. 3–41.

14. K. Marx and F. Engels, *The German Ideology*, New York 1970.

15. K. Marx and F. Engels, *The Communist Manifesto*, Harmondsworth, Middlesex 1967.

16. K. Marx, *Capital, Volume 1*, Moscow 1954.

17. Outreach funding did not allow for the hiring of a receptionist at the agency. In the absence of an 'official' receptionist, members of the staff would take turns at playing this role. However, during my fieldwork there, most of the time the agency managed to secure reception help through other grants or by volunteers. As mentioned before, I was frequently asked to help out as a receptionist when I conducted research there.

18. F. Erickson and J. Shultz, *The Counsellor as Gatekeeper: Social Interaction in Interviews*, New York 1982.

19. B. Janke and R. Yaron, 'A Report on Conditions in the Labour Market and Training Opportunities for Non-English-speaking Immigrant Women in Metro Toronto', Working Women Community Centre, October 1979, p. 7.

20. Field-notes, 2 July 1981.

21. R. Ng and T. Das Gupta, 'The Captive Labour Force of Non-English-speaking Immigrant Women', unpublished MS, Wollstonecraft Research Group, Ontario Institute for Studies in Education, Toronto. S. Arnopoulos, *Problems of Immigrant Women in the Canadian Labour Force*, Ottawa 1978.

22. Janlie and Yaron, p. 11.

23. See note 7.

24. Arnopoulos; L. Johnson, *The Seam Allowance: Industrial Home Sewing in Canada*, Toronto 1982.

25. Contemporary debates on class and ethnicity have been concerned with which one of these categories is the primary determinant of social status in

society. Women generally fall outside the frame of reference in the standard treatment of class and ethnicity. In recent years there have been increasing efforts by feminist scholars to incorporate women into the study of ethnicity and class. Frequently the similarities between racism and sexism are compared and parallels between the experience of women and the experience of minorities are drawn. In their work, Lee and Roberts attempted to provide a more encompassing approach to 'femininity', ethnicity, and class by establishing their interrelationship as three different systems of domination. These efforts are important steps forward in an area previously ignored by sociologists. While taking into account the work developed by feminist scholars in the area of gender, ethnicity and class, I am proposing a different strategy here which focuses on gender and ethnicity as they are embedded in certain relations of production rather than as interacting systems of domination. For a full discussion, see R. Ng 'Sex, Ethnicity or Class?' *Studies in Sexual Politics*, Manchester, pp. 14–15; J. Porter, *The Vertical Mosaic, An Analysis of Social Class and Power in Canada*, Toronto 1965; E. Robbins, 'Ethnicity or Class? Social Relations in a Small Canadian Industrial Community', in J. W. Bennett, ed., *The New Ethnicity: Perspectives from Ethnology*, New York 1975; D. J. Lee, 'Toward a Feminist Critique of the Sociology of Ethnic Relations', invited presentation to the Department of Sociology, Ontario Institute for Studies in Education 24 February 1981; D. J. Lee and B. Roberts, 'Ethnicity and Femininity', *Canadian Ethnic Studies*, vol. 13, no. 1 (1981), pp. 1–23; D. Smith, 'Women, Class and Family', in Ralph Miliband and John Saville, eds., *The Socialist Register 1983*, London 1983, p. 2.

Theories of the Family and Family/Authority Relationships in the Educational Sector in Québec and France, 1850–1960

This is the text of a paper presented to the conference of the Historical Institute of French America in Ottawa, October 1979, and published in the *Revue d'histoire de l'Amerique française*, vol. 34, no. 2 (September 1980).

1. F. Engels, *The Origin of the Family, Private Property and the State*, London.

2. See L. Althusser, 'Ideology and Ideological State Apparatuses', in *Lenin and Philosophy*, London 1971.

3. See in particular the following works: Michel Foucault, *Discipline and Punish*, London 1977; *La volonté de savoir*, Paris 1975; Isaac Joseph, Phillippe Fritsch and Alain Battegay, 'Disciplines à domicile, l'édification de la famille', *Recherches*, no. 28 (1977); Jacques Donzelot, *The Policing of Families*, London 1980; Philippe Meyer *L'enfant et la raison d'état*, Paris 1977.

4. Among other references, see Michael Gordon, *The American Family in Socio-historical Perspective*, New York 1973.

5. For England, see Mary McIntosh, 'The State and the Oppression of Women', in A. Kuhn and A. M. Wolpe, eds., *Feminism and Materialism*, London 1978.

6. For Italy, see Lesley Caldwell, 'Church, State and Family: The Women's Movement in Italy', in *Feminism and Materialism*. For the fascist period, see Maria A. Macchiocci, *Eléments pour une Analyse du Fascisme*, Paris 1976.

7. This is the thesis demonstrated by Ann Douglas in *The Feminization of American Culture*, New York 1977.

8. It should be said that on this level, and from our point of view, it is less a question of the family institution as such than of the family as a constituent part of a given social group. From this perspective, one should speak of families in the plural, rather than of the family.

9. The social history of Ireland and of Italy show some rather astonishing similarities with Québecois history, concerning the extent and persistence of clerical influence in the social arena.

10. We would refer the reader here to two collections which are now almost considered classics in the field of the history of education in Québec. These are the works of Louis Philippe Audet, summarized in a collection entitled *Histoire de L'Enseignement au Québec*, Montreal 1971, 2 vols., and forty years earlier the panoramic overview given by Lionel Groulx in *L'Enseignement français au Canada*, Montreal 1931 and 1935, 2 vols. Concerning college education there is also a recent work by the historian Claude Galarneau on *Les Collèges Classiques au Canada français*, Montreal 1978.

11. Certain works, which appeared throughout the period considered here (1850–1950), illustrate the above thesis most eloquently. See L. Laflèche, *Quelques considérations sur les rapports de la société civile avec la religion et la famille*, Montreal 1866; A. Mailloux, *Manuel des Parents Chrétiens*, Québec 1851. *L'éducation, ou la grande question sociale du jour. Recueil de documents*, Montreal 1886. In the twentieth century many articles appearing in the Semaines Sociales au Canada continue to designate the family as the indispensible ally of the church because it is the key element in any educational policy. On this subject, see especially accounts in the Semaines Sociales on the following themes: *La Famille* (1923), *Le Chrétien dans la Famille et la Nation* (1940), *Le Foyer Base de la Société* (1950). Father Lionel Groulx adopts a similar point of view when he writes of 'La famille canadienne-française, ses traditions, son rôle', in *Notre Maître le Passé*, Montreal 1924, pp. 101–35. The same goes for Mgr L.-A. Paquet in certain of his writings collected under the title *Études et Appreciations*. *Nouveaux mélanges canadiens*, Québec 1919.

12. On this subject see two remarkable collections by A. Prost: *Histoire de L'Enseignement en France*, Paris 1968, and M. Crubelier, *L'enfance et la Jeunesse dans la société française, 1800–1950*, Paris 1979; there is also a succinct résumé by A. L. Léon entitled *Histoire de l'Enseignement en France*, Paris 1967.

13. See J.-M. Mayeur, *La Séparation de l'eglise et de l'État*, Paris 1966. M. Ozouf, *L'École, l'Église et la Republique, 1871–1914*, Paris 1963. G. Weill, *Histoire de l'Idée Laique en France au XIXe siècle*, Paris 1925. There is also an excellent critical essay by E. Poulat, *Église contre bourgeoisie*, Paris 1977.

14. Concerning the relationship between church and state in France at primary school level, see M. Gontard, *L'Enseignement primaire en France de la Révolution à la Loi Guizot*, Paris 1959; also, by the same author, *L'Oeuvre scolaire de la Troisième République, l'enseignement primaire en France de 1876 à 1914*, Paris 1965.

15. See G. Duveau, *Les Instituteurs*, Paris 1957. J. Ozouf, *L'Enquête d'opinion en histoire. Un example: l'instituteur français 1900–1914, Le Mouvement Social*, July–September 1963, pp. 3–22. Still, the room for manoeuvre given to the lay teacher does not always seem to have been as broad as the mission he was supposed to accomplish. On this subject, see A. Querien, 'L'Enseignement', *Recherches*, no. 23 (June 1976).

16. F. Buisson, '*Discours à l'association polytechnique, 1883*', quoted by A. Prost, pp. 397–8.

478   *The Politics of Diversity*

17. A. Prost, statistical table, p. 100.

18. On the history of secondary education in France in the nineteenth century, see the remarkable synthesis by C. Weill, *Histoire de l'Enseignement secondaire en France (1820–1920)*, Paris 1921.

19. It was actually from these classes that the majority of what in the nineteenth century was called 'the school for celebrities' (see A. Prost, chapter 1).

20. On the origin of French universities and their definition as a natural prolongation of state power, see A. Aulard, *Napoléon 1er et le monopole universitaire*, Paris 1911. On the subject of a synthesis on the evolution of higher education in France, see the article by T. Zeldin entitled 'Higher Education in France, 1848–1940', *Journal of Contemporary History*, November 1967, pp. 53–80.

21. Concerning the impact of the Falloux Law on the development of denominational education and on the church–state dynamic which forms the basis of that development, see the excellent thesis by J. Maurin, *La Politique ecclésiastique du Second Empire*, Paris 1930.

22. A. Prost, p. 37.

23. Statistics for secondary education in 1898. Quoted by A. Prost, p. 45.

24. Ibid., pp. 472–82. It is worth noting here that at the beginning of the twentieth century, 'independent school' (*école libre*) was the most usual term used to designate private schools in general and, more particularly, private church schools.

25. It was only after 1959 that the Debré Law would link the extension of state aid to the official recognition of the fact that funded institutions are for the public good, and to the right of state control over that institution.

26. On the relationship between secularity and political and religious allegiances, see R. Remond, *Évolution de la Notion de Laïcité entre 1919 et 1939, Cahiers d'histoire*, 1 (1959), pp. 71–87. A. Coutrot and F.-G. Dreyfus, *Les Forces religieuses dans la société française*, Paris 1966.

27. It should nevertheless be stated that in certain areas of the north- and south-west of France agreement with the educational views of the clergy was manifest in all social groups.

28. On this subject see the writings on the school question by the principal French clerical ideologists of the second half of the nineteenth century. It is evident that as far as the 'natural' alliance between the church and the family is concerned, conservatives such as Mgr Gaume or Cardinal Pie think in much the same way as more liberal writers such as Mgr Dupanloup or Mgr Maret.

29. See J. Ozouf, *Nous, les maîtres d'école, autobiographies d'instituteurs de la Belle Epoque*, Paris 1967.

30. Speech to the Senate by M. Jouin, *Journal Officiel des débats*, 3 June 1881. Quoted by A. Prost, p. 201.

31. Regarding secondary education for girls in the nineteenth century, it should be remembered that this is of greater concern to bourgeois than to working-class families. The impact on the model of the family transmitted throughout global society remains important for all that.

32. Syntheses on girls' education are rare. However, two excellent ones have been published recently, which compensate for the neglect this field has so far suffered. The two works are by Françoise Mayeur: *L'enseignement des jeunes filles sous la Troisième République*, Paris 1977, and *L'éducation des filles en France au XIXe siècle*, Paris 1979.

33. The most significant arguments on this subject are to be found in the polemics on the question which appeared in *Le Monde, L'Univers,* above all those by the Bishop of Orléans, Mgr Dupanloup.

34. A. Prost, statistical tables, p. 205. Also F. Mayeur, *L'Education des Filles en France au XIXe Siècle,* chapter 6.

35. On the 'special features' of the girls' secondary school curriculum, see the analysis by F. Mayeur in *L'enseignement secondaire des jeunes files sous la Troisième République,* chapter 4.

Feminist Reflections on the Fertility of Women in Québec

1. Jacques Henripin and Yves Péron, 'La Transition démographique', in H. Charbonneau, ed., *La Population au Québec: études rétrospectives,* Montréal 1973, p. 42.

2. These reflections on demography developed out of discussions with the Clio collective (Micheline Dumont, Michèle Jean, Jennifer Stoddart and Marie Lavigne) while we were researching *L'Histoire des femmes au Québec depuis quatre siècles,* Montreal 1982. Some of the points made here derive from the collective's reflections and my thanks are due to my colleagues.

3. The birth cohort of 1887 consists of women who were aged sixty-five or over at the time of the 1961 census; the 1903 cohort of women aged between fifty-five and fifty-nine, and the cohort of 1913 of women aged between forty-five and forty-nine in 1961. All three groups were past childbearing age in 1961.

4. In 1926–30, the infantile mortality rate was 133 per 1,000 live births amongst French-speaking women and 89 per 1,000 amongst the rest of the population. Henripin and Péron, 'La Transition', p. 36.

5. Henripin and Péron, 'La Transition', p. 44.

6. Peter H. Uhlenberg, 'A Study of Cohort Life Cycles: Cohorts of Native-Born Massachussets Women 1830–1900', in M. A. Vinovsky, ed., *Studies in American Historical Demography,* New York 1979, pp. 507–20.

7. Given the absence of adequate statistics for mortality rates in Québec between 1750 and 1926, it is difficult to reconstruct accurately the life cycles of women who had a short cycle (because they died at an early age), of women whose fertility was interrupted by death in childbirth and of women who were widowed while still of childbearing age. We do, however, know that in 1926–30 overall mortality rates were higher for francophones than for the population as a whole (14.2 per cent as against 13.5 per cent). Compare Henripin and Péron, 'La Transition', p. 36.

8. Given that birth rates for single women were very low and that it is impossible to say how many single mothers never married, single women are regarded as never having had children in the following account.

9. Compare Marta Danylewycz, 'Taking the Veil in Montreal, 1850–1920', paper read to the Canadian Historical Association, June 1978.

10. These statistics deal with women who were still alive in 1961. Their fertility was therefore not limited by death, but it may have been limited by the death of their partners or by their failure to remarry. Mortality rates amongst men who were of an age to have children in the first half of the century were, however, low, and in 1930–32 the life expectancy of men aged between fifteen and thirty-five was greater than that of women. Jacques Henripin and Yves Périn, 'Evolution démographique récente du Québec', in *La Population du Québec,* p. 48.

11. Jacques Henripin, *Tendances et facteurs de la fécondité au Canada*, Ottawa 1968, p. 51.

12. Tamara K. Hareven and Marie A. Vinovsky, *Family and Population in Nineteenth Century America*, Princeton 1978, p. 4.

13. The work of the British writer Peter Laslett challenges the view that large complex families were characteristic of pre-industrial societies. More specifically, Laslett demonstrates that families in pre-industrial England were nuclear. Compare Peter Laslett, *The World We Have Lost*, London 1971. For a more general account see also Michael Anderson, *Approaches to the History of the Western Family 1500–1914*, London 1980.

14. Tamara K. Hareven, 'Family Time and Industrial Time: Family and Work in a Planned Corporation Town 1900–1924', in *Family and Kin in Urban Communities*, p. 202.

15. See also Joan W. Scott and Louise A. Tilly, 'Women's Work and the Family in Nineteenth Century Europe', *Comparative Studies in Society and History*, vol. 17 (January 1975).

16. Bettina Bradbury, 'The Family Economy in an Industrializing City: Montreal in the 1870s', in N. Fahmy-Eid and M. Dumont, eds., *Maîtresses d'école, maîtresses de maison*, Montréal 1983.

17. Henripin and Péron, 'La Transition', p. 40.

18. Enid Charles, *Trends in Canadian Family Size: Canada 1941*, Ottawa 1944, p. 19.

19. J.-C. Falardeau and M. Lamontagne, 'The Life Cycle of French Canadian Urban Families', *Canadian Journal of Economic and Political Science*, 1947, p. 247.

20. Phillipe Garigue, *La Famille canadienne-française* (prefaced by 'Critique de la famille canadienne-française'), Montréal 1970.

21. In 1931, 38.7 per cent of all young women in Montréal between the ages of 15 and 24 did not attend school, did not form part of the active population and were not married. The corresponding figure for Toronto was only 25.7 per cent. Marie Lavigne and Jennifer Stoddart, *Analyse du travail féminin à Montréal entre les deux guerres*, thèse de maîtrise, UQAM, 1973.

22. Chad M. Gaffield, 'Canadian Families in Cultural Context: Hypotheses from the Mid-nineteenth Century', *Canadian Historical Association Papers*, 1979, pp. 84–70.

23. Gérard Bouchard, 'Family Structure and Geographic Mobility at Laterrière 1851–1935', *Journal of Family History*, vol. 2, no. 4 (1977), pp. 350–69.

24. Marie Fleury-Giroux, 'Fécondité et mortalité en Gaspésie et dans le Bas Saint-Laurent', *Recherches sociographiques*, 1968, pp. 247–64.

25. Linda Gordon, *Birth Control in America, Woman's Body, Woman's Right*, New York 1977.

26. Angus McLaren, 'Birth Control and Abortion in Canada 1870–1920', *Canadian Historical Review*, vol. 59, no. 3, 1978.

27. Linda Gordon, *Birth Control in America*.

28. D. A. Dawson, D. J. Many and J. C. Ridlery, 'Contraceptive Practice Before the Pill: The Experience of 1901–1910 Birth Cohorts', paper read to the annual conference of the American Sociological Association, Boston, August 1976.

29. Henripin, *Tendances et facteurs*, p. 198.

30. Fadette, *Journal d'Henriette Dessaules 1874–1880*, Montréal 1971, pp. 320–21.

31. McLaren, *Birth Control.*

32. Horace Miner, *St Denis: A French Canadian Parish,* Chicago 1939, p. 170.

33. L.-F. Bouvier, 'The Spacing of Births among French Canadian Families', *Canadian Review of Sociology and Anthropology,* February 1968.

34. Ringuet (P. Panneton), *Thirty Acres,* Toronto 1970.

35. Diane Dodd, 'Women and Reproduction: The Birth Control Movement in Canada', *Social History* (Spring 1983).

36. M. Jean, interview with Léa Roback, May 1982, in Collectif Clio, *L'Histoire des femmes.*

37. *L'Union médicale du Canada,* vol. 60, no. 3 (1931), p. 209.

38. Colette Moreux, *Fin d'une religion? Monographie d'une paroisse canadienne-française,* Montreal 1969.

Nationalism and Feminism in Québec: The 'Yvettes' Phenomenon

This article is a revised version of a paper presented to a general meeting of the Canadian Research Institute for the Advancement of Women in Toronto, November 1980.

1. Laurence Bard, *L'Analyse de Contenu,* Paris 1977.

2. We have used a dossier made up by the Press Office of the Quebec Council for Women's Status. The articles used were dated from 1 March 1980 to 1 June 1980 and came from *La Presse, Le Devoir, Le Soleil, Le Journal de Montréal, Le Journal de Québec, The Gazette, The Globe and Mail, Le Nouveliste, La Tribune, Le Droit* and *Le Quotidien.*

3. Liliane Kandel, 'L'explosion de la presse feminine', in *Le Débat,* vol. 1, no. 1 (also published in *Questions feministes,* no. 7 (February 1980)).

4. Michèle Tremblay, *Journal de Montréal,* 19 March 1980, p. 31.

5. *La Presse,* national edition, 8 April 1980, p. 1.

6. Bertrand Tremblay, *Le Quotidien,* 10 April 1980, p. A4 and Marc Laurendeau, *La Presse,* 9 April 1980.

7. *Le Droit,* 8 March 1980, p. 12.

8. *Le Devoir,* 11 March 1980, p. 8.

9. Marcelle Germain-Samson, *Le Devoir,* 20 March 1980, p. 10.

10. A. St-Amand, Jonquière Liberal Association, *Le Quotidien,* 21 March 1980, p. A4.

11. *La Presse,* 5 April 1980, p. A2.

12. Marcel Adam, 10 April 1980.

13. La Presse, 11 April 1980, p. A10.

14. See *La Presse,* 19 May 1980, p. A2; *Le Devoir,* 10 April 1980, p. 2.

15. *La Presse,* 7 May 1980, p. A7; *Le Devoir,* 5 February 1980, p. 7.

16. *Le Devoir,* 25 April 1980, p. 13.

The Hidden Curriculum of School:
Reproducing Gender and Class Hierarchies

1. M. O'Brien, *The Politics of Reproduction,* London 1981. p. 2.

2. S. Russell, *Sex Role Socialization in the High School.* University of Toronto, unpublished PhD thesis, 1978; S. Russell 'Learning Sex Roles in the High School. *Interchange,* vol. 10, no. 2 (1979–80).

3. S. Bowles and H. Gintis, *Schooling in Capitalist America* ,London 1976.

4. Brief to the Management Committee of the Toronto Board of Education from the Park School Community Council. 'Downtown Kids Aren't Dumb: They Need a Better Program', in G. Martell, ed., *The Politics of The Canadian Public School,* Toronto 1974.

5. J. Gaskell, 'Sex Inequalities in Education for Work: The Case of Business Education', *Canadian Journal of Education,* vol. 6, no. 2. (1981).

6. M. Arnot, 'A Cloud over Co-education', in S. Walker and L. Barton, eds., *Gender, Class and Education,* Barcombe 1983.

7. J. Shaw, 'Education and the Individual: Schooling for Girls, or Mixed Schooling – a Mixed Blessing?', in R. Deem, ed. *Schooling for Women's Work,* London 1980.

8. A. M. Wolpe, Education and the Sexual Division of Labour', in A. Kuhn and A. M. Wolpe, eds., *Feminism and Materialism,* London 1978.

9. A. McRobbie, 'Working Class Girls and the Culture of Feminity', *Women Take Issue,* London 1978.

10. M. Llewellyn, 'Studying Girls at School: The Implication of Confusion', in *Schooling for Women's Work.*

11. M. Sharp and H. Roberts, 'Boys Will Be Boys – But What Happens to the Girls?', *Educational Research,* vol. 25, no. 2, (1983), pp. 83–97.

12. P. Willis, *Learning to Labour: How Working Class Kids Get Working Class Jobs,* Westmead 1977.

13. J. Anyon, Intersections of Gender and Class, in *Gender, Class and Education.*

14. J. Anyon, 'Intersections of Gender and Class'.

15. R. Dale, 'Education and the Capitalist State: Contributions and Contradictions, in M. Apple, ed., *Cultural and Economic Reproduction in Education,* London.

16. S. Delamont, 'The Conservative School?', in *Gender, Class and Education.*

17. J. Porter, *et al., Stations and Callings,* Toronto 1982.

18. P.Connelly, *Last Hired, First Fired,* Toronto 1978; P. Connelly, 'On Marxism and Feminism', *Studies in Political Economy,* vol. 12 (1978), pp. 153–61, reproduced in this volume.

19. This research on gender bias of guidance counsellors is strongly supported by previous research. See, for example, W. Bingham and E. House, 'Counsellors' Attitudes Towards Women and Work', in J. Pottker and A. Fishel eds., *Sex Biases in the Schools,* Associated University Presses 1977; A. Thomas and W. Stewart, 'Counsellor Response to Female Clients with Deviate and Conforming Career Goals', *Journal of Counselling Psychology,* vol. 18, (1981); J. Pietrofessa and N. Schlossberg, 'Counsellor Bias and the Female Occupational Role', in N. Glazer-Malbin, ed., *Women in a Man-made World,* Chicago 1972.

20. P. Bourdieu, quoted in P. Wexler, 'Structure, Text and Subject: A Critical Sociology of School Knowledge', in *Cultural and Economic Reproduction in Education,* p. 278.

21. N. Keddie, 'Classroom Knowledge', in M. Young, ed., *Knowledge and Control,* London 1971.

22. See, for example E. Sarah, 'Teachers and Students in the Classroom: An Examination of Classroom Interaction', and D. Spender, 'Talking in Class', in D. Spender and E. Sarah, eds., *Learning to Lose: Sexism and Education,*

London 1980; P. Sears and D. Feldman, 'Teacher Interaction with Boys and Girls', in J. Stacey, *et al.*, eds., *And Jill Came Tumbling After*, New York 1974.

23. M. Scott, 'Teach Her a Lesson: Sexist Curriculum in Patriarchal Culture', in *Learning to Lose: Sexism and Education*.

24. H. Becker, 'Social Class Variations in the Teacher–Pupil Relationship', *Journal of Educational Sociology*, vol. 25, no. 4 (1952).

25. For similar findings from research, see K. Clarricoates, 'The Importance of Being Ernest . . . Emma . . . Tom . . . Jane: The Perception and Categorization of Gender Conformity and Gender Deviation in Primary Schools', in *Schooling for Women's Work;* M. Stanworth, *Gender and Schooling: A Study of Sexual Divisions in the Classroom*, London 1983.

Conceptions of Skill and the Work of Women: Some Historical and Political Issues

I would like to thank Nancy Jackson for many discussions which have helped me clarify the ideas in this paper.

1. D. Dodge, *Labour Market Developments in the 1980's*, Ottawa 1981. G. Betcherman, *Human Resources Survey*, Ottawa 1980.

2. M. Horner, 'Femininity and Successful Achievement: A Basic Inconsistency', in Bordwick Dorevan Horner and D. Gutman, eds., *Femininity, Personality and Conflict*, Belmont, California 1970. E. Levy, 'Do Teachers Sell Girls Short?', *Today's Education*, National Education Association, 1972.

3. G. Becker, *Human Capital*, New York 1964. S. Polachek, 'Discontinuous Labor Force Participation and Its Effect on Women's Market Earnings', in Cynthia Lloyd, ed., *Sex, Discrimination, and the Division of Labor*, New York 1975. S. Polachek, 'Occupational Segregation: An Alternative Hypothesis', *Journal of Contemporary Business*, no. 5 (1976) pp. 1–12.

4. P. Armstrong and H. Armstrong, *The Double Ghetto: Canadian Women and Their Segregated Work*, Toronto 1977.

5. M. Castells, *The Economic Crisis and American Society*, Princeton 1980, p. 191.

6. Ann-Marie Wolpe, 'Education and the Sexual Division of Labour', in Annette Kuhn and Ann-Marie Wolpe, eds., *Feminism and Materialism*, London 1978, p. 294.

7. G. Picot, *The Changing Educational Profile of Canadians, 1961 to 2000*, Ottawa 1980. J. Gaskell, 'Education and Job Opportunities for Women: Patterns of Enrolment and Economic Returns', in N. Husan and D. Smith, *Women and the Canadian Labour Force*, Ottawa 1982. M. Boyd, 'Sex Differences in the Canadian Occupational Attainment Process', *Canadian Review of Sociology and Anthropology*, vol. 19, no. 1 (1982), p. 28.

8. P. Englund, 'Skill Demands and Earnings in Female and Male Occupations', *Sociology and Social Research*, vol. 66 (1982), pp. 147–68. V. Oppenheimer, *The Female Labour Force in the US*, Berkeley, California 1970.

9. R. Collins, *The Credential Society*, New York 1979.

10. H. Braverman, *Labour and Monopoly Capitalism*, New York 1974, p. 430.

11. A. Phillips and B. Taylor, 'Sex and Skill: Notes Towards a Feminist Economics', *Feminist Review*, 79–80 (1980), p. 9.

12. M. Barrett, *Women's Oppression Today: Problems in Marxist Feminist Analysis*, London 1980, pp. 166–8.

13. Department of Manpower and Immigration, Canada, *Canadian Classification and Dictionary of Occupations*, Vol 1: Classifications and Definitions, Vol. 2: Occupational Qualification Requirements, 1971; Becker.

14. T. Parsons, The School Class as a Social System: Some of Its Functions in American Society', *Harvard Education Review*, no. 29 (1959), pp. 297–318.

15. I. Berg, *Education and Jobs: The Great Training Robbery*, New York 1970. O. Hall and R. Carlton, *Basic Skills at School and Work*, Toronto 1977.

16. Collins, p. 54; see also S. Bowles and H. Gintis, 1976, *Schooling in Capitalist America: Educational Reform and the Contradictions of Economic Life*, New York 1976.

17. H. Cathcart, G. Esland and R. Johnson, *The State and Politics of Education*, Ottawa 1982. M. Apple, *Education and Power*, Boston 1982.

18. B. Reubens, 'Review of Foreign Experience', in *Youth Employment and Public Policy*, Englewood Cliffs, New Jersey 1978.

19. W. R. Dymond, *Training for Ontario's Future: Report of the Task Force on Industrial Training*, Toronto 1973.

20. M. Mitchell, 'Recent Trends in Women's Labour Force Activity in British Columbia', British Columbia Ministry of Labour, *Labor Research Bulletin*, July 1979, p. 28.

21. N. Briggs, *Women in Apprenticeship – Why Not?*, Washington, DC 1974.

22. J. Rule, *The Experience of Labour in the 18th Century*, London 1981.

23. H. Hartman, 'Capitalism, Patriarchy and Job-Segregation by Sex?', in Eisenstein, ed., *Capitalist, Patriarchy and the Case for Socialist Feminism*, New York 1979.

24. P. Foner, *Women and the American Labor Movement*, New York 1980.

25. See Rule.

26. C. More, *Skill and the English Working Class*, London 1980, chapter 3; Rule, chapter 4; E. P. Thompson, *The Making of the English Working Class*, London 1963, pp. 278–80.

27. See Thompson; B. Palmer, *A Culture in Conflict: Skilled Workers and Industrial Capitalism in Hamilton, Ontario 1860–1914*, Montréal 1979; G. Kealey, *Toronto Industrial Workers Respond to Industrial Capitalism 1867–92*, Toronto 1980; More.

28. S. Lewenhak, *Women and Trade Unions*, London 1977.

29. See Foner.

30. D. J. Lee, 'Skill, Craft and Class: A Theoretical Critique and a Critical Case', *Sociology*, no. 15 (1981), pp. 56–78.

31. J. Howell, 'Trade Unions and Apprenticeship', *Contemporary Review*, no. 30 (1977), pp. 833–57. D. Gleason and G. Mardle, *Further Education or Training?*, London 1980.

32. See More.

33. M. Ricketts, *A Time for Action: A Survey of Critical Trade Skills in the Lower Mainland*, Vancouver 1980; Dymond.

34. W. Clement, *Hard Rock Mining*, Toronto 1980.

35. Betcherman; Dodge.

36. A. Smith, *Generic Skills: Improving Transferability in Occupational Training*, Ottawa 1981.

37. See Ricketts.

38. See Braverman; D. Lockwood, *The Blackcoated Worker*, London 1958.

39. Braverman, p. 299.

40. G. Lowe, 'Women, Work and the Office', *Canadian Journal of Sociology*, vol. 5, no. 4 (1980), pp. 361–81.

41. Lowe, p. 377.

42. J. Gaskell, 'Sex Inequalities in Education for Work: The Case of Business Education', *Canadian Journal of Education*, no. 6 (1981), pp. 54–72.

43. L. Valli, 'Becoming Clerical Workers: The Relation Between Business Education and the Culture of Femininity', in M. Apple, *Cultural and Economic Reproduction in Education*, Boston 1982.

44. Hall and Carlton.

45. See J. Harp, 'Social Inequalities and the Social Transmission of Knowledge', in Harp and Hofley, *Structured Inequality in Canada*, Scarborough 1980; S. Schechter, 'Capitalism, Class and Educational Reform', in Panitch, ed., *The Canadian State*, Toronto 1977; T. Dunn, 'Teaching the Meaning of Work: Vocational Education in British Columbia, 1900–1929', in Jones, Sheehan and Stamp, eds., *Shaping the Schools of the Canadian West*, Calgary 1979; T. Dunn, 'Vocationalism and Its Promoters in British Columbia 1900–1929', *Journal of Educational Thought*, vol. 14, no. 2 (1980).

46. See Bowles and Gintis, p. 193.

47. E. Rogers and D. Tyack, 'Work, Youth and Schooling: Mapping Critical Research Areas', in Kantor and Tyack, eds., *Work, Youth and Schooling*, Stanford 1982, p. 282.

48. See Schechter.

49. K. Poss, 'The Sexual Structuring of Public High School Education, 1870–1930', paper prepared for Western Association of Women Historians conference, Asilomar, California 1981.

50. Rogers and Tyack, p. 274.

51. R. Feldberg, and E. Glen, 'Effects of Technological Change on Clerical Work: Review and Reassessment', paper presented at American Sociological Meetings, New York 1980. H. Menzies, *Women and the Chip*, Montréal 1980.

52. British Columbia Department of Education, *Business Education Curriculum Guide*, Victoria, BC 1981.

The Collusion with Patriarchy: A Psychoanalytic Account

An earlier draft of this paper was read at the annual meeting of the Canadian Sociology and Anthropology Association in Saskatoon, 1979. I would like to thank Meg Luxton, who was the discussant at that session (and, through her, Heather Jon Maroney), Pat Armstrong, John McMullan and Susan Russell for their useful criticism of that draft.

1. Christopher Lasch, 'The Family in History', *New York Review of Books*, 13 November 1975.

2. Dennis Wrong, 'The Oversocialized Conception of Man in Modern Sociology', *American Sociological Review*, 26, pp. 183–93.

3. Edward Boldt, 'Homo Sociologicus', *Society–Societe*, vol. 3, no. 1 (1979), pp. 1–4.

4. Juliet Mitchell, *Psychoanalysis and Feminism*, New York 1974. There has been a debate in the *New Left Review*: Richard Wollheim (NLR, nos. 93 and 97), Nancy Chodorow and Eli Zaretsky (NLR, no. 96), The Lacan Study Group (NLR, no. 97). Foreman, Ann, *Femininity as Alienation: Women and the Family*

in Marxism and Psychoanalysis, London 1977. Nancy Chodorow, *The Repro-duction of Mothering*, California 1978. Dinnerstein, Dorothy, *The Mermaid and the Minotaur*.

5. *Capitalism, the Family and Personal Life*, New York 1976, pp. 133–4.

6. Peggy Morton, 'Women's Work Is Never Done', in *Women Unite*, Toronto 1972, pp. 46–68; Dorothy Smith, 'Women, the Family and Corporate Capital-ism', in *Women in Canada*, Marylee Stephenson, ed., 1977; Roberta Hamilton, *The Liberation of Women*, London 1978.

7. See Pat Armstrong and Hugh Armstrong, *The Double Ghetto*, Toronto 1978.

8. Ada Farber provides a thoughtful and sympathetic insight into Freud's personal views on men and women through an analysis of his love letters to his fiancée, Martha Bernays, in 'Freud's Love Letters: Intimations of Psycho-analytic Theory', *The Psychoanalytic Review*, vol. 65, no. 1 (Spring 1978), pp. 166–89.

9. Paul A. Robinson, *The Freudian Left*, New York 1969, p. 3.

10. See Roberta Hamilton, *The Liberation of Women*, London 1978, pp. 104–5.

11. Sigmund Freud, *New Introductory Lectures in Psychoanalysis*, New York 1965, p. 116.

12. It should be clear here, as throughout the article, that I am talking only about the general case; the life history of any particular individual has its own specificity and requires its own analysis. It is equally important and interesting to investigate the conditions under which individuals depart from hetero-sexuality and from societal concepts of masculinity and femininity, but that is beyond the scope of this paper.

13. Dennis Wrong, p. 183.

14. See Shulamith Firestone, *The Dialectic of Sex*, New York 1970, p. 12.

15. See Richard Wollheim, 'Psychoanalysis and Feminism', *New Left Review*, no. 93 (1975), p. 65.

16. Karl Marx, *The Economic and Philosophical Manuscripts of 1844*, New York 1964, pp. 106–19.

17. Herbert Marcuse, *Eros and Civilization*, Boston 1955; Gad Horowitz, *Basic and Surplus Repression in Psychoanalytic Theory: Freud, Reich and Marcuse*, Toronto 1977.

18. Horowitz, pp. 44–54.

19. For example, the honey bee does not need to repress her desires in order for her to be willing to work until she dies of exhaustion.

20. See Wollheim, pp. 64–5, and Horowitz, p. 54.

21. Marcuse, p. 38.

22. Robinson, p. 232.

23. Freud, *New Introductory Lectures*, p. 116.

24. See Wollheim, p. 68.

25. Nancy Chodorow and Dorothy Dinnerstein have both provided inter-esting accounts of the implications for human development of the universality of mothering as a gendered activity.

26. Horowitz, p. 95.

27. Ibid., p. 103.

28. Ibid., p. 108.

29. Ruth Brunswick 'The Preoedipal Phase of the Libido Development' in Robert Fleiss, ed., *The Psycho-Analytic Reader*, New York 1948, p. 246.

30. Wollheim, pp. 68–9.
31. *New Introductory Lectures*, p. 119.
32. Brunswick, p. 236.
33. See Horowitz, pp. 103–4.
34. 'The Evolution of the Oedipus Complex in Women' in *The Psycho-Analytic Reader*, p. 186.
35. Lampl de Groot, p. 186.
36. Freud, p. 129.
37. *The Reproduction of Mothering*, p. 160.
38. See Horowitz, pp. 115–16.
39. Ibid., p. 106.
40. Wollheim, p. 97.
41. *Repression*, p. 123.
42. Brunswick, p. 237.
43. *Economic and Philosophical Manuscripts*, pp. 113–14.
44. Ibid., p. 114.
45. See Raymond Williams, *Marxism and Literature*, London 1977, pp. 80, 91.

Embracing Motherhood: New Feminist Theory

An earlier version of this paper was presented at the Canadian Sociology and Anthropology Association meetings (Halifax, Nova Scotia, June 1980). Thanks to Meg Luxton, Rhoda Howard, Andrew Wernick and the reviewers for the *Canadian Journal of Political and Social Theory* for their comments.

1. Although medical technology, for example *in vitro* fertilization, is increasingly capable of intervening in the process of conception in contemporary society the chief means is still adoption. Popular movements occasionally gave women such as Mother Jones the title as an honorific. Non-Western cultures have widespread and varying practices of prenatal social intervention including food taboos, beliefs about sexual intercourse, rituals, and musical or oral communication with the unborn child.

2. Aileen Kraditor, *The Ideas of the Women's Suffrage Movement*, Garden City 1971, pp. 52–5, 91; Wayne Roberts 'Rocking the Cradle for the World: The New Woman and Maternal Feminism', in L. Kealy, ed., *A Not Unreasonable Claim*, Toronto 1979.

3. Betty Friedan, *The Feminine Mystique*, Harmondsworth, Middlesex 1972; Juliet Mitchell, *Women's Estate*, Harmondsworth, Middlesex 1971, p. 36. Mitchell was the first to challenge the view that reproduction is 'an atemporal constant – part of biology rather than history', p. 107.

4. Germaine Greer, *The Female Eunuch*, New York 1972, pp. 32, 232–3. She has since revised her views in part as a critique of the imposition of Western technological rationality in the form of population control imposed on Third World women and thus also become a political exponent of the transformed view of motherhood. *Sex and Destiny*, New York 1984.

5. Shulamith Firestone, *The Dialectic of Sex: The Case for Feminist Revolution*, New York 1970. Marge Piercy, *Woman on the Edge of Time*, translates this view into fiction; in contrast, Charlotte Perkins Gilman's nineteenth-century feminist utopia, *Herland*, relies on parthenogenic reproduction in a world of mothers and daughters.

6. Philippe Aries, *Centuries of Childhood: A Social History of Family Life*, New York 1962; Lawrence Stone, *Family and Childhood in England*, Harmondsworth, Middlesex 1979. Zillah Eisenstein, *The Radical Future of Liberal Feminism*, New York 1981, links this theory with bourgeois liberal political theory.

7. The phrase is Jessie Bernard's, *The Future of Motherhood*, New York 1975, p. 20; see also Dolores Hayden, *The Grand Domestic Revolution*, Cambridge 1982; Helen Z. Lopata, *Occupation: Housewife*, Oxford 1971, for its full flowering, and Meg Luxton, *More than a Labour of Love*, Toronto 1981, for its contradictions. She demonstrates that production – of labour power – takes place in the home and that new technology has increased standards for rather than reduced the time spent in housework. Fertility peaks in Canada in 1961 and in the USA in 1957; Monica Boyd *et al.*, 'Family: Function, Formation, and Fertility', in G. Cook, ed., *Opportunity for Choice*, Ottawa 1976, and Bernard.

8. The phrase is Friedan's; Pauline B. Bart, 'Depression in Middle Aged Women', in V. Gornick and B. Moran, eds., *Women in Sexist Society*, New York 1972.

9. Helene Deutsch, *The Psychology of Women*, New York 1944, 1945; Phyllis Chesler, *Women and Madness*, New York 1972.

10. For Canada, Pat Connelly, *Last Hired, First Fired*, Toronto 1978; for the USA, Bernard, p. 144 ff.

11. Educational achievement for women is typically linked with lower marriage rates, late marriage and fewer children. Similarly, later marriage reduces the time 'at risk' for socially legitimated pregnancy and childbearing. Effective contraception permits more control over family numbers and helps to eliminate the 'extra' child; see Margrit Eichler, *Families in Canada To-day*, Toronto 1983.

12. *Time*, 22 February 1982; the reception of Oriana Fallaci's *Letter to a Child Unborn*, Garden City 1978, was a similar instance.

13. Nancy Friday, *My Mother/Myself*, New York 1978, pp. 342, 343,450.

14. *Chatelaine*, the largest Canadian women's magazine, and the *Globe and Mail* in its soft news sections have carried stories on late motherhood among the famous, unpartnered motherhood and, more recently, lesbians choosing pregnancy and motherhood. Even *Toronto Life*, September 1984 got in on the act with an article on 'muppies' – mid-thirties yuppy mothers.

15. Signe Hammer, *Daughters and Mothers*, New York 1986, p. xi.

16. Susan Harding, 'Family Reform Movement: Recent Feminism and Its Opponents', *Feminist Studies*, vol. 7, no. 1 (1981).

17. 'Female homosexuality is inseparable from the very qualities which were the perogative of women in early history. It is of no consequence to these conclusions whether the matriarchate existed as a definite period of history, which I believe, it did, or is mythology. Mythology is history, transcending concrete data and revealing their true meaning.' Charlotte Wolf, *Love Between Women*, New York 1971, p. 82; Jill Johnson sees mythology as a model for 'theory, consciousness, and action', *Lesbian Nation*, New York 1978, p. 249; Paula Webster, 'Matriarchy: A Vision of Power', in R. Reiter, ed., *Toward an Anthropology of Women*, New York 1975.

18. Juliet Mitchell, *Psychoanalysis and Feminism*, New York 1974, helped focus this interest, although her commitment to psychoanalysis pre-dates its development.

19. Rachel Blau Duplessis, 'Washing blood', *Feminist Studies*, vol. 4, no. 2 (1978), p. 2.

20. Hélène Cixous, 'The laugh of the Medusa', *Signs*, vol. 1, no. 4 (1978), p. 877; the criterion of exploring the unconscious for a new rationality is also hers. Duplessis; Anita Barrows, 'The chart'; Mary Oppen, 'Breath of life'; and Alicia Ostriker, 'From the mother/child papers' in the same special issue of *Feminist Studies*; and Jane Lazarre, *The Mother Knot*, New York 1977, illustrates this approach.

21. Robin Morgan, *Going Too Far: The Personal Chronicle of a Feminist*, New York 1977, p. 8, *et passim.*

22. Adrienne Rich, *Of Women Born*, New York 1977, p. 15.

23. Nancy Tanner and Adrienne Zihlman, 'Women in Evolution, Part I; Innovation and Selection in Human Origins', *Signs*, vol. 1, no. 3 (1981).

24. Ibid., p. 606.

25. Adrienne Zihlman, 'Women and Evolution, Part II: Subsistence and Social Organization Among Early Hominids', *Signs*, vol. 4, no. 1.

26. Merlin Stone, *When God Was a Woman*, New York 1976, p. 23; Sarah B. Pomeroy presents a counter view for a later period, *Goddesses, Whores, Wives and Slaves: Women in Classical Antiquity*, New York 1975.

27. Ibid., chapter 4.

28. Anne Barstow, 'The uses of Archeology for Women's History: James Mellaart's Work on Neolithic Goddesses at Çatal Hüyük', *Feminist Studies*, vol. 4, no. 3 (1978).

29. Ruby Rohrlich, 'State Formation in Sumer and the Subjugation of Women', *Feminist Studies*, vol. 6, no. 1 (1980).

30. Charles T. Wood, 'The Doctors' Dilemma: Sin, Salvation and the Menstrual Cycle in Medieval Thought', *Speculum*, vol. 56, no. 4 (1981).

31. Jean-Jacques Rousseau, *La nouvelle Heloise, Julie or the new Eloise*, J. H. McDowell, ed., University Park, Pa. 1968; on Rousseau see Susan Moller Okin, *Women in Western Political Thought*, Princeton 1978; and Eisenstein, chapter 4.

32. Elizabeth Badinter argues that social practices among the aristocracy in eighteenth-century France – wet-nursing, governesses or tutors and boarding-schools – indicate that mothers were relatively indifferent to the child's social welfare, preferring to emerge from social seclusion into court circles of political power, intellectual enlightenment and sociability. These were later adopted by the Parisian bourgeoises: *The Myth of Motherhood*, London 1981, p. 180.

33. The extent and character of maternal power is debated. Badinter, pp. 168 ff, accepts it uncritically; Jacques Donzelot, *The Policing of Families*, New York 1979 and Christopher Lasch, *Haven in a Heartless World*, New York 1977, see it allied with state and expert agents; Michèle Barrett and Mary McIntosh, *The Anti-social Family*, London 1982, criticized their anti-feminism but failed to note their matriphobia.

34. Barbara Ehrenreich and Deidre English, *For Her Own Good: 150 Years of the Experts' Advice to Women*, Garden City 1978, p. 15.

35. Ibid., pp. 63, 19–20. Both of these solutions remain androcentric, assuming that the real world lies outside the home in spheres of production, politics and science occupied by men.

36. Ibid., p. 172.

37. Ibid., p. 174.

38. Mary P. Ryan, 'Femininity and Capitalism in Anti-bellum America', in Z. Eisenstein, ed., *Capitalist Patriarchy and the Case for Socialist Feminism*, New York 1979.

39. See Phillip Wylie, *A Generation of Vipers*, New York 1955.

40. Shirley Radl, *Mother's Day Is Over*, New York 1978, p. 207; a content analysis of fifteen mass market books published between 1972 and 1980 revealed that all referred to the women's movement and that the most frequent citation was Ellen Peck, *The Baby Trap*, New York 1971, which argues an anti-natalist position in part on ecological grounds.

41. For example: Virginia Barber and Merril M. Skaggs, *The Mother Person*, New York 1977; Barbara Belford, ed., *Redbook's The Young Mothers*, New York 1977; Jean Curtis, *Working Mothers*, New York 1976; Elaine Hoffer, *Mothering: The Emotional Experience of Motherhood after Freud and Feminism*, Garden City 1978; Lazarre 1977; Angela Barron McBride, *The Growth and Development of Mothers*, New York 1973; Liz Smith, *The Mother Book*, Garden City 1978; exceptions are Luxton; Harriet Rosenberg, 'Motherhood and Social Reproduction', unpublished paper', Anne Oakley, *Becoming a Mother*, New York 1980.

42. Curtis, p. 42.

43. Barber and Skaggs, pp. 15, 98; Susan (Contrertto) Weisskopf, 'Maternal Sexuality and Asexual Motherhood', *Signs*, vol. 5, no. 4 (Summer 1984); 'Maternalism, Sexuality and the New Feminism', in Zubin and J. Meney, eds., *Contemporary Sexual Behavior, Critical Issues in the 1970s*, Baltimore 1973.

44. Doris Bernstein, 'Female Identity Synthesis', in Alan Roland and Barbara Harris, eds., *Career and Motherhood*, New York 1979. This volume which collects papers presented at the 1976 meetings of the National [USA] Psychological Association for Psychoanalysis, presents the newly hegemonic position validating the 'working mother'; see also Esther Menaker, Harriett Podhoretz and Barbara Harris in the same volume.

45. As well as the citations in note 44, see Jessie Bernard, *Women, Wives and Mothers*, Chicago 1975; Sydney C. Callaghan, ed., *The Working Mothers*, New York 1975.

46. Barber and Skaggs, p. 217.

47. Barbara Ehrenreich and Diedre English, 'Witches, Nurses and Midwives', New England, n.d.; Jean Donnisen, *Midwives and Medical Men: A History of Interprofessional Rivalries and Women's Rights*, London 1977; Anne Oakley, 'Wise Woman and Medicine Man: Changes in the Management of childbirth', in J. Mitchell and A. Oakley, eds., *The Rights and Wrongs of Women*, Harmondsworth, Middlesex 1976; Rich; Jane Lewis, *The Politics of Motherhood*, London and Montréal 1980; for Canada, *Ontario History*, vol. 75, no. 1 (1983), Anne Oakley, 'A Case of Pregnancy: Paradigms of Women in Maternity Cases, *Signs*, vol. 4, no. 4 (Summer 1979).

48. Sheila Kitzinger, *Women as Mothers*, Glasgow 1978, p. 50.

49. Dana Breen, 'The Mother and the Hospital', in S. Lipschitz, ed., *Tearing the Veil: Essays on Femininity*, London 1975, pp. 25–8.

50. Suzanne Arms, *Immaculate Deception*, Oxford 1975; Kitzinger; Rich; Selma Fraiberg, *Every Child's Birthright: In Defense of Mothering*, New York 1977; T. Chand and M. Richards, eds., *Benefits and Hazards of the New Obstetrics*, London 1977.

51. See Arms; Bridgitte Jordan, 'Birth in Four Cultures', and Ruth Watson

Lubic, 'The Politics of Childbirth Today', *Second Motherhood Symposium Proceedings*, University of Wisconsin, Madison 1981, pp. 151–66.

52. William Ray Arney, 'Maternal–Infant Bonding: The Politics of Falling in Love with Your Child', *Feminist Studies*, vol. 6, no. 3 (1980).

53. Rich, p. 237.

54. Alice Rossi, 'A Biosocial Perspective on Parenting', *Daedelus* (1977).

55. Sigmund Freud, 'Femininity', *New Introductory Lectures on Psychoanalysis*, Harmondsworth, Middlesex 1973, p. 153.

56. Nancy Chodorow, *The Reproduction of Mothering: Psychoanalysis and the Sociology of Gender*, Berkeley and Los Angeles 1978, pp. 33, 40.

57. Ibid., p. 206.

58. Ibid., p. 175 ff.

59. Ibid., p. 194.

60. Dorothy Dinnerstein claims close kinship with Asch and gestalt theory, but she relies on Freud, Klein and Brown, *The Mermaid and the Minotaur Sexual Arrangements and Human Malaise*, New York 1977, pp. xi, 43–4, 119.

61. Ibid., p. 161.

62. Chorodow, chapter 7.

63. Ibid., pp. 173–7.

64. Ibid., p. 185.

65. Jane Flax, 'The Conflict between Nurturance and Autonomy in Mother–Daughter Relationships and within Feminism', *Feminist Studies*, vol. 4, no. 2 (1978).

66. Mary O'Brien, *The Politics of Reproduction*, London 1981, p. 21.

67. Ibid., p. 50.

68. Ibid., pp. 29, 34.

69. Ibid., p. 32.

70. Ibid., p. 194.

71. Ibid., pp. 169 ff; for O'Brien, women's struggles for day-care, abortion and rewards for domestic labour and against legal restrictions and violence help to consolidate rational control over the process of reproduction. The further strategy she recommends, socializing children to new modes, seems inadequate to her wider vision; it is not articulated with, for example, the need to control state agencies of socialization.

72. Dinnerstein, 1973, pp. 124 ff; Sherry Ortner follows de Beauvoir to a similar conclusion, 'Is Female to Nature as Male Is to Culture?', in M. Z. Rosaldo and L. Lamphere, eds., *Woman, Culture and Society*, Stanford 1974.

73. Ibid., p. 103.

74. Ibid., p. 160 ff.

75. Mary Daly, *Gyn/ecology: The Metaethics of Radical Feminism*, Boston 1978, p. 39.

76. Mary Daly, *Beyond God the Father Toward a Philosophy of Women's Liberation*, Boston 1973, pp. 14–15.

77. Daly, *Gyn/ecology*, p. 87.

78. Daly, *Beyond God the Father*, p. 146.

79. Daly 1979, pp. 215–16.

80. Ibid., pp. 27–8, 149.

81. Daly, *Gyn/ecology*, xi ff.

82. Ibid. chapter 10.

83. Daly, *Beyond God the Father*, p. 129.
84. Ibid., chapter 6, p. 150.
85. Ibid., pp. 346–7.
86. Ibid., p. 63.